Paths of Symbolization

Paths of Symbolization explores philosophical and psychoanalytic questions about the concept of symbolization.

Alain Gibeault connects symbolization with concepts like playing, sublimation and creation. With reference to Freud's metapsychology and the French context specifically, Gibeault explores the significance of symbolization in analytic work. This book studies the theoretical questions raised by the concept of symbolization in the history of psychoanalytic thought and clarifies what is at stake when symbolization is impaired—particularly in the treatment of psychotic, borderline, and neurotic states. Through a wealth of clinical material, the author illustrates how symbolization mediates between inner and outer realities, enabling the emergence of thought, representation, and transformation. By comparing these cases, readers are invited to grasp the specific therapeutic contributions of French psychoanalysis in fostering psychic integration and the working through of unconscious conflict.

Paths of Symbolization will be of great interest to psychoanalysts in practice and in training, particularly those looking to better understand theoretical, clinical, and technical aspects of French psychoanalysis. It will also be relevant for academics and scholars of psychoanalytic studies, other areas of mental health and philosophy.

Alain Gibeault is a philosopher, psychologist, and psychoanalyst. He is a training and full member of the Paris Psychoanalytical Society and former director of the E. & J. Kestemberg Center for Psychoanalysis and Psychotherapy. He served as President of the European Psychoanalytical Federation and General Secretary of the International Psychoanalytical Association. He is also an Honorary Professor at Lomonosov Moscow State University and co-editor-in-chief of the journal *Psychanalyse et psychose* (E. & J. Kestemberg Center).

The International Psychoanalytical Association Current Challenges in Psychoanalysis Series

Series Editor: Silvia Flechner

IPA Publications Committee

Natacha Delgado, Nergis Güleç, Thomas Marcacci, Carlos Moguillansky, Rafael Mondrzak, Angela M. Vuotto, Gabriela Legorreta (consultant)

"In this creative book, the author combines a rich and nuanced reflection on mental processes of symbolization with a compelling insight into an innovative psychoanalytic practice, especially for people who suffer from symbolization disorders such as autism, hypochondria, or psychoses. It is fascinating to see how rigorously the theoretical foundation, with its discussion of the relationship between symbolizations in areas as diverse as conversion symptoms, dreams, money, and prehistoric art and, finally, in the psychoanalytic process, as well as the conceptual clarification of the relationships between symbolization, representation and sublimation, fits into a vivid synthesis of play and language in the psychoanalytic process and also in the symbolizing setting of psychoanalytic psychodrama. This book invites the reader to take a big step into often uncharted territory, and she or he is rewarded by participating in a profound conceptual reflection and deeply touching clinical case presentations".

Heribert Blass, *Member of the German Psychoanalytical Association; President of the International Psychoanalytical Association; Past President of the European Psychoanalytical Federation*

"In *Paths of Symbolization* Alain Gibeault provides a real treat for the psychoanalytic community. In what has the makings of a classic treatise, he, *inter alia*, comprehensively reviews the development of core psychoanalytic concepts and phenomena from Freud through to the evolving major French and English schools. Gibeault links these with the increasing sophisticated understandings of symbolization and its psychopathologies as understood in psychoanalysis (compared with other disciplines). How does psychoanalysis promote symbolisation? Answers are provided with fascinating clinical examples, including persons with autistic, psychosomatic, borderline and various psychotic phenomena. Also illustrated are modifications of frame such as psychoanalytic psychodrama for specific indications".

Brian Martindale, *Retired Member of the British Psychoanalytical Society; Honorary President European Federation of Psychoanalytic Psychotherapy (EFPP); Honorary Life Member International Society for Psychological and Social Approaches to Psychosis (ISPS)*

"What about symbolization for psychoanalysts? Alain Gibeault addresses this question in a particularly in-depth and convincing manner. Each chapter corresponds to a division of this symbolic function and highlights its specificity. This approach to the symbol in psychoanalysis, the *symballo*, defines it as a link between two parts, one completing the other, as well as their unity—rendered unconscious through evolution—thus requiring interpretation, the privileged psychoanalytic instrument of S. Freud. The order of the chapters follows the accidents of symbolization as revealed by

Freud's psychopathological discoveries over time. The author revisits key concepts such as projection and projective identification in his discussion of psychosis, which he considers particularly illuminating in understanding psychic functioning. He argues that psychosis not only enriches this essential process of symbolization but also contributes to the emergence and comprehension of thought activity. Let us embark on the journey through this remarkable book".

Béatrice Ithier, *Member of the Paris Psychoanalytical Society and the Italian Psychoanalytic Society; Clinical Psychologist; Recognized Child, Adolescent, and Adult Psychoanalyst by the IPA; Training Analyst at the Institute of Psychoanalysis and Psychotherapy of Warsaw*

"It is hardly surprising that the question of symbolization has been particularly studied in French psychoanalysis, given the importance that its various currents place on language and, more broadly, on the anthropological specificities of the emergence of the human species. As a psychoanalyst with a background in philosophy, Alain Gibeault is ideally positioned to explore this issue by encompassing its various aspects, taking into account not only the processes of symbolization unique to humans but also the specificity of symbolization in Freud's thought and in metapsychology. His extensive experience in the psychoanalytic treatment of non-neurotic organizations (such as psychotic and borderline states) greatly contributes to the understanding and practical application of the concept of symbolization".

Vassilis Kapsambelis, *Psychiatrist and Psychoanalyst, Member of the Paris Psychoanalytical Society; Director of the* Revue française de Psychanalyse

Paths of Symbolization

Alain Gibeault
Translated by Andrew Weller
Foreword by Howard B. Levine

Routledge
Taylor & Francis Group
LONDON AND NEW YORK

Designed cover image: © Gustav Klimt, The Tree of Life, Central part of the Stoclet Frieze, 1905-1909, Museum of Applied Arts, Vienna, Austria

First published in English 2026
by Routledge
4 Park Square, Milton Park, Abingdon, Oxon OX14 4RN

and by Routledge
605 Third Avenue, New York, NY 10158

Routledge is an imprint of the Taylor & Francis Group, an informa business

For Product Safety Concerns and Information please contact our EU representative GPSR@taylorandfrancis.com. Taylor & Francis Verlag GmbH, Kaufingerstraße 24, 80331 München, Germany.

First published in the French Chemins de la symbolisation © Presses Universitaires de France/Humensis, 2010

British Library Cataloguing-in-Publication Data
A catalogue record for this book is available from the British Library

ISBN: 9781032899909 (hbk)
ISBN: 9781032899893 (pbk)
ISBN: 9781003545651 (ebk)

DOI: 10.4324/9781003545651

Typeset in Palatino
by codeMantra

To Monique, for her unfailing support
To David and Mathieu

Acknowledgements

I would like to express my warm gratitude and recognition to Catherine Alicot, Christine Mas and Caroline Reliquet for their help in preparing this manuscript.

Nature is a temple in which living pillars
Sometimes give voice to confused words;
Man passes there through forests of symbols
Which look at him with understanding eyes.

Like prolonged echoes mingling in the distance
In a deep and tenebrous unity,
Vast as the dark of night and as the light of day,
Perfumes, sounds, and colours correspond.

There are perfumes as cool as the flesh of children,
Sweet as oboes, green as meadows
— And others are corrupt, and rich, triumphant,

With power to expand into infinity,
Like amber and incense, musk, benzoin,
That sing the ecstasy of the soul and senses.

Charles Baudelaire (1857)
The Flowers of Evil, "Correspondences"

Contents

Series editor's foreword

Silvia Flechner

The International Psychoanalytical Association Publications Committee is honoured to present a new book from the Current Challenges in Psychoanalysis series. This series explores the evolving landscape of psychoanalytic practice, addressing contemporary issues such as trauma, cultural diversity, the influence of technology, and shifts in psychoanalytic dynamics. Each volume offers concise, interdisciplinary insights from leading experts, bridging classical psychoanalytic theory with modern challenges. Designed for clinicians and researchers, this series is a vital resource for those seeking to navigate and innovate within today's complex therapeutic environment.

The IPA Publications Committee is pleased to publish Alain Gibeault's new book, *Paths of Symbolization*. His exceptional book analyses the process of symbolization from various perspectives, including psychoanalysis, linguistics, semiotics, and anthropology. It begins by exploring the sensory and linguistic connection between the material and immaterial through Baudelaire's poem "Correspondences" and the etymological origin of the symbol, stating that Freud deepens the theory of the symbol by introducing the concept of the unconscious, highlighting its interpretative and polysemic nature.

Included are discussions of theories by de Saussure and Peirce, which differentiate the symbol from the linguistic sign, and Peirce's triadic model, extended by Eco, which presents symbolization as a continuous process of meaning creation. This book discusses the evolution of symbolization in psychoanalysis, from hysteria to dream theory and the symbolic meaning of money. It also compares Freudian and Kleinian defence mechanisms, analysing their role in symbol formation.

Using clinical examples, the author illustrates symbolization in different diagnoses, from psychosis to neurosis, and examines related concepts such as representation, sublimation, and creation. Finally, prehistoric art is reflected upon as a key act of human symbolization, arguing that this process is essential at both the individual and cultural levels to create enduring forms of meaning.

In his first chapter, the author highlights how Freud discovered the concept of symbolization through the phenomenon of conversion hysteria, emphasizing its importance in psychoanalysis, giving prominence also to the role of the erogenous body in the transition from somatic experience to psychic representation, establishing symbolization as essential in the formation of symptoms and dynamics of the unconscious.

In the second chapter, the author highlights how Freud explored dream symbolism as a key development in psychoanalytic theory, demonstrating that Freud emphasized the unconscious fantasies underlying dream symbols, particularly those related to sexuality.

In his fifth chapter, the author examines how symbolization operates in various forms of psychopathology, highlighting its importance in meaning-making and psychoanalytic treatment. The relationship between sensory experience and linguistic symbolization is analysed, illustrated through clinical cases of patients with different disorders, showing how symbolization facilitates psychic integration and the transformation of internal and external reality.

Beatriz de León (2000),[1] from the Uruguayan Psychoanalytical Society in her review of W. and M. Baranger's oeuvre, cites L. Alvarez de Toledo (Argentina), who states:

> In early childhood, synesthesia occurs between sounds, smells, temperatures, shapes, and feelings: synopsias (colored hearing) are the most frequent. A sensation corresponding to a certain sense appears associated with another or others, and they regularly arise when the latter are stimulated. Thus, a mouth sound can be associated with a certain color, a certain sensation of size, a patient's perception, or a displacing sensation. This is particularly suitable for the process of symbolization.
>
> (L. Alvarez de Toledo, 1993, p. 333)[2]

Daniel Stern (1985) (USA) subsequently pointed out how the phenomenon of the unity of the senses and the amodal transposition of information, typical of the child's communication with his mother, appears as something that is taken for granted in the therapeutic relationship and in the processes of perception and artistic creation where trans sensory analogies and metaphors have a privileged place. She states that significantly, both L. Alvarez de Toledo (1996) and Daniel Stern (1985)[3] cite Baudelaire's poem "Correspondences" as the basis for their thinking. The same poem that Alain Gibeault introduces us to in his new book.

In his conclusions, the author demonstrates how symbolization serves as a dynamic psychic process that bridges material and psychic realities. It differentiates between symbolization and symbolism, underlining the importance of a transitional space for creation. Based on Freud, Lacan, and Winnicott, analytical work is presented as an elaboration that transforms experience through metaphorical interpretation, respecting ambiguity and polysemy. Psychoanalysis is revealed as a clinical and cultural act that contributes to the search for meaning and the construction of an open and provisional psychic truth.

This book will be an essential resource for psychoanalysts and scholars in related fields, such as semiotics, linguistics, anthropology, and literature, who are interested in the value of psychoanalysis, showcasing the profound and thoughtful work that Alain Gibeault has invited us to share.

Silvia Flechner
Series Editor
Chair, IPA Publications Committee

Notes

1 De León, B. (2000). *International Journal of Psychoanalysis Key Papers Series*. Key Papers on Countertransference. Karnak Books Ltd., London.
2 Alvarez De Toledo, L. (1954 in Spanish) also published in English: The analysis of "associating", "interpreting and "words". *International Journal of Psycho-Analysis*, vol. 77, Part 2 (1996): 291–318.
3 Stern, D. (1985). *The Interpersonal World of the Infant. A View from Psychoanalysis and Developments*. New York: Basic Books

Foreword

Symbolization as process interpretation, construction, and setting

Howard B. Levine

I

Freud's discovery of the symbolic relationship between manifest and latent content in neurotic symptoms, dreams, and slips of the tongue became the launching pad for the creation and development of psychoanalysis. Looked at from a social scientific perspective, symbolization as process also lies at the heart of sublimation, mankind's cultural development, and the very human response to the existential challenge of finding and creating personal meaning in our lives and investing that meaning in the otherwise incomprehensible, often incoherent experience of being-in-the-world.

Laplanche and Pontalis (1973) suggest that "The idea of a symbolic order which *structures interhuman reality* was introduced into the social sciences above all by Claude Lévi-Strauss, who took as his model the structural linguistics developed from the teaching of Ferdinand de Saussure" (p. 440, italics added).[1]

Readers of this book will learn a great deal more about this and other sociological, anthropological, philosophical, semiotic, and linguistic considerations regarding symbols and symbolization. In this short foreword, however, I will restrict myself to comments relevant to psychoanalytic clinical practice.

Viewed from a psychoanalytic clinical vertex, symbolic pairings underlie ideational psychic representation and operate in and define an intrapsychic, interpersonal, and intersubjective transitional space. They inhabit and at times help set up a force field that may simultaneously connote reciprocity, unity, bringing together and connection of elements, but that also underscores the differences that exist between those elements. For example, to say that a cigar is a phallic symbol not only points to the commonality of shape that they both share but also reminds us of the actual stark differences that exist between them. The antithetical, dialectical tension thus produced challenges our psyches to undertake a *work of symbolization* that knits together and delineates psychic elements, thoughts, and feelings in a burgeoning, elaborative process that relies on the symbolizing dimension of metaphor and polysemy in language and is central to homeostatic emotional regulation.

Alain Gibeault, who in addition to being a leading psychoanalytic clinician, theoretician, and teacher has an extensive background and knowledge of philosophy and social science, begins his exploration of symbolization by reminding us that the word, symbol, is

> derived from the Greek *symbolon*, [which] referred for the ancient Greeks to an object split in two, a stone or a tablet, whose reunion (*sumballô* = *reunite*, put together) permitted two allies or their descendants to have their common links recognized. This pact had been formed by breaking the object into two parts and by sharing it between the two persons who had previously wanted to attest thereby to their ties of alliance.
>
> (this volume, Introduction)

This original definition relies upon a pre-established unity between two elements that have been temporarily set apart. The reunification of the now separated elements restores a pre-existing state and is a guarantee or proof of previous connection. The place and work of symbolization in psychoanalytic process and theory, however, prove to be more complex. In addition to what we might think of as the identification or discovery of pre-existing, naturally occurring symbolic connections, Freud called attention to a symbolization process that not only recognized but also endowed and *created* symbolic linkages.

In regard to neurosis, as understood by Freud (1893–1895) at the time of *Studies on Hysteria*, what is of significance in symbol formation is the connection between two ideational elements, one conscious and the other repressed, *forged* (joined together) by the operations of the primary process: displacement, condensation, and symbolization. In this regard, for Freud, it is the symbolic link that often *creates* the meaning.

According to this early model, clinically relevant symbolization is initiated by and a consequence of repression. The latter begins with the disconnection of an idea from the unpleasant, unacceptable, or intolerable emotions that were initially attached (*Besetzung*) to it or that it evoked and the banishment of that ideational representation from consciousness. Although no longer accessible to conscious awareness, the idea that is removed remains intact. That is, it remains an ideationally saturated psychic representation, even as it is unavailable to being thought about or known.

For example, the wish to leave the sickbed of one's dying father and attend the ball, accompanied by anger and resentment about having to stay at home, may need to be repressed – i.e., hidden from one's awareness. Its continued presence, now in the unconscious, as memory of the wish and the attendant anger may be indicated (symbolized) by a paralysis of one's arm. Although unavailable to consciousness, the ideational elements symbolized by the paralysis remain intact. It is as if they had been locked away out of sight, rather than dismantled. Something is hidden, nothing is destroyed. If and when repression is overcome and recovery of the memory accompanied by its associated feelings happens, they are seen to be unchanged. Thus, the only changes that occur when an idea is repressed are in the status of that idea vis-à-vis recollection and the displacement of its quota of affect. If the idea later escapes from repression, then the content of the idea that emerges is the same as the idea that was repressed.

Before rediscovery happens, however, the now disconnected psychic energy – the "quota of affect" – may be displaced and attached (*Besetzung*) to different ideas that remain available to consciousness. From the perspective of a third-party observer, these secondary ideas are, objectively speaking, inherently less disturbing or unproblematic. But the investment of these secondary ideational elements with the emotions – quota of affect – belonging to the now repressed, unacceptable ideational element, may link them symbolically in meaning to the latter.

This line of reasoning offers a clinical model and metapsychological explanation for the assumption that there is an underlying basis in unconscious phantasies for hysterical symptoms. Think here, for example, of Little Hans' repression of his Oedipal desires and fears of his father leading to the displacement of his castration anxiety onto a fear of horses. It is the affect displaced from unacceptable idea A (rivalry with father; desire to possess mother; fear of father's retaliation) onto neutral idea B (horses might be dangerous) that establishes the symbolic linkage. A connection forms between the now repressed unacceptable ideas A and the once neutral or indifferent idea B that has received and now carries the displaced emotional charge.

In the case of Little Hans, the horse was presumably not initially connected in his mind to his father, his Oedipal wishes or his castration fears, until these were repressed, divested of their affective charge. That charge was then re-attached to the idea of horses, transforming them into a danger. Once this transposition takes place, then it is the horse that *becomes* the other half of the *symbolum* and is unconsciously and symbolically linked to and stands in for the imagined figure of the threatening father.

This clinical model not only enabled Freud to discover hidden layers of meaning in the minds, symptoms, and dreams of neurotic patients but also allowed him to understand and explain the phenomenon of hysterical indifference:

> how a subject can evoke an important event in his own history with indifference, while the unpleasant or intolerable nature of an experience may be associated with a harmless event rather than with the one which originally brought about the unpleasure (displacement, 'false connection').
>
> (Laplanche & Pontalis, 1973, p. 62)

It also helped establish clinical guidelines regarding therapeutic action that were encapsulated in Freud's famous dictum that in psychoanalysis, we strive to make the unconscious conscious. Freud's assumption was that the undoing of repression

> re-establishes the relation between the memory of the traumatic event and its affect by restoring the connection between the different ideas involved [and their attendant emotions] and so facilitating the [conscious recognition and] discharge of affect (abreaction).
>
> (Laplanche & Pontalis, 1973, p. 62)

II

But our understanding of the place of symbolization changed as psychoanalytic understanding developed. As I have described elsewhere (Levine, 2022), André Green (1975) noted that Freud's (1923) introduction of his second topography (The Structural Theory)

> contained within it the nascent outlines of … an *action model* intended to supplement, rather than replace, the *dream model* of the Topographic Theory. While the latter focused on psychic ideational representations in the form of wishes, desires, phantasies and repressed traumatic memories of childhood, the new model opened up the examination of the implications of the presence within the ego of the drives. Freud conceived of the latter as purely energic entities – force or pressure without differentiated aim, object or meaning – that, in their initial, not yet transformed state, were represented in the psyche by non-ideational registrations that were unknown and unknowable.[2] This theoretical change posed an implicit challenge to psychoanalysts that led them to expand their theory and technique, so as to better address the difficulties presented by non-neurotic [borderline] patients and psychic organizations.
>
> (Levine, 2025)[3]

A major element of this theoretical reorganization and advance was Freud's recognition that psychic ideational representation was not a hard-wired, built-in aspect of perception or thought, but was an ego function and a developmental achievement. The latter implicated the role of environmental provision of primary objects at key points in early development (Winnicott) and the unconscious, intersubjective regulation-enhancing activity of the analyst at key moments in the analytic process (Bion). Another consequence of Freud's theoretical shift was the change in emphasis of our clinical model from a theory centred on psychic *contents* (ideational *representations*) to a theory about *process* and the movements needed to create affectively imbued ideational representations in order to tame the unstructured, not yet represented aspects of *the drive* – that is, emotion, impulse, and somatic discharge – within the psychic apparatus.

When Freud (1923) formulated the turbulent, energic centre of the psyche that he called the id, he characterized it as

> the dark, inaccessible part of our personality ... something that we must approach ... with analogies: we call it chaos, a cauldron full of seething excitations... It is filled with energy reaching it from the instincts, but *it has no organization, produces no collective will, but only a striving to bring about the satisfaction of the instinctual needs subject to the observance of the pleasure principle... Instinctual cathexes seeking discharge – that, in our view, is all there is in the id.*
>
> (pp. 73–74, italics added)

He further asserted that that the quality of the cathexes of the id differs so completely from those of the ego that we cannot speak of or expect to find in the Id "what in the ego we should call an idea" (Freud, 1923, p. 75).

This – and extensive clinical experience – justified Green's (1998) caution that it would, therefore, at times be misleading for analysts to "speak of desire ... [when] it is legitimate to ask ... if this category is really present, ... [R]aw and barely nuanced forms [of action], expressions of imperious instinctual demands, throw a doubt over the relevance of this qualification" (p. 102).

What Green is saying is that "imperious instinctual demands" should not be thought about as or assumed to be the organized carriers of the specifiable aims and objects that we speak of as wish and desire. They are instead non-specific forces and pressures that must be contained and transformed into specifiable wishes and desires by being assigned object and aim, after which they become the emotional fuel so to speak of the drive derivatives that we refer to as unconscious phantasy.[4]

If we add to the seething force-cauldron of the id the turbulence created by traumatic disturbances of the ego's regulatory processing – the latter a subject that Freud (1920) began to address in detail in *Beyond the Pleasure Principle* – then we are left with the recognition that a significant portion of psychic activity and clinical focus is now seen as involved with the development processes of ideational representation and symbolization, whose aims are those of qualifying – i.e., containing, taming, and directing – previously undirected and unqualified force. The means through which these transformations are seen to take place is through the *creation* of emotionally linked ideational psychic representations in an intersubjective, two-person process of *psychic figurability*. The latter is analogous to early infantile psychic development and has been an important subject of much debate in non-Lacanian French psychoanalysis.[5]

III

Along with the changes post-1920 and post-1923 noted in Freud's Structural Theory, there was a concomitant change in his theory of technique. In his paper Constructions in analysis, Freud (1937) made the remarkable admission that it is not always possible to uncover a repressed, pathogenic thought, wish, fantasy, or traumatic memory. Some pathogenic events occurred in the pre-verbal period, before the infant or very young child had the capacity to record or retain fully formed memories that would subsequently be recollectable. Later traumatic events could be so disorganizing to the psyche that they defied organization and inscription in retrievable narrative forms. Sometimes the "events" in question are actually *non-events,* failures of environmental provision at crucial moments of development and so it may be much more difficult to know and therefore recall what "could have" or "should have happened", but didn't (Green, 1980; Winnicott, 1974).

Encountering the patient's structural inability to retrieve, describe, and think about past events as memory challenged Freud's earlier assumption that the recovery of a previously repressed traumatic memory of childhood was an essential component of the analytic cure. Despite this obstacle, however, there was still hope for some remediation. Freud (1937) recognized that a construction, a *presumptive hypothesis* offered by the analyst, can sometimes serve the same dynamic role in the analytic cure as the recovery of a repressed traumatic childhood memory.

Rather than reaching for historical veracity, constructions aim at plausibility. They fill an explanatory void and can produce a sense of conviction in the patient that is signalled by some salutary movements in the subsequent analytic process. These may include a change in affective tone in the sessions, the appearance of significant dreams or new material in the analysis, an enlarged space for greater freedom of thought and feeling, etc. Many of these changes reflect a strengthened capacity for symbolization.

In retrospect, we can now see that Freud's (1937) discussion of construction is a specific instance of what generally proves true in the treatment of non-neurotic patients, such as Green's (1975) limit cases and other patients included in the widening scope of psychoanalytic treatment – e.g., borderline and primitive narcissistic personalities, impulse disorders, some panic attacks, psychoses, perversions, addictions, and somatic discharges. In the treatments of these patients, what is often required is that the analyst must intersubjectively and interactively participate in, catalyse, or even sometimes initiate an inductive, intuitive process of figurability, symbol formation, and meaning making. Non-neurotic patients cannot easily string together symbolically linked sequences of thoughts to form free associations or use the analytic setting as a facilitating environment. Following these patients' verbal productions and assuming that these are meaningful, symbol-laden indicators of unconscious content is not always sufficient to ensure analytic progress. Something more must be added:

> The presence ... and the help of the object are essential. What is demanded of the analyst is more than his affective capacity and empathy. It is his mental functions which are demanded, for the patient's structures of meaning have been put out of action.
>
> (Green, 1975, p. 6)

The analyst's internal psychic processes and active interventions are needed to catalyse and support the patient's capacity for symbolization in the service of affective regulation (Green, 1975, p. 11). This need places an emphasis on the actuality of the presence and quality of functioning of the analyst's mind and being – on the countertransference, a term that for Green (1975) "includes the whole mental functioning of the analyst" (p. 3).

Technically, this may require a more active stance than is needed in the treatment of neurosis and the neurotic parts of the mind (Levine, 2022). In neurosis, the analytic relationship unconsciously symbolizes and *repeats* a past relationship. In limit-cases, "the actuality of the encounter becomes ... the essential concern of the session... [W]hat takes place in the session is the process of internalization, and not work on something that has already been internalized" (Green, 2025, p. 70).

IV

Expansion of our treatment model and its application to a broader population of patients calls attention to the fine line that may exist between construction and impingement and inevitably raises concerns about suggestion and compliance. It often necessitates making compromises in the classical setting regarding frequency of sessions and use of the couch and may require a more active stance on the part of the analyst, who must lend his or her psychic functioning to the patient in order to become a central figure in the patient's emotional homeostasis. It is not enough to say that the analyst of the widening-scope patient needs a broader theory than that required for the treatment of neurosis. Each patient requires being met by their analyst within an external setting that respects and is sensitive to the limits of what the patient can tolerate and make use of: "one must not try to cure a patient beyond his need and his psychic resources to sustain and live from that cure" (Khan, 1986, p. 18).

Meeting the patient at the level at which the patient requires and in ways that the patient can use requires flexibility, patience, negative capability, and creativity. Bleger (1967) noted that patients often enter analysis with their own unconscious internal frame, one that is very different from that of the classical analyst. This difference may have to be accepted, tolerated, adapted to, and worked within by the analyst for extended periods of time before the patient can develop the capacity to enter into a more traditional analytic use of the resources of the psychoanalytic site (Donnet, 2009). In such circumstances, in order to maintain the potential for an *analytic* process that may eventually become manifest within the treatment, each analyst must possess a suitable *internal frame* (Green, 1997; Levine, 2024) and an analytic sensibility and attitude. Together, these may enable an on-going, silent, internal analytic processing of the treatment by the analyst for long periods, until such time as the patient can begin to internalize a congruent analytic frame and attitude that will allow the patient's perspective and understanding to shift from everyday socially, consensually validatable external reality to a recognition and appreciation of psychic reality.

The changes and expansion in our clinical model that require a more active stance should not be construed as an invitation to wild analysis or self-disclosure or a denial of the possibility of the patient's oppositional, evacuative, or destructive action. Freud's original cautions about the countertransference as an analyst-derived obstruction to the analytic process still apply. However, our appreciation of the complexity of this dimension of the analytic relationship is heightened by our understanding of the mutuality, inevitability, and value of enactments (which will require analytic understanding) and the need to unconsciously actualize micro-traumatic problematic repetitions in the transference (so that their presumed origins may be uncovered or constructed). Analytic understanding therefore requires an appreciation of the communicative dimension of projective identification and the thin – perhaps non-existent – line between an obstructive countertransference, the analyst's receptivity to the patient's projective identification and the analyst's subjectivity.

It is the analyst's countertransference in the original narrow sense of the term that may become the point of reception and actualization within the analytic relationship of a patient's unconscious projective identification, a "bringing to life" of the problematic object of the patient's past or inner world, that can then be recognized and addressed analytically in the here-and-now of the session and analytic relationship (Levine, 2022). Recall Freud's (1914) admonition that the enemy cannot be slain in absentia or in effigy! It is precisely the analyst's countertransference, subjectivity, and intuition that may need to take precedence as a source of information about the analytic moment, rather than just the "typescript" (semantic) meaning of the patient's words. We are therefore well advised to implement Bion's (1970) suggestion of trying to listen to our patients without memory and desire in an attempt to engage a kind of free-floating attention (*reverie*) that does not focus exclusively on the lexical meanings of words as signifiers.

The presence of an internal psychoanalytic frame and attitude within the analyst can silently help keep alive and temporarily compensate for a transitional space in the analytic dyad that the patient is not yet ready to tolerate or make use of. From this perspective, forms of analytic psychotherapy conducted sitting up at reduced frequencies may be seen as useful, *analytic* variations of a more classical setting in an analytic process of cure. This includes the application of more radical analytic therapeutic variations such as the French individual psychoanalytic psychodrama that Gibeault describes in detail in Chapter 5. The external setting of this type of treatment is, of course, very different from that of the analytic psychotherapy models employed in the English-speaking world. However, the presence of a strong internal psychoanalytic frame and analytic sensibility in all of the analyst participants in the psychodrama can qualify this treatment as truly analytic despite its unusual form. And as Gibeault and his French colleagues have demonstrated, it can be used to good effect in the treatment of psychosis.

An essay on the metapsychology of psychosis lies beyond the scope of this preface. However, since individual psychoanalytic psychodrama is so unfamiliar to Anglophone readers, it may be useful to offer a brief description of both the psychoanalytic understanding of psychosis and the way the psychodrama is seen to function in that treatment.

The *psychic thought functions* that enable an individual to understand psychic experience have been grouped together by De Masi (2009) under the heading of the *emotional unconscious*, which he suggests includes a series of vitality and self-organizing functions that are disabled and destroyed in the progressive process of psychosis. These include the capacities to dream, play, symbolize, form, allow for, and work with classical transferences along with – or based upon – self-object differentiation, affect (frustration) tolerance, and maintenance of Bion's (1962) "contact barrier" that separates conscious from unconscious, etc.

> The emotional unconscious is fueled by affective life and early infantile relational experiences; it constantly constructs the sense of personal identity, determines the subject's mode of relating to the world, generates the capacity to perceive and deal with emotions, and defines *the unaware consciousness of existence (of the self)* .... Whereas neurosis is the result of inharmonious functioning of the dynamic unconscious, psychosis stems from an alteration of the emotional unconscious: that is, of the mental apparatus that can symbolize emotions and use the function of thought.... During the course of the psychotic process the emotional unconscious undergoes a series of transformations, initially gradual and then later radical, that completely destroy its function of intrapsychic and relational communication.
>
> (De Masi, 2009, pp. 60–61, original italics)

When this occurs, what is lost is the potential space of the self and the mental functions needed for the continuous unconscious perception of one's psychic identity. Foremost among these functions are the capacities for symbolization, ideational linkage, and associative elaboration of thought. Without these functions, one cannot adapt to or learn from experience.

> Psychosis alters the unaware elements that underlie the construction of psychic reality. Hence, the aim of *making the unconscious conscious* remains appropriate for a neurotic patient who, while repressing truth, preserves it unconsciously, and does not destroy it. The destruction of meaning in the psychotic state stems from an attack – not experienced as such – on the functions of learning from emotional experience, and generates an ever closer dependence on an omnipotent system, that proves to be a parasitic production of the mind.
>
> (De Masi, 2009, p. 67, original italics)

In place of "representation of veridical reality", the future psychotic patient begins, *often early in infancy*, to build an alternative universe of omnipotent thought and, initially, a protective and compensatory world (psychic retreat) of endless power and/or pleasure. Psychotic disorders originate out of this dissociated world that builds up from childhood. It is not so much destructiveness that spurs the child who is destined to become psychotic, but a particular kind of pleasure – perhaps a desperate, autoerotic or auto-stimulating need – that drives him to leave the relational world in order to build "another world" that he himself creates and governs. In order to build this world of total pleasure, perceived as safer than or superior to all psychic reality, the patient must alter his sense organs and destroy the psychic organs of knowledge.

Sometimes this dissociated world can be of use to the child as a defence against an uninhabitable world, made so due to trauma or prolonged maternal depression, a lack of parental emotional involvement, or other sources of early or severe frustrations that drive the organism "beyond" existential pain. Initially, the patient is seduced by the pleasurable state of this psychic retreat and does not understand the danger that comes with this kind of operation.

However, once this dissociated world is constructed and takes hold instituting the psychotic state, the problem may function like that of an addiction. Can patients maintain reality contact in the face of pain, frustration, annihilation anxiety, and other primitive agonies or do they retreat to the psychotic world, where their minds no longer work as a *thought organ* but rather as a *perceptive organ* that continuously produces sensorial phantasies, which are felt as real?

The ability to create a sensory world separated from reality, which gives rise to delusions and hallucinations, originates from the dissociated reality that has been created in psychic withdrawal. In the delusional state, the patient does not think: he "sees" and "hears". He "sees" via the mind's eyes and "hears" via the mind's ears. The mind behaves as if it were a sensorial organ instead of a meaning making organ. Through the intersubjective, dramaturgical assistance of the psychodrama, however, support for symbolization, thought, play, and reflection may help restore and maintain an internal psychic space where reality can be perceived and tolerated and meaning may be made of one's experience. Patients may be helped to symbolize, imaginatively "play", and therefore integrate and regulate a more cohesive, reality adapted sense of self, object, and meaning in the world. They can be helped in these sessions to develop an assisted capacity to create symbolic correspondences and associatively elaborate. If successful, these processes can help build a stronger identity and sense of self and achieve and maintain a more competent level of psychic functioning.

Notes

1 Laplanche and Pontalis (1973) quote Levi-Strauss (1950) as saying that "Any culture may be looked upon as an ensemble of symbolic systems, in the front rank of which are to be found language, marriage laws, economic relations, art, science and religion" (p. 440).
2 Increasingly, Freud saw the inherent aim of the drive as generalized tension reduction via discharge. The specific circumstances that permitted discharge, i.e., the selection and assignment of a specific, real world aim and object, were the provenance of the drive's derivatives. See Laplanche and Pontalis (1973) for the difference between drive and instinct and Levine (2022) for further discussion.
3 See also Levine (2022) for an extended discussion.
4 Note the distinction here between this assumption and that of Klein and others, who assume that phantasy and ideational organization, i.e., aim and object, are intrinsic components of the drive *ab initio*.
5 See for example Botella and Botella (2005) and Levine (2012, 2022).

References

Bion, W.R. (1962). *Learning from Experience*. London: Heinemann.
Bion, W.R. (1970). *Attention and Interpretation*. New York: Basic Books.
Bleger, J. (1967). Psycho-analysis of the psycho-analytic frame. *International Journal of Psycho-Analysis*, 48: 511–519.
Botella, C., Botella, S. (2005). *The Work of Psychic Figurability*, trans. A. Weller. London: Routledge.
De Masi, F. (2009). *Vulnerability to Psychosis*. London: Karnac.
Donnet, J.-L. (2009). *The Analyzing Situation*, trans. A. Weller. London: Karnac Books.
Freud, S. (1893–1895). *Studies on Hysteria. S.E.* 2. London: Hogarth Press, 1955.
Freud, S. (1914). Remembering, repeating and working-through. *S.E.* 12. London: Hogarth Press, pp. 145–156.
Freud, S. (1920). *Beyond the Pleasure Principle. S.E.* 18. London: Hogarth Press, pp. 3–64.
Freud, S. (1923). *The Ego and the Id. S.E.* 19. London: Hogarth Press, pp. 1–66.
Freud, S. (1937). Constructions in analysis. *S.E.* 23. London: Hogarth Press, pp. 255–270.

Green, A. (1975). The analyst, symbolization and absence in the analytic setting (on changes in analytic practice and analytic experience)—In memory of D.W. Winnicott. *International Journal of Psychoanalysis*, 56: 1–22.

Green, A. (1997 [1980]). The dead mother. In: A. Green (Ed.) *On Private Madness*. London: Karnac, pp. 142–173.

Green, A. (2023 [1997]). The psychoanalytic frame: Its internalization by the analyst and its application in practice. In: A. Green (Ed.) *The Freudian Matrix of André Green. Towards a Psychoanalysis for the Twenty-First Century*, ed. H. B. Levine, trans. Dorotheé Bonnigal-Katz and Andrew Weller. London and New York: IPA/Routledge, pp. 120–140.

Green, A. (1998). The primordial mind and the work of the negative. *International Journal of Psychoanalysis*, 79: 649–665.

Green, A. (2025). *Contemporary Psychoanalytic Practice*, ed. H. B. Levine and trans. A. Jacobs. London: Karnac (forthcoming).

Khan, M. (1986 [1972]). Introduction. In: D.W. Winnicott (Ed.) *Holding and Interpretation. Fragment of an Analysis.* New York: Grove Press, pp. 1–18.

Laplanche, J., Pontalis, J.B. (1973). *The Language of Psychoanalysis*. New York and London: Norton.

Levi-Strauss, C. (1950). Introduction to Mauss, M. *Sociologie et Anthropologie*. Paris: Presses Universitaires de France.

Levine, H.B. (2012). The colourless canvas: Representation, therapeutic action and the creation of mind. *International Journal of Psychoanalysis*, 93: 607–629.

Levine, H.B. (2022). *Affect, Representation and Language. Between the Silence and the Cry*. Abingdon, Oxon and New York: Routledge/IPA.

Levine, H.B. (Ed.) (2024). On the question of the internal frame. *International Journal of Psychoanalysis*, 105: 234–241.

Levine, H.B. (2025). Introduction. In: A. Green (Ed.) *Contemporary Psychoanalytic Practice*, ed. H. B. Levine and trans. A. Jacobs. London: Karnac (forthcoming).

Winnicott, D.W. (1974). Fear of breakdown. *International Review of Psychoanalysis*, 1: 103–107.

Introduction

In his poem "Correspondences", Baudelaire invites us to enter the domain of symbolization, to dream in it and endeavour to understand the principles on which it rests. Between man and nature, a nexus of relationships is woven in which something will represent something else for someone, whether it is man in nature, the writer, or the eventual reader. Symbolization brings different elements into relationship and establishes "correspondences" according to a natural analogy in which the relationship between the symbol and what is symbolized will have a motivation based on a certain similarity ranging from the concrete to the abstract (night, symbol of the irrational) or from the concrete to the concrete (nature, symbol of the mother).

In these analogies and correspondences, the body and sensoriality in general play a major role that Baudelaire does not fail to highlight, since "perfumes, sounds, and colours correspond". Sensoriality and sensuality converge in these relations that are interwoven, where the body conveys in an indivisible unity "the ecstasy of the soul and senses".

But in order to evoke the semantics of the symbol, it is necessary to use language, which itself has a symbolic dimension since it is made up of signs; by virtue of an arbitrary convention, signs will establish a correspondence between a sensible event and something else that belongs to another order.

We can then wonder about the origins of this convention and, through the etymology of the word, rediscover the original social dimension of the symbol. The word "symbol", derived from the Greek *symbolon*, referred for the ancient Greeks to an object split in two, a stone or a tablet, whose reunion (*sumballô = reunite*, put together) permitted two allies or their descendants to have their common links recognized. This pact had been formed by breaking the object into two parts and by sharing it between the two persons who had previously wanted to attest thereby to their ties of alliance.

It was into this adventure of symbolization that Freud introduced a new dimension by establishing a link between conscious symbols and unconscious symbolized elements. In the correspondence between the two terms, the raison d'être for the analogy was lost due to the introduction of this topographical dimension. The need for interpretation became all the more compelling in that unconscious symbolism was initially not available to

DOI: 10.4324/9781003545651-1

understanding. The history of psychoanalysis has shown that multiple issues emerged, first in the very development of Freud's thought, and then in that of his successors who ultimately merely confirmed the polysemy of the concept of symbolization which, with its corollary notions such as symbol, symbolic function, metaphor, and so on, constitutes the legacy of our whole civilization.

The term "symbol" has been used by all thinkers for the last two thousand years, as has been pointed out by Umberto Eco (1986, see chapter 4, pp. 130–162)[1] who has endeavoured to define the distinctiveness of the "symbolic mode" and to distinguish it from all closely related notions. His reflections allow the symbol to be situated within a theory of signs where, once again, a great deal of confusion exists. Symbolism can thus be likened to *semiotics* as a capacity to produce verbal and nonverbal signs capable of organizing experience. The conceptions of Ernst Cassirer, Claude Lévi-Strauss, and Jacques Lacan are related to a theory of the symbolic function, identified here with semiotics, which attests to the primacy of linguistics. The definition of the symbol in Charles Sanders Peirce's work as a dimension of what is conventional and arbitrary has its place in this perspective of semiotics which ultimately proves to be too broad a definition of the category of the symbolic.

This issue lies at the heart of the semantic confusion between the sign and the symbol. I should like to recall here some well-known distinctions from a linguistic point of view. Sometimes, as in Ferdinand de Saussure's work, the sign refers within language to the relations of meaning between the signifier and the signified; these relations are necessarily *unmotivated*, for they are of a different nature, while nonetheless being *necessary* insofar as one of the terms cannot exist without the other and vice-versa. The symbol, on the contrary, refers to a more or less stable association between two units of the same level, either two signifiers or two signifieds: a relationship that is both unnecessary and motivated, according to relations of contiguity and similarity. As Saussure (2011) says, "One characteristic of the symbol is that it is never wholly arbitrary; it is not empty, for there is the rudiment of a natural bond between the signifier and the signified. The symbol of justice, a pair of scales, could not be replaced by just any other symbol, such as a chariot" (p. 68). Owing to this "analogical correspondence" between what is symbolizing and what is symbolized, the concept of symbol is excluded from the definition of the linguistic sign, which is related to the principle of the "arbitrariness of the sign".

C.S. Peirce (1931–1958), on the other hand, defines the sign beyond the Saussurian restriction to the linguistic sign, as "something which stands to somebody for something in some respect or capacity" (*CP* 2:228). This definition implies substitutive relations between two terms for a given subject, thus a triadic relationship, in contrast to that proposed by Saussure, who eliminates both the subject and the object from his definition of the sign, only retaining a difference within language. Peirce adds that this substitutive relationship occurs "in some respect or capacity", which implies that the sign does not represent the totality of the object but only a certain aspect of it, thereby excluding any idea of a complete duplication or reproduction of the object.

For Peirce, the symbol becomes, then, a category of the sign defining the "conventional rule" between the signifier and the signified, that is, the linguistic sign in its arbitrary dimension. Conversely, the symbol in Saussure's sense is closer is to the two other categories of signs: the icon, corresponding to a factual likeness between its signifier and its signified, for instance between the representation of an animal and the animal represented; the index, operating by virtue of factual contiguity, between its signifier and its signified, as in the classical example of smoke indicating fire.

This is reminiscent of the reference to perceptual experience and to the essence of natural analogy and the symbol, as a motivated sign; the symbol, in Peirce's sense, denotes, on the contrary, the arbitrary sign. It may be added that, for him, language implies the relation between three types of signs which in reality are more like semiotic categories; this represents an interesting solution to the alternative of Plato's *Cratylus*[2] between convention and nature: he also points out that the most perfect signs are those in which the iconic, index-based and symbolic aspects are amalgamated in as equal proportions as possible. This perspective is very instructive when it comes to approaching the processes of symbolization in psychoanalysis which should be able to unite the richness of images with the precision of linguistic signs.

The very elaboration of this triadic conception of the sign attests to the conditions of its functioning: the condition of a sign is not only one of substitution but also one of a possible interpretation, implying three terms: the sign, the interpretant of the sign which is another sign, and the object to which it refers, first the *immediate object* or semiotic signified and, beyond that, the *dynamic object* or perceptual signified. Here we have a perspective that represents a logic of the *action* of the sign, where the dynamism of the relations of meaning is due to the functioning of the third term, the interpretant, which is both a component of the sign and a sign itself, an intermediate and mediating term that determines an infinite process of symbolization. It is also a conception of the sign that opens out, as Umberto Eco (1986, pp. 68–86) has suggested, on to the encyclopaedia of the world, rather than confining itself to the dictionary, as evoked by Saussure's dyadic conception of the sign.

The category of the symbolic may also be likened to *rhetoric*, but once again we do not have access to a specific meaning because, while it is a matter of a general strategy where an indirect meaning is substituted for a direct meaning, the actualized content has in reality to be clarified by reference to a context that fixes the pertinent elements. The connection with dream symbolism perhaps adds the unconscious connotation but tends, in Freud's work, to link up with the dimension of the code and univocity. As for allegory, it implies a visual or verbal text where the first meaning of each image is replaced by a second meaning, according to a rather precise code, and therefore cannot account for the multivocity that is suggested by the dimension of the symbol. From this point of view, neither equivalence with the motivated sign, the symbol according to Saussure, nor with the arbitrary sign, the symbol according to Peirce, would succeed in defining specifically the category of the symbolic.

The symbolic mode, as a means of production or textual interpretation, should be able to avoid the dimension of the code which refers to univocity, leaving open the possibility of "infinite derivation"; while the word "symbol" evokes "something that stands in for something else", it possesses an original reflexivity suggested by its etymology according to which "the expression and the inexpressible content become one and the same thing". It is not the indefinite referral inherent to the linguistic sign, but "the sensation that what is conveyed by the expression, however nebulous and rich it may be, lives at that moment *in* the expression" (1986, p. 218). This view of the truth of symbols may be likened to mystical and magical experience, of which Carl Gustav Jung and George Groddeck made themselves representatives.

The dimension of ineffability and individuality connoted by this dimension of the symbolic nonetheless requires the rule of interpretation if it is not to become confined within silence and incommunicability. The social and communicable dimension should be part of the symbol, but the appeal to the interpreter involves the contrary risk, namely that the symbolic mode will not engender the allegorical mode and will not be fixed in univocity.

What individual narcissism gains in terms of infinite openness, it loses in the transition to social recognition which seeks the reference to the code. Furthermore, as someone who holds the keys of interpretation necessarily has power, the dimension of social recognition can be totally undermined, since power is exerted on the basis of the code. It is well known how psychoanalytic theories have high stakes in these power struggles. They are related to the need to legitimize by means of a theology, even if negative and secularized, the practice of the symbolic mode.

This adventure of the symbolic mode, briefly touched on above, comprises in its different moments, what psychoanalysis was and is confronted with when it strives to understand symbolization. This is what I would like to show by looking at the major issues in the history of this discovery, first with regard to hysteria and the theory of mnemic symbols (Chapter 1), then through the theory of dream symbolism (Chapter 2).

The Freudian approach to symbolism will be illustrated by looking at the issue of the symbolic significance of money in analysis. As symbolization is a process that makes use of projection, I will then go on to explore the relations between projection and projective identification by showing the points of convergence between Freudian and Kleinian thought in the theory of projection as a process and mechanism of defence (Chapter 4). Symbolization in analysis, based on clinical illustrations ranging from psychosis to neurosis, in both children and adults, should help the reader to measure the clinical and technical significance of the theoretical issues outlined (Chapter 5). As the concept of symbolization was not directly theorized by Sigmund Freud, it will then be interesting to point out the similarities and differences with the corollary concepts of representation, sublimation, and creation (Chapter 6). Since the adventure of symbolization is coextensive with the emergence of *Homo sapiens*, the evocation of prehistoric art during the Palaeolithic age will give me an opportunity of showing how prehistoric artists were the first to attest to this instinctual drive experience that is characteristic of the process of hominization (Chapter 7).

Freud (1920) was sensitive to this crucial question of nature and culture in the history of humanity, since the invention of tools, the domestication of fire, and the building of dwelling-places had, according to him, all been conquests of man with a view to protecting himself against nature; although human culture also implied the "inter-regulation of human beings" and consequently symbolic institutions in general, he did not mention amongst its cultural productions the place of prehistoric art as an exceptional witness to the adventure of symbolization from the moment modern man arrived in Europe around 40,000 B.P. (Before Present). Symbolization as a process is therefore part of an individual and collective adventure which is equally one of human creativity stimulated by the awareness of death and the urgent need to create indestructible traces, images, and forms in order to overcome man's "state of distress" or primordial helplessness.[3]

Notes

1 Translator's note: The 1986 English edition of Eco's *Semiotics and the Philosophy of Language* is an abridged version of the 1988 French translation from the Italian original in 1984. Some of the author's citations cannot be found in the English edition, in which cases I have referred to the French edition.

2 In the dialogue of Plato's (1997) *Cratylus*, it is a matter of deciding on the origin of meaning: either meaning is in language and depends on a convention related to the arbitrariness of the sign or it is first in things and pre-exists language, which leads to the hypothesis of a primitive motivation of the sign, which, just like a painting, is an "imitation" of reality.

3 This book takes up again, in part, the report "Destins de la symbolisation" presented at the 49th Congress of French-Speaking Psychoanalysts and published in the *Revue Française de Psychanalyse*, 1989, 53(6):1517–1617 (Gibeault, 1989).

References

Baudelaire, C. (1857). *The Flowers of Evil*, trans. William Aggeler. Fresno, CA: Academy Library Guild, 1954.

Eco, U. (1986/1984). *Semiotics and the Philosophy of Language*. Bloomington and Indianapolis: Indiana University Press.

Saussure, F. de (2011/1916). *Course of General Linguistics*. Columbia University Press.

Peirce, C.S. (1931–1958). *Collected Papers of Charles Sanders Peirce*, vols. 1–6, 1931–35, Charles Hartshorne and Paul Weiss. Cambridge, MA: Harvard University Press.

Plato (1997) *Cratylus*, trans. C.D.C. Reeve, Indianapolis: Hackett Publishing Inc.

1 Conversion hysteria

The discovery of symbolization

Freud's first texts on conversion hysteria show how psychoanalysis was discovered through the very possibility of identifying a process of symbolization. One of the first signs of this adventure can be found in the article of 1893 suggested by Jean-Martin Charcot and written in French: "Some points for a comparative study of organic and hysterical motor paralyses" (Freud, 1893). The difference between cerebral paralyses is explained by the anatomy of the nervous system, whereas, as Freud notes,

> what is in question in hysterical paralysis, just as in anaesthesia, etc., is the everyday, popular conception of the organs and of the body in general. That conception is not founded on a deep knowledge of neuro-anatomy, but on our tactile and above all on our visual perceptions.
>
> (p. 170)

This is what emerges from hysterical paralysis, which may be marked by both excessive intensity and exact limitation: these are two characteristics that are excluded in organic paralysis, and cerebral anatomy cannot explain their simultaneity. In other words, while organic paralysis can be explained by the objective body, hysterical paralysis can only be understood in terms of the subject's own body.

However, as was the case with Charcot, the clinical-anatomical method, a method of differences, introduced, as a necessity, the maintenance of an identity between organic cerebral paralysis and hysterical paralysis. Yet in organic diseases of the nervous system, the reference to lesions remained the basic explanatory hypothesis. In order to match the organic lesions observed in neurological affections, they also had to be observed in hysteria, even if they were only dynamic, that is without any gross organic alteration.

Freud used, then, the same explanatory hypothesis. But his understanding of the notion of dynamic lesions was different from Charcot's. For Charcot, a dynamic lesion remained a real lesion: it was not an organic lesion that could be identified in an autopsy, but it was nonetheless thought of as an organic modification like an oedema, anaemia or active hyperaemia.

DOI: 10.4324/9781003545651-2

For Freud, any organic modification was excluded because hysteria could not be explained by the anatomy of the nervous system. In order to imagine this functional alteration without a concomitant organic lesion, fleeting or mobile, Freud "asked permission to move onto psychological ground". And so the lesion in question in hysteria no longer had anything but a metaphorical meaning:

> Considered psychologically, the paralysis of the arm consists in the fact that the conception of the arm cannot enter into association with the other ideas constituting the ego of which the subject's body forms an important part. The lesion would therefore be *the abolition of the associative accessibility of the conception of the arm.*
> (Freud, 1893, p. 170, Freud's emphasis)

It remained for Freud to explain why there was a dynamic lesion in hysteria, in the sense of this inaccessibility of an idea for "the associations of the conscious ego". The solution envisaged was that which he and Joseph Breuer had just put forward in their "Preliminary communication" titled "On the psychical mechanism of hysterical phenomena" (Freud & Breuer, 1893), published a few months earlier, at the beginning of 1893: this "purely functional alteration" corresponded to an unconscious fixation of this idea with the memory of the trauma.

According to this theory, the development of hysterical symptoms was attributed to the recollection of an actual psychic trauma. For Breuer and Freud, this was an "*extension* of Charcot's concept of traumatic hysteria". Charcot had observed that, in this type of hysteria, somatic symptoms, in particular paralyses, often appeared after a period of latency and following a physical trauma, even though the latter did not account mechanically for the symptoms in question. As he said himself, these phenomena appear "following and consequence of a 'shock' with or without injury" – by which he meant a physical trauma – "but where emotion plays a great part" (Charcot, 2015/1890, p. 232). In other words, hysteria occurred not as a result of a physical trauma but of a psychical trauma. Breuer and Freud extended the role of the affect of fright to common non-traumatic hysteria, and each case of hysteria therefore was to be traced back to an actual psychical trauma. On this aspect, Charcot's influence remained predominant.

But in reality, the originality of Freud and Breuer resided in the reversal of the *understanding* of the concept of hysteria. Charcot had noticed a period of latency between the physical trauma and the appearance of symptoms. But Breuer and Freud were to discover the psychological meaning of this observation and insisted on the fact that the psychical trauma did not act, to use their expression, like an *agent provocateur,* as was suggested in Charcot's conception by the relationship between the physical shock and the appearance of hysterical phenomena: even if they spoke of "a causal relationship between the motivating incident and the phenomenon", it could not be one involving operative linear causality. Rather, the pathogenic effect of the trauma was due to a *memory* that was still active. Charcot's mechanical conception thus needed to be replaced by a much more psychological conception whereby "hysterics suffer mainly from reminiscences", according to the famous formula in the "Preliminary communication" (Freud & Breuer, 1893, p. 7). In fact, the dimension of memory opened up the space of representation, leading Freud to evoke for the first time, in this joint work with Breuer, the idea of "this sort of symbolization" (Freud & Breuer, 1893, p. 5) between the hysterical symptom and its motivation. Following an intuition that would subsequently have major consequences, the authors note that this symbolic relation is similar to that which "healthy people form in dreams" (Freud & Breuer, 1893).

Somatic conversion and mnemic symbols

This theory of hysterical symbolization nonetheless requires us to clarify the connection between the conception of affect underlying the problem of somatic conversion and that of representation, which governs the definition of the symptom as a mnemic symbol. The equivalence between the affect and a quantity is, as we know, at the basis of the theory of abreaction: an event has acquired traumatic power by virtue of the intensity of the affect that was linked to it and which, for various reasons – hypnoid state, for Breuer; defence, for Freud – could not be elaborated associatively, that is to say brought into relationship with other ideas capable of correcting the disturbing effect of this event, nor discharged, "abreacted", at the motor level through an adequate reaction such as tears or anger.

The notion of abreaction puts the emphasis on the discharge of this quantity of affect and the cathartic method is efficient insofar as language is "a substitute for action" and permits, under hypnosis, both the recollection of the memory and the discharge of the affect.

Freud and Breuer note that language serves as "a substitute for action; by its help, an affect can be 'abreacted' *almost as effectively*" (Freud & Breuer, 1893, p. 8, my emphasis), which implies a similar but not identical reaction. The path through language determines quite a different status for representation and affect, respectively: in one case, the immediate affective reaction – tears or anger – to a traumatic *perception* is in the order of a signal, which subsequently seeks to suppress language and governs an automatic reflex, a reaction at the level of behaviour; in the other, the affective reaction mediated by language is in the order of a *sign*, which gives rise to an idea and permits an attenuated discharge of affect. Between perception and representation, between the signal and the sign, there is a gap in which the crucial aspects of both the discovery of hysterical symbolization and of human communication proper lie.

This gap can be found at a theoretical level in the two approaches to the relations between psyche and soma elaborated by Freud in connection with conversion hysteria. The leap from the psychical to the somatic is defined as the transposition, in the body, of the sum of excitation attached to the incompatible idea, whereas abreaction is so to speak a "conversion in the opposite direction" (Freud, 1894, p. 49), making it possible to link up once again the idea and its sum of excitation.

In contrast with Pierre Janet who saw the splitting of consciousness as the characteristic feature of hysteria, Freud distinguished in this "capacity for conversion" an "important part of the disposition to hysteria – a disposition which in other respects is still unknown – a psychical-physical aptitude for transposing very large sums of excitation into the somatic innervation" (Freud, 1894, p. 50). This psycho-physical theory is one of a complete and global expression of psychical emotion at the somatic level. The disadvantages may be surmised: in what way would the somatic symptom be pathological and different from any other expression of emotions?

At the same time as this psycho-physical conception of hysteria, Freud nonetheless introduced another conception of the relations between the psychical and the somatic when he described the somatic symptom as the *mnemic symbol* of the repressed idea. The hysterical symptom is a physical "parasite" that refers to a forgotten history and to a genuine "dynamic of representation", which he compares with a complex structure with a pathogenic *central nucleus* containing the memories of repressed events or thoughts and *concentric strata* containing themes that are further and further removed from the centre (Freud & Breuer, 1895a, p. 289). Hence, the idea that psychoanalytic work involves radial penetration towards the inner layers, corresponding to activity.

In *Studies on Hysteria*, Freud is led to wonder about the links between hysterical symptoms and buried memories and to postulate a psychical topography based on the "bar" between the conscious and the unconscious indicated by the patient's resistances during analytic work. While the metaphor of the nucleus and concentric circles clearly emphasizes the idea of a cut between the two psychic spaces, in other respects, it risks signifying a reification of the psychical apparatus and a conception of the unconscious as a treasure of memories, foreign bodies to be eradicated. However, this comparison is corrected by the idea of an infiltration which precludes the possibility of easily locating the *boundary* between "the elements of the normal ego" and the "pathogenic organization", between the shell and the kernel, giving a glimpse of analytic work that is centred more on looking for logical sequences between thoughts – and, I would say, between phantasies – than on the discovery of an external trauma.

In the "Project for a scientific psychology", Freud (1950 [1895]) clarifies the notion of mnemic symbol which he compares with a symbol, in the usual sense of the word. In a "normal" symbol, the link between the symbol and what is symbolized is maintained: he gives the example of the knight who fights for his lady's glove and "who knows that the glove owes its importance to the lady". In this synecdoche of the part for the whole, the conjunction of meaning is manifest. In hysteria, on the contrary, it is the loss of the link between the symbol and what it symbolizes that is observed:

> The *hysteric* who weeps at A is quite unaware of the fact that he/she is doing so on account of the association A–B, and B itself plays no part at all in his/her psychical life. The symbol has in this case taken the place of the *thing* entirely.
>
> (Freud, 1950 [1895]), p. 349)

In this disjunction of meaning, the affect normally attached to what is symbolized is now attached to the symbol. In both cases, the substitution implies both an affirmation, namely, the identity between the symbol and what is symbolized, and a negation, namely, the non-identity between the symbol and what is symbolized (A ≠ B). Hence, the tension, within the symbolic substitution itself, between a literal interpretation that leads to nonsense and a symbolic interpretation which adds meaning, owing to the negation that prohibits purely and simply equating the two terms in question. In hysterical symbolization, the impossibility of bringing negation into play explains the apparent nonsense of the symptom.

What may appear here to be a mere relation of substitution between two terms, the symbol and what is symbolized, implies in fact the existence of a possible interpretation, of a sequence of propositions that makes it possible to attribute a meaning in relation to the *context*. In Peirce's language of semiology, what is involved is essentially a *triadic* relation, where the sign is "something, A, which brings something, B, its *interpretant* sign determined or created by it, into the same sort of correspondence with something, C, its *object*, as that in which itself stands to C" (Peirce, 1976/1902, 4:20–21): a semantics of discourse based on "usage", corresponding in fact, according to Umberto Eco's (1986, pp. 43–45) remarks, to the structure of implication that generates interpretation. According to this propositional logic, a sign is in place of something else, not by virtue of a fixed correlation established by the code, in an *equivalence* between expression and content, but according to the modes of an *inference* that establishes an interpretative *process* (1986, pp. 34–36): if there is a somatic symptom, *then* there is a traumatic scene or phantasy.

Between the symptom and the repressed scene, real or phantasized, Freud describes this interpretive sequence in a threefold order: a linear chronological order, within each theme, which evokes well-arranged files; a concentric sequence in terms of themes, whose discovery is increasingly difficult as one approaches the central nucleus due to the patient's resistances; and finally, a logical thread which reaches as far as the nucleus, following a twisting path, corresponding to a ramified system of lines "and more particularly to a converging one" with "nodal points at which two or more threads meet" (Freud & Breuer, 1895a, p. 290).

This logical sequence is the most essential one according to Freud because it is the only one that has a dynamic character, the two other dispositions being more morphological in character. The search for the logical thread through the psychic material must succeed in overcoming the patient's resistances in order to reach the nucleus, and it is in this respect that this disposition has a dynamic character, since it reveals a conflict between contrary forces and, as Freud points out, *the existence of hidden unconscious motives* (Freud & Breuer, 1895a, p. 293, Freud's emphasis).[1] The discovery that "several threads which run independently, or which are connected at various points by side-paths, debouch into the nucleus" (p. 290) leads Freud to think that a symptom as a mnemic symbol "is over-determined in several ways" (Freud & Breuer, 1895, p. 293). The process of inference linked to interpretive research necessarily implies multivocity and, in this period during which he discovered the dynamics of the unconscious, symbolization covered the whole field of distortion linked to repression.

Between the clinical attitude that permits the appearance of the method of free association and the theoretical attitude, Freud was nonetheless divided between the respect for multivocity and the quest for univocity, based on physical "reality" or material "reality". This is why somatic conversion, as a global transposition of a quota of affect from the psychical to the somatic, and symbolization, are in fact two complementary factors.

In the case of Frau Emmy von N., for instance, certain symptomatic movements, such as the expression on her face, the expression of terror when stretching out her hands in front of her, her tightly clasped fingers, corresponded only to the "expression of the emotions". Other movements, such as playing restlessly with her fingers, rubbing her hands together to prevent herself from screaming, were "directly related to her pains". Freud refers in this connection to a psycho-physiological principle laid down by Charles Darwin, "the principle of the overflow of excitation" to "explain the expression of the emotions", for instance "for dogs wagging their tails" (Freud & Breuer, 1895a, p. 91). Finally, certain motor symptoms such as clacking, stuttering, screaming, and the longer formula, serving "as protective measures", all had "one thing in common. They can be shown to have an original or long-standing connection with traumas, and stand as symbols for them in the activities of memory" (Freud & Breuer, 1895a, p. 95).

The specificity of hysterical symptoms could only therefore be clarified insofar as they were considered mnemic symbols of traumatic memories and not as a global expression of a sum of psychical excitation in the body or *vice-versa*: this transition nonetheless remained enigmatic and for clinical practice, it was of little importance.

There remained the problem of the link between traumatic memories and the symptom. Why would this or that memory have produced this or that symptom? Freud refers to two fundamental types of association put forward by every theory of associationism since the classical period of hysteria: association by contiguity and association by similarity.

Thus, concerning the astasia-abasia of Elisabeth von R., one of the clinical cases in *Studies on Hysteria,* Freud first speaks of "conversion based on simultaneity" (Freud & Breuer, 1895a, p. 176), where there is simultaneity between an organic pain and a psychical affect: thus moral suffering is replaced by pains in the legs because pains of a somatic order – in this case muscular rheumatic pains – had really existed at the outset and the path was already traced so that the neurosis could make use of it, increase it, and maintain it; it sufficed for the pains to coincide in consciousness with the emotions. There is also simultaneity between this somatic pain and a real fact: the contact between one of the painful legs of Elisabeth with her father's swollen leg while the bandages were being changed had transformed this area of the leg into an artificial hysterogenic zone.

In this astasia-abasia, there are also associations by similarity, which Freud calls *conversion by symbolization*: the distressing impression of "not being able to take a single step forward" in life, of "standing still" of "not having anything to lean on" found expression in a somatic symptom which made walking extremely difficult. The patient "had done nothing more or less than look for a symbolic expression of her painful thoughts and that she had found it in the intensification of her sufferings" (Freud & Breuer, 1895a, p. 152). Freud clearly states that in this case, the symbolization did not *create* the astasia-abasia, but simply reinforced a symptom that was already present owing to associations by simultaneity. This seemed to him to be the general rule: the reference as a last resort to physical reality ought to allow for a really rational explanation.

Freud nevertheless found himself faced with examples that contradicted this rule, that is, cases where a formation of somatic symptoms occurred simply through symbolization. Thus, Frau Cäcilie had felt a penetrating pain in her forehead when her grandmother, who seemed very severe to her, "had given her a look so 'piercing' that it had gone right into her brain" (Freud & Breuer, 1895a, p. 180). On another occasion, the feeling of being slighted had been accompanied by a stabbing sensation in the region of the heart.

In these examples, there was no organic pain that could serve as a basis for conversion, no path already traced that could explain the determination of the symptom. Freud noted that verbal expressions like "a stab in the heart" or a "slap in the face", "I shall have to swallow this" had served as an intermediate link between the psychical emotion and the physical sensation. He assumes then that "the hysteric is not taking liberties with words, but is simply reviving once more the sensations to which the verbal expression owes its justification" (Freud & Breuer, 1895a, p. 181): originally, these expressions appeared when the emotions felt in response to a slight had in fact been accompanied by real physical sensations such as a precordial sensation or one of a constriction of the throat. This contiguity was in all probability lost thereafter because these verbal expressions had become so weakened that they were no more than figurative translations, weakened by triviality. By restoring the literal meaning of these statements and by actually reviving a physical sensation, the hysteric is merely returning to the very origin of these expressions.

Now, if the hysterical symbol leads to a literal interpretation of the metaphor and evokes the origin of language, what about this "common source"? In *Studies on Hysteria*, Freud leaves the question open: but we can already point out that with this hypothesis, Freud was basing associations by symbolization on associations by contiguity, which announced the future limitation of symbolism to the cultural stereotype, as he would do in his considerations on dream symbolism.

New light is thrown on this issue if we refer to Charles Peirce's sign theory. The determinants of the hysterical symptom can in fact be linked to the three types of signs distinguished by Peirce in the relation of the sign to its object, which defines the existential or semantic dimension of the sign. In Elisabeth's astasia-abasia, the association by contiguity between the painful leg, the muscular rheumatic pains, the father's swollen leg and the erotic effects – for her childhood friend, but also for her father – are in the order of the *index* which operates first and foremost by an experienced factual contiguity between the sign and its object. The associations by similarity between the expression "being stuck to the spot" and its utilization in its literal sense in a symptom of motor inhibition, or between the expression "I shall be obliged to swallow this" and the sensation of a hysterical aura in the throat, are in the order of the *icon* which operates above all by a factual similarity between the sign and its object. But these expressions are linguistic signs, belonging to the order of the *symbol* which operates first and foremost by a contiguity *established* between the sign and its object; this connection is in the nature of a convention which fixes a rule of interpretation: a symbol is "a sign which refers to the object that it denotes by virtue of a law, usually an association of general ideas, which operates to cause the symbol to be interpreted as referring to that object" (Peirce, 1931–1958, 2: 249).

It does not depend, like the index or the icon, on the presence of some factual contiguity or similarity, and thus designates the whole field of language: as Peirce points out, "all words, sentences, books, and other conventional signs are Symbols" (1931- 1958, 2: 292, 2: 292).

The dialectic between the index and the symbol is very informative here. The index refers to a given object in time and space, and is based mainly on a *natural link*; the symbol refers more to a general object and is characterized particularly by the predominance of an *artificial* link. Freud followed the index-related mode when, in his search for the determining causes of hysterical symptoms, he discovered associations by simultaneity in time and space: this is the path followed by medical semiology, which sees the symptom as a sign of illness. The index is related to the *positive fact* and *the perception* that grasps a relationship between two things or between two facts. It is the order of "sense certainty" (Hegel, 1807) and of the apparent reality that gives the feeling of immediately grasping things and their properties. For example, the objective truth of Elizabeth's astasia-abasia is found in this reference to an organic illness or to a real circumstance that can be situated precisely in time.

And yet, had Freud left matters there, he would never have discovered psychoanalysis. He did not reject the *uncertainties* that associations by symbolization without a real support represented for him, and subsequently the challenge to his *neurotica* presented by the discovery of infantile sexuality. For this, apparently objective reality, which is a feature of all positivism and empirism, overlooks the fact that this sense certainty is already informed by our linguistic knowledge: the objective relationship between the facts – for instance, here, between the effect and the cause – implies a logical relationship to the objectivity of this first relation that designates this object within our knowledge. Ultimately, it is to this fundamental intentionality of the object that Peirce's triadic definition of the sign refers, something that is clarified by the dimension of the symbol, as a convention. Freud's reference to the verbal expressions taken in their literal sense in hysteria led him to reflect on the dimension of language and meaning, about the origin of the convention that specifies the symbol.

It is clear that these expressions are statements or propositions that cannot be accounted for by the index-related dimension; language is not an immediate fact, but rather the manifestation itself of a mediation that is translated by the Peircean symbol: from this point of view the symbol refers less to a property, to an essence of things, than to a *function* of language: namely, of proposing the objective form of experience as a logical possibility. The Stoics had already pointed this out when they distinguished between the "representation" of a thing or its "image" which is produced by the thing itself, and that which is "expressible" (the linguistic sign) corresponding to what we can say about it, to what the soul expresses (signification) in relation to this thing (denotation) and which is no longer what the thing produces in the soul (representation): the dialectic pertained not to things but to the true or false statements pertaining to things (Diogenes, 1962, pp. 42–43), that is, not to the objective relations between the facts but to their logical relations.

This is what Eco (1984) highlights: "The Stoic model of sign assumes, therefore, the form of the inference ($p > q$), where the variables are neither physical realities nor events, but the propositions that express the events" (p. 31). The triadic dimension of the sign in Peirce's work does not refer to anything different: this implies that perception does not in itself have the power to create meaning, unless I possess the *general* law of antecedents to consequences that permits me to render the sensible fact meaningful.

That is why, if hysterical symptoms led Freud to the discovery of the unconscious and of infantile sexuality, it was because he took seriously this law of *inference* by not dwelling on index-related induction but by reflecting on the origins of these symbolizations without indicators, as manifested by Frau Cäcilie: the definition of the hysterical symptom as a mnemic symbol led him to want to understand the foundations of the conventionality and arbitrariness of the sign; the enigma of the leap from the somatic to the psychic drew him towards another enigma, that in which "a sense event refers to something of another order than itself" (Ortigues, 1962, p. 43), the leap from the sensible to the intelligible, which is equally one of the transition from the necessary to the contingent, from the physical to the non-physical, from certainty to uncertainty.

It is true that, initially, Freud provided an answer in the order of sense certainty with his hypothesis of words taken in their literal sense to explain certain hysterical conversions. Markers had nonetheless been laid down as to the importance of the body and the drive as "sources" of symbolization and language: the particular idiosyncrasy of hysteria thus opened out on to the universality of the symbolic function. It still remained for him to understand what had the potential of fostering the constitution of a bodily language and to explain the indefinitely symbolizable character of the sexual drive. The discovery of the *transference* as a "false connection" (Freud & Breuer, 1895a, p. 303) made it a particular case of the displacement of one idea to another and the equivalent of a *symptom* and *a symbol*. He was already placing emphasis on the relationship between the wish and the prohibition at the origin of the symptomatic displacement, of the "compulsion to associate" (Freud & Breuer, 1895a, p. 303) that Freud was to describe as a "primary process"; and, above all, he had surmised the role and importance of the lost object in the appearance of a process of symbolization.

Hysteria and sexuality

Actual neurosis and/or conversion hysteria: body and symbol

It is worth comparing Freud's studies on conversion hysteria with those of the same period on the actual neuroses. These studies illustrate the questions that he must have asked himself at the outset concerning the factors involved in the symbolization of the body: in fact it was his observations on the actual neuroses – neurasthenia and anxiety neurosis – which at that time he called "sexual neuroses" (Letter from Freud to Fliess, Draft B, dated 8 February, 1893 in Masson, 1985, p. 39)[2] that led him from the beginning to attach importance to the sexual aetiology of the neuroses and to reflect on the difficulties of the psychic integration of sexuality.

It was in connection with the actual neuroses that Freud presented his views of the sexual process from a purely physiological perspective of the accumulation of somatic sexual excitation that could be psychically bound by coming into contact with certain groups of ideas and lead to the specific action providing satisfaction. An anxiety neurosis appears when, for lack of any psychic elaboration, this somatic excitation is transformed into anxiety and is deployed somewhere on the boundary between the somatic and the psychic (Letter from Freud to Fliess dated June 6 1894, Draft E, in Masson, 1985, pp. 79–82).

In this schema, the inverse process of hysterical conversion can be recognized, as Freud described it at that time in his article "The neuro-psychoses of defence" (Freud, 1894). Moreover, in Draft E, he mentions this inverse relationship between anxiety neurosis and hysteria:

> This is once again a kind of *conversion* in anxiety neurosis, just as occurs in hysteria (another instance of their similarity); but in hysteria it is *psychic* excitation that takes a wrong path exclusively into the somatic field, whereas here it is a *physical* tension, which cannot enter the psychic field and therefore remains on the physical path.
> (Masson, 1985, p. 82)

From this physiological point of view, the description is perhaps clear, but the problem remains unresolved concerning the relationship between somatic excitation and psychic excitation. It is conceived as a series of periodic transformations of a physical quantity into a psychical quantity, governed by crossing a certain threshold. In this schema, it is always the totality of the excitation that is transformed globally and periodically, with the possibility of the process being reversed, which excludes any particular determination and any vicissitude separate from the psychic elements corresponding to the transformation of somatic excitation.

It is worth noting, however, that in describing the mechanism of hysterical conversion on the basis of the functional schema that he used in his description of the actual neuroses, Freud nonetheless maintained a difference concerning the nature of the excitation in question in each neurosis: in hysteria, the psychical excitation that flows into the somatic field is not necessarily sexual excitation; it may be excitation aroused by fear or anger; on the contrary, the somatic excitation in question in the actual neuroses is always sexual.

At the time of *Studies on Hysteria*, Freud did not believe, moreover, in the sexual aetiology of hysteria, something he was to confirm later:

> At the time at which I was attributing to sexuality this important part in the production of the *simple* neuroses, I was still faithful to a purely psychological theory in regard to the *psychoneuroses* [hysteria and compulsive ideas] – a theory in which the sexual factor was regarded as no more significant than any other emotional source of feeling.
> (Freud, 1906, p. 272)

In fact, for Freud, at this time, hysteria was an illness of a psychic and not a sexual origin, whose treatment could only be psychological, whereas "sexual neuroses" were regarded as illnesses of a somatic and sexual origin, pertaining more to the domain of physiology than psychology. This theoretical distinction was so categorical that, if clinical experience revealed a sexual factor in a case of hysteria, it was attributed to the aspect of "sexual neurosis" that was mixed up with "hysteria". Indeed, in *Studies on Hysteria*, Freud points out that "the neuroses which commonly occur are mostly to be described as 'mixed'" and he regretted having overlooked "the points of view that were of importance as regards sexual neuroses" (Freud & Breuer, 1895, pp. 259, 260).

The clinical observations related to the therapeutic efficacy of the cathartic method confirmed, moreover, this nosographical distinction: this psychological method "is – as a matter of theory – very well able to get rid of any hysterical symptom" but "is completely powerless against the phenomena of neurasthenia" and "is only able rarely and in roundabout ways to influence the psychical effects of anxiety neurosis" (Freud & Breuer, 1895, p. 261).

In fact, hysteria had acquired a psychical status insofar as Freud and Breuer had attributed the cause of the somatic symptom not to the immediate reality of the trauma, but to the *memory* of it, which opened up the possibility of psychological research introducing the *temporality* of the subject. In the actual neuroses, on the contrary, the symptoms resulted from the present effect of a real cause – continence, coitus reservatus, masturbation – in principle, it sufficed therefore to remove the pathogenic action for the effect, the symptom, to disappear, as in an organic illness.

Furthermore, the origin of the disorder was somatic – absence of discharge of sexual excitation in anxiety neurosis, inadequate relief of excitation in masturbation – and the appearance of a neurosis of this type depended on a "quantitative factor", that is "on the total load upon the nervous system (in proportion to its capacity to carry the load)" (Freud, 1895b, p. 131). From thereon, every symptom could be explained by the effect of an operative, real, somatic, and determinant cause, owing to its quantity, which left no room for psychic elucidation based on the subject's history. This linear psycho-physical causality, devoid of any "psychical elaboration" of the affects of pleasure/unpleasure linked to genital sexuality, excluded any possibility of symbolizing the erogenous body: the body of actual neurosis was nothing more than the objective body of biology, where the absence of psychic elaboration of bodily affects condemns the subject to somatic "acting out", a body oriented towards the "actual", towards material reality, and totally excluded from psychic life.

Concerning the actual neuroses, all of the contemporary research into psychosomatic disorganizations had their starting-point in Freud's work.[3] But what is interesting to note is that the Freudian functional schema "signifies" here the fundamental equivalence between *sexual drive, purely economic factors, and traumatic automatic anxiety*: the incapacity to symbolize the body, that is, to transform bodily messages into representations, is equally the mark of a somatic and vital risk. The psycho-physiological theory of the objective body is related here to a clinical truth concerning mental functioning, since it is possible for the psychic and phenomenal body to be so decathected that, for certain subjects, it is no more than an objective, biological body.

Consequently, the definition that Freud gave of the drive in 1915 as "a measure of the demand made upon the mind for work in consequence of its connection with the body" (Freud, 1915a, p. 122)[4] takes on full significance, since it relates to the need to internalize the body and its affects so that psychic life and somatic life can continue: the process of symbolization is to be conceived here as an activity of binding affects, which finds in the body both its limits, its source and its reason for being.

Contrary to the actual neuroses, the psychoneuroses, and in particular conversion hysteria, showed Freud the path that he needed to follow in order to highlight the symbolizing function of the body. This meant Freud had to distance himself from a "quantitative" approach to a spatialized and a-historical body in order to make use of his intuition concerning a body open to temporality: the definition of the hysterical symptom as a *mnemic symbol* could not better designate the essential connection between the symbolizing body and memory. In order to decipher the bodily marks of hysterics, which Freud compared to hieroglyphs, it was necessary to determine why a pathological defence was used in place of a normal defence; that is to say, why, in the case of psychic conflict between two ideas, a mnemic symbol is formed instead of the repressed idea rather than a simple act of forgetting with the possibility of a return that is faithful to consciousness. In the terms of the "Project", it is a matter of knowing why a primary process is used instead of a secondary process.

Between 1894 and 1896, Freud's answers were based less and less on quantitative differences. In the article of 1894 titled "The psycho-neuroses of defence", Freud leaves the question open. In the *Studies on Hysteria*, the explanation is of a quantitative order: the impulsion towards conversion is given when the dose of affect not disposed of increases owing to an accumulation of traumatic experiences and exceeds the limits of what the individual's temperament allows him to tolerate (Freud & Breuer, 1895a, pp. 173–174). The difference lies therefore in each individual's constitutional capacity to tolerate an increase of quantity, which amounted to explaining hysteria in terms of constitution, as Charcot did. This boiled down to raising the problem without resolving it.

In the "Project", Freud (1950 [1895]) denies that there is any relationship between the utilization of a pathological defence and the intensity of the affect attached to the incompatible idea, for more distressing memories exist that are neither repressed nor replaced by symbols, for instance, memories of remorse caused by bad actions; and further sexual affects are no more intense than nonsexual affects (p. 352). The explanation lies in a specific characteristic of sexual memories: the pathological defence is operative owing to the *early nature* of a *sexual* trauma.

But this explanation would have been in the order of a linear causality from past to present if Freud had not insisted on the *après-coup* effect of this infantile memory at puberty (Freud (1950 [1895]), pp. 351–356). The biphasic structure of sexuality accounts for a *retroactive causality* from the present to the past; this is constitutive of the trauma, for sure, but also a precondition for the registration of the body in psychic life and in history. As we know, with the subsequent possibility of transference, analytic treatment found this to be both an obstacle and a solution.

It is true that Freud maintains further on that the delay of puberty is a non-specific general factor, that hysteria occurs only in "individuals of whom one knows in part that they have become *prematurely* sexually excitable owing to mechanical and emotional stimulation", and that this factor is a quantitative one, for "premature *beginning* of sexual release or prematurely *intensified* sexual release are clearly equivalent" (p. 357).

In reality, the structural factor seems more decisive than the quantitative factor, which is confirmed by the position he adopted in his article "Further remarks on the neuro-psychoses of defence" (Freud, 1896a). Hysteria could not be entirely explained by the effect of trauma, for it had been noted that individuals exposed to the same traumas had remained healthy. Reliance was thus placed in the hypothesis of a susceptibility to hysterical reactions. Freud then stated: "The place of this indefinite hysterical disposition can now be taken, wholly or in part, by the posthumous operation of a sexual trauma in childhood" (p. 166).

The clinical significance of sexuality, which emerged in the second part of the "Project", was thus totally different from the theoretical significance that it had in the first part. It is true that the functional schema needed to be taken into account in the second phase of the trauma, since it was biological maturation and the possibility of somatic sexual excitation that explained the deferred effect of the memory. But the reference to the physiological sexual process was secondary in relation to the biphasic structure of sexuality: hysterical repression could only be explained by "the retardation of puberty as compared with the rest of the individual's development" (1950 [1895], p. 356).

Hysteria and infantile sexuality

In his article "The aetiology of hysteria", Freud (1896b) soon asked himself whether the activation of a pathological defence was due more to the *content* of the experiences than to the *period* at which they occurred (p. 211). The importance attributed to the reality of the traumas drove him temporarily to make the choice of neurosis depend on chronological circumstances, hence his efforts to clarify the upper and lower limits of the dates of each scene.

Now we know that as soon as the reality of the scenes of seduction was challenged, Freud focused his interest on the content of the experiences, on the dimension of phantasy and the discovery of infantile sexuality. Thus, in his letter to Wilhelm Fliess dated 14 November 1897, he linked the setting-up of a pathological defence to the content of the experiences: only memories of excitation arising from abandoned sexual zones, that is, the mouth, the anus, and the throat are subsequently subjected to repression and neurosis; memories of irritation of the genital organs subsequently only produce compulsive masturbation and libido. Hence, it must be assumed that

> in infancy the release of sexuality is not yet so much localized as it is later, so that the zones which are later abandoned (and perhaps *the whole surface of the body as well*) also instigate something that is analogous to the later release of sexuality.
>
> (Masson, 1985, p. 279, my emphasis)

For Freud, calling into question the theory of trauma gave him the impression that he had lost the structural point of view on which his theory of the neuroses was based: it amounted to calling into question, on the theoretical level, every psychological theory and the loss of the indexed reference to factual reality on which the truth of his "system" was based. The door was thus open to individual polysemic symbolization. Freud had no alternative but to replace a theory of the exogenous development of sexuality with a theory of endogenous development and to substitute the psychological conception of defence with a theory of "organic 'sexual repression'" (Freud, 1906, p. 278). This had the effect of making him transfer the heuristic function ascribed to external reality to internal reality, but only somatic internal reality, and of increasing the importance of the point of view of the global *expression* of the somatic in the psychic sphere.

But the dimension of history with the biphasic structure of sexuality retained its importance, and the erogeneity of the body – "the whole surface of the body", Freud adds, with its possibilities of multiple symbolic substitutions, was appreciated in a new light: primacy was now accorded to the oral zone, but this concealed the importance of the genital zone to the point that interpretive work aimed to reveal the genitalization of the subject's own body through the different bodily configurations other than genital ones. In this truly *vertical symbolism*, the psychic elaboration of somatic excitation was to be conceived, following Sandor Ferenczi, as the transition from a quantity to a "qualitative differentiation", which, in turn, made it "a symbolic means of expressing complex psychic contents": hence the leap from the psychic to the somatic as a phantasied "phenomenon of materialization". This hysterical symptom was consequently neither a hallucination nor an illusion, "since its essence consists in the realization of a wish, as though by magic, out of the material in the body at its disposal and – even if in primitive fashion – by a plastic representation" (Ferenczi, 1919a, p. 58). The auto-plasticity of the body "worked on" by the hysteric revealed creative possibilities that were evocative for Freud (1912–1913, p. 73) of a caricature of art and for Ferenczi (1919a, p. 104) of the body performances of the actor and the materials shaped by the artist in his own way.

However, the hysterical symptom also expressed a theatrical scene with multiple characters that underlay the "case histories" written by Freud; moreover, he reproached them for reading "like short stories" and for "lacking, as one might say, the serious stamp of science" (Freud & Breuer, 1895a, p. 160). This *horizontal symbolism* was certainly inherent to the historical dimension of theory of trauma: in the very process of his self-analysis, the emphasis placed on the "theory of sexuality" and the dimension of phantasy rather than on the dating of the traumatic scenes would permit Freud to discover the theatre of hysteria.

In a letter to Fliess written at the time when he was treating Dora, he noted, with a degree of pertinence that prefigured the subsequent metapsychological developments, the importance of identificatory factors in the vicissitudes of auto-erotism:

> The lowest of the sexual strata is autoerotism, which dispenses with any psycho-sexual aim and seeks only locally gratifying sensations. It is then succeeded by alloerotism (homo- or heteroerotism), but certainly continues to exist as an undercurrent. Hysteria (and its variant, obsessional neurosis) is alloerotic, since its main path is identification with the loved one. Paranoia again dissolves the identification, re-establishes all the loved ones of childhood who have been abandoned (compare the discussion of exhibitionist dreams), and dissolves the ego itself into extraneous persons. So I have come to regard paranoia as a forward surge of the autoerotic current, as a return to a former state.
>
> (Letter dated 9 December 1899, in Masson, 1985, p. 390)

These remarks go well beyond hysteria and locate the autoerotism characteristic of infantile sexuality within its relations to the role of object and identificatory processes: they also announce the discoveries concerning the different modes of functioning of the ego – denial and splitting of the ego or repression – in psychosis or neurosis. Freud was to say nothing different when, in the case of Schreber, he remarked that "paranoia decomposes just as hysteria condenses" insofar as "paranoia resolves once more into their elements the products of the condensations and identifications which are effected in the unconscious" (Freud, 1911, p. 49).

What Freud had learnt from hysteria, and particularly the case of Dora, was precisely the importance of "these products of condensation" in relation to identificatory processes. In connection with Dora's cough and hoarseness, he speaks of different psychic layers or stratifications that cover over somatic excitation which is the "grain of sand at the centre of the pearl" (Freud, 1912, p. 248). This somatic process only occurred once and therefore has no history if it does not have, as Freud says, "psychic significance, meaning" that is attached to it thereby giving it the faculty of repetition: this is the notion of a s̲omatic compliance (Freud, 1905a, p. 40)[5] that Freud introduced for the first time in the case of Dora to describe a normal or pathological process in, or connected with, an organ of the body which offers a locus of expression for repressed ideas.

This point of anchorage in the body has no explanatory value except for evoking, from a psycho-physiological perspective, the necessity of a fundamental reciprocal relationship between the somatic sphere, which constitutes "an already existing path of discharge", and the psychic sphere, which gives it meaning, as between matter and form. Freud nonetheless had the same concern as in the *Studies on Hysteria* to render the transition of psychic meaning into the somatic sphere less "arbitrary". The discovery of infantile sexuality and the erogenous zones offered him this connection, since the erogenous zone is defined as a *source* of somatic compliance allowing for the expression of an unconscious phantasy.

Thus, Dora's attacks of coughing and hoarseness could be related to sucking in childhood, corresponding to a precocious and intense activity of the mouth, the thumb sucking having taken over from sucking the breast; for Freud what was involved was an influence or impression that might have a "similar effect to that produced by a trauma" and in fact became the source of a subsequent somatic compliance. From this point of view, the intensity of this behaviour and its maintenance until the age of four or five underlined the fragility of the hysterical organization: the emphasis placed by Freud on the traumatic reality could be understood here, following the hypothesis of Francis Pasche (1988, p. 102), in relation to the "permeability of the stimulus barrier" and to the failure of the containing function of the mother; she, in fact, is the one who is most notably absent in Dora's story, as is the elaboration of unconscious homosexuality in the transference relationship with Freud.

That is why, though Freud describes a series of "psychic coatings" linked to her identification with her mother and with Frau K., he leaves in the shadows her identification with her father out of a wish to replace him in the relationship with Frau K., and with her mother. He assumes that at puberty a commonplace irritation of the throat – somatic compliance based on an erogenous zone – was the "grain of sand" around which different psychic strata settled: first, the "imitation" of the sick father out of compassion for him and the self-accusations on account of the genital "catarrh" through displacement, from below to above, owing to the homonymy of the word "catarrh"[6]; then later, Dora's expression of love for Herr K., the loved man who was temporarily absent; and finally, after the second scene on the edge of the lake with Herr K., through identification with Frau K., the wish for oral coitus with her father (Freud, 1905a, p. 83).

But the fact that Dora broke off the treatment helped Freud to realize that the most intense current in the somatic symptom concerned masculine identification and homosexuality. One of the essential significations of the hysterical symptom was thus related to the "representation – the realization – of a phantasy with sexual content, that is to say, it signifies a sexual situation" (Freud, 1905a, p. 47): a phantasy depicting a primal scene, which was also a bisexual phantasy with reversible roles (Freud, 1908). The hysterical condensation could be explained by these multiple identifications: the definition given by Freud of Dora's hysterical identification with her father as an imitation was therefore incomplete because, as he says himself in *The Interpretation of Dreams*, while imitation indicates the "path followed", it does not explain the "process itself", which is unconscious: "Thus identification is not simple imitation but assimilation on the basis of a similar aetiological pretension; it expresses a resemblance and is derived from a common element which remains in the unconscious" (Freud, 1900, p. 150). In other words, hysterical symbolization reveals a movement of identification with the object that both shows and hides itself in the physical symptom. Dora's nervous cough evidences a chain of ideas and affects that operates like a smokescreen: a wish to be like her father – which masks the wish to be like Frau K., which, in turn, conceals her wish to be like the mother; love for the father, which is also hatred of the father and hides her love for her mother, thereby concealing her hatred towards her. Thus a network of characters and affects emerges, serving at the same time as screens and borrowings, which are operative at the heart of a sexual scene, oral coitus: likewise, orality shows and masks the wish to introject the genital drive; the genitalization of orality is a sign of the "hysteric's grudge" and the wish to introject a sufficiently protective[7] stimulus barrier mother, to substitute the erotic breast, a source of sexual excitation, with the maternal breast, a source of tenderness.[8]

It is true that in this mirror game, Dora always knew that she was neither her father nor Frau K., nor her mother, which later led Freud (1921) to say that hysterical identification is "a partial and extremely limited one and only borrows a single trait from the person who is its object" (p. 107). It is an assimilating identification which, according to the felicitous expression of Jean Gillibert (1985), suppresses the object while respecting the alterity of others. It is a process that seizes on similarities, while preserving the differences between the subject and the object, which is an essential precondition for the operation of negation between the symbol and the symbolized.

However, although in this hysterical enactment a certain unconscious enjoyment is obtained by proxy, like in the theatre, it dispossesses itself with regard to the representation of different movements or modes of being of the object which are not comforting or structuring for its narcissism; from this point of view, hysterical identification is opposed to narcissistic identification which, in its progressive function, implies the assimilation of an "idealized" quality. Hence, the paradoxical aspect of this identification, as Jacqueline Schaeffer (1986, p. 932) has pointed out, where the identification is used not to desexualize the relationship to incestuous objects, but to maintain an erotic relationship with these objects.

Furthermore, somatization concerns issues where affect prevails over representation, and action prevails over thinking. In connection with the subject of hysteria, Augustin Jeanneau (1985) has spoken of its hallucinatory position and its language of action which makes the suspension of motor discharge that is necessary for thought difficult. Therein lies the whole interest of Freud's discovery of the analytic treatment, of the abreaction of affects in the process of psychic working-over.

Somatic conversion is in this sense like *acting out* in the body to avoid *acting out* towards the object, in particular the maternal object. In his letters to Fliess, Freud had already noted that "A hysterical attack is not a discharge but an *action;* and it retains the original characteristic of every action – of being a means to the reproduction of pleasure" (Masson, 1985, p. 212).[9] He also notes, in connection with Dora, that the child was "really a wild creature" who, after the appearance of nervous asthma, had become calm and well-mannered (Freud, 1905a, p. 82).

As Melitta Sperling (1973, p. 769) suggests, the somatic symptom should perhaps be seen as the wish to re-establish union with the mother symbolically at a pregenital level when the Oedipal situation involves a major danger of losing her and when the satisfaction of destructive impulses is prohibited in reality. Dora's hypersexualization of her body and of her bodily functions, and her increased auto-erotic activity – thumb-sucking, bed-wetting and masturbation – could be understood, among other things, as a way of mastering destructive impulses towards the mother's body; this behavioural auto-eroticism, which Freud describes as an *analogon* of the traumatic event, could be considered an appeal to transform an *action* into *representation.*

This brings us back to the crucial role of symbolization, described by Freud in connection with the formation of hysterical symptoms, whereas conversion hysteria reveals a failure in the work of representing and linking affects: hence the idea of the symptom as a "crypto-symbol" (Ferenczi, 1949), which would thus be a "pseudo-symbol" (Pasche, 1960, p. 160) that exaggerates an interpretive work of "deconstruction" and "decondensation". A progressive symbolization could be thought of as a process of moving away from the sensory and hallucinatory images of hysteria, and of "putting things into words": the discovery of the unconscious by Freud was immediately conceptualized as a requirement to substitute representation for perception, language for motor or hallucinatory action.

Dream analysis would help Freud understand more deeply the psychic mechanisms identified in hysteria, which always led him to say that the key to hysteria lay in the study of dreams. The fact remains that the affective efflorescence of hysteria had confronted Freud immediately with the dimension of mental conflict as a requirement to integrate bodily messages; hence the definition of the instinctual drive as a frontier concept between the mind and the body, and the description of its two principle representatives, the quota of affect and the ideational representative.

This reference to the drive has been the focus of multiple criticisms (see Anzieu et al., 1984). The contradictory definitions of the drive in Freud's work, in a *biological* sense depending on the psychopathological schema, or in a more *metapsychological* sense, as a relationship of representation between the somatic and the psychic, have often been recalled. In both cases, it would be tempting to evoke the economy of endogenous "somatic excitation" as the ultimate explanatory factor, which would simply be reifying a concept. But the drive is not so much a biological reality as a concept that makes it possible to understand the relations between the somatic and the psychic which, as soon as they are "reintegrated with existence", can no longer be distinguished. It is like "the order of the in-itself and the order of the for itself", or "a collision between the order of causes and the order of ends" (Merleau-Ponty, 1945, p. 90).[10] According to Merleau-Ponty, the issue, on the contrary, is one of rediscovering the intentionality of desiring man towards the world, involved in a dialectic of meaning and non-meaning, which, although it evokes the opposition between the psychic and the somatic, is never reduced to it.

The psychophysiological models that we have identified in the approach to conversion hysteria and the actual neuroses are perhaps open to criticism at the level of their positivism; but they can be considered metaphors of this possible non-meaning, linked to the erotogenic body, which establishes through the dynamic of its symbolic substitutions a reference to *another scene*, the unconscious: a body that is both psychic and somatic, since the substitutions of *erotogenic zones* are also related to substitutions of *objects*. The interest of an epistemological and historical approach, as we have taken in connection with the *Studies on Hysteria*, consists in revealing the truth of Freudian empiricism: the reified models of positivism attest to the origins of those other reified symbols, hysterical symptoms, which Freud compared to "commemorative monuments", and which refer to the weight of a reality that he defined as the "material reality" of the soma and of "external objects". The interest of a work of symbolization lies in the reference to this activity of transforming this twofold material reality precisely because of the existence of an erotogenic body governed by the pleasure/unpleasure principle. Piera Aulagnier (1975) defined this activity of representation as an activity of metabolizing heterogeneous and unknowable elements within the psyche, which Freud had compared to the Kantian thing-in-itself.

The subject's own body, the erotogenic body, and the phantasized body

What relations can we imagine between the three perspectives on the body: the subject's own body, the erotogenic body and the phantasized body? The clinical experience of hysteria had taught Freud (1905b) that "erotogenic hysterogenic zones show the same characteristics" (p. 184), and that the subject's own body could become an erotogenic body, a source of sensual pleasure. In a short article, "The psycho-analytic view of psychogenic disturbance of vision", Freud (1910) supposes that an exaggeration "in itself" of the erogeneity of an organ, comparable to the endogenous accumulation of sexual excitation in the actual neuroses, is sufficient for a defensive conflict at a psychic level to find expression in the subject's own body (p. 218).

Freud could be reproached for placing the psychic and the somatic alongside each other by comparing the schema of the defensive conflict of a psychic order with the physiological schema of the actual neuroses. He even suggested that these toxic modifications' characteristic of the exaggeration of the erogeneity of an organ could not occur without the constitutional factor represented by the notion of "somatic compliance", which seemed to make this notion the explanatory factor of organ erotogenicity, whereas in the case of Dora, it was precisely the erotogenic zone that explained the presence of a later somatic compliance.

It is rather as if, from the theoretical point of view, Freud was trying to establish, as Breuer sought to do, a "structure with several levels" with, at the bottom, a nonsexual somatic sphere from which a sexual somatic sphere emerged that explained in turn the organization of a defensive conflict. But, from a clinical point of view, the defensive conflict came first and made it possible to reveal the role of the erotogenic zones through the somatic symptom. In this article, Freud even goes as far as to suppose that the defensive conflict is the "expression of the struggle" that opposes the subject's own body – instincts of self-preservation or ego-instincts) and the erotogenic body (sexual instincts [p. 215]), contrary to all clinical evidence, showing that the subject's own body was more the terrain on which the conflict was played out than one of the poles of this conflict.

The ambiguity of this conceptualization was explainable by the reference to the reversible psychosomatic structure, characteristic of physiology, a relationship that never ceased to be enigmatic. In the *Three Essays*, Freud (1905b) said it was to be suspected that "all the connecting pathways that lead from other functions to sexuality must also be traversable in the reverse direction" (p. 205).

This psychophysiological view left entirely out of account the specificity of the Freudian discovery: the fact that the hysterical symptom was a mnemic symbol of an unconscious scene did not mean that the somatic symptom was the expression of a psychic meaning, but that the parts of the body, the organs, as well as positions and attitudes, are originally involved in the imaginary scene of the most archaic phantasies and refer to "something else" that is hidden, which it is their function to conceal and to reveal at one and the same time.

From this point of view, psychoanalysis, as it appeared from research into conversion hysteria, was irreducible to any psychological or physiological science, as these could only be attentive to relations of expression between the body and the mind. What had Freud detected, then, other than the fact that the hysterical symptom was a *concrete sign* that was related neither to a metaphorical pictorial surface, as with Charcot, nor to an event that had already occurred in a subject's life and which needed to be *expressed*, as with Breuer, but rather one that was inscribed in phantasy in the body of the hysteric and needed to be deciphered, taking us back to what had not occurred in the time of the subject and whose existence revealed a prohibited wish? The method of free association, which for Freud had replaced Breuer's cathartic method, proved to be related to an *interpretive* approach to the hysterical symptom, something the study of dreams was going to clarify (Freud, 1916–1917, pp. 390–391).

And yet, Freud's constant reference to the symptom of an actual neurosis – neurasthenia and anxiety neurosis – as the "nucleus and first stage of a psychoneurotic symptom", had, as we have seen, a heuristic function, namely, of reminding us of the sexual and heterogeneous dimension of the body. The hypothesis of hypochondria, as a third actual neurosis in the narcissistic sphere of the psychoses, as Freud (1911, pp. 56–57) had characterized it in the case of Schreber, clarified this issue: the assimilation of the organic pain in hypochondria with the painful sensibility of "the genital organ in its states of excitation" led Freud (1914, p. 84) to regard "erotogenicity as a general characteristic of all organs", whether internal or external.

Now, by defining the erotogenicity of a part of the body as the "activity of sending sexually exciting stimuli to the mind" which are liable to quantitative variations (1914, p. 84), Freud was referring indirectly to the definition of the sexual drive, the only drive strictly speaking, corresponding to the "measure of the demand made upon the mind for work" (Freud, 1915a, p. 122) which acquires a quality through its reference to its somatic *sources*, its erogenous zones and its *aims*, organ pleasure, a local pleasure taken at the level of the body, which may or not include the phantasized object.

Jean Laplanche notes that the relationship between the drive and its sources is not easy to define: first, it is not always possible to find a somatic source for all the drives, for example in the case of voyeurism and sadism; and, though the theory assumes a direct causality between the somatic and the psychic, it is more in keeping with clinical experience to speak, in connection with the drive, of the "effect of repressed source-objects on the body" (Laplanche, 1984, p. 21). From a similar perspective, René Angelergues (1989) has also pointed out that the only leap from the somatic to the psychic that it is possible to describe is "a leap in biological theorization", an epistemological break linked to the introduction of the variable pleasure/unpleasure in the functioning of the body.

It is true that Freud always insisted on the fact that the drive can never be known directly, but only through its representatives; consequently, the opposition between quantity and quality is reduplicated at the psychic level, that of the quota of affect and of the ideational representative. However, the opposition between quantity and quality cannot be conceived in positive terms: the drive is neither a pure quantity nor a pure quality, but rather a perpetual relation between the two, designating the transition from non-meaning to meaning, from unsymbolized to symbolized, which Freud suggests with the idea of a leap from quantity to quality. The concept of the drive has the function here within the theory of recalling the importance of an *economic point of view* in every theoretical and clinical appreciation of a psychical phenomenon: as Laplanche emphasizes, this boils down to taking into account both a *quantitative aspect,* which designates less a quantifiable force than "the demand for work exerted by the unconscious prototypes", and a *processual* aspect, which is to be conceived as the demand for binding cathexes which will determine whether a circulation of meaning and a process of symbolization is possible or not (Laplanche, 1984, pp. 21–22).

From this economic point of view, it was questionable what the idea of hypochondria as a third actual neurosis offered. Analogies existed between hypochondria and conversion hysteria, since the two psychopathological organizations showed the same capacity to transfer the sexual organ on to other parts of the body. In *On narcissism: An introduction* Freud (1914) was even led to suppose that "in the case of the other neuroses a small amount of hypochondria was regularly formed at the same time as well" (p. 83). From the same perspective, Ferenczi (1919b) also supposed that "the same stagnation of organ libido can – depending according to the patient's sexual constitution – have either a purely hypochondriacal or conversion hysteria superstructure" (p. 124). The extension of hypochondria to all the psychopathological organizations could in fact be considered a reference to the minimal libidinal cathexis of the subject's own body that is necessary for psychic functioning, and of the issues at stake for the erotogenic body in every psychic conflict. The importance of the hypochondriacal dimension of every neurosis is related to the introduction of drive dualism, narcissistic libido and object-libido. The idea of stagnation evokes, of course, a danger, that of the accumulation of a quantity of somatic excitation which risks overwhelming the ego; but we know that the role of the object is decisive here in permitting the integration of these "bodily messages" into the mind and the creation of a "stagnation" of the ego-libido, thereby favouring a relative stability of the form of the ego.[11]

In this sense, if conversion hysteria indicated an exclusion of a part of the body, it is nonetheless after an inclusion of the object: hence, as Paul Schilder (1968, pp. 186–188) has pointed out, the possibility of countless condensations in the hysterical symptom and of a work of allo-erotic representation. On the contrary, in hypochondria, the narcissistic withdrawal that excludes the object leads to the rejection of parts of the body or of the body itself, which is felt to be a "foreign body" that has to be expelled, like a "piece" of external reality. Such a body has lost its symbolizing function and is ultimately nothing more than "organ language" (Freud, 1915b, p. 197): it is not the "body language" of the hysteric which enacts and represents, but rather a "language about the body" which is much poorer at the level of condensations, corresponding to ego-splitting and to the abolition of representation.

This is what, phenomenologically speaking, Freud had already pointed out in his *Studies on Hysteria* (Freud & Breuer, 1895a) when he compared the reaction of the hypochondriac and the hysteric to physical pain. The hypochondriac has great difficulty in describing this pain; language is too poor to allow him to depict his sensations and to make himself understood by his interlocutor; if the painful zone is touched, it always creates an impression of physical pain. For the hysteric, on the contrary, the pain is never considered in itself, but only mentioned in relation to the moral suffering that it causes; moreover, if the painful zone is touched, it is a source of pleasure rather than pain (pp. 135–136).

Hypochondriacal anxiety nonetheless attests to less watertight splitting between the somatic and the psychic – contrary to the *non-language of the body* of psychosomatic states – and confirms, according to Angelergues (1988), the paradoxical and privileged position of the body which is both a *part* of external reality and a *source* of psychic reality. Merleau-Ponty (1968) had already spoken about this in connection with the reflexivity of the body: a body that is both touching and touched, seeing and visible, and which is also "a being of two leaves, from one side a thing among things, and otherwise what sees them and touches them" (p. 137). The reference to pain, which either remains pain or is transformed into a source of ecstatic enjoyment (*jouissance*), is a reminder of the danger that threatens the psychical apparatus: as early as the "Project" (Freud, 1950 [1895]) described, Freud described psychical trauma on the model of a physical trauma, where the organism has to deal with quantities of excitation and protect itself against any increase of excitation, at the risk of being submerged by pain which "no doubt leaves permanent facilitations behind in ψ – as though there had been a stroke of lightening" (p. 307).

However, when, twenty-four years later, Freud (1923b) considered the constitution of the body image on the basis of the internal and external perceptions of the subject's own body, he ascribed a predominant function to pain:

> Pain, too, seems to play a part in the process, and the way in which we gain new knowledge of our organs during painful illness is perhaps a model of the way by which in general we arrive at the idea of our body.
>
> (pp. 25–26)

What does this mean other than that the dialectic between the subject's own body and the erotogenic body, which Freud claimed was linked to drive dualism, contains within itself the possibility of reducing the subject's own body to the objective body, that of scientific anatomy, or of considering it a phantasized body, which refers more to a phantasized anatomy. The work of symbolization is related here to the constitution of the body image, concerning which Schilder (1968) pointed out that it is not a given, but something that develops and is formed depending on the libidinal quality of the exchanges with the world (pp. 139–143). This was underlining the fact that Freud (1923b) had already defined the ego as being "first and foremost a bodily ego" (p. 26) and that psychic work involves appropriating the erotogenic body, transforming a body experienced as outside oneself into an internalized body. The symbolism of the body in dreams would provide Freud with reference points on the path towards this integration: as a complementary approach to the hysterical symptom as a mnemic symbol, the theory of dream symbolism would both clarify and give added complexity to the issues at stake in this question.

Notes

1 It is this dimension of conflict that Nicolas Abraham (1978) wanted to stress when he noted: "Symbolization does not consist in substituting one thing for another, but in resolving a determined conflict by transposing it on to a level on which the incompatible terms are subject to an indefiniteness that is capable of harmonizing them in a new mode of functioning enjoying a new determination" (p. 30).The idea of an "operation of the symbol" was a way of including the dynamic of the symbol within a mode of functioning (See Abraham, 1978).

2 The first manuscripts sent to Fliess (at the end of 1892, and the beginning of 1893) reveal this interest in the actual neuroses, and it was in Draft E (probably of June 1894) that he laid the foundations for his article of 1895 concerning the necessity to distinguish between anxiety neurosis and neurasthenia.

3 This relationship between actual neurosis and psychosomatic issues has been emphasized by several authors, in particular by Marty, Fain, and David (1968) and McDougall (1978). Moreover, two American articles confront the Freudian hypothesis of actual neurosis with contemporary clinical experience: Gediman (1984) and Kaplan (1984).

4 The translators of the *Oeuvres complètes* of Freud distinguish the translation of the German terms *die Seele* (mind or soul) and *seelisch* (mental) from the terms *die Psyche* (psyche) and *psychisch* (psychic). According to them "in the theory, it is this unity of the term 'mind' which is the guiding thread that allowed Freud to show how the conscious and unconscious 'processes of the mind' are projected into a 'metaphysical' representation of the mind and to set psychoanalysis the opposite task of 'transposing metaphysics into metapsychology' or of 'transferring back into the human soul what animism teaches us about the nature of things'" (Bourguignon et al., 1989, p. 77; Freud, 1912–1913, p. 91). Even if current usage prefers the terms "psyche" and "psychic", it is not without interest to note this difference in Freud's thought, which restores a metapsychological meaning to metaphysical and religious concepts.

5 The French translators of the *Oeuvres complètes* of Freud have preferred a new translation of the German expression *somatisches Entgegenkommen*: hitherto translated by "compliance somatique", they propose the term "prévenance somatique" to convey the idea that "in such a hysterical symptom the body "comes to meet" phantasy in order to "pro-pose" a point of anchorage for the conversion" (see Bourguignon et al., 1989, p. 129).

6 Freud nonetheless supposes that the genital catarrh also corresponds to an identification with the mother, contaminated by the father: see Freud (1905a [1901], p. 75).

7 A. Jeanneau (1985) speaks, in this sense, of the deficient mother of the hysteric who is unable to constitute herself as a supportive object.
8 It is this movement of identification that E. Kestemberg (1984) described in evoking primary homosexuality.
9 The analysis of a case of conversion hysteria in a man with arc-de-cercle on the couch confirms this dimension close to acting (see Bonnafé-Villechenoux, 1989). Clearly, the hypothesis of bisexuality did not suffice to explain this hysterical symptom. This man's thought disorders were more reminiscent of borderline states, and the hysterical attack was not a matter of a repressed wish but of the annihilation of the double.
10 Nicolas Abraham (1978) speaks from the same perspective of an anasemic discourse in connection with the principle Freudian concepts: bringing these concepts into relation with the discovery of the unconscious makes it necessary to designify them and, consequently, not to attribute somatic and psychic with the signification of naïve empiricism. Rather, the drive should be seen as a symbol of the messenger between the somatic and the psychic, which cannot be equated with a relation of expression insofar as it refers to the unconscious kernel.
11 Concerning this double valency of hypochondria, see Aisenstein and Gibeault (1991).

References

Abraham, N. (1987 [1978]). Le symbole ou l'au-dela du phénomène. In: *L'écorce et le noyau*. Paris: Aubier-Flammarion, pp. 25–76.

Aisenstein, M., & Gibeault, A. (1991). A contribution to the study of the specificity of hypochondria, in particular to hysterical conversion and organic disease. *International Journal of Psycho-Analysis*, 72 (4): 669–680.

Angelergues, R. (1988). Réflexions sur le corps, la sexualité et le sexe. *Les Cahiers du Centre de psychanalyse et de psychothérapie*, 16–17: 7–22.

Angelergues, R. (1989). *La psychiatrie devant la qualité de l'homme*. Paris: Presses Universitaires de France.

Anzieu, D., Dorey, R., Laplanche, J., & Widlöcher, D. (1984). La pulsion: pour quoi faire? *Colloquium of the French Psychoanalytical Association*, 12 May, 1984, Paris.

Aulagnier, P. (1975). *The Violence of Interpretation*, trans. A. Sheridan. London: Brunner-Routledge, 2001.

Bonnafé-Villechenoux, M. (1989). Fantasme de bisexualité, hystérie motrice et processus de symbolization. *Revue française de psychanalyse*, 53 (6): 1813–1821.

Bourguignon, A., Cotet, P., Laplanche, J., & Robert, F. (1989). *Traduire Freud*. Paris: Presses Universitaires de France.

Charcot, J.-M. (2018/1889). *Clinical Lectures on Diseases of the Nervous System*, trans. Thomas Saville, Vol. 3, Lecture XVIII. London: The New Sydenham Society, pp. 220–243 (Classic Reprint Series).

Diogenes, L. (1962). *Vies et opinions des philosophes*, livre VII, *Les stoiciens*. Paris: Gallimard.

Eco, U. (1984). *Semiotics and the Philosophy of Language*. Bloomington and Indianapolis: Indiana University Press.

Ferenczi, S. ([1919a] 1950). The phenomena of hysterical materialization. In: *Further Contributions to the Theory and Technique of Psychoanalysis*. London: Hogarth Press, pp. 89–104.

Ferenczi, S. ([1919b] 1950). Psychoanalysis of a case of hysterical hypochondria. In: *Further Contributions to the Theory and Technique of Psychoanalysis*. London: Hogarth Press, pp. 118–124.

Ferenczi, S. (1949). Ten Letters to Freud (letter dated 10 November 1912) (1908–1933). *The International Journal of Psychoanalysis*, 30 (4): 243–250.

Freud, S. (1893). Some points for a comparative study of organic and hysterical motor paralyses. *S.E.* 1. London: Hogarth, pp. 160–172.

Freud, S. (with Breuer) (1893). On the psychical mechanism of hysterical phenomena. Preliminary communication *S.E.* 2. London: Hogarth.

Freud, S. (1894). The neuro-psychoses of defence. *S.E.* 3. London: Hogarth, pp. 45–68.

Freud, S. (with Breuer, J.) (1895). *Studies on Hysteria* (1893–1895). *S.E.* 2. London: Hogarth.

Freud, S. (1895a) (with Breuer). *Studies on Hysteria. S.E.* 2. London: Hogarth.

Freud, S. (1895b). A reply to criticisms of my paper on anxiety neurosis. *S.E.* 3. London: Hogarth, pp. 123–139.

Freud, S. (1896a). Further remarks on the neuro-psychoses of defence. *S.E.* 3. London: Hogarth, pp. 157–185.

Freud, S. (1896b). The aetiology of hysteria. *S.E.* 3. London: Hogarth, pp. 191–221.

Freud, S. (1900). *The Interpretation of Dreams. S.E.* 4–5. London: Hogarth.

Freud, S. (1905a [1901]). Fragment of an analysis of a case of hysteria. *S.E.* 7. London: Hogarth, pp. 7–122.

Freud, S. (1905b). *Three Essays on the Theory of Sexuality. S.E.* 7. London: Hogarth, pp. 135–243.

Freud, S. (1906). My views on the part played by sexuality in the aetiology of the neuroses. *S.E.* 7. London: Hogarth.

Freud, S. (1908). Hysterical phantasies and their relation to bisexuality. *S.E.* 9. London: Hogarth, pp. 159–166.

Freud, S. (1910). The psychoanalytic view of psychogenic disturbance of vision. *S.E.* 11. London: Hogarth, pp. 211–218.

Freud, S. (1911 [1910]). Psychoanalytic notes on an autobiographical account of a case of paranoia (Dementia paranoides). *S.E.* 12. London: Hogarth, pp. 12–82.

Freud, S. (1912). Contributions to a discussion on masturbation. *S.E.* 12. London: Hogarth, pp. 243–254.

Freud, S. (1912–1913). *Totem and Taboo. S.E.* 13. London: Hogarth, pp. 1–161.

Freud, S. (1914). On narcissism: An introduction. *S.E.* 14. London: Hogarth, pp. 69–102.

Freud, S. (1915a). Instincts and their vicissitudes. *S.E.* 14. London: Hogarth, pp. 109–140.

Freud, S. (1915b). The unconscious. *S.E.* 14. London: Hogarth, pp. 166–215.

Freud, S. (1916–1917). *Introductory Lectures on Psychoanalysis. S.E.* 16. London: Hogarth.

Freud, S. (1921). *Group Psychology and the Analysis of the Ego. S.E.* 18. London: Hogarth, pp. 69–143.

Freud, S. (1923b). *The Ego and the Id. S.E.* 19. London: Hogarth, pp. 3–66.

Freud, S. (1950 [1895]). *Project for a Scientific Psychology. S.E.* 1. London: Hogarth, pp. 295–397.

Gediman, H.K. (1984). Actual neurosis and psychoneurosis. *The International Journal of Psychoanalysis*, 65 (2): 191–203.

Gillibert, J. (1985). *Le psychodrama de la psychanalyse*. Seyssel: Champ Vallon.

Hegel, G.W. (1807). *The Phenomenology of Mind*, trans. J.B. Baillie. London: Cosimo Classics.

Jeanneau, A. (1985). L'hystérie. Unité et diversité. *Revue française de Psychanalyse*, 49 (1): 133–326.

Kaplan, D.P. (1984). Some conceptual and technical aspects of the actual neurosis. *The International Journal of Psychoanalysis*, 65 (3): 295–305.

Kestemberg, E. (Ed.). (1984). Astrid ou homosexualité, identité, adolescence. Quelques propositions hypothéthiques. In: *L'adolescence à vif*. Paris: Presses Universitaires de France, 1999, pp. 239–265.

Laplanche, J. (1984). La pulsion et son objet-source: son destin dans le transfert. *La pulsion, pour quoi faire*? Colloquium of the French Psychoanalytical Association, 12 May, 1984, Paris.

Marty, P., Fain, M., & David, C. (1968). Le cas Dora et le point de vue psychosomatique. *Revue française de Psychanalyse*, 32 (4): 679–714.

Masson, J.M. (Ed.) (1985). *The Complete Letters of Sigmund Freud to Wilhelm Fliess, 1887–1904*. Cambridge, MA: Belknap Press.

McDougall, J. (Ed.). (1978). The psychosoma and the psychoanalytic process. In: *Plea for a Measure of Abnormality*. New York: Brunner/Mazel, pp. 337–396.

Merleau-Ponty, M. (1945). *The Phenomenology of Perception*. London: Routledge, 2012.

Merleau-Ponty, M. (1968). *The Visible and the Invisible*. Evanston, IL: Northwestern University Press.

Ortigues, E. (1962). *Le discours et le symbole*. Paris: Aubier.

Pasche, F. (1960). *Le symbole personnel. À partir de Freud*. Paris: Payot, 1969.

Pasche, F. (Ed.). (1988). L'origine de l'hystérie. In: *Le sens de la psychanalyse*. Paris: Presses Universitaires de France, pp. 99–106.

Peirce, C.S. (1931–1935). *Collected Papers of Charles Sanders Peirce*, vols. 1–6, 1931–35, Charles Hartshorne and Paul Weiss. Cambridge, MA: Harvard University Press.

Peirce, C.S. (1976/1902). *The New Elements of Mathematics by Charles S. Peirce*, Vol. 4, ed. Carolyn Eisele, The Hague: Mouton Publishers, 1976. Atlantic Highlands, NJ: Humanities Press.

Schaeffer, J. (1986). Le rubis a horreur du rouge. Relation et contre-investissement hystériques. *Revue française de psychanalyse*, 50 (3): 923–944.

Schilder, P. (1968). *L'image du corps*. Paris: Gallimard.

Sperling, M. (1973). Conversion hysteria and conversion symptoms: A revision of classification and concepts. *Journal of the American Psychoanalytic Association*, 21 (4): 745–771.

2 Dream symbolism

While hysterical symptoms enabled Freud to discover a process of symbolization, his research into dreams gradually led him to introduce a closer definition of the symbol. In the first edition of *The Interpretation of Dreams*, Freud referred to the studies by Karl A. Scherner on the existence of dream symbolism, of a "symbolizing activity of the imagination" (Freud, 1900, p. 84), which primarily portrays the body and its organs in images where the house plays a predominant role.

He is certainly critical of this theory which recalls popular methods of interpretation, both the symbolic method of interpretation, where the manifest content is given a complete and equivalent translation in terms of latent thoughts, and the method of decoding elements of a dream point by point according to a key of dreams. But, at the same time, he pays him tribute for having elaborated a psychic theory of dreams that takes account of the somatic sources, and after citing him on several occasions, he concludes, towards the end of his book:

> If as Scherner has said, dreams appear to engage in making symbolic representations of the body, we know now that those representations are the product of certain unconscious phantasies (deriving probably from sexual impulses) which find expression not only in dreams but also in hysterical phobias and other symptoms.
>
> (p. 613)[1]

And yet, about ten years later,[2] Freud was led to make a generalization of this imaginary symbolism of the body when he assumed the existence of a symbolism employed in the dream-work. On the technical level, it was the dreamer's associative silence concerning certain dream elements that led him to make this hypothesis. He nonetheless nuanced this assertion by noting that it is still necessary to take associations into account because these symbols "often have several meanings" and "the correct interpretation can only be arrived at on each occasion from the context" (p. 353), but this is because certain symbols are over-determined. Let us now consider the issues related to this theory of symbolism.

DOI: 10.4324/9781003545651-3

The dream writing: symbolism and/or symbolization

The relationship between the manifest element and the latent element eludes the dreamer and reveals a constant, fixed relationship, like the "grammalogues" in shorthand, with a permanently fixed meaning (p. 351). The existence of such a stereotyped and univocal symbolic relationship seemed therefore to reduce the interpretation of dreams to an activity of translation based on a "dream-book" using a "key of dreams", which Freud denounced precisely in connection with popular methods of interpretation.

We are no longer dealing with a conception of the sign based on implication, but rather, according to Eco (1984), on the equivalence between the expression and the content, on equality, the fixed correlation established by the code (pp. 14–28). In this bipartite conception of the sign symbolizing and symbolized reproduce Saussure's division of the signifier and the signified, evacuating the dimension of the interpretant.[3] From a logical point of view, the meaning is no longer the function of a term, which presupposes both an *object* that is signified and a *subject* that uses the term, but a quality, a characteristic of a term. The risk, then, is the very one that Freud was to deplore later on in certain analysts who sought "the essence of dreams in their latent content" and who, in so doing, overlooked "the distinction between the latent dream-thoughts and the *dream-work*", thus forgetting that the latter is the essence of the dream (Freud, 1900, p. 506, footnote 2, added in 1925). This was Georges Politzer's (1928) error, who conceived the relations between the manifest and the latent in terms of that which exists between the letter and the meaning, according to expressive relations that do not take into account the "proportional" representation caused by condensation and displacement.

In reality, even if Freud was tempted to establish a dream code, as evidenced by the enumeration of symbols in the 1914 edition of *The Interpretation of Dreams*, he showed difficulty and reticence in referring to this method of unambiguous "translation". Indeed, it was during the decade from 1905 to 1915, corresponding to the enthusiasm for research into symbolism, that he reproached Wilhelm Stekel for establishing arbitrary connections. He also noted the difficulties represented by the discovery of the common factor of comparison between the symbol and what is symbolized. The latter is often obscure and hidden; while it is mainly based on relations of similarity, it is also sometimes based on relations of contiguity, for example, nakedness symbolized by clothes and uniforms. It is customary to distinguish between the symbol and the sign, based on the criterion of motivation: if the sign is necessary and unmotivated, the symbol is contingent and motivated. However, while analogy predominates between the symbol and what is symbolized, it does not always suffice to justify the factor of comparison.

It is remarkable that, although there are numerous symbols, the objects symbolized are much more limited and give the impression of a monotonous translation. What is there to justify the validity of the link between the symbol and what is symbolized? Freud (1916–1917) gives a list of symbolized objects: "the human body as a whole, parents, children, brothers and sisters, birth, death, nakedness" and, he adds, "something else besides", namely, the whole "field of sexual life, the genitals, sexual processes, sexual intercourse" (p. 153).

This empirical list calls for a criticism, however, in the name of logic: this is what Charles Rycroft (1981, pp. 76–79) points out when he objects to two logical errors in the Freudian theory of "dream symbolism". First, Freud compares terms that belong to different logical categories and levels of abstraction: the elements symbolized refer to general categories that are arrived at by abstraction, whereas symbols represent specific objects. Hence, there are more symbols than topics symbolized, since "the entities classified must of necessity be more numerous than the classes into which they are classified" (1981, p. 77). Then, he seems to consider sexuality as an

> additional theme, when in fact it determines all the themes symbolized: not only genital sexuality to which he often refers, but also pregenital sexuality. The human body, a source of symbolization, is in reality an erotogenic body; the range of symbolized elements concerns the field of sexual impulses, which leads him, moreover to say that 'the very great majority of symbols in dreams are sexual symbols'.
> (Freud, 1916–1917, p. 153)

Drawing up a list of symbolized objects represents, in fact, a pitfall of classical associatianism; it is also an error of language, which reifies a dynamic.

In addition, it was what Freud learnt from clinical experience. His mistrust of arbitrary iconic symbolism as practised by Stekel led him to seek a motivation along other associative chains – in this case, contiguity – than simple "natural" analogy, but above all by the "symptomal usage" of the symptom (Assoun, 1998, pp. 95–96).[4] A short article of 1916, "A connection between a symbol and a symptom" attests to this. In it, Freud notes that if "experience in the analysis of dreams has sufficiently well established the hat as a symbol of the genital organ, most frequently of the male organ, [it] cannot be said, however, that the symbol is an intelligible one" (Freud, 1916, p. 339). In other words, it is a matter of finding a motive, a "theory" that can justify the analogical association. Freud speaks both of the contiguity hat-head and an obsessional symptom linked to the salutation made with a hat that obeys the unconscious association between taking off one's hat, beheading and castration. From this perspective, it is the castration complex that strengthens and confirms the symbolic connection: hence the underlying idea that the symbolism of dreams and sexual interpretation find their raison d'être through the reference to a primal phantasy.[5]

Furthermore, as soon as Freud was able to propose an analogical association that was based more on a *linguistic usage* of symbols, he found two reasons in it to reduce the arbitrary nature of interpretation: first, owing to the *clinical* necessity of taking the dreamer's associations into account, and secondly, due to the *theoretical* requirement of limiting symbolic activity and thereby of preserving the dream-work. The analysis of the screen memory of the "Wolf Man" related to his anxiety while chasing after a big butterfly with yellow stripes illustrates Freud's concern to take into account the dreamer's associations rather than taking the easy path of offering a symbolic interpretation. Freud (1918 [1914]) chose in fact not to fall back on a "facile" interpretation according to which "the points or stick-like projections of the butterfly's wings might have had the meaning of genital symbols" (p. 90). The Wolf Man's associations led him, in fact, to recollect childhood memories which provided the key for the interpretation. As the patient was Russian, in his language a "butterfly" was called *babushka*, meaning "granny", and thus was related to the idea of a woman: moreover, the memory of pears in the store-room allowed him to make a link between the yellow stripes on the pears (pears are called *grusha* in Russian) and the first name of the nursery-maid who had taken care of him, who was called *Gruscha*. Linguistic usage – that is a play on words – had helped him to make a connection between the memory of the butterfly and that of the nursery maid, called *Gruscha*. When he was about two and a half years old, he had seen this young woman on her knees washing the floor, and the movement of her legs which exposed her sexual organs had subsequently been associated with the movement of the butterfly's wings. His anxiety on seeing the butterfly with yellow stripes had thus been associated with the excitation of the child who had urinated on seeing this woman, and with the threat of castration to which he may have been subjected.

While Freud insists on the "unconscious" aspect of the term "comparison" between the symbol and the object symbolized, he also notes that "these comparisons are not freshly made on each occasion; they lie ready to hand and are complete, once and for all" and elude individual initiatives: these symbolic relations "[agree] in the case of different individuals – possibly, indeed, agreeing in spite of differences of language" (Freud, 1916–1917, p. 165). The symbolism of dreams goes beyond the differences between people, languages and cultures.

This universality of symbolism does not only concern individual dreams; but it can also be found in collective creations such as "myths and fairy tales", "sayings and songs", and "colloquial linguistic usage and poetic imagination" (Freud, 1916–1917, p. 166.) Moreover, it is the similarities between these different domains that enabled Freud to justify the existence of a "symbolism of dreams" independent of the dreamer. John Forrester (1980) has clearly shown the benefits of this *linguistic* method of interpretation, which in fact reduces the arbitrary nature of the popular symbolic method by operating a "fusion of the individual and the collective" (p. 134): the adoption by a patient of a figure of speech is absolutely individual, but at the same time, it opens out onto a universality that goes beyond the patient and the analyst, because it belongs to a work of culture.

It is surprising that Freud sought in this way to evacuate all symbolic activity from the dream-work, for the latter determines a set of relations between the manifest content and the latent content which can, in fact, be described as symbolic: one meaning is substituted for another, which both conceals and expresses it. From this point of view all forms of representations, indirect and pictorial, – dreams, parapraxes, symptoms, bungled actions, and so on – of an unconscious wish, are symbolic, and the dream-work thus accomplishes a genuine work of *symbolization* through its effects of distortion (*Entstellung*).

It is always a particular form of symbolization since, in this substitution of representations, the connection between the manifest symbol and the element that is symbolized latently is not obvious. Contrary to the phenomena of meaning characteristic of language, dreams are initially closed to meaning: they are not intended to be recounted; they are first and foremost "the guardians of sleep and not its disturbers" (Freud, 1900, p. 233). This is why Freud says that dreams "do not think", but are content to "find another form": they contain no communicative purposes.

As for symptoms, the mnemic symbols of a recollection or of a repressed phantasy, this substitution of representations only has meaning in relation to the separation of affects and ideational elements. The dream-work is a work of symbolization, not only by substituting one representation for another, but through its attempt to link up and master affects. Condensation in dreams can only be explained in relation to the displacement of affect towards elements extrinsic to the network of the initial ideational elements: concerning this "transference and displacement of psychical intensities", Freud is quite clear: "The process we are here presuming is nothing less than the essential portion of the dream-work" (Freud, 1900, p. 308). This requirement to link up affects accounts for the specificity of the symbolization inherent to the formations of the unconscious, of the concealment of the relations between the symbol and what is symbolized.

As Freud points out, the language of dreams is not "a faithful translation or a point-for-point projection of the dream-thoughts" (Freud, 1900, p. 281) owing to the mechanisms of condensation and displacement; but it obeys a certain logic limiting the arbitrary relationship between the manifest content and the latent content: the aptitude for representability, which makes use of the ready-made stereotyped symbols in the unconscious, determines a relationship in which the characteristics of the manifest content reproduce certain characteristics of the latent content.[6] Freud compares this ideographic system of writing to the hieroglyphic writing of the Egyptians which is different from the alphabetic language. "A dream is a picture-puzzle, a rebus" whose signs are not to be read, Freud says, according to their "pictorial value", but according to their "symbolic relation") (*Zeichenbeziehung*): it relates to a meaning that is not contained homogenously in the manifest content, but arises from a chain of images that have to be deciphered at the level of their significance as signs in order to find the underlying phrase "of beauty and significance".

Hieroglyphic writing, a mixture of ideographs and alphabet, lends itself to a comparison with dreams. It used the principle of homophony to represent abstract words, without succeeding, however, in making full use of this phonetic writing. Dreams take the opposite path by subordinating phonetic writing and using words as things, exploiting their signifying function. Freud (1917 [1915]) points out, though, that dreams do not modify "words" as in schizophrenia, but only "thing-presentations, to which the words have been taken back" (p. 229). What else can this mean other than that dreams only *partly* call into question the relations of meaning between word-presentations and thing-presentations? Freud makes this clear by emphasizing that dreams undergo a topographical regression, which presupposes the existence of a psychical topography that guarantees the exercise of the referential function of signs (Gibeault, 1983).

The comparison between dreams and hieroglyphs is also justified by the means used to reduce the polysemy. Egyptian writing was faced with the difficulty of overcoming the possible ambiguity between an ideograph and a homophone, and the ambiguity that could result from the interpretation of the word as a whole. This was the reason for the invention of *unilateral* signs, simple ideographs that played a complementary phonetic role and thus opened up the perspective of not only alphabetic writing but also the *determinatives*, ideographs that are not meant to be read but serve to classify the word in a definite category. Freud (1900) found the same recourse to this system in dreams, for example when a "composition" aimed at uniting in one and the same person "features which are peculiar to one or other of the persons concerned but not common to them" (p. 320) fails: in a dream, there may therefore be two people, one of whom is outside the scene and explains the presence of the person who is the principal actor. The importance ascribed by Freud to the *context*, here within the dream but also outside it in the person of the dreamer, is characteristic of this need to have recourse to "determinatives" making it possible to resolve the ambiguity of the "ideographs" of dreams.

The language of dreams is nonetheless linked to discursive language, since latent thoughts have this form; moreover, Freud examines with great attention the processes of the transformation of the logical relations of these thoughts in a visual form. The contrast between the *optative* dimension of language and the *non-optative* dimension of the hallucinatory dream-image opens up a path that is highly instructive: a dream "is the transformation of a thought into an experience", the transition from "I wish", "I would like", which is characteristic of verbal expression, linking the future and the past, to the fulfilled wish which is experienced in the indicative mood: "The present tense is the one in which wishes are represented as fulfilled" (1900, p. 535).

Conversely, the contrast between the "experience of the dream" and the "account of the dream" reintroduces time and negation ("It was only a dream") and relies on the same distancing, even though Freud insists on the fact that in "the process of interpreting a dream this alteration [from the optative into the non-optative] must first be undone", and the dimension of the optative, that is of desire, re-established: *"I saw my brother in a box* is not to be translated *my brother is restricting himself* but *I should like my brother to restrict himself"* (p. 129). This distance between the hallucinated wish and the dream account entails the need to take into account the style of the dream, in contrast with the style of the account of the dream, as well as similarities and differences between the two forms of "rhetoric".[7]

The interpreting dimension of dreams requires us to add to the vertical coordinate (manifest content/latent content), the horizontal coordinate (experience/account) where the factors of context (who is the dream being related to?), and the forms of the account (oral account or written account) that play a direct role in the production of meaning. A series of parameters appear, then, which justify the tripartite dimension of signs, ranging from the *modalities* of the transformation of a syntax and a verbal vocabulary into iconic syntax and vocabulary, to the importance of the *form* of the dream, on which Freud had already insisted with regard to both its internal aspects (female genital organs symbolized by a gap in the dream images (1900, p. 331)) and its external aspects (the length of segments) including the *function* of the dream in the psychical economy, which may vary greatly depending on the psychopathological organizations (Segal, 1981). If a patient dreams, for instance, of mathematical formula to depict the primal scene, when considering the elements depicted in the dream, we must take into account other elements than those pertaining to a simple natural analogy, and think about the modalities of transformation not only of words into images but also from one image to another.

Such a perspective may seem to involve a "hermeneutics" centred on the dream-content; but in fact it opens out, to use Masud Khan's (1975) expression, on to the *dreaming experience* as an incommunicable experience, different both from the latent content and the lived experience of the dream: if the dream must be replaced within the dynamics of the transference relationship, it also needs to be considered a quest for oneself, for the "true self" (Winnicott, 1960), at the origin of both the sense of existing and of the capacity to *create*. This point of view is related to the study of the conditions of possibility of adequate dream-work, seen as the success or failure of the dreaming experience; while the dream bears witness to a return to the origins, revealed by the immediateness of the hallucinatory realization in the present, it is at the same time the "guardian of sleep". The psychic quality of the dream is related here to the capacity to utilize symbolization, which is measured by the balance between the productions of the dream and sleep. This dreaming experience may evoke the mystical temptation of a return to the ineffable; but, in fact, it only gives rise to a search for immediateness and the unrepresentable if it does not succeed in constituting itself.

The language of dreams and verbal language

Freud also raises a problem of particular interest, namely, that of words in dreams. We know that he insists on the fact that dreams call into question linguistic competence and that, if words appear in the manifest content of a dream, they only have the value of day residues: they are not to be taken as signifieds but as signifiers that are among the elements of the picture puzzle that have to be deciphered. And yet, in the case of the "Rat man" (Freud, 1909), he asserts that obsessions in the form of linguistic expressions are a dream creation (p. 223). Hence the temptation to reattribute dream language with linguistic competence and to bring together the different modes of symbolization within a single symbolic function, that of spoken language. Certain authors (Edelson, 1972; Heynick, 1981) have made this choice out of a wish to unite Freud and Noam Chomsky; however, while the attempt to establish an isomorphism between the deep structure and superficial structure of language and the structure of dream activity may highlight certain operations of transformation in the dream-work, it often only has a metaphorical value and leads to a tendency to overlook the importance of censorship and of the role of affects in dreams.[8]

This was also the option taken by Jacques Lacan in his wish to draw parallels between Freud on the one hand and Ferdinand de Saussure and Roman Jakobson on the other. The issue at stake, in fact, was one of bringing together unconscious symbolism and the symbolism of language within the *two-way structure* common to the various expressions of symbols (dreams, myths, poems). This was what Jakobson attempted when he emphasized the analogies between the structure of the functioning of language[9] and the tropes of rhetoric: hence the generalization that gives a linguistic status to the problem of symbolism, according to which "the competition between the two devices, metonymical and metaphorical, is manifest in *every symbolic process*, be it intrasubjective or social" (Jakobson, 1956, p. 132, my emphasis). The question arises as to whether there is an *identity* between the two domains or a *similarity*, a simple *metaphor*, which would require us not to overlook the differences that organize these different symbolic domains.

It is worth noting that, notwithstanding the analogies at the levels of the modes of association and substitution, condensation and displacement are distinguished from metaphor and metonymy as figures of classical rhetoric. As Howard Shevrin (1972) has pointed out, tropes serve the purposes of integration and *conjunction* of meaning, whereas dream mechanisms are characterized by a *disjunction* of meaning (p. 123). Thus, displacement is defined by a disjunction of the relations of causality linked to the withdrawal of affect which, according to Freud, "serves the purposes of condensation" (Freud, 1900, p. 294). A displacement then occurs towards an element extrinsic to the network of ideas present in the condensation: hence the disguised ideas and the rupture of links with physical events. There is nothing similar in the tropes of rhetoric: for example, the metaphor leads a psychical event back to its physical reality and preserves this link "both externally through its signification and internally through its rhythm" (Shevrin, 1972, p. 125). Furthermore, the dreaming experience is opposed to metaphorical construction insofar as the disjunction of meaning in the dream also dissolves the link with the dreamer who is having his dream, whereas the subject participates actively in the creation of metaphors. Metaphorical construction does not appear in front of the intrapsychic conflict but behind it, just as sublimation presupposes that repressed conflicts have been overcome. Finally, this was what Freud was saying when he compared the hysterical symptom with the "normal symbol": in one case, the relation of similarity was lost and a disjunction of meaning occurred, whereas it was preserved in the symbol in the usual sense of the term.

The application of the tropes of classical rhetoric to dream mechanisms thus leads to more nuances. It is well known that Lacan took up Jakobson's hypothesis, but it is important to point out that Jakobson's assimilations and Lacan's are not the same where the mechanisms of dreams are concerned: for Jakobson, contiguity brings together metonymical "displacement" and "synecdochic" condensation, whereas metaphor designates unconscious identification and symbolism. For Lacan, metaphor applies to condensation and metonymy to displacement. This first deviation shows the difficulties involved in identifying analogies that claim to be identities.

At the level of the dream-work, the Lacanian equation accounts at first sight for the relations between manifest content and latent content. Rhetorical substitutions can be subsumed under the binary system of metaphor and metonymy and, provided the linguistic sign is replaced by the non-referential signifier, one could account in this way for the substitutions and nonsensical effects that are characteristic of dream mechanisms. From this perspective, it matters little that the tropes of classical rhetoric have lost their meaning, provided that the hegemony of language is maintained, while highlighting the disjunction of meaning.

However, it is difficult to enclose metaphor and metonymy within the opposition between the paradigmatic and the syntagmatic. Although he takes up these rhetorical references, Guy Rosolato (1978) does not fail to point out the disadvantages related to these reductions. Leaving aside the difficulty of bringing together under "contiguity" alone the effects of meaning of metonymy (corresponding to exclusive relations between objects) and of synecdoche (corresponding to inclusive relations (Gibeault, 1981a)), it is interesting to recall Freud's intention to include the two principles of association – similarity and contiguity – in the category of *contact*:

> Association by contiguity is contact in the literal sense; association by similarity is contact in the metaphorical sense. The use of the same word for the two kinds of relation is no doubt accounted for by some identity in the psychical processes concerned which we have not yet grasped.
>
> (Freud, 1912–1913, p. 85)

Thus, metonymy may be said to correspond to this "higher unity" of contact and to account for the connection between dreams and magic as a wish-fulfilment governed by the technique of the animistic mode of thinking – namely, the "omnipotence of thoughts".

In contrast, metaphor corresponds to a substitution of one signifier by another signifier, one following the other without it being possible on the face of it to justify the attraction; hence the effect of nonsense of which Lacan speaks. Rosolato (1978) notes that this association can be called paradigmatic, but that "paradigmatic substitution does not suffice to define metaphor" (p. 80). It is an association by similarity that cannot be limited to a single circuit without incurring the risk of no longer being a metaphor but a catachresis. It is formed from different semantic and metonymic circuits, but it cannot be limited to any one of them. It establishes a *rupture*, which confers on it both its nonsense at first sight and its creative value retrospectively: its circuits are open, variable and multiple. The equivalence with the paradigmatic raises the risk of losing sight of the creative and prospective function of the metaphor; it would therefore be useful to separate the metaphorical from the paradigmatic, even if, at a certain level, this equivalence can give a linguistic status to the problem of symbolism.

Out of this concern not to completely identify the pair metaphor/metonymy with the pair paradigmatic/syntagmatic and to give preference to the opposition contact/rupture, Rosolato concurs with Paul Ricoeur (1975) who, having considered the benefits to be gained from this analogy, rightly notes that "the price to be paid is heavy". We lose sight of the "predictive character of metaphor" and, with it, "the difference between a metaphor of invention and a metaphor of usage, insofar as the degrees of freedom in the combination affect the syntagmatic and not the paradigmatic aspect of language" (p. 229). He recalls Pierre Fontanier's (1977) distinction between catachresis, whose usage is forced, and metaphor, whose usage is free. It is this freedom, this rupture inherent to the metaphor, which gives it its creative value. Jakobson's model minimizes, in fact, the difference between sign and discourse and limits the metaphor to a substitution of one term for another. The metaphor thus loses its "secret" of being a "new" combination created by the context and resulting from an unexpected syntagmatic connection.

This is a perspective that Rosolato (1983) took up again concerning the formation of symbols, in the opposition between the metonymic coherence aimed at producing a univocal discourse and the metaphorical symbol that is open to polysemy and multivocity. There is a definite advantage with regard to the need to account for the ambiguities of Freudian conceptions on symbolism. The risk, however, is that the notions of condensation and displacement lose their originality of being mechanisms that operate prior to language and its rhetoric, and that, in their "effects of meaning", are essentially concerned with mastering the irruption of affects. The unity of the symbolisms in the structure of language is in fact related to a conception of meaning and the object that rests essentially on the function of language. Rosolato subscribes, moreover, to Lacan's (1956a) assertion that "it is the world of words that creates the world of things" (p. 229). This implies that the "images" of things are considered duplications of the real world, which is not always excluded from the notion of the mnemic image in Freud's work; it remains, however, to be determined whether this primacy of language is the only and last word in Freudian associationism. The alternation between contact and rupture suggested by Rosolato could prove to be more instructive than the oscillation between metonymy and metaphor, owing to the evocation of a relation to the object that is independent of the linguistic relation.

It is not certain, moreover, that dreams and poetry, among other units of discourse, retain their differences in this unification at the heart of linguistic structure. Lacan certainly finds again the predicative function of the metaphor, but in its dimension of connotation rather than denotation. But the dream cannot be defined by communication, even if means "signifying" to the subject his place in a chain of signifiers. When he says that condensation (*Verdichtung*) is related to metaphor, and therefore to listening to poetry (*Dichtung*), owing to the "condensation" that occurs in *Dichtung* (Lacan, 1957, p. 425), he short-circuits the difference between dreams and poetry by a homonymic appeal that is not at all justified by etymology.[10] The metaphor certainly has its roots in condensation and ends in a process in which the rhythm recalls the vibration of the drive impulses and affect; but it differs at the level of the integration of meaning and affects that occur in it.

The status of the metaphor is paradoxical here. On the one hand, it is only one word for another and slides under the bar; it can therefore evoke dream functioning through the exclusion of meaning that it operates. On the other hand, it makes it possible to "cross the bar" between the psychic systems and to ensure a poetic creativity corresponding to its function of "rupture" and "freedom". This status of the metaphor is paradoxical in relation to that of the "signifier" in Lacanian interpretation, which, in seeking to unify the various fields of symbolization, does not necessarily preserve their specificity.

Primitive language

In fact, in these equations between the language of dreams and language, Lacan was following a path that had already been traced by Freud when, in order to evoke the language of dreams, he saw them as the survival of an archaic language. The unity of language continued to include verbal thought and nonverbal thought. This was the subject of Freud's (1910) article, "The antithetical meaning of primal words", where the simultaneous coexistence of opposites confirms the analogy between the language of dreams and primitive language. Freud refers to the work by Karl Abel who discovered in the Egyptian language words with two meanings, one of which was the exact opposite of the other. He gives the example of the word *ken*, which means both "strong" and "weak"; the ambiguity is removed thanks to the determinative signs invented by Egyptian writing: when *ken* means "strong", it is followed by the picture of an armed man standing upright; when it means "weak" it is followed by the picture of a squatting, limp figure. These ideographs were equivalent to the gesture in spoken language. Freud saw this correspondence as a confirmation of the "regressive, archaic character of the expression of thoughts in dreams" (p. 161), the language of dreams perpetuating the system of a primitive language.

What is the value of this correspondence? The linguist Émile Benveniste had already called it into question by criticizing Karl Abel's thesis, both on account of methodological principles in the comparison of languages and of the "logic" of language, which cannot escape the "principle of contradiction", however archaic the language may be. Benveniste demonstrates this in particular in connection with the correspondences established by Abel in Western languages based on an alphabetical system, where, it is true, there are significant errors of reasoning. This must also be true for hieroglyphic writing insofar as, like every language, it aims to "communicate"; for Benveniste (1956), every language is an "instrument for ordering the world and society" and, consequently, "applies to a world considered as real and reflects a real world" (p. 82). Every language and every system of writing, however archaic they may be, are thus a priori coherent and cannot attribute one expression to two notions that are mutually exclusive or contrary, which is confirmed by the study of languages.[11]

Abel's example of the Egyptian word *ken* (strong/weak) bears comparison in particular with the ambiguity of homonyms in alphabetical writing, where it is the context that determines the meaning, just as it is determiners that remove the ambiguity of antithetical words. Inasmuch as they are concerned with communication, language and writing have a logic that requires the principle of contradiction to be maintained. This may not be the case, however, if the writing in question does not seek to communicate but rather to conceal and hide: this is the case in particular with secret codes, and it seems that hieroglyphic writing had the purpose, at a certain moment, not of divulging the laws enacted by the authorities, as was the case originally, but to keep the secrets of Egyptian science hidden and to serve the power of the Egyptian priests (Warburton, 1977, p. 407). The very possibility of antithetical words was part of this project, and there is a strange truth here in the comparison between the language of dreams and hieroglyphic writing insofar as, in both cases, it is less a matter of revealing than of concealing.

It was also in the reference to a primitive language that Freud found a foundation for the "cultural" and "sexual" symbolism that can be found in dreams. After referring to Abel, he takes up the argument of the linguist Hans Sperber for whom the origin of language was linked to summoning the speaker's sexual partner and was marked by the identity of sexual words and the words used in work activities: "The words enunciated during work in common thus had two meanings; they denoted sexual acts as well as the working activity equated with them" (Freud, 1916–1917, p. 167).

At a time when linguistics had been led to set aside the problems of the origins of language, Freud returned to the question and found a basis for the universality of dream symbolism by taking literally the hypothesis of a basic language: "Things that are symbolically connected today were probably united in prehistoric times by conceptual and linguistic identity. The symbolic relation seems to be a relic and a mark of former identity" (Freud, 1900, p. 352).

Whether it was in relation to hysterical symptoms, contradictions in dreams, or here with the symbolism of dreams, Freud overcame the individual arbitrary factor by having recourse to the universality of a primitive language; this amounted to placing in real anteriority, in an association, or even an identity, by contiguity, that which belonged to an association by similarity and to a process of symbolization that still had to be explained. In fact, it is not really a primitive language at all since it evokes the concrete and demetaphorized thinking of schizophrenics, where the referential function of signs is totally called into question (Gibeault, 1983, pp. 138–139). Concrete thinking is the contrary of a language, as can be seen from Daniel Paul Schreber's "basic language" with which Freud (1916–1917) compared this primitive language (p. 166): an excessively sexualized language that uses euphemism to the point of antiphrasis – for example, "reward" for "punishment", "poison" for "food", "juice" for "venim", and so on (Schreber, 1903, pp. 49–50; see also Menahem, 1986, pp. 158–160; Arrivé, 1986, pp. 110–112) – attesting both to the destruction of signs and to the risk of psychic death, thus calling into question the function of the communication of language since "all nonsense will be cancelled out", as Schreber says. This certainly is related to the process of transforming one sexual gender into another but also, and above all, to the undecidable ontological paradox according to which it is necessary to be in order not to be, and not to be in order to be (Racamier, 1980, pp. 143–159).

Faced with this two-way structure, which defines as much the symbolism of the unconscious as the symbolism of language, Freud had, in fact, to find the regulating principles that permitted the effectuation of meaning. The language of dreams confronted him with the alternative between on the one hand an over-determination of dreams, removing any possibility of establishing the meaning, the infinite sequences of which may be valued, as by Carl Gustav Jung; and, on the other, a key to dreams, as in the methods of interpreting dreams that he criticizes, and to which he returns in his research into dream symbolism with constant meanings that exist independently of the dream-work.

Freud found in the dreamer's associative context a specific requirement for dream interpretation that established the pertinent features and made it possible to avoid the arbitrary nature of the key to dreams; on the other hand, Jung's calling into question of the sexual dimension of the libido and the need to account for the universality of symbolism led him to evoke a code of dreams that functioned as a system and law and made it possible to establish meaning beyond the limits of the dreamer. The hypothesis of a primitive sexual language that continues to inhabit the dreamer's nights lent support to the technical choice made by Freud to give priority to the linguistic usage of symbols used in dreams.

In the controversy with Jung, the gain was immense. If Freud was able to save his discovery of the unconscious and infantile sexuality, it was by giving priority to verbal thought over nonverbal thought, language over the contemplative aims of the ineffable: Jung, on the contrary, from the outset, opposed symbolic thought to verbal thought, thereby taking up the opposition between psychosis and neurosis, between the universal and the individual. The insistence on dream mechanisms and the work of contextual deciphering represented a way beyond these alternatives through the reference to individual history and to symbolism linked to linguistic usage. The contextual orientation of the Freudian method of interpretation corresponded in reality on the clinical level to the requirement for a universalism exempt from arbitrariness; the theoretical hypothesis of a primitive language simply postponed the debate concerning the foundations of a process of symbolism. We can imagine how the recourse to philological analysis, as John Forrester (1980, pp. 254–311) has showed, contained the germ of the Lacanian interpretation of the unconscious.

There is nevertheless a remainder and it concerns thing-presentations, since the linguistic usage to which Freud refers does not exhaust all the sexual symbols: "dream symbolism is only a small part of it" (Freud, 1916–1917, p. 166), he writes. Moreover, though he excludes the idea of a symbolic language peculiar to the unconscious, the relations between symbolism and sublimation, between thought and language, still needed to be understood. The difference between the terms presentation or idea (*Vorstellung*) and visual representation (*Darstellung*) is an indication here of a difference that needs to be respected at the level of psychic materials. Finally, while he attributes a major role to language in delusional reconstruction, as evidenced by the emphasis placed on the basic language in the case of Schreber, it is important to remember that the hypercathexis of word-presentations does not suffice to explain delusion and that the hallucinatory hypercathexis of thing-presentations constitutes primary delusional experience (Gibeault, 1985). This was the argument Jung used against Freud, but in order to foster an ineffable experience of the unconscious that seemed unacceptable to him.

Symbolism and sublimation

Jones' (1916) article, "The theory of symbolism", which was published at the same time as Freud was reflecting on the question, does not provide an answer to these questions and tends to confirm the empiricist conception of the theory of symbolism which Lacan (1960) had no difficulty in criticizing. Indeed, for Ernest Jones, all true symbolism is the substitute for repressed drives; he is categorical: "Only that which is repressed is symbolized; only what is repressed needs to be symbolized. This conclusion is the touchstone of the psychoanalytic theory of symbolism" (Jones, 1916, p. 116). He thus rejects any theory of symbolism that seeks to reverse the link established by Freud between symbols and repressed sexual impulses, making sexuality the symbol of something else. This is the reproach he made of Jung's conception of the "libido-symbol" which amounts to denying quite simply the importance of unconscious factors in the formation of symbols; indeed, for Jung, the libido-symbol signifies "any mental process that replaces another" since, for him, the libido loses its sexual specificity and the term "symbol" applies to all forms of indirect representation (Jones, 1916, p. 117).

But Jones is more particularly interested in the theory of functional symbolism developed by Herbert Silberer. In this, he follows Freud, who discusses it in relation to *considerations of representability* and the transformation of thoughts into images during the process of forming dreams (Freud, 1900, p. 344). The interest of the discussion of this theory is to clarify the psychoanalytic theory of symbolism in relation to other conceptions and to underline what is at stake in this problem of dream symbolism.

In dream symbolism, Silberer places the accent on the pictorial and concrete representation of how the mind functions at the moment of falling asleep or waking up, on the depiction of the psychic state in place of the object, and thus opposes a "functional phenomenon" that symbolizes the modalities of thought-activity, in which *what* the mind is thinking is symbolized. For Jones, symbolism becomes in this way "a representative of sublimations, instead of being the representative of unconscious complexes" (Jones, 1916, p. 141). He therefore agrees with Freud who also reproached Silberer's functional symbolism for having "led to many abuses; for it has been regarded as lending support to the old inclination to give abstract and symbolic interpretations to dreams" (Freud, 1900, p. 505). Freud, moreover, likens Silberer's functional phenomenon with secondary elaboration, but nonetheless sees "this self-observing agency" as special evidence of the "dream-censor" (Freud, 1900, p. 505).[12]

The example of the symbol of the serpent illustrates this point of view well. For Jung and Silberer, a serpent in dreams symbolizes the abstract idea of sexuality, whereas for Freud and Jones it symbolizes the concrete idea of the phallus, while being generally *associated* with the abstract idea of sexuality (Jones, 1916, pp. 106–107). On this subject, Jones stresses the importance of the *affects* linked to the symbol, and remarks that Silberer insists more on the symbolization of negative and reactive affects, for instance affects of fear and disgust related to the serpent, linked to the preconscious-conscious, than on that of positive unconscious affects, in this case, the desire for the phallus (Jones, 1916, pp. 122–123).

Based on a symbolic equivalence between two objects linked by a relation of "identification", that is, of similarity, Jones distinguishes between a process of *symbolization* corresponding to the substitution of one object for another, but without a change of affect, and a process of sublimation corresponding to the development of the real, objective intrinsic meanings of the second object, as well as to the modification of the affects invested in the first object (Jones, 1916, pp. 138–139). The formation of symbols thus appears to be a regressive rather than progressive process and, contrary to the opinion of Jung, Adler and Silberer, "symbolism is an obstacle to progress" (p. 141) as indicated by neurotic symptoms, dreams, and delusions.

This is why he distinguishes the *symbol* from all the other forms of indirect representation, and in particular from the *metaphor*: a common point between them is that they highlight a resemblance between objects with the help of an image, and are based on a symbolic equivalence between two objects. The same symbolic image, a snake for example, can thus be a symbol when it serves as a substitute for an unconscious object (the phallus), but ceases to be a symbol, strictly speaking, and becomes a metaphor when it serves as a substitute for censorship or sublimated tendencies – the snake as a symbol of sexuality or wisdom.

Symbol and metaphor are differentiated due to their links with the unconscious. Their common point is that they both seek to create an image and are thus close to the pleasure principle: "The simile is the primary process", asserts Jones. It is interesting to note that he is not far from thinking that it is a very subjective, poetic device, which seeks the path of least resistance by wanting to render an idea with its affect, and that the "decadence of the metaphor" is a mark of progress, from the point of view of objectivity, the reality-principle and science: when the figurative sense has become the usual, literal sense, the "figurative" symbol has acquired its own objective reality in place of the subjective reality that it had during the earlier phases. He rightly points out that the evolution of the metaphor is a process that is "no doubt parallel to the gradual extension and evolution of the ideas themselves that are denoted by the words" (Jones, 1916, p. 134).

What poses a problem, however, is this manner of conceiving symbolization as the failure of sublimation rather than as its promotion. And yet Jones did not betray Freud's thinking on symbolism, during these years that were basically contemporaneous with the polemic with Jung. This opposition marks too radically an opposition between the symbolism of the unconscious and the symbolism of language, whereas, as Hanna Segal (1957) points out, following many others:[13] "There are great advantages in extending the definition of the symbol to cover those used in sublimation" (p. 392).

In the first place, she writes, "a wider definition of the word 'symbol' corresponds better to common linguistic usage and includes what is called 'symbol' in other sciences and everyday language". She then points out that there seems to be "a continuous development from the primitive symbols as described by Jones, and the symbols used in self-expression, commu-nication, discovery, creation, etc." Finally, a wider concept of symbolism must be admitted if we want to understand *how* "the child's interest in the external world is determined by a series of displacements of affects and interests, from the earliest to ever new objects" (Segal (1957).)

Furthermore, the univocal and irreversible fixedness of this symbolism is contradicted by clinical experience itself. This is what Ferenczi had already pointed out in connection with the symbolism of the tooth: while it can be a symbol of the penis, it is not contradictory to see the penis as a symbol of the tooth owing to the predominance of the oral conflict: "It is not that the tooth is the symbol of the penis, but rather, to speak paradoxically, that the later maturing penis is the symbol of the more primitive boring implement, the tooth" (Ferenczi, 1924, p. 22). Lacan was to make a similar critique, reproaching Jones for "certain erroneous approaches, such as his remark … that while a church bell can symbolize the phallus, the phallus will never symbolize a bell tower" (Lacan, 1966, p. 594). The opposition of the sexual and the non-sexual to which Jones refers to describe the true symbol does not govern the "substitutions of signifiers" revealed by clinical experience.

The study of dream symbolism thus leads us to accord a place both to the symbolism of the unconscious and to the symbolism of language, and to stress their continuity, without however fixing them in the opposition between stereotyped sexual symbolism and the "anagogical" function (Silberer) or "prospective" function (Jung) of symbols. If we oppose true symbolism and sublimation, we are necessarily led like Jones to oppose symbolic (or mythological) knowledge and scientific knowledge, and to believe that "the symbolic use of symbols impedes, precisely, the idea from being formulated". In keeping with this opinion, scientific knowledge is related to the detachment of the symbolic associations obeying the pleasure principle: "a surrendering of the personal, subjective factor, and an attend-ing, which might also be called sensorial, to the objective attributes of the new percept" (Jones, 1916, p. 133). Scientific knowledge implies a "renun-ciation in favour of the reality-principle and its advantages, of the pleasure yielded by the easier and more primitive process of complete assimilation" (Jones, 1916, pp. 134–135).

From this empiricist perspective, symbolism and sublimation have no common ground and are opposed like primary and secondary processes, the pleasure principle and the reality principle, psychic reality and mate-rial reality. Nevertheless, it is a matter, in fact, of rediscovering, beyond this opposition between the stereotypes of fixed unconscious symbolism and the symbolism of language which is also conceived as being fixed in uni-vocal significations, a primordial symbolism linked to the foundations of objective thought. It was probably this continuity that Jones glimpsed con-cerning the generalization of the symbolism characteristic of civilization, emphasizing at the beginning of his article that it is "never-ending series of evolutionary substitutions, a ceaseless replacement of one idea, interest, capacity or tendency by another" (Jones, 1916 p. 87). Likewise, Lacan (1966) criticizes the opposition between regressive symbolic thought and progressive scientific thought, since "there has never been any other thought than symbolic thought" (p. 608).

Emphasis was thereby placed on the *processes* and forms of *symbolization* rather than on the *contents*. The hypothesis of a primitive language avoided raising the problem of the process, because it took for granted from the outset what need to be explained. It is noteworthy that the theory of symbolism – sexual stereotypy, transindividual and universal reality – corresponds to a structural requirement that can also be found in the hypothesis that Freud put forward during the same period with respect to *primal phantasies*: in one case it was a matter of accounting for typical dreams related to Oedipal themes; in the other, for typical phantasies that can be found in infantile sexual theories.

In *Moses and Monotheism* (Freud, 1939), Freud speaks in this connection of an "archaic heritage" consisting as much in dispositions as in innate contents. Dream symbolism refers to the "universality of the symbolism of language", which constitutes, according to Freud's interesting formulation, "a case of the inheritance of an intellectual disposition similar to the ordinary inheritance of an instinctual disposition" (p. 99), thereby emphasizing the inseparable link between drive and thought, drive and symbol, drive and language. In connection with Little Hans, he had already noted that "sexual symbolism – the representation of what is sexual by non-sexual objects and relations – extends back into the first years of possession of the power of speech" (Freud, 1905, p. 194, footnote 2). The origins of language in ontogenesis recapitulated the origins of language in phylogenesis. However useful the theory of symbolism was at the clinical level, insofar as it made it possible to put the accent on the individual vicissitudes of dream images, it does nothing to solve the question of the innateness of this heritage. From this point of view, the Freudian phylogenetic heritage and the Jungian collective unconscious, both of which are innate, had points in common, even though Freud (1939) always claimed otherwise. We need to understand the significance of this innateness in order to account for the processes of symbolization.

Symbolization: genesis and/or structure

We have a series of oppositions here that need to be linked up: *unconscious symbolism* based on analogy and motivation and the *symbolism of language* based on conventionality and arbitrary factors; stereotyped symbolic images that call for a univocal *translation* and processes of symbolization opening out onto a multivocal *interpretation*; the genesis and formation of symbols and the need to find a structural principle to limit the polysemic proliferation of symbols; the primacy of nonverbal thought corresponding to the unconscious or the primacy of verbal thought that makes access to the formations of the unconscious possible.

Jung's choice was to give priority to the nonverbal, the contemplative and direct access to images, as he had witnessed in his work with psychotic patients and with himself (Jung, 1961). The choice made by Lacan was to take over from Freud the need to refer to linguistic usage which confers a structural dimension. It was this dimension of the primal, close to the Kantian transcendental a priori, giving experience its conditions of possibility, that Lacan wanted to draw attention to in his conception of symbolization, as a symbolic order, a conception of mediation as negativity that is irreducible to any ontogenetic approach to symbols and to any semantic dimension. "This creation of the symbol", he writes,

> must be conceptualized as a mythical moment rather than as a genetic moment. One cannot even relate it to the constitution of the object, since it concerns the relation between the subject and being and not between the subject and the world.
>
> (Lacan, 1956a, p. 319)

The recourse to archetypes in Jung or to the symbolic order in Lacan – one in the recourse to the magical symbolism of the image and the other to the symbolism of language and the algorithm – appeared to be two analogous solutions due to the reference to a unique signification of the symbol, motivated sign or arbitrary sign, concealing a power of mastery and fascination over others. There is then a risk that structure prevails over the person, abstraction over the power of phantasy specific to each individual. Between the empiricist explanation that relies on phylogenesis and ontogenesis and the more intellectualist explanation that refers to the a priori of the structure, there is room for the description of a metapsychological sequence based on the reference to the primal, as a phantasized time of origins through and in the differentiation of the secondary process. This perspective is linked to the effect of retroaction, corresponding to a causality that is not linear (i.e., merely a deferred action, a latent cause) but dialectical, namely, a retroactive causality of the present on the past, which alone can account for the relations between history and structure, between nature and culture, between the stage of symbolic equation and the stage of symbolization.

Moreover, Ernest Jones and his contemporaries, Sandor Ferenczi and Melanie Klein, described a genesis of symbolization in which the semantic dimension and the dimension of duality prevail. All of them insist on a two-stage process. A stage of identification and assimilation, of symbolic equivalence (Klein and the post-Kleinians) where the symbol is a *substitute* for the object in the sense of being *identical*; and a stage of repression during which symbolization proper emerges, and where a displacement occurs of affect onto objects and interests which had previously been assimilated and sexualized owing to their similarity: this is cryptosymbolism (Ferenczi),[14] where the symbol represents what is symbolized, in the sense of a similarity that respects differences and is not just a substitute.

For Melanie Klein, this movement is not necessarily opposed to the formation of symbols in sublimation; according to her, the process is the same (identification – formation of symbols – fixation) both for the formation of a symptomatic compromise and for sublimation. The difference between the two vicissitudes depends on the moment of the fixation: in the case of sublimation, thus of a utilization of symbols not only by the primary process but also by the secondary process, there is not only a libidinal fixation but the possibility of a "transference" onto the ego-impulses, which implies introducing a delay in the search for satisfaction. She also speaks of the existence of a "highly developed faculty for identification with the objects of the world" that surround the subject, corresponding to the early and massive transformation of the narcissistic libido into object-libido. The example of Leonardo da Vinci lends support to her thesis:

> In Leonardo's case, not only was an identification established between nipple, penis and bird's tail, but this identification became merged into an interest in the motion of this object, in the bird itself and its flight and the space in which it flew.
>
> (Klein, 1923, p. 87)

The psychic *motives* underlying this assimilation are naturally debatable and those that are alleged are often more descriptive than explanatory. Jones evokes factors that belong on the one hand to the pleasure principle, concerning the dimension of pleasure attached to the association and fusion between a new idea and an older familiar idea, and on the other to the reality-principle, relating to the assimilation between the known and the unknown fostering a more efficient effect on reality (Jones, 1916, pp. 138–139). Ferenczi (1913a, p. 228; see also 1913b, p. 279) insists on the importance of *projection* in this "sexualization of everything", in this animism, where an equation between the sexual and nonsexual organs of the body occurs, as well as between the organs and bodily functions and the objects and events of the external world. For Ferenczi, these processes entail the possibility of the symbolization of one domain by another, a two-way circulation – for example, tooth and penis can be symbols for each other reciprocally – contrary to what Jones argued, who, in his opposition to Jungian polysemic efflorescence, had sought to *fix* univocally the nonsexual to the sexual.

Ferenczi also points out that two aspects govern this projective "equation": the sensory similarity, certainly, but especially the identical affect that makes it possible to equate two ideas that are only slightly similar (e.g., the extraction of a tooth and castration) (Ferenczi, 1949, pp. 243–244, letter dated 3 June, 1911). Hence, the idea that the choice of a symbol does not only have value as a representation, but gives an indication about the affect in question: if snakes and aeroplanes are symbols of the penis, the choice of the symbol will not necessarily have the same affective significance.

Ferenczi, it is true, adopted the point of view that ontogenesis recapitulates phylogenesis: the aptitude for symbolic representation has its place in an animistic period of childhood, which is also a phase of projection in ego-development. But the emphasis placed on the work of projection opens up horizons onto the psychic issues involved in the establishment of the process of symbolization. On what conditions will the child be able to organize these "symbolic relations with the world" so that he can both see in the world "reproductions of his corporeality" and learn to "represent with his body the whole the diversity of the external world"? (Ferenczi, 1913a, p. 228). His remarks on the importance of gestural symbolism with its dimension of "mimetic representation" and magical acts, as well as on the importance of verbal symbolism where economy and precision in the expression of wishes does not exclude the magic of words, underline here the full importance of the choice of verbal and gestural analogies in the organization of psychic functioning and the vicissitudes of symbolization.

Klein adheres to this current of thought, but accords greater importance than her predecessors to the destructive impulses involved in the movement of projection that governs the establishment of the assimilating symbolic equations. The motive and primary function of this identification linked to projection, which, as one may suppose, announces the concept of projective identification, resides in the anxiety resulting from attacks on the father's and mother's organs; the fear of reprisals drives the child to "equate these organs with other things", which contributes to the development of phantasy life as well as to the apprehension of reality. The example of Dick, a four-year-old autistic child, in treatment with Melanie Klein, illustrates this aspect of symbolization: a "sufficient quantity of anxiety", an "awakening of anxiety" facilitating this first phase of "symbolic assimilation" and a "good aptitude of the ego for tolerating anxiety" permitting the appearance of symbolization proper, are both equally necessary. Hence the mediating function of the symbol between the pleasure principle and the reality principle: "Not only does symbolism come to be the foundation of all phantasy and sublimation but, more than that, it is the basis of the subject's relation to the outside world and to reality in general" (Klein, 1930, p. 221).

Whether this identification occurs in the sense of the identical that does away with differences or the similarity that respects them is indicated here on the basis of a supposed temporality. It is a question of understanding the significance of this "history" of symbolization. It can be seen here that the process of thought, the sensory identification between two things, and the drive process, "the identification of oneself with others or of others with oneself", are entirely correlative; this reflects the pertinence and relevance of what Freud said concerning the "hereditary" transmission of a thought disposition, as "relations of thought between ideas", linked to a drive disposition. The drive determines here a process in which images and words, symbols and signs, analogical purpose and structural purpose have their place and echo each other.

Lacan gave priority to the structural purpose in the examination of these two phases that govern the birth of symbolization. His commentary on Klein's (1930) article "The importance of symbol-formation in the development of the ego" speaks volumes here (Lacan, 1988, pp. 68–88). He emphasizes the absence of anxiety in Dick, whose indifference towards the object seems to suggest he is completely *in reality*, in the pure state, unconstituted, according to a Heideggerian conception, where what is real is what can only be described *from the inside* of a mind that has already had access to the symbol, like the part of the unknown that is beyond: Dick is thus in reality and outside reality, since it is not constituted and is "undifferentiated". The awakening of anxiety, which Klein seeks, leads according to Lacan to the "beginnings of an imaginification of the external world": Kleinian symbolic equation corresponds to the interplay of imaginary equations, which can substitute each other infinitely, in a series of metonymic equivalences. Klein's interpretative work, which "brought in verbalization" and "plastered on the symbolization of the Oedipal myth" makes it possible to enter "the symbolic" both in the sense of the discovery of natural language and of the law of the Oedipal myth.

Klein's "jilted" discourse is, of course, related to a conception of the drive that is aimed immediately at an object: in spite of Dick's indifference, Klein assumes that "the child's earliest reality is wholly phantastic" (Klein, 1930, p. 221). Lacan does not fail to criticize this conception and this interpretative work which, faced with this "primitive real" which is equally ineffable, might just as well rely on arbitrary factors. "As long as he does not tell us anything about it, we have no means of gaining access to it, except through *symbolic extrapolations* which constitute the ambiguity of all systems such as Melanie Klein's" (Lacan, 1988, pp. 86–87, my italics). With his sense of irony, he wonders if we can "really" follow Melanie Klein when she builds this "empire of the maternal body" with the father's penis, Dick, his brother's, and so on. And his answer is: "It doesn't matter", since thanks to a "significative speech", this whole process in which "the imaginary and real begin to be structured ... has its point of departure" (Lacan, 1988, pp. 86–87). In other words, Lacan is not far from subscribing to what Freud (1937) says concerning "constructions in analysis", where the efficacy of the construction matters more than the truth of remembering and reconstruction (p. 266). In connection with an autistic child, where clearly one cannot imagine the existence of an unconscious, Lacan sees the "sensational manifestation" of the formula "the unconscious is the discourse of the other" (Lacan, 1988, p. 85). If the analyst's words are structuring, the question still remains as to whether the "discourse of the other" will lead to imposing or proposing an interpretation. This takes us back to the question of arbitrariness which Freud feared in connection with the theory of symbolism and which is related to the *theoretical* problem of truth.

Autism raises here the question of origins which are at the limits of the possibilities of psychic work: the origins of symbolization, the origins of the psyche in the functioning of its topography, the origins of the drive and of language, and the origins of the ego. Concerning Dick, Melanie Klein presupposes a beginning and a premature arrest in symbolic formation. Lacan is close to thinking that, in spite of his rudimentary language, Dick had never had access to symbolization, for he is "eyeball to eyeball with reality", unless one imagines "an anticipated, fixed symbolism, with a single and unique primary identification, with the following names – the *void*, the *dark*" (Lacan, 1988, p. 69). These images refer to Dick's need to take refuge in the "dark" between two doors, which Melanie Klein interprets as taking refuge "in the phantasies of the dark, empty mother's body" (Klein, 1930, p. 227). Is it a phantasy or the expression of the "gaping hole" that is constitutive of the subject's own structure, as Lacan suggests?

To the semantic and imaginary content proposed by Melanie Klein, which is not untainted by a certain psychological realism, Lacan ultimately opposes the intellectualist reference to the "point of origin" of the relations between symbolism and the real, the "anticipated" experience of the *autonomy of the signifier*. The *semantic function* of the symbol, associated with the dimension of the image and the imaginary which attest to the *metonymic* value of desire, is opposed to the *syntactic function* of the symbol defined here as an algorithm, that is, as a sign that does not signify. The symbol is no longer conceived here as an unnecessary and motivated relationship as in iconic symbolism; rather, it is likened to the symbolism of language, as defined by Saussure, that is, as a necessary and unmotivated relationship between the signifier and the signified. However, if for Saussure, the sign is arbitrary, thus unmotivated, it rediscovers a relative motivation owing to the systematic organization of language. By positing the autonomy of the signifier, Lacan circumvented the Saussurian sign and apparently excluded all possible motivation for the linguistic sign: he eliminated both the function of signification (the signifying/signified relation) and the referential function of the sign (the sign/thing relation). If, for Lacan, the sign is "that which represents something to someone" (Lacan, 1966, p. 712), the signifier as an algorithm has no other function than that of referring to a certain syntactical form, without reference to a content except to "something in general". With the abandonment of the reference, the referent, the one for whom there may be a reference to something, is also called into question. To account for the contestation of the power of consciousness by the unconscious, and of the rhetoric of the latter which breaks the solidarity of the two aspects of the sign, Lacan calls into question both the meaning and the subject for whom meaning is constituted: the subject is no more a subject capable of *wanting to speak* than of *not wanting to speak*, of disguising or of hiding.

The function of language is "more worthy" than that of signifying "something" openly or in a disguised manner and consists in "indicating the place of this subject in the search for truth" (Lacan, 1957, p. 421). The subject is thus defined by his *position* in the chain, as the function of its concatenation itself; as Lacan puts it, "the subject is what the signifier represents, and the latter cannot represent anything except to another signifier" (Lacan, 1964, p. 708), that is to say the very structure of the signifying chain as spacing or a hole. While the decentring of the subject and his "dehiscence" can evoke the autistic menace of the void and darkness experienced by Dick, it is not certain that the "killing of the thing" (Lacan, 1956b, p. 262) can define the symbol and the access to language and account for the experience of the subject.

This brings us back to the opposition between psychosis and neurosis which overlaps that of the nonverbal and the verbal, as in Jung's work. This explains the reversal effected by Lacan concerning the place of negation in the constitution of a process of symbolization.[15] If, for Freud, the negative is at the origin of thought-processes and language insofar as it recalls the work of the definitive reality-ego, for Lacan it is part of the series primary expulsion (deflection of the death drive)-projection-negation, which in fact engenders with the mechanism of foreclosure imaginary equations and non-symbolization. Furthermore, while, for Freud, affirmation, as a substitute for unification, and the order of the life drive can evoke the assimilations and "equations" characteristic of the purified pleasure ego, for Lacan it accounts for the process of symbolization as a "symbolic introjection" of the speech of the other and of the function of the post-Oedipal superego. In fact, the radical "cuts" between processes and domains prevent Lacan from promoting the articulations,[16] except at the price of a "coup de force" which brings back univocal fixedness just when access to polysemic symbolization is being promoted. A practically unbridgeable gulf opens up between psychosis and neurosis whose mechanisms are irreducible. It is the price to be paid for a conception of symbolization that opposes and separates the relation between the "subject to the world" and that of the "subject to being".

This reference to the symbolic order nonetheless has the interest of marking the limits of an empiricist approach that confines itself within the symbolism of the image and seeks to construct the world on the basis of associationism and contiguity which leave the problem of meaning entirely unresolved. For Lacan (1957, pp. 435–436), meaning is manifested by language: based on convention, it makes every convention possible, and in particular what represents its most "accomplished" *effect*, mathematical symbolism. The symbolic function of the algorithm is, in fact, to obey a certain syntactical form, a law without any other reference than to "something in general" – a wish of reason that aims to make the rational real in an "absolute knowledge" which, as in the Hegelian project, leaves no room for a possible "remainder", since it is a matter of constituting a structure that is coextensive with the real. "Imaginary equations" must be replaced with "mathematical equations" which guarantee absolute mastery of the object.

But, according to a "metonymic" usage of language, the symbolic in the strict sense of the algorithm also refers to the broader sense of social symbolism, as the source of all convention. What we have here is the essential reflexivity of the symbol that returns to itself and marks a junction with the origin, through the reference to the Other in general or to the Absent. The transition from the imaginary to the symbolic represents the conquest of *mediate* relations. The very principle of symbolism is the meeting-point between two isolated terms, whose significant combination has the effect of linking together subjects who recognize each other as being committed to the same pact, the same law. This is the essential link between the symbolic order and the original sense of the symbol: *sumballô* (reuniting, putting together). From a perspective in which language has primacy, etymology confirms the reference to social symbolism. Hence the essential relationship between the two fundamental "formulations" of Lacan: if "the unconscious is structured like a language" (algebraic) and attests to the importance of the signifier conceived in terms of this syntactical function of the symbol, this only has meaning because "the unconscious is the discourse of the Other with a capital O", denoting the law of affiliation governing the relations between human beings at the level of desire.

This symbolism of the rule, setting itself up against the domination of magical symbolism, is nonetheless marked by its principles: the recourse to repetitive, if not incantatory, "formulas" is a common point between Jung and Lacan even though they did not think they shared a will to exert power and fascination over others. The reference to the monism of symbolic thought, whether it is that of the archetype and magic (Jung) or that of language (Lacan), leaves aside what Freud always stressed, albeit sometimes awkwardly, namely, the need for a dualism, a distinction, and an articulation between the symbolism of the image (magic) and the symbolism of language. The truth of Freudian empiricism in the hypothesis of the primitive language, as contiguous with the origin of the symbol, no doubt lies in marking the importance of this fundamental contiguity of the mind with the body as an articulation between representation and affect, between meaning and the "primitive" magic of hallucinatory wish-fulfilment. In other words, it would be unjustifiable, in the name of mastery, to hypostacize such essential mediation and duality in the unity of reason or the ineffable.

Primal phantasies, archetypes, and the symbolic order

The search for the universal foundations of unconscious phantasy was always a concern of Freud's, in particular in his opposition to Jung who reproached him for not justifying the link between the unconscious and infantile sexuality and therefore for laying himself open to the accusation of arbitrary interpretation. To account for the repetitive character of the phantasies observed in the analytic work with his patients, even though it could not be confirmed by individual history, Freud introduced the hypothesis of primal phantasies (*Urphantasie*), which he regarded as "innate phylogenetic schemas", following in so doing a biological point of view: as he pointed out himself, "his own archaic heritage [of the human animal] corresponds to the instincts [*Instinkt*] of animals, even though it is different in its compass and contents" (Freud, 1939, p. 100).

Freud always sought to underpin the link discovered between sexuality, trauma and defence, and to determine why sexuality is traumatizing and gives rise to a defensive conflict. He initially found an answer in the theory of early seduction; then, when he found he could not always discover real scenes at the origin of traumas, he rallied to a biological realism, where hereditary predisposition was supposed to explain the appearance of sexuality, as well as the stability, efficacy and relatively organized character of phantasy life.

It was in order to account for these nuclei of phantasy life which permitted the child to answer the enigmas raised by the sexual life of the parents, through the difference of the sexes and through his own sexuality, that Freud introduced his theory of primal phantasies. He assumed that these phantasies had actually been lived out in the prehistory of humanity, according to the scenario reported in *Totem and Taboo*, and phylogenetically transmitted. These phantasies are limited in number: the primal scene, seduction and castration, to which Freud (1905, p. 226, note 2 (added in 1920)) added the return to the maternal womb; the murder of the father could also be included in this non-exhaustive list and thereby confirm that these phantasies clarify all the issues involved in the Oedipal myth.

This conception of the primal phantasies, which is equivalent to the "far-reaching *instinctive* knowledge of animals" (Freud, 1918 [1914], p. 120), is related to a biological realism which, at the same time, does not exclude a Kantian approach. Thus, Freud remarks in the case of the "Wolf Man" that "phylogenetically inherited schemata, like the categories of philosophy, are concerned with the business of 'placing' the impressions derived from actual experience" (p. 119). What philosophical categories was he referring to? Freud was an heir of the neo-Kantism of his era and referred to the Kantian hypothesis of a priori forms of sensibility, that is to say space and time and the categories of understanding[17] corresponding to the transcendental[18] point of view aimed at clarifying the conditions of possibility of experience.

It is important to stress that this is a psychological interpretation of Kant's thought, because Freud often compared his metapsychological approach to psychic life with the Kantian critique. Thus, in 1915, in "The unconscious", he asserted that "the psychoanalytic assumption of unconscious mental activity appears to us as … an extension of the corrections undertaken by Kant on our views of external perception" (Freud, 1915a, p. 171). Freud seems here to be establishing the double equation conscious = phenomenon, unconscious = thing-in-itself, which suggests that the topographical opposition between the preconscious-conscious and the unconscious repeats the opposition between the positive and the negative.

Moreover, in the "Project" (1950 [1895]), and later in "On negation" (1925), Freud introduced a theory of judgement that may be likened to the Kantian theory of knowledge. Indeed, for Kant, as for Freud, the transition from the judgement of attribution to the judgement of existence raises the problem of accession to the dimension of existence which, as such, is an irreducible fact of thought. Reality is no longer conceived as being accessible to all subjects, but as that which escapes them, justifying for Freud, the need to distinguish between the judgement of attribution and the judgement of existence (Freud, 1925, pp. 236–237) in correlation with the opposition between a "purified pleasure-ego" and a "reality- ego" (Freud, 1915b, p. 136). There is a separation here between essence and existence, where the problem is raised of access to this reality, which, assumed from the outset with the hypothesis of an "original reality-ego", does not escape the subject any less. The realism of existence, which could equally be a naïve realism here, is compensated for by an idealist position, where the negativity of the subject renders accession to this reality extremely problematic.

However, Kant does not seek to know what reality is beyond appearances; he only asserts that the object of knowledge cannot be reduced to its appearance, to the phenomenon, to what we know of it, and that in it there is something that surpasses us. This assertion expresses a requirement that imposes on all reflection on knowledge the *realistic* affirmation implied in intentionality. From the Kantian perspective, the theory of judgement represents an original solution to the problem of perception and the relations between the sensible and the intelligible, between existence and essence. The problem of perception boils down, in fact, to understanding how *for us* there can be something *in-itself*, thereby satisfying the two conditions of intentionality: guaranteeing the subject an *object*, and an object that *is*. There is, in fact, no knowledge that does not concern an object that is, something that is. This concept of "something in general", Kant tells us, is required for knowledge to exist; but it is knowledge of an entirely indeterminate object that can be called the transcendental object, the thing-in-itself; this is X, the unknown to be determined by the operations of understanding, the aim proposed for knowledge (Kant, 1781, p. 233).

But in order to achieve this determination of the object, we can only make use of the subjective modifications of our thought, sensible intuitions; our understanding cannot grasp the object directly in itself; it can only *link together* the sensible intuitions, a point Freud emphasizes by evoking the categories that have the function of "placing the impressions derived from actual experience". Therein lies the function of judgement. Kant concludes, then, that in order to have definite objects, these objects must be thought about, that is, their diverse aspects must be linked together by this faculty of thinking and judging which is understanding. These diverse links themselves depend on a higher unity, a fixed and permanent ego which Kant calls *I think* or *pure apperception,* constituting both the original function of understanding and the supreme condition of experience.

The determinations thus effected by the understanding in the field of phenomena still remain, however, short of the object concerned, the transcendental object: thus, beyond the empirical object, constituted of phenomena and corresponding to our knowledge, we still conceive of the object-in-itself which is *unknowable,* but is necessarily *thought about,* and which Kant calls for this reason the *noumenon.* This concept shows that our knowledge always falls short of its aim, and that the object of our knowledge does not include the absolute, does not go beyond the phenomenon. This concept does not have a positive, but only a *negative* sense: it is a *limiting* concept, aimed at restricting the pretensions of our knowledge.

It is important to emphasize the transcendental rather than psychological character of Kant's research. It is not research into the functioning of the mind and its psychic contents. Yet Freud uses Kantian thought to rule on the phantasy contents to which he accords a value of reality through his reference to phylogenetic schemata transmitted hereditarily. There is a confusion between the transcendental point of view and the search for a scientific foundation based on biological realism and the quest for an origin that has a structural function; there is also the temptation not to stay with the phenomenon, but to accede to the dimension of the noumenon, thereby denying its definition as a limiting concept. In reality, the recourse to Kantian thought was mediated by the thought of Arthur Schopenhauer, whose neo-Kantianism largely consisted in giving an anthropological interpretation to Kantian subjectivity, authorizing Freudian comparisons. In Schopenhauer's psychological version, the spatio-temporal forms are equated with the sense organs, while the understanding is reduced to a mere function of the brain and traced back to sensibility (Assoun, 1976, pp. 159–175), which eliminates the transcendental dimension.

This is what authorized Freud, at the end of his work, to go beyond his assumptions concerning primal phantasies. In *Moses and Monotheism* (1939), he reiterates his hypothesis of an innate archaic heritage determining the organization of phantasy life. He continues to draw on Lamarck's theory concerning the transmission of a phylogenetic heritage, even if, he notes, "biological science ... refuses to hear of the inheritance of acquired characters by succeeding generations" (Freud, 1939, p. 100). And he adds, "I must, however, in all modesty confess that nevertheless I cannot do without this factor in biological evolution", for psychoanalysis provides evidence of the reality of "external impressions", namely, the murder of the father of the primal horde. Jones (1957) says that this passage was added by Freud to confirm his deep belief in this hypothesis, notwithstanding the advice that he had given him to remove the reference to the Lamarckian point of view (p. 313). But the hypothesis is backed up by Freud at three levels. First, that of the "[innate] dispositions such as are characteristic of all living organisms" corresponding in particular to the "instinctive knowledge" of animals. This may be compared with the innate behavioural schemata in man, which can be observed in babies, and which Freud speaks of as the "inheritance of an instinctual disposition" (Freud, 1939, pp. 98–99). Then in support of his thesis, he also speaks of "the universality of symbolism in language", the "original knowledge" represented by man's capacity to use language irrespective of the languages and cultures. But he adds a third argument which reveals the difficulty of providing evidence: "The archaic heritage of human beings comprises not only dispositions but also subject-matter – memory traces of the experience of earlier generations In this way, the compass as well as the importance of the archaic heritage would be significantly extended" (Freud, 1939, p. 99, my italics). The universality of the Oedipus complex and of the castration complex finds its rationale in a biological hypothesis which was supposed to validate the existence of the primal phantasies, even if it was no longer accepted by the biological science of its time.

It is interesting to compare Freud's approach with Jung's. In a debate with Freud, Jung introduced his hypothesis of archetypes and of the collective unconscious.[19] Just like Freud, Jung is sensitive to typical forms that "defy reduction to individual determinants" (Jung, 1956a, p. 254) and are repeated in the dreams and delusions of patients; Jung is therefore astonished to find them in myths, tales, and the productions of humanity, which is reminiscent of Freud's approach to dream symbolism as belonging to a work of culture: "Over the whole of this psychic realm there reign certain motifs, certain typical figures which we can follow far back into history, and even into prehistory… they seem to me to be built into the very structure of man's unconscious, for in no other way can I explain why it is that they occur universally and in identical form" (Jung, 1954, p. 124).

This "structural" dimension is justified, as by Freud, by the reference to their biological registration and the parallelism with the animal world: "It was manifestly not a question of inherited ideas, but of an inborn disposition to produce parallel thought-formations, or rather of identical structures common to all men, which I later called the archetypes of the collective unconscious" (Jung, 1956b, p 158). Jung distinguishes, moreover, between *archetypes* that belong more to a biological framework and *archetypical images,* corresponding to their manifestations in consciousness.

Contrary to Freud, Jung rejects, therefore, the reference to Lamarck's hypothesis and to the hereditary transmission of archetypes; he prefers to evoke the biological and ethological concept of "pattern of behaviour" which makes recourse to the transmission of phantasy contents unnecessary. But he is not satisfied with this empiricist solution and refers to a Kantian conception when he adds that the archetype "itself is empty and purely formal, nothing but a *facultas praeformandi*, a possibility of representation which is given a priori" (Jung, 1935, p. 79).

The Jungian archetype thus has a biological and psychological aspect, which leads us to conceive it both from the side of instinct which contains energy and affects and from the side of archetypical images like symbols, which, as a result, contain an immense "potential of psychic energy" and a power of fascination and action connoted by the concept of "numinous". Hence, the idea that the archetypical image can have a mesmerizing power that presents a risk of possession both at the individual level, as in psychotic hallucinations, (Jung, 1935, p. 101) and at a collective level, as in groups subject to a charismatic leader:

> The archetype, as a glance at the history of religious phenomena will show, has a characteristically numinous effect, so that the subject is gripped by it as though by an instinct. What is more, instinct itself can be restrained and even overcome by this power.
>
> (Jung, 1956b, p. 159)

Unlike Freud who accords major importance to the sexual instinct in primal phantasies and only lists a limited number of unconscious phantasies, Jung leaves the question of the number of archetypes open, which covers the whole symbolic field of man's ideas about the world and himself. He certainly stresses the major role played by the sexual instinct:

> It is not possible to discuss the problem of symbol-formation without reference to the instinctual processes, because it is from them that the symbol derives its motive power ... Hence a discussion of one of the strongest instincts, sexuality, is unavoidable, since perhaps the majority of symbols are more or less close analogies of this instinct.
>
> (Jung, 1956b, p. 228)

But his theory of the libido is desexualized and denotes all psychic energy, which led to the separation between Freud and Jung, whom he considered a son whose task was to contribute to the international expansion of psychoanalysis:

> We know far too little about the nature of human instincts and their psychic dynamism to risk giving priority to any one instinct. We would be better advised, therefore, when speaking of libido, to understand it as an energy-value which is able to communicate itself to any field of activity whatsoever, be it power, hunger, hatred, sexuality, or religion, without ever being itself a specific instinct.
>
> (Jung, 1956b, p. 137)

According to Jung, the libido is the equivalent of the "thrust" of the instinctual drive according to Freud, but cut off from its erotogenic bodily source: it is equivalent for Jung to the notion of "tending towards" (Jung, 1956b, p. 137).[20]

This is why, when Freud and Jung were in disagreement about the hypothesis of the phylogenetic transmission of memory traces, they were in fact not so far removed from one another. Jung introduced very early on alongside the *personal unconscious,* corresponding to the Freudian repressed unconscious, the notion of *collective unconscious* defined as the receptacle of all the archetypes: "These, so far as psychological experience is concerned, are the archetypal contents of the (collective) unconscious, the archaic heritage of humanity, the legacy left behind by all differentiation and development and bestowed upon all men like sunlight and air" (Jung, 1956b, p. 178). This transcendent reality corresponding to the imaginary and cultural heritage of humanity is cathected with numinous energy which has a creative or prospective function in itself, insofar as it contains a teleological dimension and is the equivalent of "absolute knowledge". Jung himself refers to Kant while limiting this hypothesis to a working hypothesis: "For me this concept is only epistemological … In a certain sense I could say of the collective unconscious exactly what Kant said of the *Ding an sich*" (Letter from C. J. Jung to A. Vetter dated 8 April 1932, in Adler & Jaffé, 1984, p. 15). But, just like Freud, his anthropological version of the transcendental point of view leads him to misappreciate the limits of human knowledge.

Right up until the end of his work, Freud reflected on this "archaic heritage", "this something in a people's life which is past, lost to view, superseded" and was opposed to the Jungian conception of the collective unconscious:

> It is not easy for us to carry over the concepts of individual psychology into group psychology; and I do not think we gain anything by introducing the concept of a 'collective' unconscious. The content of the unconscious indeed, is in any case, a collective universal property of mankind.
>
> (Freud, 1939, p. 132)

However, Freud and Jung both referred to a hypothesis that grounds the universality of universal symbolism in reality: Freud in *sensible reality* and Jung in *intelligible reality.* Even if both referred to Kant, they did not follow him with regard to his recommendation of knowledge limited to the phenomenon without the possibility for man of knowing the noumenon. Their opposition thus rests less on their epistemological approach to psychic functioning than on the place given to the sexual drive and to the status of symbolization, sublimation, and creation in psychoanalysis. Concerning his definition of primal phantasies, Freud clearly highlights this issue of the sexual and the non-sexual:

> If human beings too possessed an instinctive endowment such as this, it would not be surprising that it should be very particularly concerned with the processes of sexual life, even though it could not be by any means confined to them. This instinctive factor would then be the nucleus of the unconscious, a primitive kind of mental activity, which would later be dethroned and overlaid by human reason, when that faculty came to be acquired.
>
> (Freud, 1918, p. 120)

The epistemological difficulties and ambiguities related to the status of primal phantasies were discussed in the context of French structuralism. Lacan, in particular, played an important role in differentiating between the foundational return to origins, according to a temporal conception contained within the Freudian hypothesis of a phylogenetic heritage, and the recourse to the primal as a reference to a foundational moment of a science (Perron, 2003). It was this distinction, moreover, that led Laplanche & Pontalis to translate the "Ur" in *Urphantasie* by primal (*originaire*) rather than by *primitive or primary*. The structuralists see the hypothesis of a phylogenetic heritage as a nostalgic return to psychic conflicts grounded in reality. Reality is no longer that of the individual, but now that of humanity. The same dilemma of events and what is constitutional in mental functioning can be found in the prehistory of humanity. In order not to go back in time infinitely, a primal moment is therefore posited when the peripeteia of the species were supposedly fixed: explanation is a matter for mythology.

We could then recognize in this "real", which informs the imaginary realm and imposes its law on it, a prefiguration of the "symbolic order" as elaborated by Lacan and Lévi-Strauss. Behind the myth of a prehistory, the requirement of a structure transcending the initiatives of the subject is affirmed: the symbolic order, in Lacan's terms, could thus also be likened to the Kantian transcendental a priori.[21] Concerning the symbolism of money, I will have occasion to explore in more detail the issues related to this approach which does not escape the hypothesis of the reality of the intelligible. But, as Laplanche and Pontalis (1964) point out, primal phantasies are first and foremost phantasies and, even if they provide experience with its conditions of possibility, they are ordered by contingent elements.

Now the Freudian explanation can only have a comparative value if we take into account the specificity of the psychoanalytic point of view. The concept of the drive makes it possible in fact to do without ancestral memory. It is only possible to understand this difficulty if one takes into consideration the elaboration of the concept of the drive in relation to the ambivalence of the object relationship. Eighth-month anxiety and the negative reaction to the stranger constitute, in fact, an anti-depressive defence mechanism; the phantasy of the primal scene is simply the development of this same process. If one wants to avoid considering primal phantasies as fixed contents of the unconscious – phylogenetic traces or transcendental schema – they must be conceived, as Diatkine and Simon (1972) rightly point out, as "a defensive elaboration to attenuate the distressing consequences of object-related ambivalence" (p. 389). They add that it is precisely because "the object-cathexis is ambivalent at a very early stage that phantasying cannot be considered as the effect of the pleasure principle alone"; it is not only the appearance of phantasying that constitutes a defence against the absence of the object, but its internal organization itself which appears to be a defensive elaboration.

This is how the role of primal repression can be understood; as Freud says, it permits an impulse to become fixed to an idea, and its only mechanism is anti-cathexis. It aims in fact to contain the tendency to the absolute discharge of excitation, and to defend itself against the hallucination of satisfaction through the creation of a process of phantasy and the constitution of primal phantasies. At the same time, this fixation is at the origin of the "power of the compulsion to repeat" and of the "attraction" exerted by the "unconscious prototypes", of which Freud speaks in connection with the resistance of the id (Freud, 1926, p. 159).

In this psychic work, the mother plays a role of stimulus barrier: she induces in her infant, from birth, the capacity to master excitation and anxiety, and contributes to creating bodily limits by binding the excitation she creates at the level of the erogenous zones and the skin; by promoting his auto-eroticism in this period when "the object is cathected, then perceived" (Lebovici, 1961, p. 167), she helps the infant to defend himself against the ordeals imposed on him by reality by hypercathecting pleasure and the erogenous zones. This is only possible, as several authors have pointed out, if the mother herself can anti-cathect the imaginary child, the nighttime child, in order to allow the real child, the daytime child, to exist by himself (see Braunschweig & Fain, 1975; Castoriadis-Aulagnier, 1975).

From this point of view, the importance of a pre-object auto-erotism and a cathexis of the object before it is perceived as a whole object calls into question the distinction between the *sensible* and the *intelligible,* between the *thing-in-itself* and the *I think,* characteristic of Kantian thought (Gibeault, 1981b). Here we are at the level of "feeling" prior to the Kantian "I think": the reflections of the late Husserl (1954, pp. 105–107) and those of Merleau-Ponty (1945, p. 69) are of more help than Kant in understanding how the judgement of existence only has meaning when based on an "experience that is ante-predicative" to the world, both a reprise of the world by the body and primitive influence of the world on the body. The primordial passivity of the body, its anonymity, explain how the thing and the world are always *for me* and immanent, and no less *in itself* and transcendent to my life. Consequently, we do not start from zero but from +1, "where there is something", as Merleau-Ponty said (1964, p. 130).

It is by referring to this experience of reality that we can understand what Freud (1925) writes in his article "Negation": "Originally, the mere existence of presentation was a guarantee of the reality of what was presented. The antithesis between subjective and objective does not exist from the first" (p. 237). Freud was alluding here to the original "reality-ego" which he said possesses a "sound objective criterion" "by the experience that it can silence *external* stimuli by means of muscular action, but is defenceless against *instinctual* stimuli" (Freud, 1915b, p. 134). If this exploration corresponding to what Freud calls "reality-testing" can be understood in terms of the anti-narcissistic movement which marks a movement of separation from the object, in "Negation" reality is directly linked to the hallucination of satisfaction which shows the necessity for a primitive reflexivity of the body, a "sensory experience of oneself" prior to any representation, in order for the object to exist. This reflexive movement is described by Freud, moreover, in connection with the emergence of auto-erotism as a *double turning round* of the drive: the reversal of drive activity into passivity and the turning round upon the subject's own self (Freud, 1915b, p. 126). Here we are dealing with a question that is prior to the opposition between "I think" and the "thing-in-itself": the object is given in its existence, prior to the judgement of existence which only occurs after the loss of the object when the object is perceived as a whole object.

Indeed, the repression of this primordial sensory experience, of this hallucination of satisfaction, must take place first in order to allow for the differentiation between the psychic systems and thereby for the emergence of a psychic topography permitting the objective apprehension of reality. There is thus no need to oppose, as Jung does, a personal unconscious connoted negatively by repression, and a collective unconscious connoted positively, which may seek to reunite with this primordial sensory experience to which the concept of "mystical participation" may refer. Likewise, Merleau-Ponty's hypothesis of a primordial unconscious distinct from a repressed unconscious gives value to the idea of an unconscious – the source of a primordial symbolism – that would in fact be closer to the Freudian preconscious than to the unconscious. Repression presupposes a conquest at the heart of the libido and requires the subject to let go of this "primordial undividedness" and to accept that he does not create the object alone. This is also what Freud (1925) emphasizes in "Negation" when he writes, in connection with the judgement of existence, that "a precondition for the setting up of reality-testing is that objects shall have been lost which once brought real satisfaction" (p. 238). But, in return, this is also the precondition for the capacity to represent the world.

Repression is in fact consequential to the loss of the object and the working over of this loss as not definitive: the permanence of the object guarantees its appearance/disappearance and the symbolic substitutions of its reappearance. In "Negation", Freud points out that

> thinking possesses the capacity to bring before the mind once more something that has once been perceived, by reproducing it as a presentation without the external object having still to be there. The first and immediate aim, therefore, of reality testing is, not to *find* an object in real perception which corresponds to the one presented, but to *refind* such an object, to convince oneself that it is still there.
> (Freud, 19251925, pp. 237–238)

André Green (1999) described this psychic movement in relation to negative hallucination (pp. 274–279); if the object is to be represented, it has to be accepted that it can no longer be perceived. It is when the loss is experienced as definitive, as in psychosis, that the recourse to perceptual activity becomes indispensable for ensuring the subject's narcissistic continuity: fixedness replaces permanence, mobilism replaces movement, and the juxtaposition of opposites replaces contradiction. Repression gives way to more restrictive psychic mechanisms such as denial and ego-splitting.

The pre-object relationship thus modulates the economy and dynamics of auto-erotism and narcissism after the object relationship has been established. The quality of maternal care, from the beginning of life, determines the subsequent fate of the struggle against anxiety through recourse to auto-erotic activities, and the cathexis of the subject's own body thus ensures a foundation for the subsequent evolution of the narcissistic libido. This is a register where the quantitative aspect plays an important role: the affective *excesses* or *deprivations* of the mother, or of her substitute, can determine a regressive tendency to auto-erotism as a behaviour without phantasying after the recognition of the whole object.

It is this economic function of the mother, and of adults close to the child, that Ferenczi (1933) also highlights in his article "Confusion of tongues between adults and the child: the language of tenderness and passion". Following Freud (1905), who had already insisted in his *Three Essays on Sexuality* on the importance of the "seduction" by the mother in her ministrations to the infant, Ferenczi points out that in this phase of tenderness, the excess or deprivation of love have the same consequences as a real seduction: the language of passion, which comprises the adult's guilt feelings, accentuates the importance of hate over love and impedes the binding of drive affects which allows for a favourable evolution of the child.

Sexual impulses are thus a source of conflict in themselves and give rise to a process of binding-unbinding. Starting from an openness to the world that comes with the establishment of the object relationship, this can explain either a process of dedifferentiation and destruction, as in schizophrenia, or on the contrary, a process of differentiation and structuring that is revealed by the mechanisms of displacement and condensation found in the most evolved neurotic organizations. That is the rationale for the drive dualism to which Freud always adhered, and for the last theory of the drives which, through a biological myth, confronts us with the struggle between Eros and Thanatos, union and disunion, love and hate.

Notes

1 The translators of the *Œuvres complètes* chose to translate the German term *Phantasie* by "*fantaisie*", which they prefer to "*fantasme*", for it refers to the activity *and* its result. However, the term "*fantasme*" still has its "rightful place" in psychoanalysis and in everyday language (Bourguignon et al., 1989, pp. 104–106).
2 Between 1905 and 1920, the attention of Freud and his disciples was focused on the problem of symbolism, in particular under the influence of Stekel and Jung, and of their preoccupations with the correspondences between psychoanalysis and culture. These studies led Freud to add a section on dream symbolism

to the chapter on the dream-work in the 1914 edition of *The Interpretation of Dreams*, and to devote a special Lesson to this problem in his *Introductory Lessons on Psychoanalysis* (Freud, 1916–1917).

3 E. Ortigues (1962, pp. 57–58) makes the interesting remark that if, in Antiquity and the Middle Ages, priority was given to a tripartite conception of the sign where it was a matter of interpreting a story, it was with the logic of Port-Royal in the 17th century that a bipartite conception of the sign emerged again, corresponding to the wish to analyse the conditions of certainty in judgements. This perspective of truth, which had the ambition of analysing language formally, conveyed the wish for an unambiguous and scientific language.

4 The reference to the concept of usage according to Wittgenstein is particularly felicitous in that it shows the difficulty of the notion of a symbolism of dreams, which refers to a conception of signification as substance, whereas the notion of the usage of a term, in the sense of the usage that is made *in* language as an institution, highlights the importance of relating the symbol to its function within in a theoretical and clinical ensemble to which the symptom bears witness. While the benefit for clinical practice is undeniable, the notion of usage does not, however, dispense with the ontological problem of meaning.

5 While linguistics may call into question the analogical motivation of the symbol in order to emphasize the "internal motivation of the discourse" (see Arrivé, 1986, p. 102; Todorov, 1978, p. 16), we can imagine here which theoretical issue goes beyond the linguistic discourse.

6 U. Eco (1984) defines this mode of sign-production ruled by *ratio difficilis*, insofar as the projection goes from selected characteristics of the content to characteristics of expression: such visual iconism and isomorphism is used, for instance, in the diagram, where the relations at the level of the content are characteristics on the level of expression. Signs are produced on the contrary according to *ratio facilis* when the expression is arbitrarily correlated to the content (pp. 206–207 and p. 252).

7 On the style of dreams, see Danon-Boileau, 1987, pp. 55–66; Mahony, 1987.

8 For a critique of Edelson's approach, see Mahony and Singh (1975).

9 A structure corresponding to the double articulation of language: that of the syntagmatic relations that Jakobson defines as the combination of successive entities related to the context, and that of paradigmatic relations, which he describes as the selection and substitution of simultaneous entities referring to the associated units in the code. These two fundamental linguistic operations, which take up the opposition between contiguity and similarity, apply both to phonemes and to words.

10 This etymological difference is pointed out by Lyotard (1971); he notes that *Verdichtung* is linked by *Dicht* to the old German *dihan* (like *gedeiben*, prosper); *Dichtung* comes from the Latin *dictare* (in *Discours, figure*, p. 254).

11 From the same perspective, Claude Hagège (1985) shows that these words with contrary meanings have a function in language: not of leading to contradiction, but of *facilitating generality*. They are "Janus-headed" and have the characteristic of including two opposite means within a global meaning, as, for example, in the case of verbs derived from nouns in Semitic languages: these verbs refer to the idea of "doing something in general" corresponding to what the noun designates, and can therefore be fulfilled by two actions of opposite meaning. It is not a matter therefore of both affirming or denying the same content, which would indeed be calling into question the principle of contradiction; furthermore, this cannot be found in any language (see pp. 149–151).

12 Freud added these remarks on Silberer in the 1914 edition of *The Interpretation of Dreams*; this commentary can also be found in "On narcissism: an introduction" (Freud, 1914), where he links the "dream censor" to the ego ideal and to the dynamic manifestations of moral conscience (pp. 95–98).

13 This is the case in particular of Charles Rycroft: according to him, Jones distinguishes, in fact, between two sorts of affects with which symbols can be cathected, and not between two sorts of symbolism (see Rycroft, 1956, p. 14).

14 It was in a letter to Freud dated 10 November 1912 that Ferenczi put forward the concepts of phanerosymbolism and cryptosymbolism to denote the two phases of symbolization (before and after repression) (see Ferenczi, 1949, p. 244).

15 This is what emerges from Lacan's text on negation presented one week before the commentary on the case of little Dick: see Lacan's text "Response to Jean Hyppolite's commentary on Freud's 'Verneinung'" (10 February, 1954) (Lacan, 1956a).

16 This sense of unease is patent when Lacan seeks to indicate "the correlate of projection". "It would be necessary", he says, "to find another word than *introjection*"; for between "psychotic" projection and "neurotic" introjection, an entire field of expression is not covered by this radical separation between the imaginary and the symbolic. This recalls from a certain point of view the difficulties Jones had in articulating the pleasure principle and the reality principle.

17 Kant distinguishes two a priori forms of sensibility, space and time, and classes the categories of the understanding in four groups of three: the categories of quantity (unity, plurality, totality), of quality (reality, negation, limitation), of relation (substance and accident, cause and effect, reciprocal linking), and of modality (possibility, existence, necessity).

18 For Kant, the transcendental point of view refers to any approach related to the search for the foundations of knowledge and science: "I apply the term *transcendental* to all knowledge which is not so much occupied with objects as with the mode of our cognition of these objects, so far as this mode of cognition is possible *a priori*" (Kant, 1781, p. 149), that is to say independent of our experience. The epistemological status of unconscious phantasies, primal or primitive phantasies, is part of this problem.

19 For a discussion of Jung's approach, the reader is referred to the following books: from a Freudian perspective, see Kaswin-Bonnefond (2003); from a Jungian perspective, see Humbert (1982); Gaillard (2007). For a definition of the main Jungian concepts, see Agnel (2008).

20 Since the separation of Freud and Jung in 1914, the Jungian movement of "analytical psychology" has diversified into three main schools or tendencies, which means the Jungian approach to the unconscious and analysis must be nuanced: the *classical* school or Zurich School which has maintained the heritage of the theory and practice of Jung; the *developmental* or London School, which is close to the psychoanalysts of the British Psychoanalytic Society and has explored more thoroughly the transference/countertransference issues in the analytic session; and the *archetypal* school, which is no longer strictly a clinical group and has placed value on research into the concept of archetype as a basis for exploring imaginary life (see Hillman (1975); Young-Eisendrath and Dawson (1997); Samuels (1985)). In France, the French Society of Analytical Psychology (SFPA), since its foundation in 1969, has fostered the collaboration between these different "schools" in all its governing bodies, which is not always the case in each of the fifty schools, and a National and Regional Society which make up the International Association of Analytical Psychology (IAAP). Christian Gaillard, former president of both the SFPA and the AIPA, was actively involved in collaboration and debate with the different Freudian psychoanalytic societies within the IPA.

21 Bion's theory of the preconception can also be likened to this Kantian perspective. Bion describes the infant's experience of satisfaction at the breast by referring to Freud's hypotheses of the two stages in this experience: the stage of the first satisfaction, corresponding to the actual experience of the breast, and then the stage of hallucinatory reliving; but he inverses the two stages and assumes

that the first stage is one of the juxtaposition of a *preconception* of the breast or a priori knowledge of the breast and a non-realization of the breast; the second stage corresponds to the realization of the breast and to the interactions between the infant and its mother (Bion, 1962, pp. 34–36). While the intellectualist reference to the Kantian a priori leads him to point out that hallucination precedes perception and gives it meaning, on the other hand Bion does not stray from an empiricist approach when he assumes that this preconception of the breast is *innate,* which enables him to support the Kleinian hypothesis of an object-relation from the very beginning of life. Moreover, the theory of the levels of symbolization, from beta elements to algebraic formalization, which follow a movement from the particular to the general, from the concrete to the abstract, does not escape these associationist origins and refers to the "I think" which is separate from the "thing-in-itself" (see Gibeault, 1982).

References

Adler, G., & Jaffé, A. (Eds.) (1984). *Selected Letters of C. G Jung, 1909–1961.* Princeton, NJ: Princeton University Press.

Agnel, A. (Ed.) (2008). *Dictionnaire Jung.* Paris: Ellipses.

Arrivé, M. (1986). *Linguistique et psychanalyse.* Paris: Méridiens-Klincksieck.

Assoun, P. (1976). *Freud, la philosophie et les philosophes.* Paris: Presses universitaires de France.

Assoun, P. (1988). *Freud and Wittgenstein.* Paris: Presses Universitaires de France.

Benveniste, E. (Ed.) (1956). Remarques sur la fonction du langage dans la découverte freudienne. In: *Problèmes de linguistique générale.* Paris: Gallimard, 1966.

Bion, W.R. (Ed.) (1962). *Learning from Experience.* London: Heinemann.

Bourguignon, A., Cotet, P., Laplanche, J., & Robert, F. (1989). *Traduire Freud.* Paris: Presses Universitaires de France.

Braunschweig, D., & Fain, M. (1975). *La nuit, le jour.* Paris: Presses Universitaires de France.

Castoriadis-Aulagnier, P. (1975). *The Violence of Interpretation,* trans. A. Sheridan. London: Routledge.

Danon-Boileau, L. (1987). *Le sujet de l'énonciation. Psychanalyse et linguistique.* Paris: Ophrys.

Diatkine, R., & Janine, S. (1972). *La psychanalyse précoce.* Paris: Presses Universitaires de France.

Eco, U. (1986). *Semiotics and the Philosophy of Language.* Bloomington and Indianapolis: Indiana University Press

Edelson, M. (1972). Language and dreams. The interpretation of dreams revisited. *The Psychoanalytic Study of the Child,* 27: 203–282.

Ferenczi (1913a). Stages in the development of the sense of reality. In: E. Jones (Trans.) *First Contributions to Psychoanalysis.* London: Routledge, 2018, pp. 213–239.

Ferenczi (1913b). The ontogenesis of symbols. In: E. Jones (Trans.) *First Contributions to Psychoanalysis.* London: Routledge, 2018, pp. 276–281.

Ferenczi, S. (1924). *Thalassa, A Theory of Genitality,* trans. A.H. Bunker. New York: Psychoanalytic Quarterly, 1938.

Ferenczi, S. (Ed.) (1933). The confusion of tongues between adults and the child: the language of tenderness and passion: In: *Final Contributions to the Problems and Methods of Psychoanalysis.* London: Hogarth, 1955, pp. 155–167.

Ferenczi, S. (1949). Ten letters to Freud (letter dated 10 November 1912) (1908–1933). *The International Journal of Psychoanalysis,* 30 (4): 243–250.

Fontanier, P. (1977). *Les figures du discours* (1821–1830). Paris: Flammarion.

Forrester, J. (1980). *Le langage aux origines de la psychanalyse.* Paris: Gallimard, 1984.

Freud, S. (1900). *The Interpretation of Dreams. S.E.* 4–5. London: Hogarth.

Freud, S. (1905). *Three Essays on the Theory of Sexuality. S.E.* 7. London: Hogarth, pp. 135–243.

Freud, S. (1909). Notes upon a case of obsessional neurosis. *S.E.* 10. London: Hogarth, pp. 151–249.

Freud, S. (1910). The antithetical meaning of primal words. *S.E.* 11. London: Hogarth, pp. 155–161.

Freud, S. (1912–1913). *Totem and Taboo. S.E.*13. London: Hogarth, pp. 1–161.

Freud, S. (1914). On narcissism: An introduction. *S.E.* 14. London: Hogarth, pp. 69–102.

Freud, S. (1915a). The unconscious. *S.E.* 14. London: Hogarth, pp. 166–215.

Freud, S. (1915b). Instincts and their vicissitudes. *S.E.* 14. London: Hogarth, pp. 109–140.

Freud, S. (1916). A connection between a symbol and a symptom. *S.E.* 14. London: Hogarth, pp. 339–340.

Freud, S. (1916–1917). *Introductory Lectures on Psychoanalysis. S.E.* 16. London: Hogarth.

Freud, S. (1917 [1915]). A metapsychological supplement to the theory of dreams. *S.E.* 14. London: Hogarth, pp. 222–235.

Freud, S. (1918 [1914]). From the history of an infantile neurosis. *S.E.* 17. London: Hogarth, pp. 7–122.

Freud, S. (1925). Negation. *S.E.* 19. London: Hogarth, pp. 235–242.

Freud, S. (1926). *Inhibitions, Symptoms and Anxiety. S.E.* 20. London: Hogarth.

Freud, S. (1937). Constructions in analysis. London: Hogarth, pp. 257–269.

Freud, S. (1939). *Moses and Monotheism. S.E.* 23. London: Hogarth, pp. 1–137.

Freud, S. (1950 [1895]). *Project for a Scientific Psychology. S.E.* 1. London: Hogarth, pp. 295–397.

Gaillard, C. (2007). *Jung.* Paris: Presses Universitaires de France, "Que sais-je?".

Gibeault, A. (1981a). Symbolisme inconscient et symbolisme du langage. *Revue française de psychanalyse,* 45 (1): 144–145.

Gibeault, A. (1981b). Jugement et négation. De la théorie du jugement chez Kant et Freud. *Les cahiers du Centre de psychanalyse et de psychothérapie,* 2: 91–131.

Gibeault, A. (1982). Symbolisme primitif et formation des symboles. De l'apport des post-Kleiniens à la théorie de la symbolisation. *Nouvelle Revue de Psychanalyse,* 26 (L'archaïque): 303–313.

Gibeault, A. (1983). Pulsion et langage. Des concepts de représentation de chose et de mot dans l'œuvre de Freud. *Les Cahiers du Centre de psychanalyse et de psychothérapie,* 7: 87–160.

Gibeault, A. (1985). Travail de la pulsion et représentation: représentation de chose et représentation de mot. *Revue française de psychanalyse,* 49 (3): 753–772.

Green, A. (1999/1993). *The Work of the Negative,* trans. A. Weller. London: Free Association Books.

Hagège, C. (1985). *L'homme de paroles.* Paris: Fayard.

Heynick, F. (1981). Linguistic aspects of Freud's dream model. *The International Review of Psychoanalysis,* 8: 299–314.

Hillman, J. (1975). *Revisioning Psychology.* New York: Harper & Row.

Humbert, E.G. (1982). *Jung.* Paris: Hachette, 2004.

Husserl, E. (1954). *Expérience et jugement.* Paris: Presses Universitaires de France, 1970.

Jakobson, R. (Ed.) (1995 [1956]). Two aspects of language and two types of aphasia. In: *On Language*. Cambridge, MA: Harvard University Press, pp. 115–133.

Jones, E. (Ed.) (1916). The theory of symbolism. In: *Papers on Psychoanalysis*. London: Ballière, Tindall, and Cox, 1950, pp. 87–144; *British Journal of Psychology*, 9 (2): 181–229.

Jones, E. (1957). *The Life and Work of Sigmund Freud, vol. 3, The Last Phase, 1919–1933*. London: Hogarth.

Jung, C.J. (1935). The archetypes and the collective unconscious. In: H. Read, M. Fordham, & G. Adler (Eds.), *The Collected Works of C.J. Jung*, trans. R.F.C. Hull, Vol. 9.1. Princeton, NJ: Princeton University Press.

Jung, C. (1954). Fundamental questions of psychotherapy. In: R.F.C. Hull (Trans.) *The Practice of Psychotherapy*. Bollingen Series XX, New York: Pantheon Books, pp. 111–126.

Jung, C. (Ed.). (1956a). Recent thoughts on schizophrenia. In: *Collected Works of C.J. Jung, Vol. 3. Psychogenesis of Mental Disease*. Princeton, NJ: Princeton University Press, pp. 250–255.

Jung, C. (1956b). *Symbols of Transformation*, trans. R. F.C. Hull. New York: Bollingen Series/Princeton University Press.

Jung, C. (1963 [1961]). *Memories, Dreams, Reflections*. New York: Pantheon Books.

Kant, E. (1998 [1781]). *Critique of Pure Reason*. Cambridge: Cambridge University Press.

Kaswin-Bonnefond (2003). *Carl Gustav Jung*. Paris: Presses Universitaires de France.

Khan, M. (1975). De l'expérience du rêve à la réalité psychique. *Nouvelle Revue de Psychanalyse*, 12: 89–99.

Klein, M. (Ed.) (1975 [1923]). Early analysis. In: *The Collected Works of Melanie Klein*, Vol. I. London: Hogarth Press, pp. 77–105.

Klein, M. (Ed.) (1975 [1930]). The importance of symbol-formation in the development of the ego. In: *The Collected Works of Melanie Klein*, Vol. I. London: Hogarth Press, pp. 219–232.

Lacan, J. (1956a). Response to Jean Hyppolite's commentary on Freud's 'Verneinung' (10 February, 1954). In: B. Fink (Trans.) *Écrits*. New York: W.W. Norton & Co. pp. 318–333.

Lacan, J. (1956b). The function and field of speech and language in psychoanalysis. In: B. Fink (Trans.) *Écrits*. New York: W.W. Norton & Co. pp. 197–268.

Lacan, J. (1957). The instance of the letter in the unconscious. In: B. Fink (Trans.) *Écrits*. New York: W.W. Norton & Co., pp. 493–441.

Lacan, J. (1960). In memory of Ernest Jones: On his theory of symbolism. In: B. Fink (Trans.) *Écrits*. New York: Norton & Co, pp. 585–601.

Lacan, J. (1964). Position of the unconscious. In: B. Fink (Trans.) *Écrits*. New York: W.W. Norton & Co. pp. 703–725.

Lacan, J. (1966). *Écrits*, trans. B. Fink. New York: W.W. Norton & Co.

Lacan, J. (1988/1975). *Freud's Papers on Technique, 1953–1954. The Seminar of Jacques Lacan, Book I*. New York: Norton & Co.

Laplanche, J., & Pontalis, J.-P. (1964). Fantasme originaire, fantasme des origines, origines du fantasme. *Les Temps modernes*, 215: 158–182.

Lebovici, S. (1961). La relation objectale chez l'enfant. *La psychiatrie de l'enfant*, 3, fasc. 1: 154–162.

Lyotard, J.-F. (1971). *Discours, Figure*. Paris: Klincksieck.

Mahony, P. (1987). *Psychoanalysis and Discourse*. London and New York: Tavistock Publications.

Mahony, P., & Singh, R. (1975). The interpretation of dreams, semiology and Chomskian linguistics. A radical critique. *The Psychoanalytic Study of the Child*, 30: 221–241.

Menahem, R. (1986). *Langage et folie*. Paris: Les Belles Lettres.

Merleau-Ponty, M. (1945). *La phénoménologie de la perception*. Paris: Gallimard.

Merleau-Ponty, M. (1964). *Le visible et l'invisible*. Paris: Gallimard.

Ortigues, E. (1962). *Le discours et le symbole*. Paris: Aubier.

Perron, R. (2003). *La passion des origines. Être et ne pas être*. Lonay: Delachaux & Nestlié.

Politzer, G. (1928). *Critique des fondements de la psychologie*. Paris: Presses Universitaires de France.

Racamier, P.-C. (1980). *Les schizophrènes*. Paris: Payot.

Ricoeur, P. (1975). *La métaphore vive*. Paris: Seuil.

Rosolato, G. (Ed.) (1978). L'oscillation métaphoro-métonymique. In: *La relation d'inconnu*. Paris: Gallimard, pp. 52–80.

Rosolato, G. (1983). Le symbole comme formation. *Psychanalyse à la université*, 9 (30): 225–242.

Rycroft, C. (1956). Symbolism and its relationship to the primary and secondary processes. *International Journal of Psychoanalysis*, 37 (2–3): 137–146.

Rycroft, C. (1981). *The Innocence of Dreams*. Oxford: Oxford University Press.

Samuels, A. (1985). *Jung and the Post-Jungians*. London: Routledge.

Schreber, P. (1903). *Memoirs of My Nervous Illness*. London: W. Dawson, 1955.

Segal, H. (1957). Notes on symbol formation. *International Journal of Psychoanalysis*, 38: 391–397.

Segal, H. (Ed.) (1981). The function of dreams. In: *The Work of Hanna Segal*. Northvale, NJ: Aronson, 1986, pp. 89–100.

Shevrin, H. (1972). Condensation et métaphore. *Nouvelle Revue de Psychanalyse*, 5: 115–130.

Todorov, T. (1978). *Symbolisme et interprétation*. Paris: Seuil.

Warburton, W. (1977/1744). *Essais sur les hieroglyphs égyptiens*. Paris: Aubier-Flammarion.

Winnicott, D.W. (Ed.) (1960). Ego-distortion in terms of true and false self. In: *The Maturational Processes and the Facilitating Environment*. London: Karnac, 1965, pp. 140–152.

Young-Eisendrath, P., & Dawson, T. (Eds.) (1997). *The Cambridge Companion to Jung*. Cambridge: Cambridge University Press.

3   The symbolism of money and psychoanalytic treatment

Money in analysis makes it possible to illustrate the essential interest of symbolism as a universal or personal symbol and to reflect on the importance of symbolization from the angle of its function in mediation. If clinical work shows that money is polysemic and refers to orality, genitality, and anality, why, both in the analytic treatment and in culture, does anality appear to be the essential referent of this symbolization? While we can recognize the importance of symbolization in connection with money in sublimatory processes, what sort of dialectical relationship can be envisaged between psychic reality and social reality? These are all questions raised by the symbolism of money from a psychoanalytic perspective, ones I will try to answer while taking into account both the semantic and syntactical (Gibeault, 1981) dimension of this essential symbol in analysis. The validity of free analysis rests in part on theoretical arguments that can be retained.

The semantic function of money

Gold-money: a symbol of faeces

Freud insisted very early on in his work on the "intimate relations" in the unconscious between gold and money on the one hand, and excrement on the other. In his letters to Fliess, he observed the correspondence between what had already been noted in myths and folklore and the productions of his patients:

> I read one day that the gold the devil gives his victims regularly turns into excrement; and the next day Mr E., who reports that his nurse had money deliria, suddenly told me (by way of Cagliostro – alchemist – *Dukatenscheisser* [one who defecates ducats]) that Louise's money always was excrement. So in the witch stories it is merely transformed back into the substance from which it arose.
>
> (Letter from Freud to Fliess, dated 24 January 1897, in Masson, 1985, p. 227)

DOI: 10.4324/9781003545651-4

He was thus led to compare an unconscious equivalence in dreams and neurosis with what has always been encountered in ancient civilizations, in myths and folklore. From this point of view, the symbolism of money was part of the more general context of a work of symbolization independent of the dream-work.

In the 1900 edition of *The Interpretation of Dreams,* Freud recognized that "the dream-work is doing nothing original in making substitutions of this kind" (1900, pp. 345–346) and that "there is no necessity to assume that any particular symbolizing activity of the mind is operating in the dream-work" (1900, p. 349). Just as the dreamer meets with a language and cultural objects that he has not created, he makes use of "symbolizations which are already present in unconscious thinking": it is these that "fit in better with the requirements of dream-construction on account of their representability, and also because as a rule they escape censorship" (1900, p. 349).

Freud continued to give increasing importance to this idea in the successive editions of *The Interpretation of Dreams* and to accord an ever greater place to a work of culture. The symbolism of money did not escape this perspective: "Dreams with an intestinal stimulus throw light in an analogous fashion on the symbolism involved in them, and at the same time confirm the connection between gold and faeces, which is also supported by copious evidence from social anthropology" (1900, p. 403). Moreover, the existence of a stereotyped symbolic relationship seems to reduce the interpretation of dreams to ancient methods of decoding which relied on a "key of dreams" that made it possible to interpret them without taking the dreamer into account. Hence the idea of a one-to-one relationship between the symbol and what is symbolized: "In dreams in folklore, gold is seen in the most unambiguous way to be a symbol of faeces" (Freud, 1957 [1911], p. 187).

The symbol of gold does not escape the questions raised by every symbol relating to the unconscious. The common factor of the comparison between the symbol and what is symbolized is often difficult to determine, because the work of substitution does not belong to the individual but to culture. Unconscious symbolism is often repetitive but, as a result, universal, and has to do with the repression of genital and pregenital sexuality.

The genesis of money

How do these displacements concerning money occur? Ferenczi's (1914) study "On the ontogenesis of the interest in money", which was in fact contemporary with Freud's reflections on symbolization, will help us to explore the question in more depth. It is certainly a matter of *ontogenesis,* since it is a question of determining the factors that are involved in this work of symbolization, but ontogenesis should be linked to *phylogenesis,* with the hereditary acquisition of the preceding generations as it can be observed in the correspondences with "social-psychological productions (myths, fairy-tales, folk-lore)" (p. 319).

Ferenczi insists on two factors. First, *the pleasure of holding back* stools, a matter Karl Abraham would return to more explicitly, making it the characteristic of the second anal-sadistic-stage:

> The excrementa thus held back are really the first 'savings' of the growing being, and as such remain in a constant, unconscious inter-relationship with every *bodily activity or mental* striving that has anything to do with collecting, hoarding, and saving.
>
> (1914, p. 321, my emphasis)

It is worth noting here the importance of displacement according to contiguity and similitude in the process of *representing the drive:* the latter obeys both the *contiguity* of physical pleasure and of psychic pleasure and the *metaphorization* of the physical pleasure of retaining stools as a psychic pleasure of holding back, collecting and conserving in its many different forms. Ferenczi insists here, then, on a displacement of interest based on a contiguity and similarity of the function and aim of the drive guaranteeing in both cases *auto-erotic satisfaction.* If the anal sexual impulse is based on the process of defecation, on a need in the order of self-preservation, it distances itself from it by means of all the possibilities of displacement of the *action* and the *aim* at the level of the contrasting pair retaining-expelling.

But a second factor plays a role in the transition from anal erotism to an interest in money. This *auto-erotic* pleasure is transformed into *object-love* as soon as the child's interest gets displaced "from the neutral sensations of certain organs on to the material itself that caused these feelings" (1914, pp. 321–322). The expulsion of faeces means at the same time that they are "introjected", in the sense that "they count as a valuable toy, from which the child is to be weaned only through deterrents and threats of punishment" (1914, p. 322).[1]

Hence the possibilities of displacement at the level of the *object* through a process of symbolization by means of the contrary: from odorous, humid, soft, and dull stools, the child passes over to odourless, dry, hard, and shining coins. Objects of "transition" favour this displacement which on each occasion substitutes a contrary quality: along this symbolic chain, we have odorous mud that removes the disagreeable smell of faeces, *dry* sand that removes their humidity, stones that favour the transition from soft to *hard*, and *finally shining* coins that are the contrary of dull faeces: "With this the development of the money symbol is in its main outlines complete. Pleasure in the intestinal contents becomes enjoyment of money, which, is seen to be nothing other than" (1914, p. 327).[2]

Ferenczi assumes that, in this movement, the interest pertains more to the materiality of money as an object arousing the pleasure of the senses than its economic value. In order for money to establish itself as a "standard of value", another genesis is necessary whose continuity is less direct. He points out that this investment in value is also due to "the respect in which [shining pieces of money] are held by adults, as well as to the seductive possibilities of obtaining through them everything that the child's heart can desire" (1914). This is a common fact of observation which merely raises the problem rather than explaining it.

From this point of view, Freud went further a few years later when he introduced the connecting link of *gift* between excrement and *gold-money* to account for this ontogenesis:

> The child knows no money apart from what is given to him – no money acquired and no money of his own. Since his faeces are his first gift, the child easily transfers his interest from that substance to the new one which he comes across as the most valuable gift in life.
>
> (Freud, 1917, p. 131)

Money acquires an economic value as an object of exchange between the child's parents and himself, reflecting a movement of identification. This movement is part of both a *narcissistic* and *object-related* cathexis of faeces. Freud clarifies Ferenczi's thinking in connection with this twofold cathexis when he links object-love for faeces with love for the whole object:

> Defecation affords the first occasion on which the child must decide between a narcissistic and an object-loving attitude. He either parts obediently with his faeces, 'sacrifices' them to his love, or else retains them for purposes of auto-erotic satisfaction and later as a means of asserting his own will.
>
> (Freud, 1917, p. 130)

Insofar as they are a *part of his body*, the child cathects his faeces narcissistically, an interest that will subsequently be transferred onto money. Insofar as it is a *part that is separate from his body*, he can cathect it in an object-related manner as a part-object and enter into relations with the whole object where a possession can become a gift offered and a means of exchange.[3] The economic value of money has its place more in the exchange between parents and children than in the materiality of money, which makes all financial abstractions possible.

Ferenczi pointed out, moreover, this "logical" evolution of the "faculty of thinking" insofar as "the symbolic interest in money" gets extended not only to objects with similar physical attributes, but to all sorts of things that in any way signify value or possession: paper money, shares, bank book, etc. (Ferenczi, 1914, pp. 327–328), and today we could add: checks, bank cards, etc.

In reality, it is not a question of choosing between two geneses, for in fact they are complementary and sometimes a source of conflict; Ferenczi points out with a great deal of pertinence that

> many people are ready enough to sign documents that bind them to pay large sums, and can easily expend large amounts in paper money, but are striking tardy in giving out gold coins or even the smallest copper coins. The coins seem to 'stick' to their fingers.
>
> (Ferenczi, 1914, p. 330)

The materiality of money retains from its origins an erotic pleasure related to the senses that money loses in terms of economic value.

Symbolism of gold-money and repression

In this respect, the symbolism of gold-money thus appears to be essentially in the service of repression, in keeping with the conception of unconscious symbolism, as Jones developed it by opposing symbolism and sublimation (see Chapter 2). Money may be regarded both as a symbol of faeces and a metaphor of wealth. As several authors have pointed out, this approach to symbolism opposed to sublimation is problematic.

The elaboration of the loss of the object shows on the contrary, how symbolization, as a process of substituting one representation for another and of binding affects, coincides with the process of inhibiting the drive aim, connoted by the concept of sublimation. We must bear in mind here the genesis of psychic life as described by Freud. It is when we witness the displacement on to the maternal object of the experiences of pleasure/unpleasure linked to the satisfaction of needs that the drive proper, the unconscious, and phantasy emerge. Primitive splitting between the ego and the external world, which occurs as soon as the mother is recognized as a whole object different from every other object,[4] is a defensive process which may be equated with what Freud called primal repression: it is the first stage when the creation of unconscious phantasies fixes the drive to its representatives, when the binding of affects of anxiety occurs, linked to the mother's absence and to representations that make it possible to tolerate this absence. Primal repression has its rationale in the need to organize at the same time the libidinal and destructive aspects experienced in relation to the maternal object.

It is on the basis of what is being played out at that moment that the loss of the object can be elaborated from the angle of annihilation and terror, as in psychosis, or from the angle of negation of presence and signal anxiety,[5] as in neurosis, and that there will be rejection or denial, or repression proper. In this sense, symbolism and, consequently, language, are linked to an *economic* process, as drive activity shows. Symbolization appears not only to be the substitution of one representation for another, but also primarily an anti-depressive mechanism making it possible to limit the circulation of affects. It is a process linking two heterogeneous psychic representatives, and links to the symbol an affect which without it, would remain floating.

This is illustrated by the wooden reel game, which Freud mentions in connection with his grandson. This game evidences the mastery of distressing affects aroused by the mother's disappearance and shows the success of a process through words, gestures and visual perception.[6] Thus, when the child says *fort* and *da*, it is the introjected mother that is speaking in him. The mother says "gone" (*fort*) and the child-wooden reel has gone. The mother says: "There again" (*da*), and the child-wooden reel reappears. Symbolization is organized on the model of this object manipulation, and it can be seen how language develops at the end of this process of symbolization.

We can understand, then, why Hanna Segal (1964) described this genesis of the symbol as the "outcome of a loss" and as a "creative work involving the pain and the whole work of mourning" (p. 76). This description accounts for the notion of sublimation, which Freud thought was one of the possible vicissitudes of the drive: the process of inhibiting the drive in its aim, that is to say the transition from a sexual aim to a socially valued nonsexual aim to which the concept of sublimation refers, is linked to a genuine process of mourning the maternal object.

It is still the case that along this trajectory within which symbolization is organized, we can sometimes recognize a tendency in which *repression* is operative, and sometimes another tendency where, on the contrary, *sublimation* comes into play more. The different vicissitudes of the representatives of the part-drives are in question here. Concerning anal-erotism, the symbolism of money could also be subject to a movement of gradual desexualization and sublimation; in this case social reality is taken into account more by psychic reality or, on the contrary, remains involved in constant sexualization, where the possession of money retains its links with repressed anal erotism. Analysis necessarily faces the analysand with a resexualization of money and possibly with the need to engage in a work of desexualization.

After Freud and Ferenczi, only the primacy of the anal drive was linked to the symbolism of money, from the perspective of an unambiguous link, which is in fact debatable, between the symbol and what is symbolized. And yet, Freud himself, in the case of the "Wolf Man" (Freud, 1918 [1914], p. 82),[7] completes his schema of the "transpositions of instincts as exemplified in anal erotism" by showing that through the link *gift* which is common both to the equation faeces-gift-money, money can also be the symbolic substitute for the child and be related to the genital drive (Figure 3.1).

The first screen-memory of the "Wolf Man" was related, moreover, to the latter's feelings of anger because he had not received enough presents for Christmas; according to Freud, this had to do with his disappointment with regard to his expectations of anal satisfaction. Money subsequently

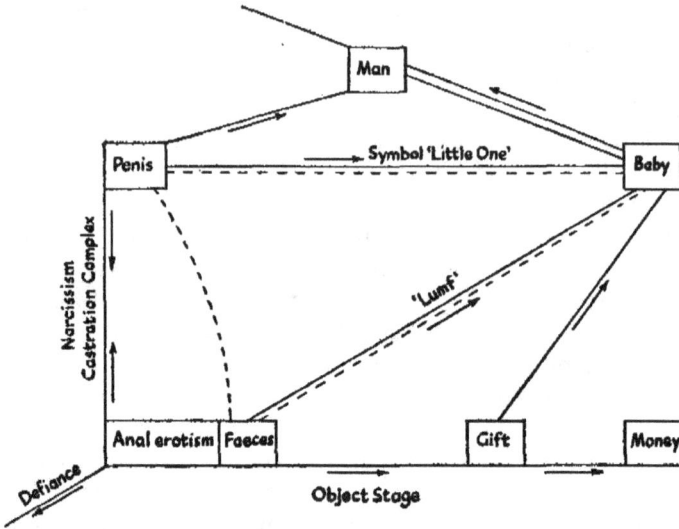

Figure 3.1 Freud's diagram on anal erotism.

took over from this childhood wish when one day, probably after the age of six, he was very jealous of his sister whom he had seen receiving "two big banknotes" from their father. When he was alone with her, he had claimed his share so vigorously that his sister had given him everything. Hence Freud's conclusion: "What had excited him was not merely the actual money, but rather the 'baby' – anal satisfaction from his father" (Freud, 1918 [1914], p. 83). In the same way, he had claimed a share of his mother's inheritance after his father's death, which is reminiscent of the "Rat Man's" wish to obtain part of his mother's inheritance and thereby to realize his wish for a child (see Aisenstein, 1985).

Money and anal erotism

The symbolism of money is certainly polysemic, but anal erotism has a particular role that calls for an explanation: we may ask ourselves if this anchoring in anality is not precisely what allows for the organization of this polysemic process. It is true that, from this point of view, money only comes into the equation afterwards and is not the object of a primary infantile wish; as an inherent aspect of social reality, it only subsequently offers a representation for psychic reality.

Freud himself noted this retrospective dimension concerning the equation between faeces and money. Interest in defecation subsides "in the years of maturity"; the narcissistic and object-related issues it refers to find favourable soil in an *interest in money* concerning which Freud (1908) says that it "makes its appearance as a new interest which had been absent in childhood" (p. 175). This is the reason, he says, for the change of aim concerning the earlier longing; or perhaps it could be said rather that it is a metaphorization of the same action, of the same aim, namely, conserving-expelling.

Carine and her interest in defecation

An early case of analysis should enable us to follow this movement better, in both its progressive and regressive dimensions; and also to clarify both the role of anality and the symbolism of money in this transition from early childhood to the "years of maturity". Carine, who was aged 3½ when she began her analysis with Janine Simon (Diatkine & Simon, 1972) shows very well the challenge and conflict aroused by sphincter control, and the function that money can play in this process. In the fifty-second session, Carine began by drawing a house, demonstrating technical progress which showed that she had acquired greater control over her affects. The drawing of a little girl with phallic attributes, hair and legs, and a mouth with the threatening teeth of a wolf caused an oral regression and the projection of her destructive oral greed, biting and taking possession of the breast, on to her analyst. She recovered by enacting a mother putting her daughter on the potty and a girl who did not want to "give her poo" because, if she gave it, she would no longer have it in her belly (Diatkine & Simon, 1972, pp. 173–175). Sphincter control – retaining faeces – thus allows the child to acquire the "narcissistic clinging" Freud (1917, p. 130) speaks of, by means of which he or she can struggle against the danger of maternal aggression, recover control, and exert sway over the object, which had been undermined by the intensity of the oral impulses.

The advantages of this sphincter control are multiple. The beginnings of acting out during this psychodramatic representation of toilet training show how *control of mental activity* and *sphincter control* are cathected in the same way (Diatkine & Simon, 1972, p. 202). Carine wanted to take hold of her analyst's skirt, but stopped herself and said: "Oh, it's true, here we don't do things, we talk", thereby announcing the fundamental rule of analysis, even though it had never been formulated to her.

Mentalization can replace action, provided that oral-sadistic and anal-sadistic destructiveness is relatively controlled. Thus, sphincter control, implying voluntary opening and closing of the anal sphincter, helps to differentiate better the inside and the outside of the body and to ensure a function of narcissistic restoration. But, at the same time, one may suppose that it was the binding of affects by representations that made it possible for this sphincter control to organize itself and to have this progressive value.

Confirmation of this can be found in an earlier session (the twentieth, pp. 67–68), when Carine had a strong urge to defecate at the beginning of the session. She went to the toilet and came back declaring with great satisfaction that she had done a big poo and that she had used a big piece of paper. This joy was quickly called into question when she wondered if her analyst used a greater quantity of paper, which faced her with disturbing feelings of rivalry and obliged her to resort to coprolalia. This phantasy of an anal penis, which is in keeping with the unconscious equation highlighted by Freud between faeces and the penis, nonetheless allowed her to defend herself against her feelings of helplessness and incompleteness as a child and her wishes to attack and take possession of the maternal anal penis, corresponding to the omnipotence of mastery and possession attributed to her mother.

Sphincter control thus clearly has a defensive function insofar as it promotes the mastery of destructive impulses. But it is itself the result of the working over of psychic conflicts, as the clearing up of Carine's symptoms of bed-wetting shows. She had not yet acquired control of the urethral sphincter, which inevitably reminded her of her anxiety about losing control of her anal sphincter. In this same session, the interpretation of the defensive use of this bed-wetting to struggle against her Oedipal wishes towards her father made it possible to remove this symptom.

In this sense, anal mastery as an erotization of retention helps to establish a delay in the search for satisfaction and the development of "secret phantasy activity, isolated from the world" (Fain, Kreisler, & Soulé, 1974, p. 239). The processes of retention and expulsion which apply to the faecal object also apply to voluntary motricity, thought and language, and constitute the basis of the development of mentalization: the pleasure of retaining faeces, which is the source of a narcissistic gain, thus becomes economically identical with both the pleasure of keeping and evoking memories and with that of thinking instead of acting (Diatkine & Simon, 1972, pp. 320–321).[8]

The differentiation between the inside and outside of the body occurs, as Michel Fain emphasizes, because defecation loses its public character and fosters phantasying "in a place that is radically separated from the rest of the family house" while "retaining the significance of a close link with this same house thanks to the acceptance of the ritualization that it symbolizes" (Fain, Kreisler, & Soulé, 1974, pp. 238–239). The open and boundless oral-narcissistic universe is now opposed by the anal-object-related universe, one could say; according to Bela Grunberger (1971) the latter fosters the movement of independence in relation to the external object and separation between the subject and object (pp. 173–174). This is not to say that orality is not object-related, but rather that anal erotism is a major experience in the movement of objectalization outlined in oral erotism.

There cannot be any question here of describing a genetic sequence in the sense of a succession of stages as determined by the writings of Karl Abraham. The evolution from one stage to another can be attributed to biological *maturation*, which gives rise at a certain moment to the more or less important activity of an erogenous zone; but, clinically, the reality of this transition from one stage to another is secondary compared with the history of the *conflict* that comes into play at this time.

At the metapsychological rather than genetic level, orality and anality are less successive stages than *parallel and inseparable* modes of cathecting the object: if orality thus has to do with the narcissistic and boundless dimension, anality represents the object-related dimension, which makes it possible to structure the object-relation and to facilitate both the appearance and the decline of the Oedipus complex.[9]

From this point of view, the dialectic of conserving/losing inherent to anal erotism confirms that the aptitude for symbolization is a process of binding affects and mastering excitation. The wooden reel game, which often embodies the first experience that reveals the setting-up of symbolization, presupposes this manipulation of an internal object, at once conserved and expelled, which defines anal erotism. It is an experience of mastery that shows that the fear of being engulfed by the object, which is specific to orality – emptying or being emptied – is here contained within limits thanks to the use of a third object.

Encopresis is the sign, on the contrary, of a deficiency[10] in the elaboration of these psychic processes, because it is more a hypercathexis of acting which reveals an immediate need for discharge and is opposed to the psychic displacement of the pleasure of retention. The eroticized activity of retaining faeces and their expulsion acts, in fact, as a brake on the development of psychic activity; for it is more concerned with making up for a weakness in the organization of the boundaries between the inside and the outside of the body, between the ego and the external world (Fain, Kreisler, & Soulé, 1974, p. 236), than promoting a work of symbolization and sublimation of anal erotism. The refusal in encopresis to separate the activity of defecation from the external world is thus confirmed, thereby forcing the presence of the external object rather than fostering the constitution of the internal object. This is expressed in the scene enacted by Carine of her mother watching her daughter defecate: this absence of distance between the mother and the child defecating is related to the danger of maternal intrusion.

Carine's analysis shows very well how the anti-cathexis of anal erotism, rather than its hypercathexis, contributes to the development of mentalization. After this session, where she allowed herself to find "another place" to defecate and returned triumphantly, she began to develop an interest in metalanguage: replying to her analyst who pointed out to her that we say *"nombrils"* and not *"zombries"*, she said: "We say *un nombril (a navel), les zombries)…* You should go back to school and learn your declensions"; she also learnt to differentiate representation from perception and declared, reading a book on wild animals: "Fortunately, it's a book; they cannot move, otherwise I would be afraid" (Fain, Kreisler, & Soulé, 1974).

Anal erotism and sadomasochism

It would be arbitrary, however, not to emphasize the essential link established between anal erotism and sadomasochism. In "The disposition to obsessional neurosis" (Freud, 1913a), Freud puts forward the hypothesis of a pregenital organization of sexual life in which "the component instincts that have already come together for the choice of an object" are combined and dominated by "the anal-erotic and sadistic ones" (p. 321): anal erotism is related to auto-erotic *passivity* centred on the anus, whereas sadism takes up the nonsexual *activity* "due to the common instinct for mastery" (Freud, 1913a, p. 322) and puts it "in the service of the sexual function" (Freud, 1913a), which thus becomes allo-erotic. Freud does not connect anal erotism with masochism, but in 1905, in the *Three Essays,* he pointed out that in this interplay of retention and expulsion characteristic of anal erotism, holding back the stool "must no doubt cause not only painful but also highly pleasurable sensations" (Freud, 1905, p. 186). In so doing, he was already stressing the connection between the passivity specific to anal erotism and that which characterizes erotogenic masochism.

Without taking up again the whole question of sadomasochism, it is nonetheless worth pointing out that the organization of primary masochism, as a cathexis of the pain related to hallucinatory satisfaction, contributes in an essential way to the progressive dimension of anal erotism as a pleasure of retention favouring the delay of satisfaction. On the other hand, it is sadism that opens the way to the object, both in the desire to *destroy* it and in that of *dominating* it; that is why, if sadism can account for the pleasure of mastering and dominating the object in the narcissistic challenge of holding back stools, it also underlies the *gift* of these stools, which does not always occur under the auspices of love, but is motivated by impulses of hating and attacking the object. It can be seen, then, that the aims of the component drives included in the anal-sadistic pregenital organization can participate in different alliances, depending on the degree of drive fusion or defusion: the activity of holding back/giving will take on different forms depending on whether it is determined by hate or love. In the progressive movement, the pleasure of giving becomes linked to the pleasure of receiving and underpins the processes of introjection.

The integration of anal erotism in the functioning of the ego implies that the contrary aims of the anal impulses, holding back/losing, and of the sadistic impulses, dominating/destroying,[11] are dialectalized rather than fixed in a single direction. The functioning that is necessary for negation, as a movement of *Aufhebung*[12] which both suppresses and conserves, can be found here. The appearance of thought-processes indicates the sublimation of anal-erotism and implies recognizing in analysis this dual direction of the anal-sadistic impulses, while emphasizing the positive dimension of "conserving" and the negative dimension of "suppressing"; it also shows that this ambivalence not only concerns part-objects but also whole objects (Diatkine & Simon, 1972, p. 215).

Carine and interest in money

It was in this process of integrating anal eroticism that Carine referred to money. At the end of this session, the fifty-second, where she resorted to anal mastery to fight against her oral greed, she nonetheless failed to maintain this mastery: in the waiting room, when her mother came to pay the analyst, Carine snatched the banknote and fled into the office, obliging her mother to go and take it back from her; but, taking her mother as a witness in a projective movement, she attributed her analyst with full responsibility for the anal-erotism and reproached her for having spoken more than ever about "poo and crap" (Diatkine & Simon, 1972, p. 175). Money appeared here to be a substitute for her mother's anal power, without it being possible to infer that Carine saw an economic value in it. It was a case of acting out, which marked a movement of withdrawal in relation to the psychic elaboration of the session; but, in the following session, it was most interesting to see Carine take up the question in the form, this time, of a well-mastered game which consisted in fabricating money, notes and coins, in a very large number, which led her to ask for more and more sheets of paper. It was this control of her sphincters as a means of fighting against her analyst's intrusion that Janine Simon interpreted to her, pointing out, after what they had said to each other the last time, that "she was amassing big reserves of money and poo and was being very careful to keep her mouth closed and her buttocks squeezed tight so that nothing would come out" (Diatkine & Simon, 1972).

The retention and possession of faeces are represented symbolically here by the accumulation of money, but the genesis of this symbolic representation is probably not in keeping with that which Ferenczi described, because it seems that more value is placed on the displacement between the big roll of toilet paper and the large number of sheets of paper. Nor can we overlook the importance of an object (the banknote) that her mother possessed and that was exchanged between her and the analyst. Here we come up against the limits of a genetic and empiricist approach which aims to describe the genesis of symbolism based on a real sequence proceeding from the concrete to the abstract, from the material to the *pictorial*,[13] without explaining what makes this process of symbolization possible.

The intervention of money in analysis which occurs here in a defensive and regressive movement of recourse to anality is a struggle against castration-anxiety. At the beginning of her analysis, it already underlay Carine's designation of the vagina as a "piggy bank", which marked the anal cathexis of her genital organs: although it is possible to see this memory as reflection of "family symbolism" which values money, she used it nonetheless to deny the difference between the sexes; likewise, the sphincter control that she possessed, unlike her little brother, allowed her, as the authors point out, to "diminish anxiety connected with difference between her parents and herself concerning possession of the coveted object" (Diatkine & Simon, 1972, p. 299).

Money nonetheless acquired both a *polysemic* and *economic* function from the moment it elaborated the Oedipal conflict. In the sixty-third session (pp. 190–191), Carine, who was now five years old, evoked and spoke about money which makes it possible to buy things, but is not inexhaustible: she was growing up quickly and needed a new dress and coat, but had to wait until she had more money. The session then turned around two important purchases: her father had bought a car for her mother, and her mother, with her father's money, had bought roller skates for Carine. In fact money was what her father gave to her mother and therefore symbolized the father's penis: money condenses both the phantasy of incorporation of the part-object (faeces, penis) exchanged by the parents and Oedipal desire towards the father, in a movement of secondary identification with the mother as a whole object. As Diatkine and Simon point out, Carine is thus led to

> desire what the mother desires based on the common origin of her objects, the possession of which has great value in terms of narcissistic restoration: it is the father who gives money, it is the father that the child desires, as her mother desires him.
>
> (Diatkine & Simon, 1972, p. 226)

It is not difficult to imagine that money could symbolize both the child desired by the father and, regressively, the maternal breast, completing the symbolic equivalence faeces-penis-baby described by Freud. The organization of anality facilitates the structuring elaboration of the Oedipus configuration which permits money to acquire its economic and polysemic value. The double reference of faeces as both a possession and a ritualized object of exchange with others finds a privileged substitute in money, explaining the unambiguous and exclusive relation that has often be attributed to them. But it is precisely this double reference that authorizes their polysemic symbolization. The dialectic of being and having to which the opposition between bound cathexes and unbound[14] cathexes refers is represented by money retrospectively and allows it to play a role of mediation, as evoked, in the case of Carine, by the role of the father who provides it.

The syntactic function of money

The ontogenesis of the symbolism of money helped me to understand what lies *at the basis* of symbolization, namely, the substitution of one representation for another and the binding of affects. But Carine's analysis also led me to get a glimpse of the *effect* of this symbolization in the relation between money and the role of the Oedipal father, which is related to the mediating function of money and its social dimension.

The symbolism of money, as a phenomenon of indirect expression, is only significant insofar as it is linked to a social structure in which one participates, taking the form of a pact, contract, or alliance. Money, as an essential dimension of the analytic contract, has thus been likened to the original sense of the symbol in the image of the ancient *tessera*. Like the latter, money is a materialized symbol which may, of course, refer to representations that confer on it its possibilities of expression and substitution by analogy; but in its mediating function, money denotes a law of recognition and difference, which makes it impossible to identify the symbolic relation with the terms of substitution. This syntactic function of the symbol, whose purpose is to introduce us to an order of meaning and importance, was developed, as we know, by Lacan in a conception of mediation as negativity that cannot be reduced to any ontogenetic approach to symbols.

Money: sign and signifier

The publication of an important study on money and psychoanalysis by Pierre Martin (1984) has the interest of clarifying what is at stake in this structural efficiency of money as a mediating third element. Following Lacan, the author deplores any attempt to consider money solely as a content of phantasy, not only at the level of the conduct that it involves – gratification, love, hate, etc. – but also of psychological references (the father, the phallic mother, the devouring mother, etc.) and of anatomical forms – breast, faeces, and penis. In other words, in the subject's relationship to the world, "money represents the *sign* of an exchange", based on need, demand and jouissance, and on "their corollaries in social intersubjectivity: production, power, security, and even provocation, the affirmation of indigence" (p. 16). The money paid in analysis has the purpose of "buying" knowledge, power, jouissance: money as a sign is the imaginary register of the "commerce of analysis" and of the question of "how to *deal with* money in psychoanalysis".

But money also has the function of being a *pure signifier* which contests any idea of a reference between the sign and the thing or of a relation between the signifier and the signified: Lacan (1957) remarked that money is "the signifier that most thoroughly annihilates every signification" (p. 27). Thus, as Martin points out, money is a *primordial signifier* which "makes every signification vacillate, that is, every conjectural relationship between an identity of the subject and being" (Martin, 1984, pp. 69–70), revealing, on the contrary, as in Martin Heidegger, the dehiscence of being, the relation "of the subject to being". Money in analysis must aim less to satisfy a jouissance that is always unsatisfied than to reveal the dimension of the "lack of being" (*manque-à-être*), that of a fundamental inadequacy of the subject in relation to desire.

In the register of analysis, money is a *master signifier* which, like the Name-of-the-Father and the symbolic phallus, introduces into the Oedipal scene the dimension of the *third*, the lost object of the mother's desire, and marks all objects with the sign of castration. Hence the conclusion: "At the end of analysis, the patient has only paid for the 'emptiness' of his initial demand: he has exchanged nothing .... Ultimately, this money pays nothing more" (pp. 50–51).

If money as a sign is power over the other (*l'autre*), enacted power, money as a signifier is power of the Other (*l'Autre*), the total dispossession of the imaginary aim of added enjoyment (*plus-de-jouir*) of added value. The question, therefore, is not: "How to deal with money in psychoanalysis?" but rather, "What is the *place* of money in analysis?" (Martin, 1984, p. 14). From this perspective, the materialization of the *act of payment* is essential to analysis insofar as it is "evidence of an infinite demand" and sends the subject back to the very cause of the discourse and of the demand: this act is a "sensitive sign" which makes it possible to reveal this function of money as a revelation of the subject to himself, a subject, however, who is no more *someone* for whom there is a reference in general than there is *something* that refers to the signifier.

It is understandable, then, that from this perspective in which money has the essential function of revealing symbolic castration, the idea of free analysis is unthinkable. It could only result in the inhibition of the discourse or pure seduction: "Faced with the rule of abstinence, there would remain no other exchange for the demand than the imaginary passion whereby the image of each protagonist is alienated in that of the other" (Martin, 1984, pp. 51–52).

This underlines the risk of collusion between the analyst and the analysand, and the need for a materialized third element that is the "sign of what is prohibited (*l'inter-dit*), which is essential to the transference" (Martin, 1984, p. 152). Though certain analysts seek to justify the possibility of free analysis, this can only be "a phantasy of analyzing": in other words, if the analysand does not pay with money, he is condemned to pay with his person, and the analyst is in collusion with this situation.

As for analysis adapted to those who are "economically weak", with or without the intervention of a third-party payment, it can lead to symptomatic modifications but it cannot be called analysis: the right to health entails a limitation of analysis to psychotherapy because the "indispensable 'singularity' of the act of payment no longer evokes the debt of One to the Other, but the *commerce* of everyone" (Martin, 1984, pp. 153–154). The act of payment in analysis cannot refer to a demand for *treatment* any more than it refers to a demand for *knowledge:* hence the rupture with any perspective that proposes to ask for fees "reduced by society" as in analysis approved by social security or in certain institutions, or "in proportion to the patient's earnings" (Martin, 1984, p. 156). This conception of money in analysis is consistent with the idea that the subject in analysis has nothing to do with someone, with the psychological, existential, or anthropological subject.

Money: a polysemic and personal symbol

The Lacanian conception of money in analysis brings to light some important aspects. There is no doubt that genetic perspectives have often failed in their associationism in revealing the conditions of possibility of the symbolization of money. Incidentally, the mediating function of money was not always perceived by Freud, if we refer, for example, to the "Wolf Man": the gifts of money received prevented Freud from analysing the Wolf Man's idealized transference towards him, as was revealed by the subsequent analysis he did with Ruth Mack Brunswick (1971).[15] Furthermore, the right to health has often led to distorting the very purpose of analysis, as evidenced by its status in certain countries where it is almost always reimbursed by health organizations.

It is nonetheless true that money is diverted from its function both of symbolizing the body and of its power in phantasy, owing to the negative connotation attached by Lacan to the dimension of the imaginary. On the one hand, the reference of money to the body and resexualization are invalidated, placing value finally on its power of abstraction: "Money is a signifier without signification: something everyone had long sensed with their noses: *Pecunia non olet*" (Martin, 1984, p. 15). On the other hand, the reference of money to the body, thereby dispossessed of its power of phantasy, is reintroduced at the level of the act of payment, an act that is said to be essential to the analytic contract, but which in reality is the only *acting out* authorized by the analytic situation: "Of this subject, the *act* of payment marks the place physically and it is … for nothing" (Martin, 1984).

It is an obligatory act which, in fact, leads to negating the phantasized function of money in analysis, as well as the reference to the erogenous zones and to affects, while only retaining its mediating function which is likened more to an abstract power imposed on the analysand, the necessity of "going through" symbolic castration; it is more a matter of power that may sometimes potentialize sadomasochism rather than lifting the repression inherent to the symbolization of money. In this hardline conception of analysis it is by no means certain that the collusion between the analyst and the analysand that is so decried in the name of the mediating function of money does not reappear through this reference to unambiguous symbolization: the function of money in analysis finally only has one meaning, that of introducing the symbolic order. Just when money acquires a *universal and unambiguous dimension*, it loses its *personal and polysemic* value: money contributes to making sure that structure prevails over the person, abstraction over the power of phantasy specific to each person.

It is true, as Martin points out, that often the "object of the phantasy mobilized by money" is the "wish for murder", that is, "the refusal of all filiation, the affirmation of being born of oneself (that is the denial of difference)". Money as a primordial signifier contributes to representing this phantasy and to revealing "the father who is already dead, that is the symbolic father announced by the Name-of-the-father" (p. 192). This is what the anal regression of the "Wolf Man" showed, for example, since his obsessions with money had in particular the function of repressing the wish for murder inherent to the oedipal conflict; his analysis with Freud had allowed him to rediscover a filiation in phantasy both represented and repressed by the symbolism of money (Aisenstein, 1985). But this symbolism, in its polysemic richness, is not limited to representing the mediation of the paternal third and the death wish towards him. Here we come up against the limits of a critique of genetic empiricism which, by seeking to give priority to the structural dimension of mediation, positions itself in a radical situation of rupture between nature and culture, between history and structure, between the subject's relationship to the world and the subject's relationship to being, between the semantic function and the syntactic function of symbols.

The symbolism of money shows on the contrary that it is in no way a universal and unambiguous symbolism. In clinical practice, money has a polysemic symbolic power and, although its materiality often seems indispensable for making the transference experience tolerable and manageable, it is not always indispensable and can even sometimes impede phantasy activity. Money, as far as it is resexualized in analysis, is one of these "pseudo-symbols" that needs to be analysed in order to find the "personal symbol" of the patient (Pasche, 1960, pp. 157–159). The universality of symbolism – whether it is of a semantic order, as in Freud, Jones and Ferenczi in the years of the polemic with Jung, or whether it is of a syntactical order, as in Lacan, with the constant reference to symbolic castration – leaves out of the picture what constitutes the process of symbolization: a process that is essentially polysemic and individual which must make it possible at the same time, as Segal has already pointed out, to bring together and integrate "the internal with the external, the subject with the object and the earlier experiences with new ones" (Segal, 1957, p. 397).

Symbolism in analysis is a process that is not always accomplished or acquired, and it is a matter of imagining more or less open possibilities. This symbolization which is closed and abstract to begin with may tend to become increasingly fixed to the point of losing its function; the drive defusion that can be encountered can lead, in psychosis, to a process of desymbolization or excessive symbolization, as Bion (1970) noted, in fact an essentially *private* experience (p. 68). The impossibility of an anchoring in anality, constitutive of the differentiation between the subject and the object, is opposed in this case to the development of polysemy. The risk is also that money is caught up in a perverse tendency, and eludes all symbolization, retaining its unique dimension as currency.

Although it is in the service of repression, the symbolization of money allows us on the contrary to rediscover bodily exchanges and the concrete experience of each person, and manifests its essentially *social* dimension by letting its elements open up to new meanings (1970, pp. 64–65). The resexualization of money in analysis and its elaboration in phantasy, with or without materialized mediation, thus leads to a convergence between symbolization and sublimation, psychic reality and social reality. The psychic work resulting from the integration of anality makes it possible for the symbolism of money to acquire its polysemic value retrospectively and in response to the Oedipus complex; and further, to function as a mediator in phantasy referring to the paternal *imago,* permitting ideally the absence of its materialization, as in free analyses.

Money in analysis, whether real or phantasized, is thus an essential marker on the path that leads from closed and repetitive sexual symbolism to an open and nonrepetitive personal symbolism. What it loses at the level of universality permits it to rediscover singularity, a real concreteness, as is revealed by the rediscovery of the physical and historical meanings that money can assume. This does not mean, however, that this singular work, which shows that the symbolism of money only finds its place retrospectively in infantile sexuality, should be closed to a certain extension revealed by cultural correspondences, the "work of culture" of symbolism. It cannot, however, be the universality of the *sumbolon* which, taken up by Lacan in symbolism, shows the risk of a materialization that is simply the reverse side of an even greater degree of abstraction.

In spite of the theoretical insistence on delimiting dream symbolism, which was reminiscent of the key to dreams, Freud did not fail to emphasize the importance of a work of individual symbolization and of the detour via the dreamer's associations. Likewise, the symbolization of money follows both singular and multiple paths, but this does not exclude identifying the general conditions of its efficacy. In fact, it is in the same movement, where psychic reality and social reality coincide in the elaboration of the Oedipal conflict, that the symbolism of money finds both its temporality retrospectively and its efficacy at the level of its polysemic possibilities. From this angle, the anchoring in anality, structuring the object relationship, appeared to be decisive in the transition from the univocity to the polysemy of this symbolism. This was perhaps what Freud suspected when, in connection with the "Wolf Man", he remarked:

> We are accustomed to trace back interest in money, in so far as it is of a libidinal and not of a rational character, to excretory pleasure, and we expect normal people to keep their relations to money entirely free from libidinal influences and regulate them according to the demands of reality.
>
> (1918 [1914], p. 72)

Is money indispensable, then, to the unfolding of the psychoanalytic treatment? Even though he sometimes practised analytic treatments freely, Freud (1913b) considered money an important parameter in the analytic process:

> The absence of the regulating effect offered by the payment of a fee to the doctor makes itself very painfully felt; the whole relationship is removed from the real world, and the patient is deprived of a strong motive for endeavouring to bring the treatment to an end.
>
> (p. 132)

Free treatment could be an insurmountable source of resistance and a major obstacle to the continuation of the analysis.

Freud's remarks still retain their share of truth. It is said of money that it has no smell, thus marking the special connection between money and anality. In this sense, it permits the *neutralized* mediation which undoubtedly fosters the repression of the corporeality of primitive exchanges; but, at the same time, it authorizes symbolic substitutions for them and their elaboration in the treatment, shielded precisely from this isolation of the sensual and corporal contents.

Money is effectively the *reified* third element which makes it possible to manage the transference relationship and the erotism, both loving and aggressive, that it implies, in a tolerable way. Without this mediation, there is a great risk of collusion between the analyst and the patient, which removes the object-related dimension of the analytic relationship: the analyst might then become an omnipotent character who impedes the individuation of his or her patient and obliges him or her to pay with their person rather than with money. The payment has the advantage of modulating the relationship of dependence between the patient and the analyst because, although the analytic relationship represents a very great situation of dependence of the patient on the analyst, the money given by the patient makes it possible to inverse this relationship of dependence; from this point of view, it is the analyst who depends on the patient.

Money in analysis thus has a symbolic function which, due to its very materiality, compensates for the insufficiency of the phantasized mediator in the form of the paternal *imago*; this is indispensable for the constitution of the object-relationship, for reducing omnipotence. As a real mediator that is indispensable for the efficacy of the analytic treatment, money thus echoes the very origins of symbolization.

And yet free analysis is possible, perhaps less in private practice (Freud had experience of this and denounced the dangers and risks of it) than in an institution which takes over the mediating function ascribed to money. This implies according more importance to the money phantasized than to the money paid and evaluating under what conditions this phantasy activity can be encouraged or, on the contrary, hindered. Experience shows that it is not always the money paid that permits its elaboration in phantasy.

Notes

1 It was Ferenczi who introduced the concept of introjection into psychoanalytic theory to refer to a psychic process relating to the drives and permitting an awakening of the ego. Freud took up this concept and clearly contrasted it with the concept of projection: this movement of differentiation between the ego and the external world is organized on the basis of the opposition between the introjection into the ego of everything that is a source of pleasure and the projection outside of everything that is a source of unpleasure. The introjection of faeces signifies, therefore, that anality acquires meaning for the subject and becomes both a source of auto-erotic pleasure and a means of exchange with the external world.

2 From this perspective, certain meeting points between "ontogenesis" and "phylogenesis" can be highlighted. It seems that in the beginning the genesis of money had nothing to do with operations of exchange. For primitive peoples, money was allegedly invested with magic and mysterious virtues related to its material quality (its shine, for example) and linked in the first place to cultural acts; its function of economic exchange appeared gradually in connection with the selection and distribution of sacrificed animals: "The path leading from thesaurization to money as a sign is one of the gradual detachment of the archaic representation of a *qualitas occulta* from its material object; by taking on a quantitative aspect, money became a means in the service of the economy" (Schacht, 1973, p. 92).

3 Part-objects correspond to the objects of part sexual impulses (specified according to their *source*, as with the oral and anal impulses, or according to their *aim*, as with the impulses to see or to exhibit oneself) and concern mainly actual or fantasized parts of the body (breast, faeces, penis) and their symbolic equivalents; they stand in contrast with whole objects, corresponding to persons as such (father, mother, child). The dialectic part-object/whole object is at the centre of psychic conflict and of the problem of having and being, since it is a matter of having the part-object that the whole object possesses in order to be the whole object and identify with it.

4 It is during the second semester of the first year of life that the "object stage" is organized according to Freud, that is to say the structuring moment when the child is capable of perceiving and forming a picture of his mother as a distinct person different from every not-mother object. The baby's stranger anxiety bears witness to this experience.

5 In *Inhibitions, Symptoms and Anxiety*, Freud (1926) distinguishes between *automatic and traumatic anxiety* related to the infant's unsatisfying expectations of his mother, corresponding to a quantity of excitation that is liable to completely overwhelm the ego, and *signal anxiety* which indicates that the ego has the possibility of experiencing this automatic anxiety in an attenuated way and to cope with it without being submerged by it. It is to this capacity to elaborate the loss of the maternal object, through the organization of unconscious phantasies, and to substitute signal anxiety for automatic anxiety, that the following fundamental affirmation of Freud refers: "When the infant has found out by experience that an external, perceptible object can put an end to the dangerous situation which is reminiscent of birth, the content of the danger it fears is displaced from the economic situation on to the condition which determined that situation, viz., the loss of object. It is the absence of the mother that is now the danger; and as soon as that danger arises the infant gives the signal of anxiety, before the dread economic situation has set in" (1926, pp. 137–138), my italics).

6 This wooden reel game corresponds to a case observation described by Freud (1920) in *Beyond the Pleasure Principle* concerning a game played by his grandson

in his mother's absence: "The child had a wooden reel with a piece of string tied behind it. It never occurred to him to pull it along the floor behind him, for instance, and play at its being a carriage. What he did was to hold the reel by the string and very skilfully throw it over the edge of his curtained cot, so that it disappeared into it, at the same time uttering his expressive 'o-o-o-o'. He then pulled the reel out of the cot again by the string and hailed its reappearance with a joyful 'da' ['there']" (p. 15).

7 It is therefore necessary to add to Freud's schema in his article "On transformations of instinct as exemplified in anal erotism" (1917), an arrow between *money and the child*, in addition to those marking the processes of symbolization between the gift and money and between the gift and the child.

8 The development of phantasying and thought-processes makes it possible to suspend momentarily the discharge of the quantity of excitation corresponding to the libidinal satisfaction, and is opposed to behaviours and acts which represent *immediate* discharges without any possibility of delay and waiting in the search for satisfaction. This distinction between thinking and acting stems from the model of the experience of satisfaction as described by Freud in "Project for a scientific psychology" (1950 [1895]) on the model of the child at the breast: faced with an organic need, the infant may react either immediately and inadequately (screams, crying), and risk being overwhelmed by the inflow of excitation or in a mediate and specific way through the organization of thought-processes which make it possible to introduce a delay in satisfaction and to find the "specific [or adequate] action". According to Freud, the transition from the primary process to the secondary process depends on a "sufficient ego-cathexis" capable of anti-cathecting the tendency to absolute discharge of the quantity of excitation according to the pleasure principle. From this point of view, impulsive acting out (*passages à l'acte*) and somatizations all represent weaknesses in the possibility of elaborating psychically and in phantasy this tendency towards the absolute discharge of tensions.

9 In orality, if the mother feeds the infant, the infant can only devour; cannibalistic phantasies of incorporation and anxieties of reincorporation and engulfment by the mother confront him with the risks of the loss of limits. As E. Kestemberg has pointed out in an oral communication, it is only in anality that the infant rediscovers the identification with the giving mother, in the sense that giving his faecal matter is also giving food. This identification with the nourishing mother contributes in an essential way to mastering the act of giving and to the establishment of limits between the one who devours and the one who is devoured.

10 A disorder that consists, in a child beyond the normal age for acquiring control of the sphincters (between the ages of two and three), in defecating in his pants more or less regularly, without a neurological impairment or dysfunction of the anal sphincter.

11 We can see what makes Abraham's (1924) distinction between two phases in the anal-sadistic stage problematic: the earliest phase is marked by hostile tendencies (losing/destroying) and the later phase by conservative tendencies (holding back/dominating). For it not so much a matter of describing two successive phases in time as of evoking a dialectical movement, a conflict between contrary aims which sometimes assume a progressive and sometimes a regressive value, depending on the predominance of love or hate. Furthermore, without denying the importance of moments of development where the prevalence of an exchange at a bodily level is privileged, the idea of an anal stage or of regression to the anal stage suggests the possibility of a dual relationship of exchange with the mother which would exist in itself, whereas what is involved, in fact,

is a defensive phantasy whose aim is to repress the death wishes towards the Oedipal rival.

12 The Hegelian concept of *Aufhebung* (resolution), which is difficult to translate into French, refers to the process of overcoming a dialectical contradiction between a negative meaning and a positive meaning.

13 As in the genesis of symbolism described by Jones (1916, pp. 104–116).

14 The opposition between unbound cathexes and bound cathexes translates the economic dimension of the Freudian distinction between primary and secondary processes: in one case, energy is *free*, insofar as it circulates from one representation to another according to the principle of the most immediate and rapid satisfaction; in the other, energy is bound insofar as it permits delay and waiting in the search for satisfaction.

15 It is interesting to note that this period of analysis with R. Mack Brunswick ended among other things by a dream about money, which both recalls the reasons for the psychotic episode of the Wolf Man and shows the solution. The free analysis with Freud in 1919–1920 and the money Freud collected for him after this for six years contributed, as we know, to generating in the Wolf Man the fantasy of being Freud's favourite son and to accentuating his feminine position, which found in particular a form of expression in his hypochondria and his persecutory experience towards doctors. However, in this dream in which the patient consulted a doctor, he agreed to *pay for* his consultation rather than being treated for free, at the price, however, of depreciating both the currency in which he paid and the value of the doctor. Moreover, although the latter subsequently sought to *give* and not to sell his patient "old music" and "coloured postcards", they were gifts without value, as Freud's gifts became. At the end of the dream, the patient was also able to express a positive Oedipal desire towards his female analyst (Mack Brunswick, 1971, pp. 293–295). In this case, the money had not played its mediating role, and it was only the work of de-idealizing Freud undertaken by Ruth Mack Brunswick that enabled the Wolf Man to elaborate his ambivalence and to free himself from his homosexual passivity towards Freud, which was reminiscent of his infantile quest for his father's gifts and money.

References

Abraham, K. (2018 [1924]). A short study of the development of the libido, viewed in the light of mental disorders. In: D. Bryan & A. Strachey (Trans.) *Selected Papers on Psychoanalysis*. London: Routledge, pp. 418–501.

Aisenstein, M. (1985). Quelques réflexions sur argent et névrose de transfert à propos d 'L'Homme aux rats'. *Cahiers du Centre de Psychanalyse et de Psychothérapie*, 11: 31–52.

Bion, W.R. (1970). *Attention and Interpretation*. London: Tavistock.

Diatkine, R., Simon, J. (1972). *La psychanalyse précoce*. Paris: Presses Universitaires de France.

Fain, M., Kreisler, L., & Soulé, M. (1974). *L'enfant et son corps*. Paris: Presses Universitaires de France.

Ferenczi, S. (Ed.). (1914). On the ontogenesis of the interest in money. In: *First Contributions to the Problems and Methods of Psychoanalysis*. London: Hogarth, pp. 274–275.

Freud, S. (1900). *The Interpretation of Dreams*. S.E. 4–5. London: Hogarth.

Freud, S. (1905). *Three Essays on the Theory of Sexuality. S.E.* 7. London: Hogarth, pp. 130–243.

Freud, S. (1908). Character and Anal Erotism. *S.E.* 9. London: Hogarth, pp. 169–175.

Freud, S. (1913a). The disposition to obsessional neurosis. *S.E.* 12. London: Hogarth, pp. 317–326.

Freud, S. (1913b). On the beginning of the treatment. *S.E.* 12. London: Hogarth, pp. 123–144.

Freud, S. (1917). On transformations of instinct as exemplified in anal erotism. *S.E* 17. London: Hogarth, pp. 127–133.

Freud, S. (1918 [1914]). From the history of an infantile neurosis. *S.E.* 17. London: Hogarth, pp. 7–122.

Freud, S. (1920). *Beyond the Pleasure Principle. S.E. 18.* London: Hogarth, pp. 1–64.

Freud, S. (1926). *Inhibitions, Symptoms and Anxiety.*

Freud, S. (1950 [1895]). *Project for a Scientific Psychology. S.E.* 1. London: Hogarth, pp. 281–397.

Freud, S. (1957 [1911]. *Dreams in Folklore. S.E.* 12. London: Hogarth, pp. pp. 180–203.

Gibeault, A. (1981). Symbolisme inconscient et symbolisme du langage. *Revue française de Psychanalyse*, 45 (1): 139–159.

Grunberger, B. (1971). *Le narcissisme.* Paris: Payot.

Jones, E. (1916). The theory of symbolism. In: *Papers on Psychoanalysis.* London: Baillière, Tindall and Cox, 1950, pp. 87–144. *British Journal of Psychology,* 9 (2):181–229.

Lacan, J. (2002 [1957]). Seminar on 'The Purloined Letter'. In: B. Fink (Trans.) *Ecrits.* New York and London: W.W. Norton & Co, pp. 6–48.

Mack Brunswick, R. (1971). A supplement to Freud's History of an infantile neurosis (1928). In: M. Gardiner (Ed.) *The Wolf Man and Sigmund Freud.* London: Routledge.

Martin, P. (1984). *Argent et psychanalyse.* Paris: Navarin.

Masson, J.M. (Ed.) (1985). *The Complete Letters of Sigmund Freud to Wilhelm Fliess, 1887–1904.* Cambridge, MA: Belknap Press.

Pasche, F. (Ed.). (1969 [1960]). Le symbole personnel. In: *À partir de Freud.* Paris: Payot, pp. 157–159.

Schacht, J. (1973). *Anthropologie culturelle de l'argent.* Paris: Payot.

Segal, H. (1957). Notes on symbol formation. *International Journal of Psychoanalysis,* 38: 391–397.

Segal, H. (1964). *Introduction to the Work of Melanie Klein.* London: The Hogarth Press and The Institute of Psychoanalysis, 1978.

4 Symbolization, projection, and projective identification

Theory does not exist outside analysis itself, the standard model of which presupposes a relationship involving two "terms", the analyst and the analysand, whose work is only possible on the condition that it is linked to the third agency of the setting: the analytic situation is thus both symbolic and symbolizing, insofar as its mode of functioning relies on a structure involving three terms which, precisely, permits a process of symbolization to unfold, with its moments of closing and opening. The emphasis Freud placed on an essentially individual symbolism, in contrast with the work of culture open to a social dimension, attests in fact to the adventure of symbolization within analysis: closed and repetitive symbolization should give way to open and non-repetitive symbolization that introduces a new system of exchanges.

Reflections on symbolization have always led to hypotheses about the *conditions of emergence,* in particular with regard to its relations with the origins of language. Freud was interested in these origins and did not always find it easy to demarcate a *descriptive* level centred on a linear genetic perspective and a theory of primitive origins, and a *metapsychological* level based on the reference to the primal, as a phantasized period of origins and of the primary dimension, through and in the de-differentiation from the secondary dimension according to the model of deferred effects. And yet, the reference to the *experience of satisfaction,* that of an infant at the breast, as Freud described it in empirical terms of images and mnemic traces, is in fact essentially a prototypical model which delimits the domain of the process of symbolization in the transition from need to the drive: in effect, Freud defines the drive as a boundary concept between the psychic and the somatic; it is constituted after the experience of hallucinatory satisfaction and its constant pressure is related to the permanence of the object when the whole object is perceived.

The constitution of hallucinatory wish-fulfilment is equally the foundational moment of symbolization in its essential function of binding affects,

DOI: 10.4324/9781003545651-5

in correlation with the issues of *cathexis* and *identification*. This was what Freud pointed out so well in a note of 1938:

> 'Having' and 'being' in children. Children like expressing an object-relation by an identification: 'I am the object.' 'Having' is the later of the two; after loss of the object it relapses into 'being'. Example: the breast. 'The breast is a part of me, I am the breast.' Only later: 'I have it' – that is, 'I am not it'.
>
> (1941 [1938], p. 299)

This can only mean that the issue of identification, in the sense of an identity that cancels out the differences with the object or a similarity that respects them, is established at this moment. Between the narcissistic cathexis ("I am the breast") and the object cathexis ("I have it" – that is, "I am not it"), the dimension of psychic space and time is organized: a space of psychic topography, which also signifies acceptance of temporality, that is, delay, waiting, the succession between the time of being and, as Freud puts it, "only later", the time of having. The symbol loses its function of mediation when it is a matter of abolishing, of reducing to the "same period of time" the time of being and the time of having. What ensues is concrete thinking, the regime of symbolic assimilation between the ego and the world, of the identity between identification and cathexis expressed by the concept of pathological projective identification as described by Melanie Klein. But symbolic assimilation corresponds here to a defensive movement aimed at avoiding recognition of the object and its differences, rather than denoting a stage of development.

Theories on the genesis of symbolization (Jones, Ferenczi, Klein, Segal) have often assumed a process in two stages representing successive periods of life, whereas in fact what is involved is a structural process: a period of identification and assimilation, of symbolic equivalence, of sexualization of the universe based on the projection of bodily organs and functions on to the objects and events of the external world; a period of repression during which symbolization proper emerges and a displacement of affect occurs on to objects and interests which had previously been assimilated and sexualized on account of their similarity. In this movement of desexualization and emergence beyond primitive animism, the symbol represents what is symbolized and is no longer identical to it.

From this point of view, the hallucinatory experience of satisfaction is a postulate that cannot be verified by the experience which determines the a priori conditions of the psychoanalytic field. It denotes the dialectic between the non-optative ("I am") and the optative (I want, I am not), which can only be expressed provided sufficient time is allowed for the dimension of the non-optative: one of the major contributions of Winnicott (1951) was that he insisted on the importance of duration in this moment of non-optative illusion as a prerequisite for the moment of the optative, of disillusionment. Hence, the importance of rhythm in the alternation between contact and rupture, between pleasure and unpleasure, a temporal factor that Freud (1924) considered to be constitutive of primary masochism and that attests to the alternation between being neither too early nor too late in the regulation of drive intensity.

In fact, it was a matter of insisting on an experience of illusion that was not in contradiction with disillusion: an articulation rather than an opposition, which refers to the necessity of what Freud said was a necessary but insufficient condition for sublimation, namely, the inhibition of the drive concerning its aim – in the transition from the discharge of excitation to the experience of the feeling of tenderness. This is probably what is at the basis of the dynamic and mutative effect of narcissistic regression in analysis.

From this perspective of the found/created object, René Roussillon (1995) has introduced the concept of *primary symbolization* which is at the basis of the nonverbal encounter with the external object and constitutive of the "bodily ego"; he distinguishes this from *secondary symbolization* which is based essentially on the internal object and language, and links thing-presentations with word-presentations. This reference to the notions of primary and secondary makes it possible to highlight the idea that *preverbal* thought linked to the economic balance between the principle of inertia and the principle of constancy must be assumed to be prior to language. In *An Outline of Psychoanalysis*, Freud (1940) speaks in this connection of a work of binding carried out by the preconscious/conscious prior to language, on which the formation of the categories of space, time, causality, and permanence at the beginning of life depend and which underpin the development of *linguistic thought* (pp. 163–164).

While the concepts of primary and secondary may suggest a genetic sequence, it is nonetheless important to point out that what is involved here is merely a metapsychological sequence that presupposes the constitution retroactively of the primary by the secondary; this is Roussillon's concern when he assumes that it is a matter of "two fundamental and structural phases". From this perspective, we may ask ourselves if the concept of primal rather than that of primary would not make it easier to bring to the fore this structural dimension, as was the case for the concepts of primal phantasy and primal repression.

The experience of the loss of the object thus governs different vicissitudes of symbolization with respect to the possibility of constituting a dialectical articulation between the time of being and the time of having. It is an essential gap that is cancelled out in the illusory wish to make the subject and object, memory and perception, meet each other in the "same moment of time", as much in the movement that aims to exclude the object as in that which aims to include it – movements that are correlative with the exclusion or inclusion of the erogenous body as a source of psychic reality.

Different modalities of symbolization are thus denoted. The symbolic assimilation governed by the search for what is identical may result in undermining the *projective work;* the only path that is then available is the search for immediate satisfaction through acting out entailing the degradation of the *symbol,* which represents the object, into a *signal.* The latter addresses itself, on the contrary, to the object's real presence with a practical reaction in view: the urgency of affect transforms language into action language in an economy of destructive auto- or hetero-acting out which de-animates the world and where erotogenic masochism is prevalent. On the contrary, the symbolic assimilation may aim to include the object in projective work which, even if it dehumanizes the world by transforming it into abstract entities, nonetheless maintains a link in a universe of index-based *signs* where the categories of what is certain, foreseeable and univocal prevail.

Depending on how the object is used, these two different economies lead in one case to a repression of affects and to a splitting of the body involving the exclusion of all symbolization: this is the register of the non-delusional psychoses and psychosomatic disorganizations where there is a noticeable correspondence with autistic withdrawal. In the other case, the economy strives to conserve these affects at a psychic level in a symbolic efflorescence which, while it aims to eliminate the gap and distance, nonetheless attests to a solution at the level of representations, as delusional psychoses show. According to Bion, the premature saturation involved here has the paradoxical effect that all acts are symbolic, and yet the patient is incapable of symbolic formation. He symbolizes excessively and prevents himself from being informed by the knowledge of the world: the psychotic symbol contains a *private* dimension which marks the rejection of any form of paternity of the world (Bion, 1970, pp. 68–69). True symbolization reveals on the contrary its essentially *social* dimension insofar as it "represents a constant conjunction which is recognized by a group to be constant" (Bion, 1970, p. 65); it thus permits its elements to remain "unsaturated" and to open themselves to new meanings. This is what, in other terms, Nicos Nicolaïdis (1989) emphasizes when he contrasts the freezing of the component affect in psychosomatic organizations and the freezing of the component ideational representative in psychosis, giving rise in particular to concrete thinking and excessive symbolization, which equally marks a failure of the process of symbolization.

We can thus see a positive and negative function in symbolic assimilation that may be compared with what has often been said about negative hallucination. Freud (1917a) himself states that positive hallucination can only be understood in relation to negative hallucination (pp. 229–230). What does this mean other than that the external world must disappear so that the space of an internal world becomes possible, and so that openness to the world and the exercise of the judgement of existence are constituted retrospectively. This is the positive dimension of negative hallucination, which presupposes both a self-presentation of the subject and the presentation of an object. André Green (1977) has spoken of the structuring function of the presentation that is organized in this negativity. It is worth emphasizing the importance, in this process, of the cathexis of unpleasure linked to hallucinatory satisfaction, correlative with the progressive organization of primary masochism and of the movement leading from the substitution of thought-identity by perceptual identity.

Different degrees are possible in this self-presentation of the subject, even to the point of losing his own self-image, like the narrator in *The Horla* by Guy de Maupassant (1887), who is plunged into terror when he is no longer able to see his image in the mirror:

> I got up so quickly, with my hands extended, that I almost fell. Horror! It was as bright as at midday, but I did not see myself in the glass! It was empty, clear, profound, full of light! But my figure was not reflected in it – and I, I was opposite to it! I saw the large, clear glass from top to bottom, and I looked at it with unsteady eyes. I did not dare advance; I did not venture to make a movement; feeling certain, nevertheless, that He was there, but that He would escape me again, He whose imperceptible body had absorbed my reflection.
>
> (p. 26)

The allusion to the image absorbed by the object reflects well the connotation of vampirism induced by psychotic anxiety. Negative hallucination refers here to the moment when the loss of the object results in both the loss of the subject and the loss of the capacity to constitute hallucinatory wish-fulfilment in its dialectical relation between the time of being and the time of having.

These are, of course, more economic than nosographical references, which can be found in the analysis of one and the same patient; I will illustrate this later with the analysis of Charles. The atypical hypochondria of this patient partook of these two economies, on the one hand through recourse to a melancholic solution which had led him to make a suicide attempt and, on the other, through recourse to a paranoiac solution which led him into a frantic quest for the object, in particular doctors. This is why it is necessary to take into account the economic differences determining structural differences, both of which require different technical approaches: this implies accepting that the link to the object and to the body is not acquired from the outset, and that the object can be an "object within a dotted line" as Évelyne Kestemberg (1981) put it in connection with the economy of non-delusional psychoses.

A different perspective lies behind the Kleinian interpretation of psychotic organizations, where the relation to the internal object governs issues of splitting and projective identification: somatic, hysterical, hypochondriac, or psychosomatic symptoms have similarities insofar as they correspond to split-off parts of the self – in particular hate towards the object – which, when projected into the body, find a space that is sufficiently dissimilar and distant. Even if we can notice similarities in the ways of treating the object, it is important to be able to determine the differences, both in the description of psychic functioning and in the interpretative approach.

Independently of these varied metapsychological approaches, there is general agreement concerning the different somatic symptoms, for example, in facilitating a rediscovery of the symbolic and symbolizing dimension of the instinctual body by re-establishing the psychic link to the internal object and external object. Nevertheless, it is interesting to reflect on the issues at stake for our concepts, which govern different technical approaches. A closer examination of the concepts of projection and projective identification will be useful here.

Ever since Melanie Klein (1946) introduced the concept of projective identification in her article "Notes on some schizoid mechanisms", there has been an ongoing controversy about whether this concept overlapped with projection, as Freud defined it, or added something. Was there an interest in replacing one concept with another, or would it have been better to consider that projective identification added nothing to what was already defined by the concept of projection? If it was deemed desirable to retain both concepts, their mutual relations still had to be defined. It is important to be able to answer all these questions, particularly as the concept of projective identification has been extended to such an extent that it has become at certain moments difficult to specify its content.

Projective identification seems to be a crossroads concept that refers through its *projective* aspect to related concepts like extrajection (Weiss, 1947),[1] excorporation (Green, 1971),[2] and externalization, and through its *identificatory* aspect to incorporation, introjection, and internalization. On the one hand, there is a centrifugal movement towards the object, and on the other a centripetal movement of the object towards the subject. This double movement also occurs in the opposition between projective identification – or identification through projection – and introjective identification – or identification through introjection. A comparison between the concept of projection in Freudian theory and the concept of projective identification in Kleinian theory should help us to clarify the issues at stake in this question which cannot be reduced in fact to a mere problem of terminology.

Projection: defence mechanism and/or process

In a letter to Jung dated April 1907, in which he puts forward some new ideas on paranoia, Freud gives an interesting definition of projection:

> Projection (like conversion, etc.) is a variety of repression in which an image becomes conscious as perception; the affect pertaining to it is detached and withdrawn into the ego with reversal into unpleasure. This affect (the libidinal cathexis) then tries, starting from the perceptual end, to force itself once more on the ego.
>
> (McGuire, 1974, p. 40)

In an effort to "explain" projection, Freud asks, in this same letter:

> What is the condition for the outward projection of an inner affectively cathected process? A glance at the normal situation: originally, our *cs.*, registers only two types of experience. From the outside, perceptions (P), which as such are not affectively cathected and have qualities; from within it experiences "sensations", which are manifestations of drives in certain organs. These are only in a small degree qualitative but are capable of strong quantitative cathexis. What shows such quantity is located within, what is qualitative and without affect, is localized outside.
>
> (McGuire, 1974, p. 38)

With these thoughts, Freud was setting out the issues involved in a metapsychological reflection on projection. Projection is clearly a *defence mechanism* which, as he emphasizes in this letter, is "a sort of repression". And yet, in the case of Schreber, Freud opposes the two defence mechanisms: repression (or rejection) which both operate in the direction of the decathexis of certain ideas and even evokes the possibility of withdrawal from the object; and projection, which is associated more with "the failure of repression, involving the breaking through and return of the repressed", which makes it possible to move towards recathecting the object and to consider delusion as "an attempt at healing". They are therefore two economically different defence mechanisms, even if their tasks can be associated, in particular in neurotic functioning (Freud, 1911c, pp. 72–73).

If in his work Freud often spoke of pathological projection as a defence mechanism, characteristic for example, of paranoia and phobia, he often referred to normal projection, to a non-defensive *process,* constitutive of the psyche. In his letter to Jung, he speaks about his conception of psychic functioning, insisting on the links between the work of the drive, marked by the reference to quantitative and economic factors, and perception, which allows for access to qualitative factors, in the Freudian perspective of "becoming conscious" related to the cathexis of "perceptual residues". Projection plays an essential role, therefore, in the process of differentiating between interior and exterior, between inside and outside.

Whether it is a defence and/or a process, projection is a complex concept on which Freud, according to Jones, wrote an article at the time of his papers on metapsychology. But we know that this contribution never reached us even if, in the case of Schreber, Freud announced the project for a later date of "a thorough investigation of the process of projection" (Freud, 1911c, p. 71). Since Freud, many studies have been made on this subject, not to mention the importance of the concept of projective identification elaborated by Klein and the post-Kleinians which, in the analytic community, appeared to be more heuristic than that of projection.

In its defensive function, projection thus aims to reject into the outside what cannot be recognized in oneself. Freud often pointed out that it is easier to protect oneself from an external danger than from an internal danger. In *Totem and Taboo*, he remarks that primitive men were unaware of unconscious hostility towards the dead when they attributed it to them and considered them as dangerous demons. Likewise, in psychopathology, projection contributes to resolving the conflict related to ambivalence by denying any feelings of hate towards the deceased (Freud, 1912–1913, p. 92).

But projection also has a function of *knowledge*, for it makes it possible to discover the external world thanks to *misrecognition* and concealment of the internal world. In paranoia, it is a matter, indeed, of recognizing in others what the subject does not want to see in himself, and thus of exploring the external world. In this connection, projection, which Freud says "has a regular share assigned to it in our attitude to the external world" (1911, p. 66), gives a representative content to the internal processes which he says are only known to us "through the sensations of pleasure and pain alone", the "sensations" without quality to which he referred in his letter to Jung. It contributes to the work of representability by permitting a detour via the "perceptual residues" originating in the external world, just as the different perceptions of the senses are related to objects in the external world.

In this function of knowledge, projection becomes, according to Freud's expression in *Totem and Taboo*, "a method of understanding" that enabled primitive man to rediscover in gods and demons what he was himself. Freud thus makes an essential link between *projection* and *identification* when he remarks in this connection that it was natural and innate for primitive man to project his own essence into the external world, to see all the events that he observed as being due to spiritual beings that were basically similar to him. Without being the equivalent of animism, projection nonetheless has close links with this way of thinking which allowed primitive man to "establish a relation" with the world and to influence it, to act on it, by favouring "psychic mastery" at the basis of physical mastery when faced with the dangers of nature.

Freud compares here the feelings of impotence and distress of primitive man with the feelings that the infant can experience at the beginning of life. Without there being any question of reducing prehistoric man to a child, which is strongly contested by our colleagues who are pre-historians, it is more a question of describing a fundamental process of the mind: projection is inherent to identification in the sense of identifying, assimilating and establishing an analogy that permits the development of identification in the reflexive sense of "identifying oneself". It is marked by misrecognition insofar as the distress in the face of the external world is ultimately more tolerable than the distress related to the internal world and to the danger of the instinctual drives. But it opens the way at the same time for an equation between oneself and the external world that is characteristic, it is true, of an animistic approach to the world, but is also at the very basis of the apprehension and constitution of the external world.

In his considerations on the evolution of culture, Freud assumed there was a transition from an animistic phase to a religious phase of humanity, prior to a scientific phase which would assume its full scope and significance particularly under the influence of psychoanalysis (Freud, 1933, pp. 164–171). But psychic functioning is such that projection and its beliefs can certainly evolve towards a more objective knowledge of the world, whereas animism and its illusions cannot be reduced totally, as dream hallucination shows. The hypothesis of hallucinatory wish-fulfilment on the model of dream hallucination shows that hallucination precedes perception and that the latter is essentially a belief as Merleau-Ponty (1945) pointed out. Projection as a process necessarily refers to the Freudian dialectic of hallucination and perception.

Projection, hallucination, and perception

It is interesting to recall here that, for Freud (1917a [1915]), "a dream is therefore, among other things, a *projection*, an externalization of an internal process" (p. 223). At a first level, it was a way for him to emphasize the defensive dimension of this projection, since for the dreamer, it is a way of struggling against unconscious instinctual impulses by avoiding the moment of waking up. But he also refers to an "internal process", which is nothing other than the essential relation between hallucination and perception.

The hallucinatory dimension of dreaming determined the essential construction of psychoanalytic theory, namely the experience of satisfaction according to the model of the infant at the breast. It is a postulate that is unverifiable by experience, according to which the hallucination is satisfaction, thereby defining the psychoanalytic approach to mental functioning. For Freud, influenced by the positivist context of his era, it was necessary to assume that there is first stage of a real experience of satisfaction, followed by a second stage of its hallucinatory repetition. Hallucination therefore follows on from perception. But in reality, it is the hallucinatory satisfaction of a wish that precedes the perception and gives it meaning, and not the real experience which is subsequently duplicated psychically. It was a matter of according full importance to the priority of instinctual drive cathexes, to psychic *work*, which transforms bodily sensations into psychical representations.

This was what Bion had understood when he assumed that, initially, the meeting of the preconception with non-realization engenders a "proto-thought", a primal thought, presenting the characteristics of a "beta element": a present bad breast – the need for a breast that is felt to be a thing-in-itself. With this reference to the Kantian a priori which refers to the conditions of possibility of the experience, Bion was thus able to highlight the primal dimension in psychoanalytic thought: before any actual experience of the breast, one must suppose there has been a hallucinatory satisfaction of the wish, just as dissatisfaction is necessary if the infant is to hallucinate pleasure. The infant's capacity to tolerate the frustration inherent to these primitive thoughts will later determine the outcome of the real perception of the breast, in particular the transformation of "beta elements", initially oriented towards discharge and evacuation, into "alpha elements" capable of being used for dream thoughts, images and phantasies (Bion, 1962, pp. 34–35).

Projection is situated both in the centrifugal movement of hallucinatory cathexis turned towards the external world with the aim of recreating the perceptual presence of the object and in the centripetal movement which aims to produce a representation of the object, distinct from its perception. Freud always insisted on the importance of distinguishing between *memory* and *perception* and, according to the model of the mystic writing-pad, of conceiving their functioning as successive rather than simultaneous. It is the basis of the psychic topography governing the possibility of representative activity. From this perspective, projection is inseparable from introjection, in this essential movement linking the subject and the object, and creates the possible conditions for their meeting and exchanges: it is a process where the hallucinatory "contact" described as perceptual identity is followed by a "rupture" with perception, which is the basis of thought-identity and representation. The process that is constitutive of the psyche depends on the cathexis of a found-created object, as described by Winnicott, corresponding to the *illusion* of having created the object and to the psychic work of projection which organizes the complex hallucination-perception. It assumes that the subject subsequently has the capacity to be *disillusioned* at not being the sole creator of the object and the world and to accept differentiation. But this stage of illusion, in connection with the setting-up of an "intermediate area of experience", shows the necessity of an "object that is cathected, then perceived" (Lebovici, 1961, p. 167), that is, a projective experience that is indistinguishable from an introjective experience and subsequently permits both the perception of the object and its psychic representation.

It is true that the Freudian reference to projection as a defence situates it in the movement of differentiation between the inside and the outside. The description in *Instincts and their Vicissitudes* (Freud, 1915) is well known: the "purified pleasure ego" "incorporates or introjects" objects which are a source of pleasure and "expels" outside itself objects that are a source of unpleasure in the movement that Freud explicitly links to the mechanism of projection (p. 136).

In "Negation" (Freud, 1925), the oral impulse provides the bodily prototypes by means of which the processes of introjection and projection are represented: according to the "language of oral instinctual impulses", "I would like to eat that" represents the first mode of acceptance by the ego and constitutes a model for future introjections; "I would like to spit it out" marks, on the contrary, the first mode of rejection and serves as a model for future projections. The processes of introjection and projection, associated with the opposition between love and hate, contribute in this way to the early splitting of the ego and the object, which helps to limit the circulation of affects in a movement linked to the elaboration of the loss of the object. By introducing in 1915 the notions of introjection and incorporation, which he opposed to the earlier concept of projection, Freud wanted to clarify this movement, both psychic and genetic, in which the ego emerges as a psychic agency and in which the differentiation between subject and object through phantasy activity occurs.

This same defensive function and its differentiation from projection is also inherent to Freud's reflections in connection with the last theory of the drives. The *mechanism* of projection accompanies the *process* of deflecting the death drive towards the objects of the external world in alliance with the life drive; the death drive opens the way to primal sadism, while the binding of the latter in the organism is at the origin of erotogenic masochism. In "The economic problem of masochism", Freud (1924) states that *projection* is related to primal sadism, whereas *introjection* is related to primal and secondary masochism:

> We shall not be surprised to hear that in certain circumstances the sadism, or instinct of destruction, which has been directed outwards, projected, can be once more introjected, turned inwards, and in this way regress to its earlier situation. If this happens, a secondary masochism is produced, which is added to the original masochism.
>
> (p. 164)

Freud is speaking here of introjection when in reality it is a movement of reintrojection of sadism; but it must be assumed that the constitution of primal masochism is related to a movement of introjection of the oral impulse, like the binding of the death drive in "libidinal sympathetic excitation".

Freud mentions here the projection and introjection of an *instinctual drive* and an *affect* but, at the same time, the *object* participates in this double movement since, in "Instincts and their vicissitudes" he evoked these processes in connection with the "stage of the object" and of the appearance of phantasy activity. What could be assumed about the time preceding the perception of the whole object and its reprise at the level of phantasy? Freud does not speak about projection, even though the object can play a role during this period that he calls the "auto-erotic stage" or "stage of primary narcissism", depending on whether he was adopting a structural or genetic conception of narcissism. The nature of what is projected – drive, affect or object – is important here: between the instinctual and affective cathexis of the object and its representation lies the dimension of the process of *projection* which is linked here essentially to that of *introjection*.

Projection and introjection are two formalized concepts describing the processes of cathexis and identification which cannot be separated without running the risk of losing sight of the essential aspects of the Freudian discovery of psychic work. The cathexis of the object goes hand in hand with a projective movement on to the object in which hallucination plays a predominant role in its relations with perception; but, at the same time, it is this cathexis that grounds identification and the introjective movement. Our concepts are involved in the function of language which has the result of distinguishing and opposing, with the risk of reifying these concepts, and of losing sight of the dimension of process. A positivist reading of Freud does not escape this trap, which is why it is important to recall with Angelergues (1984) that "identification is the *result* of the work of introjection and projection" (p. 23), just as it is the *matrix* of this work. In the same movement in which projection establishes the differentiation between the subject and the object, it must be assumed that there is a movement aimed at concealing this difference, if we want to understand how the constitution of the subject and of the object is possible.

This is probably what Freud (1917b) had in mind in his description of primary identification, where projection and introjection are concepts aimed at designating one and the same psychic process:

> Identification is a preliminary stage of object-choice, ... the first way – and one that that is expressed in an ambivalent fashion – in which the ego picks out an object. The ego wants to incorporate this object into itself, and, in accordance with the oral or cannibalistic phase of libidinal development in which it is, it wants to do so by devouring it.
>
> (pp. 249–250)

The projective process that opens the way towards the object-choice and establishes the process of introjection, portrayed here in a phantasy of incorporation, occurs at the same time.

It is not a matter here of diminishing the importance of a psychic development that distinguishes more the projective and introjective aspects of psychic work in a process in which the libidinal cathexis of external objects and objectivity are developed – a process Freud referred to by speaking about the transition from the purified pleasure-ego to the definitive reality-ego. But it is important to emphasize that projection as a primal process determines both the differentiation and non-differentiation between subject and object: this primal dimension is often portrayed by Freud by a primitive origin which must not, however, make us lose sight of the reference to the processual aspect of our concepts.

Incorporation, introjection, and identification

Introjection and projection are related processes. On the other hand, it is worth pointing out that Freud uses the concepts of incorporation and introjection in an equivalent manner to refer to these relations between the ego and the external world established by the purified pleasure-ego, and says he took over the concept of introjection from Ferenczi. Now, while for Freud (1915) *introjection* referred to the incorporation of the object in the sense of including the object in the ego and objectalizing primitive auto-erotism, Ferenczi (1909) nonetheless gave it the broader sense of a process contributing to the gradual awakening of the ego linked to the emergence of the drives as a whole. As Maria Torok (1968) suggests, it is a progressive process that can be associated with the secondary process: the object plays a role of mediation in this process ensuring exchanges between the ego and the external world and, in this sense, the *introjection of the drives* makes it possible to put an end to dependence on the external object.

On the contrary, *incorporation* corresponds to a phantasy through which the process of introjection acquires meaning in the ego; it implies in effect the loss of an object and marks the setting-up of the object in the ego in place of the lost object in order to maintain the *pleasure* linked to this object. In this sense, incorporation corresponds to the implementation of the primary process and marks more an arrest or backward step in the awakening of the ego; the incorporated object is opposed to the evolution of the ego and to its openness to reality.

The confusion between these two concepts stems from the fact that, in the case of the oral impulses corresponding to the most archaic level, the introjective process of the drives is indistinguishable from the phantasy of incorporating the object. That is why in connection with melancholia Freud speaks of an "introjection of the object" (1921, p. 109) when "the shadow of the object fell upon the ego" (1917b, p. 249) and sees it as a regression to the "primary narcissism" corresponding to the structural sense of narcissism, as a precipitation of a form of the ego during the object stage. At this primitive level, primary identification and narcissistic identification, introjection or incorporation of the object, are all concepts that seek to denote one and the same psychic reality.

Freud never really spoke of the introjection of the drives, but it seems difficult not to give it this meaning when he uses the concept of introjection to denote both the incorporation of the object in melancholia and the setting-up of Oedipal objects in the ego in the form of the superego. Freud (1924) says, in effect, concerning the Oedipal superego:

> It came into being through the introjection into the ego of the first objects of the id's libidinal impulses – namely, the two parents. In this process the relation to those objects was desexualized; it was diverted from its direct sexual aims.
>
> (p. 167)

Introjection therefore marks the process in question at the level both of primary identifications and secondary identifications: in one case it refers to a process in which the boundaries of the ego are challenged and the imagos are undifferentiated, as is suggested by the transition from the reality-ego at the beginning to the purified pleasure-ego; and in the other case, it is a process that presupposes the integration of the ego's boundaries and the differentiation of imagos, in accordance with the movement from the purified pleasure-ego to the definitive reality-ego (Freud, 1925, p. 237). The work of projection can only have a specific quality by taking into account the immediate difference that is created between the cathected external objects and the phantasized objects during the object stage, then in the course of the later evolution of the introjective processes. Ultimately, it is to this polyvalence of introjection as an instinctual drive process and to its impact on projection that a reflection on the concept of projective identification refers.

Projection and projective identification

The introduction by Melanie Klein of the concept of projective identification had the merit of confirming the importance of an essential "interaction" between projection and introjection for understanding the issues at stake in projection.

Deflection, oral introjection, and anal projection

For Melanie Klein, the last theory of the drives constituted the starting-point of her theory of mental functioning. Before introducing the concept of projective identification (Klein, 1946), she used the concepts of projection and introjection as Freud had described them in 1915, in the context of the opposition between the life drives and the death drives.

She took the step that Freud had been unwilling to take and assumed that the processes of projection and introduction are active from the outset, at birth, and that the content of these processes concerns not only affects but also objects. This conception is directly related to her theory of phantasy as a direct expression of the life and death drives: the external object has its origin in the movement of the projection of hate and love, just as the internal object is an incorporated object resulting from the introjection of this hated or loved object. The predominance of hate over love determines the persecutory dimension of this incorporated object which Melanie Klein (1932) says "at once assumes the role of a superego" (p. 127), thus of a primitive superego which precedes the appearance of the Oedipal superego. On the contrary, the predominance of love over hate allows for the projection and introjection of the good object and the transition from the paranoid-schizoid position to the depressive position.

From this perspective, which, at the time of her book *The Psychoanalysis of Children*, followed Abraham's theory of stages quite closely, projection is nonetheless linked to the movement of expulsion of excrement characteristic of the anal-sadistic stage, while introjection remains characteristic of the movement of incorporation specific to the "oral-sadistic stage". Just like introjection with incorporation, projection finds its bodily prototype in anal expulsion:

> We know that in the early anal-sadistic stage what he is ejecting is his object, which he perceives as something hostile to him and which he equates with excrement. But as I see it, what is already being ejected in the early anal-sadistic stage is the terrifying superego which he has introjected in the oral-sadistic phase. Thus his act of ejection is a means of defence employed by his fear-ridden ego against his super-ego; it expels his internalized objects and at the same time projects them into the outer world. The mechanisms of *projection* and *expulsion* in the individual are thus closely bound up with the process of super-ego formation.
>
> (Klein, 1932, pp. 140–141, my emphasis)

This is why the first movement towards the object is described more in terms of the deflection of the death drive, a process which Melanie Klein, recalling Freudian theory, says is "fundamental to the individual's relations to his objects and to the *mechanism* of projection" (Klein, 1932, p. 126). The mechanism of introjection concerns therefore the partial incorporation of a bad and persecuting object which forms the "nucleus of the superego", and the anxiety aroused by this introjected object gives rise to the mechanisms of expulsion and projection (p. 168).

This chronological succession: deflection, oral introjection, anal projection, is nonetheless purely speculative, for a process of deflection still needs to be defined that is not at the same time a projective movement. They are both necessarily closely bound up with each other, insofar as the process of displacement of the destructive drive from the inside towards the outside is at the same time a movement of attributing the object with a drive aim that is identical to that of the subject, which defines projection. In fact the link between deflection and projection enables Melanie Klein to give a metapsychological status to projection which had previously only been defined as a movement of rejection outside of oneself, leading her to use the concept of *extrajection* (Klein, 1931, p. 244; see also Petot, 1979, p. 227). Projection appears to be a mechanism that aims to protect the ego from persecuting incorporated objects by displacing the source of danger into the outer world, but that thereby contributes to the discovery and observation of the outer world "with a watchful and suspicious eye", and "increases its relations with reality, though in a one-sided way" (Klein, 1932, p. 146). In fact, persecution determines the development of symbolization as an indefinite substitution of objects beginning with primitive objects.

In spite of the elaboration in terms of successivity, projection and introjection thus acquire an essential reciprocity from the beginning of life, centred around the fear of incorporated objects and the fear of retaliation; hence Melanie Klein's conclusion: "There follows a reciprocal action between projection and introjection, which seems to be of fundamental importance not only for the formation of his superego but for the development of his object-relations and his adaptation to reality" (Klein, 1932, pp. 142–143).

Projective identification: a mechanism of defence

What contribution, then, did the concept of projective identification make? From a certain point of view, many clinical examples that preceded the introduction of the concept in 1946 show that Melanie Klein had understood the importance of this psychic mechanism: for instance, the "premature empathy" shown by the child Dick when he equated his analyst one day with the pencil shavings she had in her lap (Klein, 1930, p. 227). But in reality Melanie Klein had never before completely drawn out the theoretical significance of this *interaction*, of this *interplay*, between introjection and projection. As Jean-Michel Petot (1982) points out, projection had primarily described a mechanism pertaining to the bad object, while introjection described more the incorporation of the good object (p. 117): indeed it was in keeping with the processes of projection and introjection as described by Freud (1915) in "Instincts and their vicissitudes". The concept of projective identification was to confirm clinically and theoretically the application of these processes to *any content*, good or bad; the very importance of the identificatory element in this interaction between projection and introjection was, moreover, to lead him to describe both a projective identification (identification through projection) and an introjective identification (identification through introjection).

Projective identification thus takes up a fact of common observation where *identification* with others obeys a centrifugal movement of *projection* of one's own feelings and thoughts: thus, when the reader of novels puts himself in the shoes of the protagonists, he follows their story while equating their feelings with his own feelings; he identifies with the different characters while imagining that they are experiencing what he himself is experiencing. Moreover, Melanie Klein sees this movement of "friendly" projection as the foundation of empathy: "By attributing part of our feelings to the other person, we understand their feelings, needs, and satisfactions; in other words we are putting ourselves into the other person's shoes" (Klein, 1959, pp. 252–253). Empathy as a means of understanding others depends on an identification through projection with the *good* parts of oneself.

"Good" projective identification takes up a progressive dimension of mental functioning that had hitherto been attributed to the oral introjection of the good breast, and becomes a factor of integration and development. However, if it is carried out excessively, this "good" projective identification can become "bad", for "the good parts of the personality are felt to be lost": identification with the object then results in "weakening and impoverishing the ego" (Klein, 1946, p. 9). "Good" projective identification may well lead to a loss of ego boundaries and the danger of being engulfed by the object, just as the movement of empathy, in its "premature" dimension, can lead to the disappearance of the subject in the object: "There are people who go so far in this direction that they lose themselves entirely in others and become incapable of objective judgement" (Klein, 1959, p. 253).

In reality, "excessive" projective identification, as Melanie Klein described it in 1946 and later on,[3] has an essentially bad connotation, which certainly contains the risk inherent to identification through projection of the good parts, but also due to identification through projection of the bad parts: "If projection is predominantly hostile, real empathy and understanding of others is impaired" (Klein, 1959, p. 253).

It was from this negative perspective that Melanie Klein introduced this mechanism of projective identification to refer to "the prototype of an aggressive object-relation" which is necessarily linked to excessive *splitting* of the object and of the ego between an idealized part and a persecutory part. The aim of projective identification, which is both a mechanism and phantasy of omnipotence,[4] consists essentially in *taking possession* of the object from the inside and of *controlling*[5] it in order both to establish and erase the boundaries between the subject and the object: hence the idea of an unconscious projection *into* the object, which certainly implies a dif-ferentiation between the subject and the object, and contributes to it, but whose immediate aim is to undo it in order to rediscover a sense of identity. As Melanie Klein (1946) points out, the mother "is not felt to be a separate individual, but is felt to be the bad self" (p. 8): to take up the concepts of Edith Jacobson (1954), it is a matter of wanting to feel complete *oneness* with others, according to primary identification, a movement that can be surpassed thanks to the mediation of the double and of *sameness* in order to reach a state of *likeness*, corresponding to secondary identifications. The *identificatory* aspect of *projection* has the function of marking the aim of *iden-tity* contained in the concept of projective identification which thus repre-sents the essential mechanism of narcissistic identification.

The control exerted over the object connoted by the concept of projec-tive identification contributes to this and clarifies what Freud had already suggested in his description of the deflection of the death drive: the drive is called the *destructive drive*, the *drive for mastery* or the *will to power* over the object (Freud, 1924, p. 163). Hence the idea that, in projection, it is not only a matter of expressing a phantasy but of exerting *real* pressure on the object, of influencing it in order to verify two aspects of the phantasy: that the object possesses in an identical way the projected parts of the self and that it is controlled by the subject who has projected them. (Ogden, 1979, p. 369; Segal, 1967, p. 204). This is the reason for the external pressure in the interaction between the subject and the object to make the object think, feel and behave in accordance with the projective phantasy: in the analytic situ-ation, the analyst may be led to react to the violence of the affects thus pro-jected by counter attitudes which can also amount to a counterprojective identification towards the patient (see Grinberg, 1962; Kernberg, 1987).[6] Projective identification thus comprises a dimension that is both *intrapsychic* and *interpersonal*.

Projective identification: a principle of communication

Projective identification is consequently directly related to *introjective identification*, corresponding to the centripetal movement of the object towards the subject: it is therefore no longer a question of an identification of oneself with the object, but of an identification of the object with oneself, through the introjection of the object's attributes, both hated and admired. Melanie Klein (1959) speaks of the risk of an "excessive introjection" which endangers "the strength of the ego *because* it becomes completely dominated by the introjected object" (p. 253); it is the shadow of the object that falls upon the ego, as in melancholia. The predominance of hate over love can only give rise here to a pathological introjection which is dominated by fears of retaliation and persecution.

The predominance of love over hate nonetheless allows for the development of introjective identification in a progressive sense: Melanie Klein saw the projection of the good breast as the essential factor in the child's maturational process. It was this idea that was to lead Bion to propose an extension of projective identification and to distinguish between *excessive* projective identification, as described by Melanie Klein as a *defensive mechanism* in the service of the pleasure principle, and *realistic* projective identification as a *primitive mode of communication* in the service of the reality principle. In this case, this mechanism is not used to *take flight* from reality but to try and *modify* it by allowing the object to "digest" the bad projections, thereby favouring the reintrojection of a good object. Bion attributes "the mother's capacity for reverie" with the aptitude for transforming β (beta) elements, which are only suitable for evacuation through excessive projective identification, into α (alpha) elements "suitable for employment in unconscious waking thinking, dreams, contact-barrier and memory" (Bion, 1962, p. 26; see also Gibeault, 1982a). It is this process of transformation related to the mother's alpha function that allows introjective identification to break the cycle of retaliation and to open itself up to more evolved forms of identification – in this case post-oedipal secondary identifications.[7]

This theory of projective identification was, as we know, formulated by Bion on the basis of the metaphor of the *container* and the *contained*, insofar as this mechanism implies the differentiation of the subject and the object and the projection of a content *into* a container (Bion, 1962, pp. 87–94). The extension of projective identification as a mode of communication which calls for a work of elaboration by the object-container has prospered in post-Kleinian research. Herbert Rosenfeld was thus led to distinguish between two forms of projective identification in the treatment of psychotic patients: a *positive* form that has a communicative function with the analyst-container and suggests a relatively good prognosis; and a *negative* form which simply aims to evacuate the bad parts and undermines the analytic work through destructive *acting out* directed against the analyst (Rosenfeld, 1971, pp. 117–118). In particular, Rosenfeld sees the transference actualization of these two forms of projective identification as both what impedes and makes it possible to dislodge the "psychotic islets" contained within the psychosomatic symptoms. Taking up his earlier studies on hypochondria and psychosomatic illnesses (Rosenfeld, 1957, 1964) in light of Bion's hypotheses, he explains the appearance of these psychotic islets by the failure of the mother's containing function: hence the early splitting off of the destructive impulses that the mother is unable to take in and contain and their projection into the body or bodily organs. This excessive splitting between the subject's mind (the inside) and body (the outside) clearly shows the possibility for the body to serve as a special object for the evacuation of destructive affects by means of omnipotent projective identification. Rosenfeld sees this as the failure "of an attempted projection into an external object", a process that analysis can help to stimulate and "transform" thanks to the positive function of projective identification (Rosenfeld, 1980).[8] In this way, he underlines the differences in the modalities of projection depending on whether it seeks to include or exclude the external object.[9]

Furthermore, this model of container-contained permitted Hanna Segal to re-elaborate the theory of symbolization previously linked to the resolution of excessive projective identification (Klein, 1930; Segal, 1957). If the mother contributes to the introjection of a good breast capable of containing affects, she thereby facilitates access to the depressive position and the formation of "true symbols" where the symbol is experienced as *representing* the object. If, on the contrary, the mother cannot transform the bad projections related in particular to envy, then the relation between container/contained becomes negative and leads to concrete thinking and to "symbolic equations" where the symbol is experienced *as being* the object (Segal, 1978).

It was also this extension of the concept of projective identification that led to the distinction between projective identification as a primitive and unconscious mode of communication and intrusive identification as a defence-mechanism aimed at impinging both on external and internal objects. This is a point Donald Meltzer makes, who suggests speaking of "container" to refer to "the interior of the object receiving the projective identifications" and of *claustrum* for the "interior of the object penetrated by intrusive identification" (Meltzer et al., 1982). This is reminiscent, under different aspects, of the Freudian idea of a non-defensive normal projection and a defensive pathological projection.

Pathological defence and normal defence are thus marked by differences of an economic order: the amount of excitation involved will determine the degree of the "excessive" dimension of the defence, and a different vicissitude of projection, depending on whether it is in the service of ego-splitting or repression. Pathological projective identification always goes hand in hand with excessive splitting of the object and the ego between an idealized part and a persecuting part. Projective identification thus seems to be a primitive form of the *mechanism* of projection, which Danielle Quinodoz (2003) emphasized by taking up a dialogue with me (Gibeault, 2000) concerning the distinction between *aspects* of oneself and *parts* of oneself: according to her, in projection it is a matter of aspects of the ego – drive, affects, representations – which do not call into question the difference between the subject and the object; whereas in projective identification, there is a projection not only of the drives, represented by affects and representations, but also of the part of the ego that experiences these affects and creates these representations. Projective identification implies, then, the utilization of ego-splitting, for the patient must "have detached and split off a part of his own psyche in order to project it", which impairs the integrity of the ego and the object due to the identification of the object with the ego and mastery over the object (Quinodoz, 2002, pp. 99–101).

This is why the reference to the concept of projective identification entails the idea of an interpersonal dimension between the subject and the object on account of this compulsion for non-differentiation, which leads the subject to make the object experience affects and ideational contents, and even to make it *act* in accordance with these affects and ideational contents. Quinodoz insists on the importance of bodily and preverbal phantasies that are often involved here and on the work of transformation that leads to linking up bodily sensations, bodily experiences, and the emotional significance of these experiences.

From this perspective, projective identification necessarily calls for work on the countertransference, the aim of which is to identify these early experiences and to transform them in such a way as to go beyond splitting and to promote differentiation between oneself and others. The contribution of Heinrich Racker (1953) on the difference in the countertransference between complementary identification and concordant identification, as well as that of Leon Grinberg (1962) on projective counter-identification, have their place in this attempt to take into account this compulsion for psychic elaboration, which also constitutes a movement of differentiation in analytic work.

The difference between two forms of projective identification, one pathological with evacuation as its aim and the other normal permitting communication, led to a renewal of the concept of *empathy*, giving it a psychoanalytic dimension, in particular in the work of Stefano Bolognini (2002). The experience of empathy is then considered the product of normal projective identification with a communicative purpose. Psychoanalytic empathy implies taking into account the experience of the *countertransference* considered here in terms of both its positive and negative values, without being reduced to them; for the idea of empathy refers to the conditions of possibility of conscious and preconscious *contact* with the patient, who is not faced with the opposition between absolute distance as in indifference or absolute proximity as in emotional contagiousness. It is a question of being able to put oneself in another person's shoes while maintaining distance. Merleau Ponty's (1964) concept of "proximity through distance" comes to mind here (p. 170). In this work, the analyst is invited to *enter a participatory experience* where the dimension of feeling, sensations, and affects plays a predominant role. Bolognini insists, however, on the fact that empathy is not equivalent to a concordant identification; while it is always necessary, it is very often insufficient, in particular when it is a matter of understanding difficult patients, like psychotic patients. Otherwise there is a risk of regarding empathy and goodness as equivalent, which would leave out the necessity, at certain moments, of experiencing hate in the countertransference.

Melanie Klein's discovery of projective identification as a pathological defence mechanism thus led to the extension of the concept by Bion, as a principle of communication in the service of the reality principle. This extension has often been called into question, on the grounds that it was created to the detriment of understanding the concept. It is interesting to note that this discovery has enriched Freudian reflection on projection by showing the essential links between projection, introjection and identification.

Clinical experience of psychic mechanisms leads, according to Danielle Quinodoz (2003), to making a distinction between projection of *aspects* of the ego and projection of *parts* of the ego; this in turn makes it possible to distinguish between projection that is in the service of repression and characteristic of neurotic functioning, and projective identification that is in the service of ego-splitting and characteristic of psychotic functioning. Quinodoz (2002) finds this distinction useful in clinical work, but hesitates, at a theoretical level, to see it as the basis of a difference between these two mechanisms; she states: "Perhaps the difference between the two is enshrined to a much greater extent in the concepts espoused by each psychoanalyst when working with his patients" (p. 101).

But perhaps the theoretical solution would lie in the possibility of restoring to projection and projective identification their dimension as psychic processes. If, for Freud, projection is necessarily linked to the constitution of the object which is born in hate, it is necessary, according to Benno Rosenberg, to consider projection as a defence against internal destructiveness while attributing it to the object, which would necessarily entail a confusion between inside and outside. For Rosenberg (2000), an *essential condition* of projection lies in a certain momentary confusion between inside and outside, with the provisional loss of reality-testing (and a distortion of perception). Even if Rosenberg does not put it like this, I think that we can conclude that projection and projective identification converge in describing the *foundational* moment of the psyche. But the clinical experience of projection would lead to differentiating the two mechanisms and to seeing the aim of projection as one of distinguishing and opposing inside and outside, and the aim of projective identification as one of non-distinction and non-differentiation.

The vicissitudes of projection

From this perspective, projection is not only a defence mechanism aimed at ejecting an internal danger into the outside world but also a process that strives to describe the relations between the subject and the object, and to express the transformations of the process of identification, from its most elementary modalities to those that are more elaborate. In this evolution, the status of the representation of a psychoanalytic point of view is decisive here.

Let us recall here the issues at stake in this concept of representation, in terms of the distinction between thing-presentations and word-presentations. It is in the difference between cathected external objects and objects corresponding to the processes of projection and introjection vis-à-vis internal objects that the notion of thing-presentation has its specificity in psychoanalysis: it corresponds to the introjection and reprise of mnemic traces permitting the representation of the object at the basis of phantasy activity which has its roots in a cathexis prior to the perception of the object. It is this hallucinatory activity related to a projective movement which ultimately determines the psychoanalytic problem of representation as the "psychical representative of the drive". In fact, this work of representability and cathexis situates the thing-presentation between sensation (hallucination of satisfaction) and perception (hallucination of the object). The word-presentation in the double articulation of language takes over from reflex movement characteristic of hallucinatory wish-fulfilment and conserves the motricity inherent to this "motor image".

The distinction between sensation and perception assumes its full importance here when we consider the thing-presentation, since the "thing" presents itself first via bodily sensations and affects, and can never be either completely *depicted* or completely *expressed* in an adequate discourse. The vicissitudes of projection are correlative here with an activity of representation which, in its aim of binding affects, will always comprise a remainder.

In accordance with the alternation between memory and perception, the activity of representation is only possible if a rupture is created in the complex hallucination/perception corresponding to a process of *negative hallucination*. Green, and other authors following him, have insisted on the important role played by the negative hallucination of the mother in constituting a "framing structure" (Green, 1999), a "constituting function" (Angelergues, 1991), or alternatively a "psychic screen" (Lavallée, 1999), where the projection of unconscious ideational contents can occur. It was with a similar purpose that Pasche (1971) had evoked the importance of forming a "shield of Perseus" to protect oneself from the petrifying gaze of the Medusa, using a very eloquent metaphor to emphasize the necessity for an intermediate activity of representation between the subject and the object. It confirms the importance of the subject's reflexivity in the constitution of auto-erotism where "representing" and "being represented" are correlative with "representing oneself".

Without the possibility of constituting this negative hallucination, projection can only be directed at external reality, in a confusion between the inside and the outside corresponding to pathological positive hallucination. Hallucination in the clinical sense – that is to say positive hallucination – substitutes itself for and makes up for the failure in the introjection of hallucinatory wish-fulfilment and attests to an inner experience which is then merely projection without a work of introjection. According to the famous Freudian definition of projection in the case of Schreber: "It was incorrect to say that the perception which was suppressed internally is projected outwards; the truth is rather, as we now see, that what was abolished internally returns from without" (Freud, 1911c, p. 71). Freud speaks in this connection of the "suppression of a perception" and we may ask ourselves what the content of this perception may have been. Was it a representation, an affect or a sensation? Vassilis Kapsambelis (2001) assumes that it was "the delocalization of a bodily state as it should have been experienced by the ego", resulting in "the projection of a part of the ego", since "every bodily sensation is potentially a part of the ego" (p. 153). Denial and rejection are directed at raw bodily sensations, that is not linked to affects and representations, corresponding to what I said above about pathological projective identification. The apparent discontinuity induced by projection is merely the manifest counterpart of continuity and the danger of non-differentiation.

This vicissitude of projection confirms the intuition of Victor Tausk (1919) that projection is directed first at the body experienced as an external object, with the risk of complete psychic disappropriation. It is worth noting the projection characteristic of psychotic hallucination is distinct here from projection as Freud (1907) described it in the *Gradiva*: Norbert Hanold's delusion is defined by Freud as hysterical, in contrast to Schreber's paranoid delusion, and corresponds more to the hallucinatory state close to *onirism* and similar to the psychic mechanisms of dreams (Kapsambelis, 2001, p. 151; see also Jeanneau, 1990; Angelergues, 1994). It is also different from the hallucinations of "normal people" which César and Sára Botella (2005/2001) have described as a third hallucinatory modality corresponding to an "accident of thought", to "a momentary regression in the course of psychic processes, whether neurotic or normal" (p. 130). Hence their question: Why use the same term "hallucination" to describe phenomena whose mechanisms are so different? Their choice to distinguish between the *hallucinatory dimension* as a "permanent process of psychic life ... inseparable from the regressive path which flourishes in dreams" and psychotic *hallucination* is already one answer. The utilization of two different terms should not, however, lead us to create an unbridgeable gap between neurotic functioning and psychotic functioning and thus lose sight of the economic dimension which, in reality, determines the structural differences.

Between hallucination in the sense of wishful hallucinatory satisfaction (the hallucinatory) and psychotic hallucination, the work of projection determines different psychic solutions, where the object-related dimension is maintained, even in the creation of this neo-object that is the psychotic delusion. However, clinical experience of psychotic states reveals organizations in which the object is excluded in its function of binding and representation, and narcissistic continuity is rediscovered only in bodily pain, inflicted on oneself and on others, in a hypercathexis of erotogenic masochism. The modalities of projection determine here an essential difference between delusional psychoses and non-delusional psychoses concerning the status of representation, insofar as the delusional psychoses tend to include the object and perceptions of it, and to work *with* it, while non-delusional psychoses tend on the contrary to exclude it, and to work *against* it. The vicissitude of projection in psychotic functioning is related here to the degree of "masochistic erotization of primary distress" (Rosenberg, 2000, p. 815); the relations between the recourse to masochism and projective work are thus inversely proportional. From this point of view, the psychosomatic solution – essential depression and operational thinking – can be likened with non delusional psychoses owing to this movement of de-objectalization (Green, 1986) which calls into question the activity of representation and the utilization of projection, and leads accordingly to a much greater degree of drive defusion and destructiveness than in delusional psychoses (Rosenberg, 2001).

Projection and projective identification in analysis

After this theoretical and speculative detour, what can we say about projection in analysis? How can we interpret projection and projective identification so as to foster a movement of introjection and identification with the interpretative function of analysis? A certain number of clinical examples will serve later to illustrate the theoretical issues I have tried to outline here. As Jean-Luc Donnet (1995) has already pointed out, there is always a risk of a coincidence between the *act* of interpreting and the *content* of the interpretation. This is a way of emphasizing the importance of a dialectic between the complex hallucination/perception and the work of representation. It also implies a process of symbolization that maintains the gap between the search for perceptual identity and the acceptance of a delay in satisfaction thanks to the cathexis of an activity of representation and the search for thought-identity.

Freud often evoked the opposition between two spaces, the space of psychic reality and the space of external reality, while insisting on the importance of finding "intermediate links" characteristic of the work of the preconscious. It was in this sense that Winnicott (1971) put forward the hypothesis of an "intermediate reality" ("a potential space", p. 104) inherent to the transitional space that momentarily suspends the opposition between the two first spaces.

In a remarkable posthumous article, Paul-Claude Racamier (2000) evokes the existence of a "fourth space", the "delusional space", which has the characteristic of escaping the double attraction, the physical and material attraction of the gravity of living beings, and the affective attraction of intra-and interpsychic links. Strange but not unambiguous, and indestructible, this fourth space, derived from the transitional space, is conceived as having been constituted in a denial of origins and in the search for absolute certainties. At the end of his article, Racamier wonders what sort of therapy is possible. He excludes the perceptual confrontation between internal reality and external reality and concludes: "Only the third reality is capable of thwarting the fourth. The reality that is so often evoked as a panacea is not a remedy for delusion. Rather, the best remedy would be (in Winnicott's sense) *playing*" (p. 829).

This is a way of evoking the importance of the reciprocity between projective processes and introjective processes if psychic life is to be enriched and become creative. Thanks to this capacity for play, analytic work permits each patient, whatever his organization, to rediscover *his own desires* through emotions and representations which he then perceives no longer as a threat or an external persecution, but as an internal world to which he now has access.

Notes

1 Weiss wanted to be able to circumscribe the multiple meanings of the term projection by using three different terms : *extrajection*, representing projection in general, as any "transformation of a part of the ego into an object-representation" which conserves at the same time the boundaries of the ego and of the object; "*true projection*, corresponding to "the false imputation of traits or desires to external objects", as in hallucinations; and "*objectivation*", which represents on the contrary the attribution of characteristics to the object which correspond to something real in it (for example, in the projected jealousy evoked by Freud where the subject's desire for infidelity finds an echo in the object's unconscious desire for infidelity).

2 Green (1971) distinguishes between *excorporation* corresponding to the expulsion outside of any internal tension prior to the differentiation between the subject and object and *projection* proper, which implies differentiation between the subject and the object and the possibility that an object can "receive" what is excorporated" (p. 943).

3 See in particular the article "On identification" in which Melanie Klein (1955) comments on the novel by Julien Green (1947) *If I were you*, "a novel illustrating projective identification". The transformations of the hero, Fabien Especel, into different persons are an opportunity for her to show the aims of projective identification and the dangers that this mechanism of defence raises, in particular concerning the loss of oneself in the other.

4 If introjection and projection are psychic *processes*, that is, modes of functioning of the psychical apparatus, they are at the same time mechanisms aimed

at managing instinctual drive conflicts. However, from a Kleinian perspective, defence mechanisms are merely an abstract representation of unconscious phantasies; for, if phantasy is the expression of the instinctual drives, it also has a defensive function: as Susan Isaacs (1948) puts it, "phantasy is the link between the id impulse and the ego mechanism, the means by which the one is transmuted into the other" (p. 92). Hence the interpretation of the mechanisms to the patient, and in particular of projective identification, insofar as it is less a matter of interpreting the mechanisms than "the phantasies that are contained in the mechanisms" (Segal, 1964, p. 509). The immediate transcription of the phantasy into a mechanism or into a process may nonetheless result, conversely, in "abstracting" the phantasy from its registration in the body and leaving out the "mediation" of the external object in the psychic processes established by the work of the instinctual impulses, processes that are correlative with the deferred effect of the hallucination of satisfaction on perceiving the whole object.

5 This characteristic of projective identification is related to one of the possible senses of the concept of *externalization*, as a movement leading from the world of representations of the subject towards a modification of the world of representations of the object itself (Ogden, 1979, pp. 369–370).

6 It was from a similar perspective that Évelyne Kestemberg elaborated her distinction between counter-transference and counter-attitude. Unlike *countertransference* which implies the analyst has the possibility of binding the contradictory affects aroused by his patient with the help of representations, *counter-attitudes* are manifested by a series of more or less conscious affects, without representations binding them, apart from possible rationalizations: rather than accompanying the patient in his instinctual drive movements without exploiting them for his own benefit, the analyst is then led to engage in self-protective impulsive reactions faced with the impulsive danger presented by the patient, in an affirmation of narcissistic identity.

7 In certain studies, the concept of introjective identification often refers to secondary identifications. See Meltzer et al. (1982).

8 The studies by Tausk on the relations between identification and projection, in particular the projection of one's own body, "the aim of which is to find the object in one's own body" anticipate in an astonishing way all this research into the concept of projective identification (see Tausk, 1919).

9 It is worth pointing out, however, that the Kleinian hypothesis of the projection of the internal object into the body or into the external object leaves in the dark the differences in the projective work between the economy of erotogenic masochism in non-delusional psychoses and that of sadism in delusional psychoses: in one case it is a matter of working both against the internal object and the external object and, in the other, on the contrary, of using them (see Gibeault, 1982b).

References

Angelergues, R. (1984). La projection comme outil de travail psychique. *Cahiers du Centre de Psychanalyse et de Psychothérapie*, 9–10: 19–48.

Angelergues, R. (1991). *De l'hallucination au langage. Monographie du Centre de Psychanalyse et de Psychothérapie*, II.

Angelergues, R. (1994). Eloge de l'incertitude. Sur le problème de l'onirisme en psychopathologie. *L'Evolution psychiatrique*, 59 (1): 89–99.

Bion, W.R. (1962). *Learning from Experience*. New York: Basic Books.

Bion, W.R. (1970). *Attention and Interpretation*. London: Tavistock.

Bolognini, S. (2002). *Psychoanalytic Empathy*. London: Free Association Books, 2004.

Botella, C., & Botella, S. (2005/2001). *The Work of Psychic Figurability: Mental States Without Representation*, trans. A. Weller. London: Routledge.

Donnet, J.-L. (1995). *Le divan bien tempéré*. Paris: Presses Universitaires de France.

Ferenczi, S. (1909). Introjection and transference. In: M. Balint (Ed.) *First Contributions to the Problems and Methods of Psychoanalysis*, trans. E. Mosbacher. London: Hogarth, 1952, pp. 35–93.

Freud, S. (1907). *Dreams and delusions in Jensen's 'Gradiva'. S.E.* 9. London: Hogarth, pp. 1–95.

Freud, S. (1911c). Psychoanalytic notes on an autobiographical account of a case of paranoia (Dementia Paranoides). *S.E.* 12. London: Hogarth, pp. 9–82.

Freud, S. (1912–1913). *Totem and Taboo. S.E.* 13. London: Hogarth, pp. 1–61.

Freud, S. (1915). Instincts and their vicissitudes. *S.E.* 14. London: Hogarth, pp. 117–145.

Freud, S. (1917a [1915]). A metapsychological supplement to the theory of dreams. *S.E.* 14. London: Hogarth, pp. 222–235.

Freud, S. (1917b [1915]). Mourning and melancholia. *S.E.* 14. London: Hogarth, pp. 243–258.

Freud, S. (1921). *Group Psychology and the Analysis of the Ego. S.E.* 18. London: Hogarth, pp. 69–143.

Freud, S. (1924). The economic problem of masochism. *S.E.* 19. London: Hogarth, pp. 159–170.

Freud, S. (1925). Negation. *S.E.* 19. London: Hogarth, pp. 233–239.

Freud, S. (1933 [1932]). *New Introductory Lectures on Psychoanalysis. S.E.* 22. London: Hogarth, pp. 7–182.

Freud, S. (1940). *An Outline of Psychoanalysis. S.E.* 23. London: Hogarth, pp. 139–208.

Freud, S. (1941 [1938]). Findings, ideas and problems. *S.E.* 23. London: Hogarth, pp. 299–300.

Gibeault, A. (1982a). Symbolisme primitif et formation des symboles: de l'apport des postkleiniens à la théorie de la symbolisation. *Nouvelle Revue de Psychanalyse,* 26: 293–321.

Gibeault, A. (1982b). Questions ouvertes. Du masochisme primaire et de la pulsion de mort chez S. Freud et M. Klein. *Les Cahiers du Centre de Psychanalyse et de Psychothérapie,* 5: Masochismes, II, Le masochisme érogène, pp. 97–134.

Gibeault, A. (2000). De la projection et de l'identification projective. *Revue Française de Psychanalyse,* 64 (3): 723–742.

Green, A. (1971). La projection: de l'identification projective au projet. *Revue Française de Psychanalyse,* 35 (5–6): 939–960.

Green, A. (1999 [1977]). Negative hallucination. In: A. Weller (Trans.) *The Work of the Negative.* London: Free Association Books, pp. 274–278.

Green, A. (Ed.). (1986). Pulsion de mort, narcissisme negative, function désobjectalisante. In: A. Green, *La pulsion de mort.* Paris: Presses Universitaires de France, pp. 49–60.

Green, A. (1999/1993). In: *The Work of the Negative*, trans. A. Weller. London: Free Association Books.

Green, J. (1947). *If I were You,* trans. J.H.F. McEwen. London: Harper, 1950.

Grinberg, I. (1962). On a specific aspect of countertransference due to the patient's projective identification. *International Journal of Psychoanalysis,* 43 (6): 436–440.

Isaacs, S. (1948). On the nature and function of phantasy. *International Journal of Psychoanalysis.* 29: 73–97; republished in M. Klein, P. Heimann, S. Isaacs, & J. Riviere (Eds.) *Developments in Psychoanalysis.* London: Hogarth Press, 1952.

Jacobson, E. (1954). Contribution to the metapsychology of psychotic contributions. *Journal of the American Psychoanalytic Association*, 7 (2): 239–262.

Jeanneau, A. (1990). *Les délires non psychotiques*. Paris: Presses Universitaires de France.

Kapsambelis, V. (2001). Freud et la question des hallucinations. In: G. Charbonneau (Ed.) *Introduction à la phénoménologie des hallucinations*. Paris: *Le cercle herméneutique*, pp. 141–159.

Kernberg, O. (1987). Projection and projective identification: developmental and clinical aspects. In: J. Sandler (Ed.) *Projection, Identification, Projective Identification*. London: Routledge, pp. 93–116.

Kestemberg, E. (1981). L'appareil psychique et les organisations psychiques diverses. In: *La psychose froide*. Paris: Presses Universitaires de France, pp. 179–199.

Klein, M. (1930). The importance of symbol-formation in the development of the ego. In: *The Collected Works of Melanie Klein, Vol.1, "Love, Guilt and Reparation" and Other Works, 1921–1945*. London: Routledge, pp. 219–232.

Klein, M. (1931). A contribution to the theory of intellectual inhibition. In: *The Collected Works of Melanie Klein, Vol.1, "Love, Guilt and Reparation" and Other Works, 1921–1945*, London: Routledge, pp. 236–247.

Klein, M. (1932). *The Psychoanalysis of Children*. In: *The Collected Works of Melanie Klein, Vol. 2*. London: Routledge.

Klein, M. (1946). Notes on some schizoid mechanisms. In: *The Collected Works of Melanie Klein, Vol. 3, "Envy and Gratitude" and other Works, 1946–1963*. London: Routledge, pp. 1–24.

Klein, M. (1955). On identification. In: *The Collected Works of Melanie Klein, Vol. 3, "Envy and Gratitude" and other Works, 1946–1963*. London: Routledge, pp. 141–175.

Klein, M. (1959). Our adult world and its roots in infancy. In: *The Collected Works of Melanie Klein, Vol. 3, "Envy and Gratitude" and other Works, 1946–1963*. London: Routledge, pp. 247–263.

Lavallée, G. (1999). *L'enveloppe visuelle du moi*. Paris: Dunod.

Lebovici, S. (1961). La relation objectale chez l'enfant. *La Psychiatrie de l'enfant*, 3 (1): 147–226.

Maupassant, G. de (1887). The Horla. https://www.eastoftheweb.com/short-stories/UBooks/Horl.shtml

McGuire, H. (Ed.). (1974). *The Freud/Jung Letters: The Correspondence between Sigmund Freud and Carl J. Jung*, trans. R. Mannheim & R.F.C. Hull. Princeton, NJ: Princeton University Press.

Meltzer, D., Milano, G., Maiello, S., & Petrelli, D. (1982). The conceptual distinction between 'projective identification' (Klein) and 'container-contained' (Bion). *Journal of Child Psychotherapy*, 8: 185–202

Merleau-Ponty, M. (1945). *La phénoménologie de la perception*. Paris: Gallimard.

Nicolaïdis, N. (1989). La function symbolique dans le processus dissociatif et les déorganisations contre-évolutives. *Revue Française de Psychanalyse*, 53 (6): 1871–1877.

Ogden, Th. (1979). On projective identification. *International Journal of Psychoanalysis*, 60: 357–373.

Pasche, F. (1971). Le bouclier de Persée ou psychose et réalité. *Revue Française de Psychanalyse*, 35 (5–6): 27–41.

Petot, J.-M. (1979). *Mélanie Klein: premières découvertes et premier système, 1919–1932*. Paris: Dunod.

Petot, J.-M. (1982). *Mélanie Klein: le moi et le bon objet, 1932–1960*. Paris: Dunod.

Ponty, M. (1964). *Le visible et l'invisible*. Paris: Gallimard.

Quinodoz, D. (2002). *Des mots qui touchent*. Paris: Presses Universitaires de France.

Quinodoz, D. (2003). *Words That Touch: A Psychoanalyst learns to Speak*. London: Karnac Books Ltd.

Racamier, P.-C. (2000). Un espace pour délirer. *Revue Française de Psychanalyse*, 64 (3): 823–829.

Racker, H. (1953). The meanings and uses of countertransference. In: *Transference and Countertransference*. London: Maresfield Library, pp. 127–173.

Rosenberg, B. (2000). Essence et limites de la projection. *Revue Française de Psychanalyse*, 64 (3): 801–820.

Rosenberg, B. (2001). Le Carrefour psychose-somatose. *Psychanalyse et psychose*, 1: Violence et destructivité, Centre de Psychanalyse et Psychothérapie E and J. Kestemberg.

Rosenfeld, H. (1957). Some observations on the psychopathology of hypochondrical states. *International Journal of Psychoanalysis*, 38 (2–4): 121–124.

Rosenfeld, H. (1964). The psychopathology of hypochondriasis. In: *Psychotic States*. New York: International Universities Press, pp. 180–200.

Rosenfeld, H. (1971). Contribution to the psychopathology of psychotic states. The importance of projective identification in the ego structure and the object-relations of the psychotic patient. In: R. Doucet & C. Laurin (Eds.) *Problems of Psychosis*. Amsterdam: Excepta medica, pp. 115–128.

Rosenfeld, H. (1980). De la relation des symptômes psychosomatiques aux états psychotiques latents. Unpublished communication at a seminar in Paris (7–9 November, 1980).

Roussillon, R. (1995). La métapsychologie des processus et de la transitionnalité. *Revue Française de Psychanalyse*, 59 (Congress special edition): 135–1519.

Segal, H. (1957). Notes on symbol-formation. *The International Journal of Psychoanalysis*, 38: 391–397.

Segal, H. (1964). Contribution au symposium sur le fantasme. *Revue Française de Psychanalyse*, 28 (4): 507–513.

Segal, H. (1967). Melanie Klein's technique. In: *The Psychoanalytic Forum, Vol. 2*. New York: International Universities Press, pp. 197–211.

Segal, H. (1978). On symbolism. *The International Journal of Psychoanalysis*, 59: 315–319.

Tausk, V. (1933 [1919]). On the origin of the 'influencing machine' in schizophrenia. *Psychoanalytic Quarterly*, 2: 519–536.

Torok, M. (1968). The illness of mourning and the fantasy of the exquisite corpse. In: M. Abraham & M. Torok (Eds.), *The Shell and the Kernel, Vol.1*, trans. N.T. Rand. Chicago, IL: University of Chicago Press, pp. 107–124.

Weiss, E. (1947). Projection, extrajection and objectivation. *The Psychoanalytic Quarterly*, 16: 357–377.

Winnicott, D.W. (Ed.). (1958 [1951]). Transitional objects and transitional phenomena. In: *Collected Papers: Through Paediatrics to Psycho-Analysis*. London: Tavistock, pp. 229–242.

Winnicott, D.W. (1971). *Playing and Reality*. London: Tavistock.

5   Symbolization in analysis

The approach to symbolization thus involves appreciating several issues at stake. While it may appear to be the substitution of one object by another, it is first and foremost the result of a process that implies both the capacity to *represent* an absent *object* and a subject capable of *knowing* that the symbol is not the object symbolized. Correlatively, interpretation is not so much a question of substituting one hidden meaning by another as of appreciating a psychic conflict in which the symbol is the product of a dialectic between primary and secondary processes.

Theory can put emphasis either on a linear origin which reveals the circumstances of these substitutions involving two terms or on a symbolizing operation involving three terms which determines a structure of functioning. Theory does not exist, however, independently of analysis itself, which, in its classical model, implies a relationship involving two "terms", the analyst and the analysand. And analytic work is only possible on the condition that it is related to the third agency of the setting: the analytic situation thus appears to be both symbolic and symbolizing insofar as its mode of functioning is based on a structure involving three terms, which permits the deployment of a process of symbolization with its moments of closure and opening.

The theoretical issues at stake, as they emerged from the history of the Freudian discovery, are to be found essentially in analytic work itself, in its project of construction and/or reconstruction of history. Such work always operates in a hiatus between an inexpressible and unrepresentable experience and a discourse that is based on the search for truth, the aim of which was often, for Freud, to find a match between historical truth and material reality. Although analysis sometimes relies on interpretations and constructions with a metaphorical value, there is always a great temptation to reify metaphors for reconstructive purposes, both in clinical work and in theory.

And yet, Freud, who often had recourse to metaphor to express his discovery, warned us against the risk of "mistaking the scaffolding for the building" in his undertaking to reconstruct the psychical apparatus with the help of optical metaphors (Freud, 1900, p. 536). In truth, our metaphors are symbols that are always situated at a distance from the things to which

DOI: 10.4324/9781003545651-6

they refer; but we can assume that they have a function of representation which gives access to these things. How is this so?

The instrument used to describe this experience of symbolization is itself the object of reflection, hence the impression we have of being confined by language. This could give one the feeling that there is no other solution than the alternative between contemplative silence and totalitarian and univocal speech. Freud was faced with this enigma and he did not always find it easy to delimit a *descriptive* level based on a linear genetic perspective and a *metapsychological* level oriented more towards psychic conflict and a dialectical history.

The essential construction of psychoanalytic theory does not contradict that which Freud (1950 [1895]) imagined as early as the "Project for a scientific psychology" to describe the principles of psychic functioning: namely, the experience of satisfaction of the infant at the breast. As we know, this postulate according to which hallucination is satisfaction was founded on dream experience and is unverifiable through experience. Freud speaks, moreover, of the "fiction of a primitive psychical apparatus", and thereby evokes a structural moment. But at the same time he introduces a temporal scansion, namely, a period during which the sexual drives are underpinned by the functions of self-preservation, corresponding to the hallucination of satisfaction and the upsurge of traumatic automatic anxiety; a period of the "object stage" and of hallucination of the object, when the mother is perceived as a whole object, corresponding to the displacement on to the object of experiences of pleasure and unpleasure linked to the satisfaction of needs.

This structure involves two stages, which the deferred effect makes it possible to understand as a retroactive reorganization opening out onto the processes of symbolization, in the *gap* between the field of need (ingesting milk) and the field of the drive (incorporating the breast). It is this difference, constitutive of the symbol, that Laplanche (1971, 1980) drew attention to by evoking both a *metonymic displacement of the object* (from milk to the breast) and a *metaphorical displacement of the aim* (from ingesting to incorporating). This scenario of an action between a subject and an object corresponds to the introjection of the oral impulse and acquires meaning in a phantasy of incorporation. The cathexis of the breast as a symbol of auto-erotic satisfaction is therefore at the origin of a movement that establishes an immediate difference between cathected external objects and objects corresponding to the processes of projection and introjection, that is to say internal objects. The gap between the whole object and the part-object that is thereby created gives rise to the perpetual tension between the constant thrust of the drive – related to the permanence of the object – whose aim is to reduce this difference, and the necessity of maintaining this difference, this gap, so that psychic space and time can be constituted. Also involved here is the tension between the assimilating aim of perceptual identity and the separating aim of thought-identity, as Freud distinguished them in *The Interpretation of Dreams.* Hallucinatory wish-fulfilment is at the heart of the dialectic between symbolic assimilation and the creation of symbols.

The Freudian "fiction" provides a model of mental functioning that nonetheless has its place within history, both that of ontogenesis and that of phylogenesis. In *An Outline of Psychoanalysis*, Freud (1940) emphasizes the structural dimension of the infant's love for his mother, which goes beyond the mere satisfaction of need owing to the "other agreeable or disagreeable physical sensations" that accompany it; irrespective of whether the infant has been fed by the bottle or at the breast, the mother becomes its "first seducer" and the breast is the symbol of all the auto-erotic sensations and satisfactions conveyed by the oral relationship. As he puts it: "the nourishing breast is the first erotic object": in order to stress the structural element of this love which is the "prototype of all later love-relations", he attributes it to a "phylogenetic foundation" which "has the upper hand over personal accidental experience" (p. 188). But he also insists on the progressive function of the alternation between contact and rupture, from which we can infer an implicit answer to the questions raised before concerning points of transition between the pleasure principle and the reality principle. He notes:

> There is no doubt that, to begin with, the child does not distinguish between the breast and its own body; when the breast has to be separated from the body and shifted to the *'outside'* because the child so often finds it absent, it carries with it as an *'object'* a part of the original narcissistic libidinal cathexis. This first object is later completed into the person of the child's mother....
>
> (p. 188)

Surely this means that undifferentiated cathexis and hallucinatory contact, as well as the "absence" of the breast and separation, are essential moments in the differentiation between the inside and the outside, without it being necessary to attribute a negative or positive value to either of them.

Winnicott (1951) was to make use of this intuition by placing the accent on the field of *illusion* that must be maintained between the mother and her infant so that the experience of disillusionment connected with the object-cathexis is possible and progressive. Far from being a negative factor, the phase of identificatory assimilation and of non-discrimination, provided it has sufficient duration, is precisely what makes acceptance of the object possible; likewise unpleasure and the disruptive dimension of the object are important for the movement towards the search for the "specific action", the initiation of thought-processes and openness to reality. This is even what Bion (1962) emphasized when he spoke of the conjunction between the innate preconception of the breast and the absence of realization that is indispensable for a "proto-thought" to emerge: the bad breast – no-breast (pp. 34–35). Hence, the importance of rhythm in the alternation between contact and separation, between pleasure and unpleasure, a temporal factor that Freud saw as constitutive of primary masochism, which is also linked to primary sadism: the constitution of symbolization is marked by the importance of temporality, as if the alternation between neither too early nor too late regulated the intensity of the drives, whether at the level of the hallucination of satisfaction or at that of the hallucination of the object. Discussion of a few clinical cases should help us to grasp the issues at stake in these processes of symbolization in analysis.

From disillusionment to autistic withdrawal

François or the child of the shadows

François, a three-year-old child, was brought one day to see a psychoanalyst who had no experience of autistic children, but was ready to help a child be born to himself.[1] This little brown-haired boy, with fine features, was stuck to his mother and mute; he did not look at the person speaking to him or seem to hear what was being said to him. When his mother pushed him forwards, separating him from herself, he suddenly became agitated: he started running in all directions and breaking objects without realizing the damage he was causing, and only stopped to contemplate the shadows of things.

Armed with her analytic intuition and her experience with her own children of a young age who were developing normally, this analyst chose two strategies: she marked off an area of play within which the child had to stay and tried to "tame" the child by offering him other things than fascinating shadows. These shadows were clearly autistic shapes as defined by Frances Tustin, and for the child these objects, like his own body, were no more than a two-dimensional surface: magical and soft forms that were a source of delight and auto-sensuality, whose function was to calm the excitation and erase the traces of the "not-me" external world.[2] François seemed to oscillate between excitation without any direction and adhesion to the two-dimensional shapes to which all objects were reduced, including his mother and his analyst.

But he was also attracted by cubes, the only toys that held his attention among all those that his analyst presented to him. Cubes can evoke the autistic objects also described by Tustin, which are essentially hard objects that are also a source of hard sensations and used to mask any not-me awareness (Tustin, 1980).

Paradoxically, it was by means of these cubes that contact was established between the analyst and François, who also refused to have any form of bodily contact. The exchanges between them diversified as soon as the analyst offered the child a sensorial, tactile, olfactory, visual and gustative world that was more varied than the world of shadows in which he took refuge. She got him to sense and name the differences between hot water and cold water, between mild and strong smells, between colours – light and dark – between tastes – sweet and bitter. This appeal to the constitution of a sensorial self as the first step in coming out of the world of shadows prefigured the studies of Tustin on the importance of differentiating and integrating contrasting primary sensations in order to allow for reunion with the object. In the interpretative work, it was a matter of enabling the child to become aware that these basic sensations exist together, in the body and the external world, and that there can be an interaction between them. This discovery came quite late in Tustin's work since, on the basis of her Kleinian training she had initially interpreted the autistic world in terms of projective identification like Melanie Klein, presupposing a world of phantasy and symbols, to which in fact such children do not yet have access.

The analyst continued to tame the child by singing nursery rhymes; she thought that these little songs could foster playful and prelinguistic exchanges as with babies in their first months of life. But this met with no success until the day when, after seven or eight months, the game "Angel, my beautiful angel" marked a turning-point in the psychotherapy. This game consisted in placing the child on the table, opening out her arms to him and singing: "Angel, my beautiful angel, jump into my arms". One day, François finally jumped into her arms, rather roughly, it is true, but accepting a physical contact that had hitherto been avoided. This contact aroused in him the desire to repeat it indefinitely, something the analyst had to stop, thereby introducing an indispensable temporality into the alternation between continuity and discontinuity. This ritual led on to the game of "peek-a-boo, there he is", marking the possibility of taking a certain amount of pleasure in the succession of presence and absence.

The discovery of the object was a source of anxiety for François; he went back and forth between his mother and his analyst, as if he wanted to assure himself that they were both present. But above all he began to play at pulling the toilet chain and would plunge his head into the toilet bowl as if he was following the water that was disappearing. His analyst told him that the water disappeared but came back just as she did, and she stopped the game as soon as he started repeating it interminably. At that time, he would regularly ask the cleaning woman for a glass of water and drink it with his eyes closed. As soon as he became aware of the object, he had to cope with feelings of catastrophic anxiety to do with losing a part of his body when he lost the maternal object: the disappearance of the toilet water referred as much to the separation from the maternal breast as to the loss of faeces, which was equivalent here to the total loss of himself.

It was in this context that echolalia appeared at the very beginning of the first year of treatment, when François would repeat words without referential relevance, for the pleasure of their sounds rather than for their meaning. Now, one day, at his analyst's, when he was looking at a crane through the window, he suddenly pointed to it and uttered the word "crane", which he had already heard his analyst say, as if the word had linked up with the thing for the first time. Clearly, the crane represented his analyst's arm, which was an indication of François' projective possibilities; but if he discovered in this way the meaning of language, which implies accepting the loss of the thing and depressive feelings, we can suppose that he had not yet totally acquired it, since he also had an impulse to jump out of the window into the "arms" of the crane, without taking into account the void separating him from it. The absence of depth showed the difficulty this child had to emerge from a two-dimensional world. When the loss of the object entails the risk of killing the object, it is then that the symbol ceases to represent and becomes a mere substitute: if the word is the "murder of the thing" (Lacan), *how* can we imagine that the thing can be recreated and that language has the power to designate and reveal the world? It was probably owing to this destructiveness that François was ready to jump into the void to join the crane, in an equivalence established between touching and vision that is characteristic of autistic dismantling and the undermining of intermodal correspondences between the senses.[3]

After this discovery of oral language, François was able to take interest in written language in the form of a game of letters his analyst presented him with. On a board on which one can stick coloured magnetic letters, he played with his analyst at identifying the first letter of the word heard: "M for mummy, F for François, G for Guedeney".

Whether it was by naming things directly or by means of the letters referring to them, in both cases, the child learnt to speak about the world thanks to the complicity that existed between him and his analyst when they looked together at a third object in order to refer to it. This is a foundational element of communication that was stressed by Jérôme Bruner (1983, pp. 17, 89) and could very well be an image of the symbolic functioning of analysis: two protagonists who, protected by a setting, avoid collusion and a narcissistic struggle through a common view of a shared history.

For François and his analyst, it is not surprising that in this context of communication the mirror game to which Lacan, following Henri Wallon, accorded an organizing role for the psyche, had a mutative function. After many games in front of the mirror in which the analyst named the parts of the child's body and her own while showing them to him, François succeeded one day in saying "I" while pointing to himself, and in saying the name of his analyst while pointing to her. It was two years after the beginning of his psychotherapy, when the acquisition of the symbolic function was thus confirmed, that François was able to open himself to the full syntactical and semantic richness of language.

"Sensory feeling" and "I think"

The story of François, the child of the shadows, depicts the crucial moments in the stages of a process of symbolization. What can be constructed or reconstructed from the origins of the autistic encapsulation of a child like

François? Can we extrapolate anything from the way the analysis unfolded about the beginnings of psychic life in general? Various answers have been given to these questions about origins without always avoiding psychological realism. Meltzer and Tustin, for example, in the path traced by Bion of an "innate preconception of the breast", assume an aptitude for signification which has been undermined by a "nameless dread" such as is manifested retrospectively in the psychotic depression of the child on emerging from autism.

Tustin, for her part, likens the recourse to autistic objects to symbolic equations as Hanna Segal defined them in connection with equations, in the sense of identity, following the use of projective identification: she proposes the notion of "adhesive equations" as Esther Bick had suggested, a notion that Meltzer took up thereafter (Tustin, 1984). However, speaking about symbolic equations already assumes, surely, a differentiation between inside and outside, between the inside and outside of an object and of the self characteristic of projective identification, which is not operative here in the contiguity between the child's body and the autistic objects. Tustin (1981) speaks of a "flowing-over-at-oneness" (p. 80) prior to projection and identification, which excludes *any* sensation of a separate object.

The confusion of the points of view of innatism and structure leads in effect to assuming from the outset a primitive symbolism which, from the Kleinian perspective, coincides with the idea of the drive that is object-related from the outset. Bion's hypothesis on the innate preconception of the breast has the advantage of showing that hallucinatory wish-fulfilment is constitutive of openness to the perceptual world, contrary to Freud who assumed that first there was an experience of satisfaction, then of hallucinatory satisfaction. But it presupposes an infant who possesses from the outset access to symbolization, a perspective underpinned by the hypothesis of adhesive equations corresponding to symbolic equations and to the description by Bion of a preverbal thinking oriented from the beginning by the constitution of a primitive matrix of ideographs related to the linkage between visual images (Bion, 1957).

In spite of everything, research studies into autistic children teach us that vision does not have a privileged status and stress the importance of the other sensory impressions, in particular touching. The two-dimensionality of the object is related to the undermining of the "consensuality of the breast", corresponding to the integration of primary sensations: three-dimensionality appears here to be linked above all to the possibility of establishing correspondences between visual and tactile impressions, which appears very early on in the infant, during the first weeks of life.

The encapsulation of the shell-type autistic child tends to show that this structuring of sensations depends on the possibility of establishing very early on the rhythm between inertia and constancy, between the tendency towards lowering excitation to the level zero and the tendency to maintain excitation at a constant level. This instinctual rhythm enables the child to constitute a primitive "sensory feeling of himself" correlative with the hallucination of satisfaction, which opens the possibility, subsequently, when the mother is perceived as a whole object (when, therefore, mother/not mother are differentiated) of constituting a capacity to "represent oneself" in which vision, a privileged sense of representation, confirms the depth of the organization of the sensory field and that of the subject and object.

Bion gave a very good definition of this experience inherent to the mother's "capacity for reverie"; it requires the mother not only to satisfy the infant's oral needs, as one is led to believe by the mothers of future autistic children, but also to provide instinctual exchanges which implies free libidinal play: this is what Freud emphasized by evoking the polysensoriality of the maternal breast. The strict experience of biological care, where the protagonists are a good and docile child and a depressed and absent mother, would explain autistic withdrawal, which Diatkine (1985) does not understand as a "nameless dread", but as a simple process of returning to a state of calm and erasing cue behaviours (p. 131).

We could therefore liken Tustin's mechanism of a flowing-over-at-oneness, as a precursor mechanism of projection, with the process of excorporation, as elaborated by Green (1971): the pure ejection of excitation without distinction between inside and outside. Without the mother's gaze directed at her infant, corresponding to the cathexis of her prior to perception, this does not lead to the organization of an instinctual drive rhythm, to the alternation between inertia and constancy, but rather to the *de-animation* of the body and the world. Hence, the only solution is the primacy of masochistic autosensuality in which the alternation between autistic objects and autistic shapes is but a rigid and deadly travesty of the instinctual drive rhythm that opens out onto life and the object. From this point of view, the autistic withdrawal of the infant with a protective shell is the paradigm and image of all psychic functioning that gives priority to perverse auto-sensuality. The non-delusional psychoses show this in particular: blank psychoses (Donnet & Green, 1973) or cold psychoses (Kestemberg, 2001; E. Kestemberg, J. Kestemberg & Decobert, 1972), depending on whether vision or touch is privileged; in both cases, it is a question of excluding the object and, in so doing, of excluding the body in psychic functioning in order to hypercathect the undifferentiated sensuality of the sensorial self. The comparisons that Tustin makes between infantile autism and mental anorexia confirm the similarity of these issues concerning relations with the object.

The devitalization of the subject and the object, narcissistic anaemia, the domination of deadly masochism and auto- or hetero-destructive acting out are all metaphors to express a mode of mental functioning that is organized around the exclusion of the object – and, consequently, of the body – as sources of psychic reality. Psychosomatic disorganizations belong to this register of autistic withdrawal, and psychotic depression could also be likened to essential depression, as an unrepresentable loss which can only lead to the exclusion of the body and of life.

These are converging lines in the way the object is treated which, of course, must not lead us to overlook the differences between infantile psychoses and psychosomatic disorganizations, between psychosis and perversion. But the frequent references to the "preverbal" traumas that have occurred in these cases plead in favour of the interest in highlighting the "autistic" dimension of these instinctual drive situations.

The overcoming of infantile autism has much to teach us about the issues involved. Psychotic anxiety, with its metaphors of the black hole, endless spilling away, falling, and dissolving, confirms the importance of the loss of the object as a loss of a part of the body that no longer has any boundaries, except by finding an interposing "material reality" (Pasche, 1975) to stop the narcissistic haemorrhage: autistic objects and shapes and infantile or adult fetishes have a function of gathering and bringing bits of the body together when the body image is one of a bodily sieve. The fixed nature of recourse to these objects, which, in reality, are *things*, may acquire a symbolic dimension in fetishism, where the fetish is a symbol of the maternal penis, but it is understandable that its symbolic dimension has sometimes been challenged (Fain, 1983) when there is so little polysemic richness and when the impermeability of ego-splitting has a counterpart in the form of the fixed nature of the perverse scenario and of the "perverse" thing. The urgency of closing the body's boundaries through recourse to a "dead thing" can only result in the arrest of the processes of symbolization, leading to the paradox where, to succeed in maintaining psychic life, the only solution is to cut off the path that allows it to be irrigated.

Tustin (1986) makes an important remark when she says that one of the central images of emerging from autism is not the body being contained by its skin, but the body *as a system of pipes* (p. 228); this metaphor suggests the revitalization of the psychic realm by the body, and consequently by the object, in the image of blood circulation, the systems of digestion and defecation. It is the beginning, therefore, of a regulation of the body's orifices, which are no longer simply holes that are reminiscent of the "holes" of the rupture with the object, but reflect the renewal of relations with it. This involves a work of "transformation" of bad experiences, which enables the infant to feel that his body has a living inside, and that its "holes" are means to control what enters and what leaves his body. It is also a constituent experience of anal erotism in that it establishes the dialectic of keeping/losing, thereby offering a truly reciprocal metaphorization of the tummy and the mind in which the body acquires a psychic dimension and the psyche a physical embodiment. Such psychic depth of the body depends on the constitution of a psychic topography and reflects a cathexis both of the control of psychic activity and of sphincter control (pp. 156–157). Herein lies the truth of Bion's metaphor of the introjection of a psychic container as the "digestion" of sensations: the appearance of symbolization can thus be conceived as a reciprocal fecundation of the body and of the mind, which ceases to reproduce dualistic theories of the mind and body.

The importance of a psychic representation of a tummy finds clinical confirmation in the psychotherapy of a child presented by Nora Kurts (1988). The characters in his drawings, which were filiform at the beginning of his therapy, gradually acquired a "body" with volume in the course of the sessions; clearly, this movement was possible insofar as his analyst respected the child's attempts to isolate the object – well-executed drawing, associative silence – and recognized at an opportune moment his depressive "void". The drawing also showed that the acquisition of a body, of a tummy linking the mouth and the anus, had become possible to the extent that the primal scene and the bodies of the parents could be tolerated and portrayed: this movement was reflected in particular by the transition from a drawing with two characters to the utilization of a cartoon in three episodes with three characters.[4]

The acquisition of an animated body appears to be a consequence here of the introjection of a non-intrusive object and, in this sense, anality reflects both the regulation of bodily orifices and the regulation of relations with the object: this differentiation between an inside and an outside implies the possibility of a *delay* in the search for satisfaction, of a counter-cathexis of the hallucinatory "sensory feeling" through the defensive elaboration of unconscious phantasies and the creation of a space of representation. This "encounter" with his body and with the object is portrayed wonderfully by the "drawing of the cross" in the treatment of autistic children; noticed first by Geneviève Haag, Tustin (1981) saw it as the equivalent of a "stage" (pp. 156–157), the very sign of a psychic mutation offering the possibility both of bringing together contrary sensations into a unity without their being mutually destructive and of bringing the subject and object into contact, without necessarily implying a definitive rupture.

This presupposes being able to accept that not every sensation is under the influence of touching, since hallucinatory contact and its continuous present finds in this sensation its privileged figure, and links up with the depth of vision which is also evocative of the internalization of an *invisible* dimension in oneself and in others. The impossibility of accepting maternal castration is related to the danger represented by the invisible dimension of the mother and the threat of dissolving reincorporation.

It is this correspondence and this reciprocal articulation between the tactile and the visual, between the hand and the eye, that permits spontaneous graphic activity in drawing: the drawing of the cross confirms what Serge Tisseron (1987) has shown concerning the importance of the hand drawing as a bridge between gesture and speech, between gesture and thought (p. 33). The autistic child often cannot draw: when François, for example, took up his pencils, he contented himself with tearing up the blank sheet of paper and breaking the pencil leads. To draw one has to be able to hold back the uncontrolled motor discharge, immediate destructive satisfaction, and tolerate the deployment of the gesture in time and space.

The reflexivity of the touching-touched hand which Merleau-Ponty (1960), after Husserl, drew attention to in order to mark the openness of intersubjectivity, confirms here the importance of this bodily articulation: the touching-touched hand belongs to the movement in which the hand touched the *mouth* to constitute auto-erotism, a precondition that is essential to ensure that vision does not refer to a terrorizing infiniteness but is linked with touching. Descriptions have often been made of good autistic children who are content with looking at their hands, as well as infants who hypercathect the gaze when the object has not sufficiently facilitated the erotism of touching.[5]

This issue was brought to the fore by an adolescent in psychodrama. Following an operation at the age of fifteen months for a congenital malformation, his hands were attached for three months, leading him to withdraw into an autistic position from which he was only able to emerge by splitting vision and touching. He made us play out repetitively more or less the same scene for years on end: one student was observed by other students, which at the same time showed his difficulties in phantasying – the scene reproduced in an almost identical manner the situation of the psychodrama – and his recourse to an omnipotent position in the gaze that observes and is observed.[6]

It is this integration of the body that Paulette Letarte (1990) described so well in the psychotherapy of an adult autistic patient by showing the importance of a contradictory dual movement in the therapeutic strategy of the analyst: a movement of *rapprochement* in which "the words of the body are represented, sensations are named and feelings expressed"; and a movement of *distancing* in which "putting things into words, the reference to a third figure, the evocation of another period in the therapy and the allusion to another place created an obstacle to the rapprochement" (p. 223). Openness to symbolization depends essentially on this process of transformation from sensation to affect and representation. From a technical point of view, the author emphasizes the "structuring role" of "perhaps" in the interpretative work, which takes into account the respective limits of the patient and the analyst (p. 223).

This situation shows clearly that variations of technique in relation to standard analysis can be judged in terms of whether there is a possibility of integrating the different sensations or not: face-to-face therapy becomes necessary when the erotism of looking has to make up for the eroticism of touching and, conversely, analysis is indicated when the registration of the erotism of touching – hand/mouth, breast/mouth – allows for a certain freedom compared with the erotism of looking, to the extent that the invisible part does not necessarily result in terror of unbounded infiniteness. The capacities for psychic work can therefore be measured by the more or less important need to refer to an invisible material: language becomes the privileged tool, without the constraint of the act, as in psychodrama, or of looking, as in face-to-face psychotherapy, from the moment the third party no longer needs to be materialized to confirm the existence of boundaries and differences.

This is what the wooden-reel game, a prototypical game if ever there was one for signifying access to symbolization, shows; not because it is an organizing moment as such, but rather because it depicts the factors involved in this process. Emphasis has often been placed on the importance of the substitution of the act and speech in the search for immediate satisfaction: Freud (1920) insists on this point when he says that the game "was related to the child's great cultural achievement – the instinctual renunciation which he had made (that is, renunciation of instinctual satisfaction) in allowing his mother to go away without protesting" (p. 15). He was thus underlining the link between the processes of symbolization and the inhibition of the instinctual drive aim that is connoted by the concept of sublimation, thereby rediscovering continuity between symbolization and sublimation.

But it is noted less often that Freud added, in connection with this child, that at the time, he played at making himself disappear and return (p. 15) in the mirror and that, not long after, he recounted a dream related to the separation from his father (Freud, 1900, p. 461) All these elements attest to the constitution of the dimension of the *invisible* which is essential to the functioning of psychic life, since the intelligible, thought and words, cannot be touched by the hand; it is even on this condition that they acquire flesh. While the dream image, as an emblem of the thing-presentation, can evoke the possibility of immediate contact, it is only possible on account of the rupture with perceptual material. Distance is always already there at the very moment it wants to be suppressed, and this is what makes possible the dimension of representation and the appearance of the image.

The wooden-reel game, which reflects the existence of the "I", a subjectivity that the autistic child is unable to constitute, just as he is unable to constitute that of others, appeared in the child observed by Freud when he was eighteen months old. This is a pivotal period between the precipitation of a form of the "I" from six months onwards and the possibility of saying "I" around the age of thirty months, which confirms the constitution of a more coherent body image (p. 206). Lacan (1949) has shown the importance, in the mirror game, of being able to differentiate between a fragmented image and a unified image of the body, between the image and the reality of the body. This can be seen, it is true, as the starting-point of the narcissistic lures of the imaginary, but it is interesting to note that this "phase" indicates the possibility of organizing hallucinatory wish-fulfilment as a hallucination of the object, owing to an identificatory process that permits renunciation of immediate contact with the body and with the object. This confirms that the body image is not a consequence of the psycho-physiological functional schema but arises from a dual dialectic between hallucinatory cathexis and perception, as well as between the subject and the object (Angelergues, 1975).

Language and transitionality

But, at the same time, eighteen months is the age corresponding to the peak of transitional language, of the use of words as the equivalent of transitional objects. It corresponds to an important moment in the acquisition of language, since it is situated between the acquisition of one-word expression and two-word expression, constitutive of the very basis of syntax (Weich, 1978) and of the development of the organization of language around two intersecting axes: syntagmatic and paradigmatic. Research studies in psycholinguistics have shown that one-word expression is used to indicate a present object, while two-word expression refers to an absent object and implies the elaboration of the loss of the object.[7] Similarly, Pierre Luquet (1988) has shown that the holophrase, or one-word expression, was first centred on the object from which satisfaction is expected. This is evidenced, moreover, by the word "crane" uttered initially by François; then, later, the verb was added to the object to refer to the movement of the fantasy, and it was only subsequently that the subject of the action found its place in the enunciation and that the "I" appeared (pp. 282–283). This is what is demonstrated by François's acquisition of language in the mirror game, which is only possible on the condition that subject and object have been differentiated: the difference between the "I" and the "You" allows therefore for the reference to an "It" denoting triangulation, which is precisely what favours the emergence of language. This is an essentially an economic process, which shows that language is less a point of departure than a point of arrival, whereas its function of communication could lead us to believe that it is a constitutive principle.[8]

This origin of linguistic symbolization is part of a gestural symbolization that precedes it and accompanies it subsequently. Transitional language participates in this "intermediate area of experience" which favours the appearance of transitional phenomena and objects during the first year of life. We are in a phenomenological and behavioural register, where cognitive activity and instinctual drive activity stand in a mutual relationship to each other. Current research into early interactions have highlighted facts and experiences confirming the existence of "proto-representations" (Pinol-Douriez, 1984, p. 63) organizing the rhythm of cathexes between the mother and her child.

From this point of view, the dimension of semantics tends to be prioritized in the effort to measure the "gap" between symbolic assimilation and true symbolization. This is why the transitional object is defined as a "proto-symbol"[9] in that it is more a *substitute* than a *representation* of the maternal breast and contributes to this assimilatory and projective activity of the psyche. But the multiple controversies on this subject concerned with differentiating it from the infantile fetish show that this semantic perspective is in the end not essential. Winnicott did not accord a predominant place to this question, giving priority rather to the syntactic dimension of transitionality, its *function* in the constitution of the mind. This is what he did when, in order to differentiate the fetish from the transitional object, both of which refer to the breast and the maternal penis, he spoke of *hallucination* in one case and *illusion* in the other (Winnicott, 1951, p.11).

The transitional object is thus only the witness and instrument of a process of symbolization related to the creation of a "third world" between the internal world and the external world. The intermediate area of experience and the potential space of play denote here the crucible or the matrix of all symbolization, in the fusion of the ego and not-ego which permits their differentiation. As the first ego/not-ego possession, unlike autistic and fetishistic objects which aim, on the contrary, to deny what is not-ego, the transitional object is the sign of a psychic mutation favouring assimilation and fusion over the premature differentiation between what is internal and external: as it is an internal choice based on an external reality, it allows for the later representation of reality.

If it thus has a function as a witness and initiator, the transitional object also refers to "transitional processes" (Rose, 1978) which go well beyond the observation of a form of behaviour; for, as Winnicott points out, its fate is neither to be forgotten nor to be the object of mourning, but rather to be abandoned, after having facilitated a psychic movement organizing the area of play and culture. Although it always reveals the necessity of a "material reality" between the child and his mother, it lets itself be forgotten before being taken up again by this intermediate intrapsychic area, the preconscious, also a *third* area, whose function is essentially one of protection through the counter-cathexis and junction between what is internal and what is external.

It is no coincidence if the analytic treatment has found in this metaphor of the "intermediate area of experience" an adequate representation of its mode of functioning: if the recourse to material symbols – money, for example (Gibeault, 1986) – has seemed indispensable, the reference to transitionality makes it possible to imagine a mode of psychic functioning that no longer needs this sensible material, owing to the internalization of a process of linking which defines symbolization.

From illusion to disillusion

It is this "intermediate area of experience" which fails to establish itself in psychosis and obliges the subject to resort to autistic manoeuvres or delusional constructions. This system of mutual impingement between psychic reality and material reality calls for protective measures; in the non-delusional psychoses by excluding the object and the body and resorting to erotogenic masochistic practices, and in delusional psychoses, by including the object and the body, and the possibility of a projective efflorescence. The analyses of two patients, Charles and Raphaël, presenting a psychotic mode of functioning, will help to portray the role of delusion in the processes of symbolization. It will be seen here how adolescence is a pivotal period in the choice of the different psychotic solutions.

Charles or the hypochondriacal body

Charles was referred to me by a psychiatric colleague for psychotherapy after a suicide attempt using pills. He was a forty-seven-year-old man who looked at least fifteen years older than that, because he wore a beard and his hair was completely white. He had been prey to intense anxiety ever since his wife had died of cancer a few years earlier. He was convinced that he had cancer too and had sought reassurance from doctors concerning the integrity of his body.

A love affair with a woman, whom he had met little more than a year after the death of his wife, plunged him into an intense state of excitement and anxiety. He spoke of sexual satisfactions that he had never had with his wife; but his anxiety welled up when in connection with this woman friend, he thought of his mother who, like her, was a "pulsating woman". This friend had become unbearable for him as soon as she took an active position in their sexual relations. According to him, she had become "lesbian" because she had cut her hair and wore trousers. It was to escape the anxiety of being dispossessed of himself, aroused by this passivity, that he had made a suicide attempt. Frightened by this, his friend had left him.

During the first consultation, Charles was very mistrustful, but his grievance was lively and immediate: *What I am feeling is infernal. I feel as if I am in the final stage, as if I was going to go completely mad. I can no longer think or react.* This madness of hypochondriacal anxiety which was at risk of overwhelming the ego shows the importance of the body which, according to Tausk (1919), is the first projection of an outside (pp. 541–542): The example of Charles shows that the painful body is a mark of progress in comparison with the de-animated body of autism, insofar as it reflects a representation of it and is thus on the boundary between a paranoiac solution and a melancholic solution.

It is nonetheless a split representation since, at the very moment when the instinctual body could be introjected, it is rejected: according to the classical definition of rejection "what was abolished internally, returns from without" (Freud, 1911, p. 71), which Lacan reformulated in less topographical terms as "what is not symbolized reappears in the real" (Lacan, 1981, p. 86).

These formulations are aimed at defining psychotic projection, the hallucinatory return of what has been rejected, which confirms the hypochondriac's belief that he is suffering from a torturing, and often mortal, illness. Whether the hypothesis of a specific mechanism of psychosis is one of the denial and rejection of maternal castration or one of the foreclosure of the Name-of-the-Father, it aims to recognize an ego-organization that is distinct from that which exists in neurosis – namely, the splitting of the ego, involving the coexistence and juxtaposition of two contrary psychic tendencies, the aim of which is not so much to render a representation of reality unavailable as the history of internal objects. Thus, the searing pains that Charles told me about indefinitely were reified evidence of a history and secret that he nonetheless tried to rediscover in the course of his psychotherapy.

It was first the history of a homosexual cathexis of his father which, as in the case of the "Wolf Man", was reflected by the frantic search for a doctor who would be "the good Lord" capable of giving him a "new skin" again. The first representation of ego-splitting showed a splitting of the object between an idealized paternal object and a persecuting maternal object. I immediately appeared to him to be the saviour who was more the object of a massive cathexis than a differentiated transference, and who, as he said, *kept his ahead above water* and protected him from women *with hard faces*. With this expression, he was evoking a childhood memory in which his mother, a very good swimmer, wanted to teach him to swim in the sea by pushing his head underwater, making him feel terribly afraid. His father had "saved" him by taking him to a swimming pool for lessons with an instructor.

Sheltered by this idealized transference cathexis, Charles set about doing "research" into his psychic productions that were matched only by his hypochondriacal concerns. He brought several dreams that he thought were absurd and signs of madness: they were always premonitory dreams that generally confirmed how dangerous he was, in accordance with the thought-contact described by Freud in connection with magical thinking and the omnipotence of thoughts. The absence of a gap between psychic reality and material reality, which were thus in "direct contact" (Racamier, 1987), was a mark of disorders of symbolization in Charles insofar as the representations between thoughts led him to believe there was a relation between the things themselves.

The unpredictable nature of the dreams required immediate decoding using a key to dreams that he found in books, which was reminiscent of his research in medical textbooks to find confirmation of his hypochondriacal presuppositions and self-observations. This "paranoiac" interpretation of the world gave a systematic and unambiguous meaning, and preserved him from any surprise and uncertainty: it was a world of delusional *conviction* rather than *belief* in the world. By seeking to protect him from the slightest unforeseeable irruption of the object, it aimed to include the object totally.

Charles did not, however, develop a systematic delusion: hence the possibilities of "playing" in connection with the understanding of dreams rather than using a pre-established code: he made references to the situation he was experiencing with me, revealing a split-off history, impossible to rediscover in memories. *I have no memories of my childhood*, he repeated with regret, just as he regretted at certain moments having forgotten parts of his dreams that would have given him the "key" to his anxieties.

One of his dreams, related at the beginning of his analysis, was a constant reference: *I had a glass of beer in my hand; I was with you and blowing on the foam.* I said: *Mind out, the foam stains.* In other words, mind my moustache (he had a beard), with which erotic contact is a source of danger; beware too of anal and urethral contamination, because the glass of beer made him think of a glass full of urine, which risked making me ill. It was a warning against the homosexual danger that I represented: while the homosexual cathexis enabled him to make a spectacular "recovery" at the beginning of his psychotherapy, the fear of contaminating and of being contaminated soon came into the foreground and characterized the lateralization – or rather even the juxtaposition – of the transference cathexis onto a number of different doctors.

Like the "Wolf Man", Charles went to see a series of general practitioners and specialists to find a treatment for what he called his "dysentery", the origin of which he initially attributed to his father's alleged condition of syphilis, then, later, to parasitosis, after reading a journal article by a certain Dr X., which talked about the relations between dysentery and amoebiasis characteristic of colonial wars.

Charles had indeed taken part in one of these wars during his military service, and he attributed his physical ailments to the contamination of water-points by the Arabs: his "dysentery" had lasted almost thirty years but, since his wife's death, it had become a central theme in his hypochondriacal grievances. All examinations were highly sexualized, in particular that of his colon by a certain Dr Y.: *He blew air into my colon to the point of causing me a hernia.* The examination situation by Dr. Y. reproduced, in fact, his expectation of me, since he often repeated to me: *You are there to blow air into the ball and to help me feel well in my skin.* In other words, his hypochondriacal grievances reminded Charles of his passive desires towards his father, and of the ideas of persecution linked to the struggle against passivity and to his identification with women. The expression of self-mutilating fantasies – *I sometimes want to tear off these organs that torture me* – found an outlet in a "delusion of being harmed" by doctors who had not treated him properly, and whom he couldn't stop thinking about: hence the progressive significance of the transition from projecting into his own body to projecting into the object.

However, to overcome the persecutory situation, it was important to show him that this wish to be in a feminine position and the fact that I spoke about it with him did not mean, however, that he *was* a woman, just as the fear of having a serious illness did not mean that he *was* really ill. The equation between fantasy and reality necessitated this detour via the analysis of his way of thinking which contributed, in part, to his hypochondriacal anxiety. The interpretative work helped him to gain access to the dimension of "as if", instead of remaining in that of "it is", which amounted to taking "his wishes for realities" literally in order to avoid infantile distress and omnipotence. This work enabled him to speak about memories related to this fear of being considered a woman, which he often formulated as one of being taken for a homosexual. His wife had told him one day not to cross his legs when he was in the metro, because that was what homosexuals did. He also recalled that as a child, when he was walking with his mother, someone had said, pointing to him: "How is the little girl?"

Here, Charles' "paranoia" reflected the role of castration anxiety in hypochondria and the displacement of genital impulses into the body or the bodily organs. His pains ranged from headaches to stomach aches, including back pain – arthritis, a painful sigmoid colon, throbbing anal herpes, which led him to engage in frantic and unbearable anal masturbation and to have an inflamed penis and prostate as well as a hernia. Charles had a string of organs in a state of continual excitation, attesting to his state of sexual over-excitation – the slightest erotic or violent image seen on television faced him with a traumatic breach.

In fact, these genital and anal anxieties were directly linked to oral persecutory anxieties, which are the other aspect of the history of the split internal object in the hypochondriacal symptom. Charles' decompensation can be traced back to two circumstances: his economic redundancy – he was working in a delicatessen – at a time when his wife was still alive; and then her illness and death. One day, he said: *When I saw my wife ill, I wanted to swallow her illness so that she would recover.* He reproached himself for having given the doctors the "green light" in the terminal stage of her illness and, after her death, he was convinced that he had cancer, until a doctor was able to reassure him momentarily.

A dream indicated this pathological introjection revealing the melancholic dimension of his hypochondria: *My wife returned and she was in good health; I had cancer and I vomited three fish.* The three fish were three cancers (bladder, prostate, colon) and referred to what Dr Y. had said to him ironically when Charles complained of having cancer: *You have three big ones.* Three big cancers like his mother's three big babies, with whom Charles identified in the expression of a fantasy of procreation.

Concerning his pains, he said, one day: *I've got a crab eating up my belly,* which certainly referred to cancer (the crab), but above all to the incorporated sadistic object whose reprisals he feared. This fear of being devoured by an inhabitant of his own body was also one of being destroyed by the "shadow of the object that falls upon the ego", by the sadistic attacks of the superego on the ego already modified by the incorporation of the sadistic wife-mother. Evidence of this movement could be seen in Charles' extreme difficulty and reticence in attacking his wife in the sessions – "I cannot make reproaches to someone who is dead or criticize them for fear of their reprisals". And yet, all he could remember of her was her cancer; the same was true of his mother of whom he had no good memories, and who had died, like his father, a long time ago.

But this crab was also Charles' greed and sadistic envy, which had recently found expression in another dream: *I dreamt of three crows that were eating rotten meat.* Intrigued by these three crows, he consulted his dream book and found in it, like a Jungian analyst searching for mythical correspondences, the reference to the crows of Wotan, which, according to him, in Germanic mythology, were messengers of death. But, on my encouragement, he also thought about young Arabs who envy old people and want to take everything from them, rather like those vultures that wait until their prey are dead in order to devour them all the better. Charles lived in fear of having his pension taken away from him by Social Security, of having his apartment taken away from him, which was certainly related to the phallic rivalry of young people towards old people, but also and primarily to anal-sadistic envy projected on to the crows-babies (the three children of his family). In this sense, the fear of going mad could be attributed to the danger of being breached by generalized genital excitation, and to the fear of being submerged by envious and sadistic impulses.

The reproach made to doctors and to the analyst of having a secret – *You know what I've got, but you won't tell me, you are evasive* – could correspond to the phantasy of a good breast refused sadistically. Charles' brother had told him that when he was a baby he had cried non-stop and that he (the brother) had had the task of rocking him. He often said that he had been born at a bad moment; he was not eagerly awaited, his father had suffered a reverse of fortunes and Hitler had just come to power (p. 217). Hence, the phantasy of having been an unwanted baby and his memory of a mother with a "hard face" who, whenever she went out, "locked him up" in the house, similar to the fear that Dr R., the psychiatrist who was treating him, would confine him to a psychiatric hospital or would turn him over to a substitute, his brother or father – or his analyst. This non-recognition by his mother was related to the non-recognition by the son, to the *disavowal* of alterity, which defines in fact the rejection (*Verwerfung*) characteristic of psychosis.

Charles' hypochondria could thus be related to the inability to obtain real oral satisfactions, which might then, according to Rosenfeld (1965, p. 199) extend to the genital sphere. Since his woman friend had left him, he had not had any sexual relations, and he had no difficulty in finding a doctor to tell him that with his herpes he should abstain. Moreover, these warnings echoed with earlier recommendations. In the army, his commanding officer had told him: *Beware of women, they will be your downfall.* During his adolescence, his mother told him repeatedly: *If you continue to run after girls, you will go crazy.* What relationship can be surmised between the absence of genital satisfactions, except masturbatory ones, and hypochondria? The connection with actual neuroses is surely insufficient: the recent elaboration of envy and oral persecution split-off and projected into the body had allowed him in effect to rediscover a more positive relationship towards women.

Hypochondria raises the problem of the mutual relations between masochism and projection in primary distress. While the affected organ may represent the penis or the child, but also the faeces or the breast, it is not these symbolic contents that are significant; for, in fact, the oral, anal, and genital impulses are intertwined and do not refer to a genital organization. Rather, it is the register of the non-differentiation of imagos that is dominant, even after a few years of psychotherapy, and even if an economic modification has been achieved in the sense of a fetishistic relationship to the object described by Kestemberg (1978) as the projection of an ambisexual imago guaranteeing narcissistic continuity. This would be a solution for the economy of this hypochondriacal state, on the boundary between the masochistic erotization of primary distress, to which the melancholic solution is linked, and projective reconstruction, to which ties with the paranoiac object are linked. Though Charles often continued to complain about his pains at the beginning of a session, almost in a ritual and exorcistic way, he had nonetheless understood that if the link with the object was experienced in a less persecutory way, it could modify his relationship to his body. He had learnt not to be the object but the *subject* of his pains, and told me, one day: *I notice that I no longer have any pains when I am with people with whom I feel well.*

This was probably the reason why Charles was now able give himself more room to think about and imagine other satisfactions than those of living with his torments in order to preserve his dead relations, which is the only way to face an experience of grief that cannot be mourned. From this point of view, drawing support in analysis from a fetishistic relation to the object enabled him to enlarge the zone free of torments in comparison with the zone of torments – his "masochism", as he said himself, which, before his psychotherapy, had led him, when faced with the difficulty of organizing a delusion, to prefer suicide in order to triumph over death.

Thus, Charles' delusional potentialities developed minimally in the analysis through hypochondriacal experience which, from the body, was displaced on to the persecuting cathexis of doctors and the analyst, allowing him to rediscover a past and to give himself a history. It was, of course, atypical hypochondria and limited in its scope, unlike that of Schreber, for example, whose cosmogonic vision organized around the phantasy of procreation and self-procreation may be understood as a vast hypochondriacal delusion based on bodily hallucinations.[10] The delusional organization does not de-animate the object, but rather humanizes it in a sort of avalanche of hallucinatory satisfaction: this is what led Angelergues (1981) to say that hallucination in the psychiatric sense appears where hallucination in the psychoanalytic sense ceases.

The importance, in delusion, of fantasies of self-procreation can be understood as a deficiency, as it were, of the process of self-procreation related to hallucinatory satisfaction: delusion emerges when illusion has not been articulated with disillusionment. But the treatment of the object and its perceptual qualities authorizes the process of symbolization inherent to every delusional organization – symbolization that is nonetheless excessive, which led Bion (1970, p. 68) to say that it was private and prematurely saturated, residing essentially in an exacerbated symbolic equation. Such an illumination of the world, under the regime of contiguity, finds the identical in everything; Freud (1900), moreover, had noted such symbolic lucidity in connection with the interpretative capacities of schizophrenics who "have shown a direct understanding of dream-symbolism of this kind to a surprising extent" (p. 351). Charles had shown the fascination and powers of mastery of such a univocal reading of contents by resorting to the interpretations of the keys to dreams; but this attitude illustrated difficulties in organizing a real process of symbolization, which must leave room for what is possible and uncertain.

Symbolization has its place within a work of negation, one of the modalities of which is rejection-foreclosure. The very possibility of projection is part of this aptitude to say "no", and thus to constitute what André Green (1982) defined as a double boundary ("double limite"), between the inside and the outside and between the unconscious and the preconscious-conscious. If, in the autistic register, the preconscious is uninhabited, on the contrary, it is "hyperdense" (Racamier, 1987, p. 35) in delusions, ready to explode into imaginary efflorescence precisely on account of economic factors. Moreover, it is the economy of the narcissistic and object-related cathexes that needs to be taken into account, it seems to me, in evaluating the relations between neurosis and psychosis: this leads to conceiving mental functioning not primarily in terms of topography and contents, but chiefly in terms of the economy of negation. This is sometimes established in the mode of rejection and desire, which represents a repression of the repressing ego, and is sometimes open to repression and to the operations of negation. This is a situation in which economic differences lead to structural differences, which implies conceiving the forms of the symbol in terms of the function of symbolization, and not the contrary. The theory of the psychic mechanisms of rejection and/or repression may insist sometimes on oppositions and sometimes on similarities, depending on whether the emphasis is placed on a topographical or economic theory of castration.[11]

Adolescence and action

This dimension of the economy is essential for understanding the "intermediate" period between childhood and adulthood in adolescence. It is the time when delusional ideas may emerge from the narcissistic fragility induced by pubertal maturation and the erosion of parental idealization. Action takes precedence, since incestuous phantasies may find some realization and choices must soon be made in love and professional life. Evaluating action in relation to acting out requires considering the psychic economy rather than the act's manifest content. Some actions may be viewed as enactments that open the way to symbolization within the analytic relationship. In the analytic situation, some actions may be understood as enactments leading to symbolization.

This is what, in other terms, Winnicott highlighted with reference to the dimension of play. Play requires a potential space to be created between hallucination and perception which determines the opening of the field of symbolization with regard not only to its inventive but also its creative possibilities. I am referring here to play not in the sense of a game, which is determined by rules and limits the possibilities of illusion, but in the sense in which it is free of rules and gratuitous, for the sole pleasure of mental functioning. The child's play fosters the field of illusion in that it is based on a projective incarnation in which the characters are not living their own lives. Adolescence represents a disruption of this equilibrium, owing to the new risks of genital realization which make it necessary to take into account the desires of the "characters" (Angelergues, 1987, pp. 15–16).

This being so, there are two possibilities for the adolescent: either that of becoming an adult straight away, giving priority to action which is not far from coinciding with acting out insofar as it blocks out the possibility of illusion and resorts to the fascinations of the ideal of the narcissistic ego; or, on the contrary that of deferring for as long as possible the requirements for becoming an adult, which can be seen in the gloominess of those adolescents who are unable to go through a crisis of adolescence owing to a lack of projects and action. Whether the adolescent seeks to deny his distress by exaggerating his independence in relation to the pregenital imago or whether he abandons himself to it,[12] in both cases, there is a great risk of no longer being able to cope with the demands for reorganization specific to this period of life. The adolescent must be able to rely on the resources of the superego, a third agency, which permits the interplay of illusion/disillusion and the maintenance of a living conflictuality. Genital maturation leads, more than at any other period, to fascination for the search for immediate satisfaction and acting out which compromise the possibilities of a work of symbolization. The economic value of the *Weltanschauung* (Gibeault, 1990) that is elaborated in adolescence can serve here as a criterion of evaluation and approach: although these views of the world are very often organized around the law of all or nothing, they are nevertheless a progressive factor in openness to the domain of possible choices, interests and achievements. The relation between representation and action may vary from one adolescent to another; it is not a matter of opposing them but of evaluating the possible interplay between them depending on the narcissistic or object prevalence: the *Weltanschauung* may signify the confinement of representations within a system that is governed by the ideal of the narcissistic ego; or it may evoke reunions with object-related cathexes and foster the appearance of sublimatory and creative activities.

Acting out is therefore characteristic of a process of desymbolization, since its aim is to short-circuit the work of representation, and has thus been compared with the symbolic equation (Anastasopoulos, 1988): there is a risk of calling into question the acquisitions of the latency period. But, at the same time, the narcissistic regression characteristic of this period leads us to consider acting out as having a progressive anti-depressive and elaborative function: it can serve as a compromise between omnipotent phantasies and a temporarily weakened ego, and appear to be the only way of integrating the past with the present.

The example of Étienne (Gibeault, 1988), an adolescent who, at the age of fifteen, got involved in a homosexual relationship and drug addiction, is telling here. Although his various forms of acting out were the only way of coping with his father's bankruptcy, at the risk of leading to his own downfall, they had a function of communication within the analysis and of expressing the issues to which they were related in phantasy: the minimum level of conflictuality maintained by moral masochism in the face of the deadly fascinations of erotogenic masochism made it possible to link up his perverse forms of acting out with phantasies of being beaten by his father. Consequently, his acting out was transformed into an action governed by reunions with the post-oedipal superego and, in particular, allowed Étienne to rediscover pleasure in the functioning of thought.

It is therefore not surprising that, during a period of life when action is a major issue, it is appropriate, for some adolescents, to adopt variations of the technique, like psychodrama, where the gesture is a means of representation that makes up for difficulties in elaborating phantasy. From this perspective, the need for "intermediate" materials may appear to be a requirement which diminishes from childhood to adulthood and from psychotic functioning to neurotic functioning: if play is prevalent in childhood, action in adolescence and adulthood is defined by the prevalent use of language. But these are aspects related to the means used by the symbolic function and must not lead us to overlook, as Winnicott pointed out, that play is just as apparent in adult analyses as in work with children. It has its place in the very acquisition of language and we can find it in the different ways adult patients use language during their analysis, whether it is "in the choice of words, in the inflections of the voice and indeed in the sense of humour" (Winnicott, 1971, p. 40). These are all indirect indicators of the quality of symbolization that can serve as references for the representative dimension of affects in analysis.

The dimension of play is also inherent to the utilization of the gesture in individual analytic work and partakes of what Marie-Lise Roux has described as the "compulsion to represent". In the psychotherapy of a schizophrenic adolescent girl, she was thus led to make a gesture conveying representations that made it possible to transform the self-destructive acts of her patient. While the latter was wearing herself out by touching herself, hitting things and hitting herself hard, she had cried out: "I am the shadow of my mother". As the sun was shining brightly in the room, Marie-Lise Roux raised her hand to show her the shadow on the wall and asked her: "Like that?" –"Yes" – "So I asked her, 'Who is making the shadow?'" Delighted, the patient cried out: *Ah, so the sun, the sun, is my father?* (Roux, 1994, pp. 34–35). From that moment on, the patient calmed down and began to cathect play with images and words which made it possible to link the sensations and affects that had overwhelmed her in an experience of confusion with the maternal imago. Intuitively, the analyst had rediscovered the movement that had led *Homo sapiens* to leave the trace of absence on the walls of decorated caves: a negative hand that showed the capacity acquired in the history of humanity to leave a representation of the body in its absence.

Raphaël or the mediating function of the image in individual psychoanalytic psychodrama

One form of psychotherapy, individual psychoanalytic psychodrama, introduces a variation of the setting and technique based on play. The paradox of psychoanalytic psychodrama consists in prescribing systematically, in the form of play, what is otherwise considered an impediment to the development of the analytic process, in particular the lateralization of the transference and acting, motor or verbal. It is true that taking up the patient's conflicts in a playful form avoids the resistance characteristic of these defences which are in the order of action as such, making them a preferred means of working-through for patients who are unable to tolerate a transference relationship organized around one analyst alone. If the motor of the process, the transference, and its purpose, are those of classical analysis, in psychodrama, the differences reside in fact in the setting.

Analytic psychodrama, as it was theorized in the 1950s by Serge Lebovici (Lebovici, Diatkine & Kestemberg, 1969–1970), René Diatkine and Évelyne and Jean Kestemberg (Kestemberg & Jeammet, 1987), and more recently by Jean Gillibert (1985) and Philippe Jeammet (Jeammet & Kestemberg, 1981), provides in effect the economic and topographical conditions that allow interpretation to be heard without intrusion – and, as a result, to be introjected. Such psychodrama is centred around one patient only, with a group of therapists including the group leader who has the interpretative role, and the co-therapists, who are at least four in number, made up of members of both sexes, and who are potential players. The session is weekly and lasts approximately half an hour.

The specific setting of individual analytic psychodrama is designed for patients, adults or children, who in general present major phenomena of excitation or inhibition, often characteristics of psychotic functioning or of a phase of significant reorganization, such as the immediate period of pre-adolescence or adolescence. The diversity between the group leader and the different members of the team makes it possible to fragment a massive transference cathexis and thereby to lighten the economic weight of this excitation: interpreting alternately in and outside the role-playing leads in the best of cases to a concentration of the displaced and ambivalent transference on to the person of the group leader, and, at that moment, it can be handled like an analytic treatment with a single analyst.

In reality, the interpretative tactic aims less to analyse the transference systematically than to foster a work of representation based on the phantasies arising in the role-playing and corresponding to the establishment of formal and topographical regression. The fragmentation of the transference cathexis on to all the psychodramatists thus allows for the organization of the analytic process, and it is only later on, thanks to the temporal regression thus made possible, that it may become possible to interpret the transference on to the group leader.

This theoretical and technical perspective differs from the Kleinian approach. Évelyne Kestemberg (1957) noted:

> It seems to me ... that we must avoid as far as possible the onset of a transference psychosis and seek to bring about a neurotization of psychotic transference manifestations. This progressive neurotization alone will enable us to rediscover with psychotic patients the margin between phantasy and reality which, as Nacht said, is the one on which we can work.
>
> (p. 45)

And she added:

> In effect, if we substitute the psychotic state with a transference psychosis, the latter is a delusional construction, whose defensive character we can no longer show efficiently, since the analyst is an integral part of this construction and constitutes the reality, devoured and devouring, against which the patient is struggling and that prevents him from engaging in any autonomous action other than this type of defence whose extreme point is autism or suicide.
>
> (p. 45)

These differences between the French and English approaches do not mean we should confine ourselves within an irreducible opposition. They both aim to bring about a lasting psychic change in the psychotic states, but using different technical modalities with regard to the setting and the interpretative modalities.

These different theoretical and clinical approaches can find common ground provided the interpretation of projective identification is not understood as the mere verbalization of the mechanism of projection. This is what Danielle Quinodoz (2003, p. 115) notes in connection with interpretations that function in the mode: "You are unconsciously making me feel that..." (p. 112), which cannot fail to induce a persecutory reaction. It is interesting to note that it is often like this that the interpretation of projective identification is presented. Claude Janin (1990, pp. 157–158), for example, presented this type of interpretation comprising "the declaration of sufficient intentionality" which refers to the analyst's omnipotence and thus favours the recourse to a manic defence. Janin prefers a "shared animistic" interpretation using the reference to "I", "You", and "We", and including in its formulation the difference between the protagonists as well as the possibility of an encounter. Now, it is precisely in this way that Quinodoz (2003) understands the interpretation of projective identification, which favours differentiation and recognition between the affective movements of the subject and of the object, on the condition of avoiding "such interpretation... as wild and persecutory, as if the analyst knew better than the patient what the patient was feeling and doing" (p. 112).

Analytic work with patients with a psychotic mode of functioning aims, then, to interpret, in the transference, excess projective identification, and to enable the subject to acquire differentiation from others, thereby guaranteeing a freer and more autonomous mode of psychic functioning. The interpretation of projective identification implies taking into account the bodily dimension of phantasy involved in the projection of parts of the ego, that is to say "symbolic representations of the body bound up with unconscious bodily fantasies" (Quinodoz, 2003, pp. 102), and elaborating the emotional significance of these bodily experiences. The challenge, however, is to know how to interpret projective identification. Danielle Quinodoz (2003), following the contributions of Kleinian colleagues, in particular Leon Grinberg (1979), shows how the use of the countertransference, in its positive dimension described by her as projective counter-identification, enables the analyst to feel the affects involved and to interpret the underlying phantasy. In the case of her patient, Luc, who suffered from vertigo and wanted to stop his analysis, the analyst had really felt that she was not able to carry through the analysis of this patient successfully, which had allowed the patient to show her "his anxiety about being dropped into the void" (p.96).

This understanding of projective identification can even involve dramatizing voices and multiple roles in the mode of psychodramatic role-playing. In analytic work with children, it is often they who propose such dramatizations with adults; it may be useful to employ the same technique for patients who are unsuited to formal and topographical regression and, to use Quinodoz's (2003) expression, to be "the direct spokesperson" for the part of the patient's self projected into the analyst (p. 113). It is a matter therefore of offering them "interpretations in projection", "images" capable of enabling them to integrate their desires and their impulses without being obliged to get rid of them into the object. Quinodoz (2003) gives the example of a patient, Marie, who, identified with an impinging and reproachful mother, attacked the analyst/little girl who was unable to satisfy her; to the reproach expressed by the patient that the analysis was not going quickly enough, the analyst heard herself saying to her, speaking in the first person: *Mummy always wants me to go faster, but I can't go so fast; it's very hard not to be able to go at my own little-girl pace.* And the analyst concluded that this interpretation in this form had allowed her patient to calm down, to recognize herself in the analyst's words and to differentiate herself from her by allowing her to recover the part that she had projected into her (pp. 112–113). Individual psychoanalytic psychodrama develops such an interpretative approach through role-play promoting the recognition of projected sensations, affects and representations, while nevertheless drawing on the difference between the interpretative function of the group leader and that of the psychodramatists.

From self-procreation to the primal scene

The case of Raphaël, a psychotic patient in individual psychoanalytic psychodrama, will serve to illustrate this interpretative tactic.[13] During the first interview, Raphaël said to the consultant: *I have bought a pistol. I tried to kill myself for two days while doing a circuit along the Seine... I don't know why, but I had chosen the bridges... the plan was to shoot myself and then fall into the water... I don't understand what held me back... it was probably because with the pistol, one had to press the trigger very hard and the lapse of time between pointing the gun at myself and pressing the trigger was too long, I think,... when I realized that I would not be able to do it, well, I decided to go to the psychiatric emergency department of Saint Anne's Hospital.*

This suicide attempt led Raphaël, after several months of hospitalization, to have a consultation with Jean Gillibert, the former director of the E. & J. Kestemberg Centre:[14] this presentation left no room for play in both senses of the term, because it was both the image of an immediate realization and of the suspension of time, the "lapse of time" that impeded the murderous act.

In response to these murderous issues, the consultant suggested introducing the dimension of play of psychodrama in order to foster the creation of a psychic space and temporality that make it possible to overcome the recourse to omnipotent denial and ego-splitting. Raphaël's psychotic functioning had, in fact, brought about the failure of a psychoanalytic treatment on the couch for two years, and then face-to-face psychotherapy for a further period of two years: this work had been broken off suddenly by his suicide attempt. The analytic treatment had not made it possible to bind the violence and destructiveness of this patient, which was the only solution to avoid the annihilating threat of non-differentiation from the object, a movement that Green (1986) has described as a "conjuration of the object" (p. 243). To overcome the confusion, the only option remaining was the destruction of the object or of the subject himself.

Raphaël's psychodrama treatment, initially under the direction of Jean Gillibert for two years, and then under my direction for the last eight years, has enabled Raphaël to consider other solutions than destruction. He was in a state of great disarray. He had been made redundant two years before the consultation and could no longer work or seek work; he had "stayed in bed… pretending to be dead" until he decided to opt for the solution of suicide.

He was haunted by a humiliating and shameful paternal history, in which his paternal grandfather and his father were guilty of collaboration with the Germans during the Second World War; stories of war and destruction were the subject of his childhood readings and he felt invaded by images of pulverized bodies, which had as much to do with his fragmentation anxieties as to their mastery through the imaginary repetition of the themes that inhabited him. At the end of adolescence, according to his father's wishes, he became a soldier for five years and felt "confined to barracks" (*encaserné*), to use his expression, referring to the frightening experience of no longer being able to get out once one had joined up, corresponding to the terrifying experience of being engulfed by the object: his psychotic experience corresponded to the vision of *The Exterminating Angel*, the title of the 1962 film by Bunuel, where the guests suddenly find themselves trapped in a house after a dinner party and are unable to leave.

Faced with this confinement by the object, there was no other solution but to flee from the object and to take refuge in decathexis, "letting oneself… fall", as Raphaël said evoking his childhood memory when he was two years old: *My father was on the riverbank (on the banks of the Marne), he was very far away; he was on the left side. My mother was with me on the right side. I advanced into the water. As I was little, I must have lost my footing very quickly, unless I fell into a hole, but what I remember exactly is that I really felt myself… falling. And this lasted a long time. And it was something that was without anxiety, almost even a pleasure.*

This exit from time, this fascination with endless falling in which the primal scene is denied in favour of an experience of eternity and immortality may correspond to a phantasy of death and rebirth of which the subject is the sole master: thus a phantasy of self-procreation corresponding to the recourse to omnipotence as the only solution to avoid incestuous confusion with the mother in the absence of a father who was "very far away". His parents had got divorced when he was thirteen, and his mother had then invited him to share her bed, where, the sight of her naked breasts had made him go momentarily "blind in one eye".

After nine years of psychodrama, one sequence allowed us to see the possibility of emerging from the psychotic solution in which Raphaël had felt confined for so long. He was now fifty-four years old but looked fifteen years younger, as if he had retained a juvenile look close to adolescence. He was dressed in a relatively adult and elegant way, in contrast with his appearance at the beginning of the psychodrama: at the time he was dressed in shapeless tracksuit trousers, with either dishevelled or tightly cropped hair which gave him a lost look; in the image of his formless outer appearance, he was so passive in the scenes that he made one think of an individual without contours and without any interiority. This masochistic submission to the object was however simply the other side of a terrifying phantasy world expressed apparently without affect: with a funny look, he had suggested playing a scene in which his two younger sisters were cut up into pieces and buried in the family garden.

This patient's passive physical presence, without contours, reflected his capitulation to the object, his abandonment to his mother's body and her pleasure. In this case, the scene of the psychodrama offered him the possibility of freeing himself from this domination and this threat of non-differentiation in another way than through destructive violence. Although *passivity* was intolerable owing to this fear of being engulfed, psycho-drama offered, through its technique, the possibility of an *activity* involv-ing play whose themes and roles were prepared by the patient. It thus allowed him to regain an image of his body that had hitherto been marked by gaps, rifts, and fragmentation owing to the deficiencies of the primary maternal cathexis.

More than in individual psychotherapy, where the presence of the body and gestures already sets a limit to anxiety about non-differentiation, psy-chodrama dramatizes the body and therefore makes it possible to go beyond splitting between affects and representations. Psychodrama is based on the representative mimic expression of the body and thereby fosters the transi-tion from the body to speech.

This implies, however, that, in psychodrama, the gesture is always allusive, thereby leaving a gap between the identical and the same, between literal reproduction and its representation: the work of symboliza-tion offered by the psychodrama setting takes place precisely within this distance between the acting out in the order of symbolic equation and the *enactment* which takes place within a difference between the thing and rep-resentation. While touching is possible, it cannot be in the order of covetous and envious erotism, which would strengthen the psychotic anxieties of incorporation, but it must be addressed to another person while respecting his space. The *allusive* gesture that dramatizes the body grounds its sym-bolic aim on the third point of view of the group leader, who thus becomes the guarantor of an objectalizing aim and of the reappropriation of the body and its affects.

Raphaël had found himself in a situation where he was unable to work, and even to look for work, and this had led him to make a suicide attempt. Thanks to the psychodrama, he was able to take up again his work as a technician and to start to paint again, which had even led him one day to bring us a few of his paintings in an abstract style, in the style of Poliakoff. However, he was always asking himself why it was necessary to work and earn money. He spent everything he earned on a woman friend whom he considered vampire-like and he also had a lot of difficulty in getting paid. For him, working and being remunerated meant earning his living "like everyone else".

We had worked on this conflict previously in terms of an opposition between his narcissistic ego ideal of being a great man who did not need to work and the demands of the superego to accept limits and, consequently, to be able to give himself real satisfactions. The interpretative work, which was centred more on the modalities of psychic functioning than on unconscious phantasies, had enabled Raphaël to cope better with his destructive impulses by promoting the capacities for binding the excitation through recourse to images and words that were tolerable for the ego.

It was only later that it was possible to tackle the issues involved in his unconscious phantasies. During a scene depicting his curiosity about the sexual relations of his parents, he had expressed a denial of the primal scene: during this scene, he naturally found it intolerable that his parents could be together; the exclusion from the primal scene was suggested by the two psychodramatists expressing the wish not to be disturbed by their children when they were alone together. Raphaël felt goaded to express his wish to see and said: *I'm looking through the room; it's like a white/blank hole (trou blanc)*. A white/blank hole that was "troubling" and which could be understood as the depiction of a negative hallucination denying the primal scene at the same time as Raphaël was directly confronted with it.

In his associations after the role play, he recalled that in adolescence he thought that his parents never had a sexual life and that children were born by spontaneous generation. The elaboration of this scene made it possible to interpret the unconscious phantasy underlying his lack of pragmatism and reluctance to earn money: "Earning one's living like everyone else meant accepting the idea of being born of a father and mother like everyone else", something that for him had for a long time been both intolerable and unacceptable. Because it had been possible to depict the denial of the primal scene, we were able to go beyond the psychotic mechanisms of denial and ego-splitting and enable him to introject the interpretation, without experiencing it as a breach of his psychic world.

It is interesting to note that, for Raphaël, the primal scene was depicted in relation to the theme of concentration camps. One day, he mentioned the fact that his parents had often argued violently about the Nazi extermination of European Jews in the concentration camps; his father refused to accept the reality of the Holocaust, while his mother argued the contrary. Faced with such a violent and destructive primal scene, Raphaël had no other recourse but to transform the black hole into a white hole and to get rid of any trace of terror and violence at the price of this "rift in the ego", the image used by Freud to describe ego-splitting in psychosis.

In this transition from the phantasy of self-procreation to the elaboration of the primal scene, Raphaël found he was the *subject of his drive impulses* rather than the object of persecution by others. In the course of the following sessions, he wondered if his hatred had not distorted the way that he saw his parents and, conscious of the importance of temporality, he understood that everything he was experiencing in the present, particularly in his relations with women, stemmed from everything that he had created in his mind when he was little. At the same time, he became aware of the difference between *thinking* and *doing* and, after having had so many violent phantasies, he said, with astonishment, *I haven't slaughtered anyone up till now.* It is noteworthy that during the sessions when the themes were most violent, he preferred to take the role of an observer and to let a psychodramatist express his most primitive phantasies: cutting his sisters up into small pieces and putting them in the left-luggage office of the Paris railway station, the "Gare de Lyon" (Lyon station) which, under the pressure of the primary process, then became the "Gare des lions" (Lions' station).

Just as he was emerging from psychotic confusion and feeling able to accept himself once again as being human, Raphaël fell ill, and we would never know if what he called a big cold, for which he was hospitalized, was meningitis or not, like the invulnerable autistic child emerging from psychotic encapsulation who develops all sorts of somatic illnesses. Raphaël was physically ill for the first time, but was reluctant to speak about a mortal illness: he thought about death, "but I prefer", he said, "not to think that that could frighten me". Becoming human and subject to time implies accepting birth and death.

Time has to be renewed everyday a little bit, he said one day, thereby indicating the risk of being confined within the juxtaposition of instants, but also expressing the wish to establish himself in duration and permanence. This implies being able momentarily to suspend issues of life and death without denying them, in a *pleasure of playing* which is equally a *pleasure of thinking* and *phantasying*.

What can we say about the transference dynamics? It is quite remarkable that at the same time as Raphaël showed his capacities to overcome his ambivalent conflict concerning parental imagos, he had his first transference dream after eight years of psychodrama: *he brought me a huge bunch of colourful and scented flowers behind which I disappeared.* This strongly condensed dream evidenced a capacity to portray an inverted Oedipus by projecting onto his analyst the feminine position, while at the same time representing his own anxiety in face of the devouring "flower-woman-vagina". The theme of flowers, portraying the female sexual organs, had been an opportunity to reflect with him on his fear of *touching* the woman-flower, for fear of being sucked in, and on his need to keep these flowers at a distance by limiting himself to *smelling* their fragrance. In his transference dream, the scented flowers were certainly flowers that could be touched, but at the same time they risked leading to the disappearance of others or of the subject himself.

Photography, "that makes my head spin"

Individual psychoanalytic psychodrama offers a setting that is conducive to developing and fostering *thinking in images* in order to go beyond fixed, stereotyped and repetitive images, and to open oneself up to a *movement* of images that grounds the constitution of narrative and history. The support of psychodramatic role play observed by the group leader makes it possible to create the distance that is necessary for constituting a process of symbolization, which is simply the possibility of playing with images, representations, and language.

As Tisseron (1989) has pointed out, the image has an intermediate position between things and words, and implies that we are attentive both to its "containing virtuality", which helps the subject to find the path towards the object, and to its "spellbinding power" which risks confining the subject within a state of almost hallucinatory fascination, or within psychotic hallucination. He quite rightly points out that

> the impossibility of being able to imagine a situation may lead to action; but, at the same time, the impossibility of being able to imagine a situation as realized may also lead to the wish to realize it in order to be able to imagine it, that is, to symbolize it through an image.
>
> (p. 1996)

In other words, when patients ask us to guarantee them a reciprocity of desire, it is fitting to offer them a *reciprocity of the image.*

A recent sequence from Raphaël's psychodrama will help to illustrate this function of the image in analytic treatment, permitting the reintegration of body and the mind, sensation and perception, representations and affects. Raphaël, who used to be overwhelmed by anxieties to do with nondifferentiation with regard to the archaic maternal imago, was gradually able to draw support from the paternal transference and rediscover in himself the desire for a paternal line of descent. After reading Gérard Haddad's (2005) book *Le jour où Lacan m'a adopté* [The Day Lacan Adopted Me], he managed to express through role play his phantasy of being adopted by the group leader and the team members, his "new family".

It was in this context that he was able to express for the first time so eloquently his relation to images by talking about his visit to a photographic exhibition.

When I asked Raphaël what situation he wanted to play out, he thought for a moment, with his arms crossed, and then, looking at me for the first time since the beginning of the session, said:

R: *Well, okay, why not? I'm not quite sure, but at the FNAC there is a photo exhibition on St Petersburg… There could be Mrs E and uh… me, for example.*

AG: *Right. So, Mrs E?…*

R: *It's a lady that I saw there, in fact.*

AG: *So you are both looking at the exhibition of photos on St Petersburg.*

R: *That's right.*

AG: *O.K., good.*

[The protagonists stand up]

Beginning of the scene:

Mrs E: *Oh, I didn't know there were "white nights"*[15] *in St Petersburg; it's a strange phenomenon that, white nights, do you understand how that happens?*

R: *I knew they existed but not in that sense.*

Mrs E: *In what sense were you thinking about, then?*

R: *Well, anyway, a little while ago we passed by each other; you moved, and I thought to myself, but what on earth is she doing?*

Mrs E: *What did it look as if I was doing?*

R: *Well, you were making the sign of the cross. [he laughed]*

Mrs E: *Did it seem as if I was inspired by these Russian churches, these landscapes?*

R: *No, there is no church there. [still laughing]*

Mrs E: *No, there is no church, it's…*

R: *That's right, there's no church.*

Mrs E: *Should I have prostrated myself before that? No, but you must have dreamt that I was making the sign of the cross!*

R: *Oh, so it was me who invented it.*

Mrs E: *Yes, I think so, maybe I was a bit agitated, I think these photos are really beautiful, I was thrilled by the magnificent colours, the impression of "white" nights, but do you have "white" [sleepless] nights?*

R: *Because it's more striking.*

Mrs E: *It's a very particular colour, this milky-white space.*

R: *Gosh, I understood that it was a clear night.*

Mrs E: *And when we speak about a "white night" [nuit blanche, sleepless night]*

R: *Yes.*

Mrs E: *Do you have them sometimes?*

R: *You can't sleep.*

Mrs E: *Yes. [silence] Well, I don't think the sun sets there, does it?*

R: *Hmm. [silence]*

Mrs E: *That must be a strange thing. I think, in fact, that they dance all night-long there, they're always coming and going in St Petersburg.*

R: *There, there was no one; there was just the sea, the sea that was frozen over.*

In this sequence, Raphaël talked about the excitement aroused by the sight of the photos of St Petersburg, depicted by the "madness" of the female spectator making signs of the cross. The image of the white/sleepless night suggests his inability to cope with the excitement that stops him from sleeping, while the image of the frozen sea represents the countercathexis of this excitement. He then brought associations to the disturbing feelings provoked by the sight of the photos:

Mrs E: *And you, what do you do? Do you like photos, do you go to photo exhibitions?*

R: *Yes, I do; yes, I like that.*

Mrs E: *And you are…*

R: *But I mustn't see too many, though.*

Mrs E: *Oh, really!*

R: *It's like paintings.*

Mrs E: *They make your head spin?*

R: *Yes, that's right.*

Mrs E: *Do you think it's dangerous?*

R: *No, but it makes my head spin.*

Mrs E: *It turns, it makes your head spin?*

R: *I've soon had enough of it.*

Mrs E: *Yes, it's a bit tiring; a little while ago I was a bit agitated, when you thought I was making the sign of the cross; they exhilarate me, they excite me, perhaps that's what you feel is dangerous?*

R: *Well, yes, perhaps, because afterwards I don't know any more what to do with it.*

Mrs E: *You have to quickly go back and do something with it!*

R: *It eventually subsides.*

Mrs E: *Personally, it makes me…*

R: *Or else it remains in your head and that's it.*

The scene ends with Raphaël recalling the photos that his father used to take and the immediate link he made with the "slaps" that he used to get when he was young. In the exchange that followed with Raphaël, he talked about his inhibition with regard to painting, which I interpreted to him as "the fear that it might make his head spin, because there would be too much pleasure".

With great insight into himself, Raphaël then associated to the links between pleasure and annihilation anxiety: *Yes, because when that happened to me, when there were things I did and understood, it was as if they destroyed me, I couldn't go any further because, well yes, that's right, because it's linked to pleasure… and it's overwhelming!*

I pointed out to him, then, that psychodrama is a form of play, and that it is possible to share pleasure without being overwhelmed by it, and that this was a different experience from what he had told us about the war games he used to play with his father in his childhood, when "all of a sudden it turned into something that was no longer a game". After a moment of silence, Raphaël associated to this, saying: *"Yes, there is murder"*.

I continued: *"Yes, there is murder, so we stop playing and say to ourselves: 'I'm never going to play again'"*.

Thanks to this support from the psychodrama group leader and the other team members, Raphaël was able to speak about the double polarity of images as mental images and material images, implying a link between their function of quasi-hallucinatory non-differentiation and their containing function. For Raphaël, an image had to be a copy of reality, leaving little room for its powers of evocation and its emotional dimension, otherwise there was a risk of his head spinning, of being "saturated" or "annihilated" by it. The words used by the patient to describe the photos at the St Petersburg exhibition are impressive: the sight of an image soon turns into a source of anxiety to do with non-differentiation, from which he can only free himself by switching off from it immediately, just as a dreamer triumphs on waking up over the images of his nightmare. In this connection, Murielle Gagnebin (2002) has evoked the *shadow of the image*: "Confronting shadows *in* the image may lead to many dangers, including that of exuding a frightening and staggering pain that comes close to annihilating all meaning and awareness" (p. 10). The risk is then one of finding oneself faced with "an image deprived of shadow forever", without depth.

In this connection, Laurie Laufer (2005, 2006) has described with a great deal of talent the crucial role of the image in traumas of loss:

> In the case of a trauma, a "freeze-frame" may sometimes occur, where a state of paralysis is provoked by terror or fascination, resulting in the freezing of all affects and making it impossible for the subject to feel moved any longer, that is, to experience his instinctual body, in particular through speech.

And she adds, "What is an image without movement other than blindness or being captured by the gaze?" This gaze could also be the petrifying gaze of the Medusa. The solution can only come through "working on vision" which implies being able to "shut one's eyes" and to discover the invisible aspect on the edge of the visible world. In a relatively old nightmare, Raphaël had dreamt that "he was a surgeon, that a patient was lying on an operating table, and that the operation consisted in removing his eyelids": there could be no better depiction of the conditions required for working on *vision* with regard to the need to introduce a movement of continuity and discontinuity, of opening and closing the eyes, so that an image can have depth of field, distance, and the necessary gap between the subject who is looking and the image that he is looking at.

Working on vision is one way of describing the dimension of hallucinatory activity that seeks, of course, to ensure perceptual identity, but also to draw all *movement* towards thought-identity. Without this temporality, an image is little more than pure sensation that blinds and burns: this is what

Laufer calls the "melancholic freeze-frame". It is therefore necessary to distinguish between the status of the image in pathological hallucinations and in the hallucinatory activity related to the quality of this movement. Furthermore, the *movement* of the image opening out on to the dimension of representation and history is different from *mobility*, which places the image within a repetition without history in the service of sensation.

The analytic work with Raphael shows clearly that access to hallucinatory activity is only possible by overcoming the "murder" of the object and forming its representation in mental life. Marie-José Mondzain (2003) offers an eloquent description of the consequences of this mental work: "What cannot be represented can only expect symbolization to come from vision itself" (p. 120). Thus far, our patient had experienced psychodrama as a space that would help him recover his capacity to see: this task was not yet completed but this session showed the patient's capacity to understand what was at stake, given his increased capacity to look and be looked at as someone who could cathect and be cathected by the object, thereby making possible acceptance of a process of differentiation between self and other and access to the functioning of mental topography.

"What do I see in paintings?"

In the following session, Raphaël began by saying: *"That last session gave me a big sense of relief. And I think it's because I mentioned the word 'murder'".* This gave us an opportunity of thinking together about the difference between fantasy and reality: it is possible to talk about murder without actually killing anyone. His relief was a sign of his capacity to experience his hatred without fearing that he might destroy either himself or the object. This opened the way for differentiating between *orgasmic pleasure,* which increases in intensity and then subsides, and *transitional pleasure,* which affords access to desexualized thought and to sublimation. Winnicott (1971) pointed out that the experience of transitionality has no "climax" and differs from "phenomena that have instinctual backing, where the orgiastic element plays an essential part, and where satisfactions are closely linked with climax" (p. 98). This was also what Freud (1924) had in mind when he discussed satisfaction as being linked not to the discharge of a *quantity* of excitation, but to its *qualitative* dimension related to rhythm. From this point of view, sublimation has to do with the possibility of organizing the thought processes that Freud (1950 [1895]) described in his "Project for a scientific psychology" as involving the use of small quantities of energy; this allows for the possibility of taking pleasure in something that is not specifically linked to the discharge of a quantity of excitation, following the inertia principle, but to the preservation of a certain degree of tension, in accordance with the constancy principle.

Raphaël was now able to think about his mental functioning and, while reflecting on his desire to paint and the difficulties that he was encountering with that, he sought to understand what he sees when looking at a painting: *I cannot say that I really believe in light, but, in fact, when I look at the painting, that's what I see and I wonder why I see that.* He chose to play out a scene with Mrs V. who was to be, like him, a spectator. In the scene, he began by evoking the idea of "a great light in the painting", which brought associations to the dazzling light of the sun when it is at its zenith; in connection with the sight of a painting, he had an astonishing formulation to describe and try to push away the sensation that he felt, which was in danger of invading him: *It's the body that receives something, that's all.* He then talked for the first time since he began the psychodrama about a hallucinatory experience that took place in his childhood, one that most probably determined his traumatic view of the world:

R: *Well, [silence], no, but it's like the day I saw the Holy Virgin.*
Mrs V: *Really, you saw the Holy Virgin!*
R: *No, it's really true.*
Mrs V: *Oh, really, what was that like? Was it at your communion?*
R: *No.*
Mrs V: *No? Well how did you see her?*
R: *They were waiting to show a film called "Bernadette Soubirous".*
Mrs V: *Yes, okay and then?*
R: *Well, I saw her through the hole in the roof [he laughs].*
Mrs V: *And then she …*
R: *Like for the film, everyone was waiting, becoming more and more impatient.*
Mrs V: *And was there any light?*
        [The exchanges became animated and they were gesticulating with their hands; their voices were full of expressive intonations]
R: *Oh yes, yes!! When I told the priest that, it wasn't long ago since I went to Italy, because somebody in Marie's [his current girlfriend] family is a priest, well he asked me: "Didn't she say anything to you?"*
Mrs V: *Well then, what did she say to you?*
R: *Well, not much.*
Mrs V: *But what did she say about … after all, you did see her, didn't you?*
R: *[silence]*
Mrs V: *Didn't she say anything to you?*
R: *No, no.*
Mrs V: *And why, it frightened you, didn't it?*
R: *Oh, no! I wasn't afraid, no, not at all but, she didn't say anything.*
Mrs V: *Well now, I didn't know things like that could happen. You're, well, you're lucky to be all lit up like that because, for me, it's only in art galleries that I see light like that; sometimes I feel really gripped by something…*

R: [cutting in and speaking in a much louder voice] No, I, well anyway,
            what do I see in the paintings?
Mrs V: Yes, it's like the Holy Virgin.
R: But maybe I can see something else.
Mrs V: Yes? What do you see?
R: Well, I don't really know at all, but I can see something else.
Mrs V: There, look at that painting, the one opposite you. (see Figure 5.1 on the
            next page)

We may ask ourselves if the evocation of his hallucinatory vision of the Holy Virgin, through identification with Bernadette Soubirous, the young girl from Lourdes, did not take him back to his primary psychotic experience, in a movement that Freud described in connection with Schreber's paranoiac projection. Before the psychodrama, this patient had had a mystical delusion which could be understood as having had its origin in this hallucinatory vision.

Raphaël found appropriate words to describe what was at stake in the vision: *It's the body that receives something, that's all; Maybe I can see something else.* He then associated to a painting that he could see in the room where the psychodrama was taking place; it was blue landscape representing a mountainous relief and a strip of land going into the sea:

R: Hmm.
Mrs V: Well, what can you see?
R: The blue bit there?! [in a very lively tone of voice]
Mrs V: Yes? Can you see anything in that?
R: Well, what I see there is, uh, a vagina.
Mrs V: Ah! Well, you're quite right, it's an enormous vagina, but…
R: Well, it's always enormous.
Mrs V: No, but wait a minute, the vagina… what's that? There's something
            inside it.
R: Well yes, but I don't know what it's called.
Mrs V: Well, what is it? Because there is something in the middle of this
            vagina, isn't there? What is it? What can you see there?
R: It's…
Mrs V: Anyway, that vagina isn't empty.
R: Hmm.
Mrs V: It's something that's going back into it, or something that's coming out,
            I can't see very clearly.
            [silence]
R: That [doubtful]?
Mrs V: What can you see?
R: Well, yes, yes, I can see a phallus.

Figure 5.1 Irena Dedicova, promontory (1982).

Lithograph, 66 × 49cm ©Photo Eugenio Angel Prieto Gabriel

Mrs V:	*So it's going in. Mind you, when you say it's enormous, I might perhaps see a baby coming out; that's where it comes out, isn't it?*
R:	*Yes, well, you can't see anything.*
Mrs V:	*Okay.*
R:	*When you come out.*

Mrs V: *You are completely blinded.*
R: *Oh! I don't know anything about that.*
Mrs V: *Mind you, I imagine that you can see light, a white light.*
R: *Once outside the hole, you are, uh, dazzled.*
Mrs V: *That's right dazzled.*
A.G: *Okay, then.*

When Raphaël looked at the landscape of the painting on the wall of the psychodrama room, at first he saw a vagina; thinking in images remained sexualized in a symbolic equation mode of functioning as described by Hanna Segal (1957). But he also talked about birth and being dazzled by the excessive presence of the object which also had to do with too much absence. There was the image of a tunnel at the end of which there is a dazzling white light, rather like the experiences described by patients on coming out of a deep coma in an in-between state between life and death. When I stopped the scene, he took up again the theme of birth:

R: *Well, that makes me think about birth.*
A.G: *Can one be born without being dazzled? Blinded?*
R: *Mm, well anyway, I was blinded, uh, by the hatred I felt towards my father at that time!*
A.G: *But at the same time it is a matter not only of hate but also of love; you are able to form a picture of what happened in the past, when you were completely blinded, in your delusion, and to understand some-thing about your own history. When we speak about the individual and his history, that means History with a capital "H" [Raphaël had begun the session by mentioning a book that he had just bought called The Individual and History], but as far as you are concerned it also means you in your own history (R: "Yes"), in the history that we have shared together here and in which you have followed your own path. I think it's very important that you are much less blinded than was the case in the past (R: Yes), so that relationships are now possible without thinking about murder; and it is also possible to separate without it implying a total void. You see, you have had a deeply emotional experi-ence, one that is shared by all human beings. I think that today, thanks to all the work we have been doing together, you can put words on your past, and understand your own history – and as a result be in a better position to imagine life.*

The excitement aroused by the light of the painting had echoes for the patient, certainly, with the bedazzlement of separation from his mother at birth, but above all with the annihilation-anxiety related to rejection by the object in primary psychotic experience: the dazzling light correspond-ing to the exciting sexualization that fills the "black hole" of the psyche to use Tustin's (1986, p. 39) expression. Raphaël switched, moreover, from "the vagina" to "you can't see anything" and to "outside the hole, you are dazzled". Paul-Claude Racamier (1987) describes this psychotic catastrophe in the same terms as our patient and sees it as the consequence of a phantasy of self-procreation that is marked more by sensory feeling than by representation: He writes:

> What seems to me to be both obvious and of major importance is that the activation of this 'phantasy' [of self-procreation] brings about an extremely rare modification in the subject's state of mind. It constitutes what I would call a *blank psychic event* (and I do mean: *psychic*). Blank: something that illuminates like a flash of lightening, creating an explosion all around it and blinding you. It may as well be said right away that that this psychic event corresponds exactly to the primal catastrophe. And so we have in the history of delusion a process that is different from and more precise than a mere decathexis. Of course, it does require massive denial; but there is more to it than just denial: there is the constitution and activation of this extraordinarily *seductive* fantasy. And I say that especially as self-procreation is directly related to *narcissistic seduction*. Anyone who is in this register will be exposed to this fascinating and terrible blank event, which will empty everything out of his mind, and the only way to overcome it is by creating a delusion.
>
> (p. 38)

For her part, Piera Aulagnier (1985) compared this hallucinatory experience to the sensation of a hand clinging on to a rock that is slipping endlessly into a void, as though caught up in a breathtaking whirlwind. The only solution is to produce hallucinations and delusional images, especially of persecutors chasing you, in order not to sink into this free-fall without representations.

Raphaël understood that this psychotic crisis was linked to hatred, and he was now able to put it into words because he had recovered a capacity for love through his cathexis of the psychodrama, whose intensity could be measured by the creative cathexis to which it gave rise both in him and in all the members of the team. The work of symbolization is equally one of co-creation between the patient and the analyst in what Winnicott (1951) called "an intermediate area of experience", as materialized by the psychodrama scene. Raphaël had not yet taken up painting again, but he was giving himself the means to understand in depth the reasons for his inhibitions both in his painting activity and in his love life.

Raphaël had thus been able to work through his "aesthetic conflict", a conflict Meltzer (1988) has described as the experience of the overwhelming presence of the object, the mother's beauty, which cannot be assimilated by the child if there is too great a distance between "the outside of the 'beautiful' mother, available to the senses, and the enigmatic inside, which must be construed by creative imagination". As Meltzer points out, the child

> has, after all, come into a strange country where he knows neither the language nor the customary non-verbal cues and communications. The mother is enigmatic to him; she wears the Gioconda smile most of the time, and the music of her voice keeps shifting from major to minor key.
>
> (p. 22)

Painting and music correspond once again here, accounting for Raphaël's experience of having been unable to make sense of his mother's "ambiguous messages", thus condemning him to psychotic confusion and to the impossibility of integrating his intellectual, affective and artistic creativity. From Bion's perspective, it was a matter of transforming the *beta* elements corresponding to intrusive sensations that cannot be elaborated into alpha elements suitable for thought, dreams, and fantasies. This is in keeping with what Laplanche (1987) also described in his theory of generalized seduction concerning the need for the child to be able to make sense of the mother's "enigmatic signifiers" or messages (p. 45).

Symbolization and the synergy of sensations

In an earlier session, before the summer holiday break, Raphaël had spoken for the first time about his childhood memory of being overwhelmed by incomprehensible emotions and sensations in the presence of his parents. In thinking about why he linked the separation to feelings of emptiness, he wondered if he had not suffered from experiences of abandonment early on in his life. When I asked him about when this might have happened, he replied: *When I was four years old*, and then corrected himself by saying: *I can't remember the time when I was four, but before then, when I was still in a pushchair, there was complete silence; my parents were there but they didn't speak; they would quarrel and I couldn't understand anything, it was just soundless words.*

He explained that the quarrel was about the rent that their landlord was claiming, because his father had not paid it, and added: *"I'm a bit like that, today"*.

It was his inability to integrate all these sensations that had led Raphaël to form relationships with other people that were based either on being too present or too absent, just as the child in his pushchair had been unable to understand "soundless words", a strange expression to denote "wordless sounds", an incomprehensible noise equivalent to "soundless words", to a destructive silence on the part of the parents who, due to their quarrelling, decathected and disregarded the child's emotional life. The recollection of being a child in distress, who was unable to integrate his parents' auditory messages, had led Raphaël thereafter to hypercathect visual sensations to the point of hallucinating.

But what about his other senses? In one of his recent sessions, Raphaël had begun to think about the reasons why he felt invaded by the word "rance" [rancid]. This was an opportunity for him to become aware of how he rejected all sensoriality, since the word "rance" made him think of "errance" [wandering, roaming] and then of "lait rance" [rancid milk], the smell, taste, and colour of which he had never been able to bear. Having chosen to play the word "rance", he was led from words to things and to represent, also for the first time, his early relations to his mother based on smells and touching. After saying: *My mother smelt bad*, Raphaël associated insightfully to his drive impulse: *At a certain moment, I was smelling bad* then: *I destroy everything* and *As soon as I touch something… whoosh!* As an infant at the breast he had rejected his mother because of tactile, olfactory and gustatory sensations experienced as bad and destructive.

In the course of this scene, Raphaël spoke again about the bad smells of his father who used to "fart", which he thought at the time was a sign of virility, but it was destructive because the body gases made him think of the gas chambers in Nazi concentration camps. His grandfather's and father's collaboration had led Raphaël to cut himself off from any masculine identification, except in a sadistic mode. Through this enactment of the bad smells of both his parents, he thus gave himself the means to understand more emotionally that the primal scene had had a destructive significance for him, since it was an anal-sadistic scene.

After this sequence on the polysemic meanings of the word "rance", in the discussion with the group leader, Raphaël became aware of how he rejected his body and his sensations, along with the parental objects who had left him completely unequipped for feeling, thinking about, and discovering the world:

R: *I don't know … well yes, but I don't know why. But if I think about how my father used to fart, it makes me think about the way you said "gas", pfffft [with a look of disgust], well, after, it's still a massacre, but in fact I am still in it.*

AG: *I think what you are saying is that we all have a body (R: "Yes") and that sensations and smells are part of it.*

R: *Yes, right.*

AG: *And there's a part of you that wanted to reject those sensations, those smells.*

R: *Well, yes, without any smell, what does that mean? It's nothing.*

AG: *It's nothing.*

R: *No body at all.*

AG: *No body, that's right.*

R: *Someone who doesn't give off a smell…*

AG: *There's a saying: odourless, colourless and tasteless.*
R: *That's right, so you can't see him.*
AG: *You can't see him.*
R: *You can't smell him.*
AG: *You have no body.*
R: *You can't taste him.*
AG: *At the same time, I think...*
R: *[Cutting in on AG] Ah, yes that follows on from the sacrifice, then.*
AG: *Yes.*
R: *Last week...*
AG: *Exactly, the body had to be sacrificed. Yet, at the same time, the body is what enables you to live, to exist (R: "Yes.", to feel (R: "Yes.") and to share, too, and especially in love- relations (R: Hmm), since you were asking me about love-relations.*

Raphaël then associated to the scent of flowers and suggested playing out a scene on "good smells". The theme of flowers had already come up in sessions a few years before, in particular following the first transference dream in which I disappeared behind a huge bunch of sweet-smelling and colourful flowers that he had brought me. Now, at the end of this session, Raphaël was able to understand better his rejection of the female body due to the negative recollection of being breast-fed – *"The milk made me feel sick"* – and was consequently more accessible to a relationship with the object that was not immediately disruptive for his narcissism. The scent of the flowers, their "fragrance" can, to use the patient's expression be intoxicating and "disorienting"; but it was possible for him this time to evoke the smell of musk and vaginal secretions. Flowers could now evoke the image of a woman who was not immediately a source of anxiety and destructiveness. Raphaël ended this session by saying to the three female colleagues who were playing the role of flowers: *You can smell them, look at them and touch them, too,* attesting to a significant change in his mental economy. He could touch without "destroying" everything, just as he could be touched by the transference experience of the psychodrama without being "overwhelmed" by the presence of a threatening and intrusive object.

We can imagine that the subjective reappropriation of his body and sensations would allow him to make room for his desire to paint as well as to that of loving a woman without being overwhelmed by unspeakable anxiety. The painter's eye can go beyond the opposition between dazzling light and total darkness, insofar as the sight of colours brings with it correspondingly the whole palette of sensations, whether they be olfactory, gustatory, tactile, auditory or visual, in a synergy of what Bion (1962) called the "consensuality of the breast".

Raphaëls psychic creativity is the equivalent of a psychic birth where the visual ceases to be anxiety-provoking on the condition that there is a gathering together of sensations and that an auto-erotism emerges that includes the object and its representations. In her considerations on the French author Colette, Julia Kristeva (2004) has quite rightly drawn attention to what is at stake in this "supportive role of the senses" in the perception of the world. She writes:

> Every flower is a bouquet of synesthesias: seen, heard, inhaled, eaten, caressed, it invites all the senses to communicate and to contaminate one another at its approach: "I do more than see the tulip come back to its senses: I hear the iris flowering" (Colette, 1924, p.95). And all the sensations shore one another up to focus the gaze on the secret of floral rhythm.
>
> (p. 210)

In his famous 1857 poem with the same title, Baudelaire also stressed the importance for symbolization of these "correspondences" between sensations, of these "forests of symbols" where "scents, colours and sounds echo one another".

On illusion and disillusion

The trajectory of clinical entities leads us to place more value on the importance of identification with the analyst's interpretative function over the cathexis of his personality. In this gap, the possibilities of symbolization and elaboration find their place in analysis, in correlation with the possibilities of the displacement and differentiation of imagos, as clinical work with neurotic states teaches us.

Clinical work with borderline states shows how difficult it can sometimes be for these patients to accept, in Marion Milner's words, "a symbolic relation with the analyst instead of a literal one", to be willing to make use of the symbolism of speech and to "talk about their wants rather than taking action to satisfy them directly" (Milner, 1952, p. 194). This implies being able to use the analytic setting as a special place where "creative illusion" will develop, permitting the recognition of the essential difference between a symbolic relation and a literal one.

Borderline states confront us immediately with this issue, since they play on this boundary between the symbolic and the literal and also confront the analyst with the difficulties of the paradoxical transference (Anzieu, 1975). If delusion has sometimes seemed to be the transposition of an erotomanic relationship (Kestemberg, 1962), the transference relationship is organized around loving commitment that oscillates between using the object in terms of a phantasy of incorporation and using the object as a mediator of a process of instinctual drive introjection.[16]

A classical analysis of a case of anxiety hysteria will allow me to highlight some key issues in this "daily" work.

Marc or the anguished "soldier"

When I met Marc for the first time, he was twenty-six years old and presented a classical clinical picture of hysteria anxiety with multiple and varied symptoms: hypochondriacal anxieties and a nosography revolving around stomach cancer; disorders of depersonalization, in particular the sense of no longer being in contact with other people; he suffered from bulimia, insomnia and, transiently, premature ejaculation. He spoke abundantly and in a hurried way, leaving no room for silence, clearly manifesting a degree of excitation that left him no respite. In some ways, he was reminiscent of Charles, in particular with regard to his hypochondriacal complaints and the tonality of his excitation; but, in fact, the Oedipus complex and castration appeared from the outset to be an anchor point against oral regression.

Marc had displayed a significant degree of disorganization when, four years earlier, his mother had died of lung cancer. She had been operated on two years before for breast cancer, which had been unbearable for Marc. Unable to tolerate the situation, he decided to leave her immediately, to give up his university studies and to become a representative in a small provincial town. After his mother's death, Marc went from bad to worse: feeling anxious and depressed, he had then become bulimic and put on thirty kilos. His anxiety had taken on such proportions that he could no longer work and was hospitalized in a psychiatric hospital for ten months.

The oldest of two children, he was born when his father was fighting in a colonial war. His father had joined up voluntarily just after his marriage "to show his own father what he was capable of", since the latter had expressed doubts about his son's aptitude for becoming a husband! When his father had returned from the war, his mother soon became pregnant with his younger sister. Marc presented his father's return as a traumatic event: he had cried on seeing his father and turned away from him!

I will focus here on two important movements in Marc's analysis to show that, unlike Charles, his possibilities of psychic work enabled him to mourn his mother and to recathect his body thanks to the integration of his bisexuality. While his various forms of acting during the analysis – turning round, absences for periods of varying length, sudden changes of profession – suggested a flight in the face of intolerable anxiety, which was reflected in his fear of madness, he always showed possibilities of drawing support from the double paternal and maternal register of the transference, and an "aptitude for pictorial representability" in particular in condensed dreams to which he associated amply. Anality as a way of playing between retaining and losing seemed essential in this assault course, as he imagined the analytic adventure to be. At that time, Marc was a fervent practitioner of martial arts and walking activities, serving as a defensive hyperactivity against his passivity, which he likened with his father's war escapade.

The first dream, at the very beginning of his analysis, seemed like a programme of work for the whole analysis and was in fact worked through in the transference in the third year. The dream narrative went as follows: *I was waiting to enter the cinema. Soldiers were queuing behind me. I then went into the cinema – pornographic films were being shown. In the cinema a man wanted to seduce a woman, then moved away and climbed up on the stage. I rushed towards him and wanted to punch him, but my arm stopped before I could hit him.*

His Oedipal rivalry with his father, suggested here by the wish to hit this man, is secondary compared with the wish to take the place of the Oedipal mother, and above all of the pre-Oedipal mother, an omnipotent and always sexually aroused mother, where the penis is only a partial object of the mother: desire not for a penis but for a vagina that would allow her to enjoy infinite excitation.

The work on the legend of his birth also suggested a link to his mother, prior to his father's return, as a source of constant excitation, in the image of the actress in the pornographic film or of the spectator in danger of being seduced and raped by this man. An important moment in the analysis was rediscovering, in a dream, the phantasy of the maternal breast, not as a sexual object but as a nourishing breast: an image of analytic work and its function as a protective shield, which makes it possible to experience phantasy activity and interpretation as something other than a mutual destructive rape.

The father's return from war could then be considered a means of displacing envy of the maternal vagina onto envy of the father's idealized penis, from which support could thus be found. The analysis in the transference of passive homosexual desires was a significant structural movement: he himself evoked his first dream in his analysis and identified the soldiers behind him with the analyst and his soldier/father. In this movement, the analysis of his desire to be penetrated anally in order to take possession of the paternal penis made it possible to give meaning to a series of anxieties related to his feminine identification and his fear of homosexuality.

He understood the origin of his anxiety after his mother's death, which had led him to be hospitalized for a very long time. At that time, he could not bear the presence of his father who cooked for him and replaced his mother: the uncertainty concerning his sexual identity could only be resolved on the condition of being physically separated from his father by the walls of the psychiatric hospital.

His hypochondriacal anxieties, centred on his stomach pains and fear of cancer, had led him to undergo several invasive medical tests; but his hypochondria disappeared permanently from the moment it was worked through as a phantasy of pregnancy in relation to his father. At that time, he relapsed into his bulimia and put on weight again, this time 10 kg only, which he understood as the realization of his phantasy of pregnancy.[17]

We can therefore imagine the importance in Marc's history of his destructive impulses towards his mother and the traumatic impact of her death, considered as (or to be) the realization of his negative Oedipal wishes. The possibility of reorganizing a whole paternal image, the image of a father who was not only a part object of the mother, allowed Marc to rediscover his love for his mother and to begin a work of mourning.

This work of mourning implies undoing the links with the lost object and manifests itself – Abraham has showed this very clearly – as the expulsion of faeces, a corollary movement to the oral incorporation of the object after its disappearance (Abraham, 1924, p. 442ff; see also Chasseguet-Smirgel, 1977). One of Marc's dreams, in the fourth year of analysis, attests to this other significant movement in the analysis: *I had a strange dream last night, which is difficult to relate and unusual. I had defecated on a silver plate, and I was showing it to Catherine [the woman friend with whom he was living] who was talking on the telephone to her mother. After that, I wanted to put it under the bed; then, I went into the kitchen and I wanted to cover it with an Indian bedspread. That was when I realized that it was dirty; there was excrement everywhere.*

In his associations, he saw his excrement as something aggressive towards his girlfriend with whom he had had an argument the evening before because he had reproached her for not being available to listen to him whenever he wanted. After I had pointed out to him that his excrement was also "something precious", he talked about Catherine's indifference in the dream; I linked this to the indifference he reproached both her and me for because we did not understand what he had gone through when his mother died and because we wanted to replace her. It should be noted that his girlfriend's mother had died when she was six years old, and that it is not without significance that, in the dream, she was talking to her, reviving her, just as Marc himself had continually sought to keep his own mother alive within him through his anxiety.

Telling this dream helped Marc to speak for the very first time about the circumstances of his mother's death: *I was not there at the moment of her death, but I would've liked to have been there. I was in class teaching. My father telephoned me to announce her death. I went straight away to Marie-Claude's [his girlfriend at the time who was a great anorexic]; she was not there, so I put 50 francs under her door to induce her to join me. That makes me think of the excrement that I put under my bed in the dream. I arrived too late, my mother had already been put in a coffin.*

He then recounted the arrival of Marie-Claude who was very anxious due to her conflictual relations with her own mother; he had wanted to have sex with her, in a manic movement (Abraham, 1978), aimed at denying the loss: *We had not had complete sexual relations until then; it didn't work, it was just mutual masturbation. In fact, it wasn't really the right day for that. But it was probably a need to reassure myself that she would not drop me as my mother had done by dying.*

And he added: *I am beginning to understand many things, to feel much less anxious, thanks to you, and I am very grateful to you. I want to continue the analysis [He had often expressed the wish to stop it] and to go more deeply into all that to free myself from it. I have already said that I used to experience indissoluble anxiety. You pointed out that it was the links that were indissoluble. I want to be able to free myself from them.*

And he remained silent for a few moments until the end of the session, contrary to his usual need not to allow any "void".

It was a mutative session attesting to the correspondences between the past and the present, thanks to the transference mediation: this was initially rejected in order to keep alive both the lost object and the illusion of a loving relationship in which the child is everything for his mother, yet accepted subsequently as the only possibility of freeing himself from an unsatisfied longing that was now forbidden and buried with the object. Moments of illusion that can tolerate moments of disillusion and permit the transition from closed symbolization, confined within the symptom, to open symbolization insofar as it re-establishes the circulation between the psychic systems.

This movement makes possible the phallic and genital introjections that were hitherto closed off and barred by the incorporation of the lost object. This mode of oral cathexis certainly gives rise to anxiety concerning the loss of boundaries, but here it is nuanced by the mode of anal cathexis which maintains the libidinal cathexis of objects and the links between love and hate. Hence the possibility of an interplay between expelling and retaining, since the loss of the object does not result here in the irremediable loss of the ego, unlike in Charles's case. If Charles' case was in some ways reminiscent of the "Wolf Man", Marc's case might be compared to that of "Little Hans", according to a difference formulated by Freud (1926) in *Inhibitions, Symptoms and Anxiety* concerning the dimension of regression in the face of the Oedipus complex. In the first case, castration cannot play its anchoring role and what is involved is "a genuine regressive degradation of the genitally-directed impulse in the id"; in the second case, castration only leads to a "replacement of the [psychical] representative by a regressive form of expression" (Freud, 1926, p. 105). In other words, while for the "Wolf Man", love for the father entails the fear of being devoured by wolves and the loss of boundaries, for Little Hans, it only entails a displacement of affects and ideas in the animal phobia: the fear of being bitten by the horse. The semantics of symbolism, similar from certain points of view, needs to be articulated with its syntax, and its function in the psychic economy.

That is why, since the death of his wife, Charles had never been able to leave Paris and see the South of France again, where his parents had died, whereas Marc had been able to continue his work of mourning by returning for the first time to see his mother's tomb in a little provincial village where his mother's entire family had lived. It was not only a matter of expelling the bad mother, but also the mother who had been ill and diminished, and finally her corpse. In line with his sporting and martial arts habits, he decided to do part of the journey by bike to visit his mother for the last time. One day, he said that he had not cried when his mother was buried. It is possible that with this project he wanted to *exhume* his mother in order to *inhume* her once and for all. It was a matter of reuniting a historical child and an imaginary child, from which emerges, as Conrad Stein (1986) has pointed out, the figure of the symbolic child.

This work of mourning did not occur, however, without difficulties; Marc suddenly left his job as a teacher to become a representative and was absent more often and for longer periods from his sessions, which made me fear that he would break off the analysis. I interpreted his wish to remain close to his mother through his absence and reminded him of the difference between breaking off and terminating an analysis, and this led him to undertake a real process of termination during his last year of analysis. Thanks to this working-through, Marc was able to envisage emotional and professional commitments that he had never been able to engage in before; he decided to marry the woman friend he had been living with before his analysis and to have a child; he found a post as a teacher again corresponding to his aptitudes. He separated from me with some difficulty, reliving during the final months sudden anxiety attacks which were understood and interpreted as a way of repairing me for the anticipated loss. He wrote to me a few months after the end of his analysis, which had lasted six years, to announce the birth of a son, and took the opportunity in this letter to speak of the benefit of his analytic work and to express his recognition.

The retroactive effect (après-coup)

Marc clearly seemed to have completed a very fruitful analytic journey, involving topographical, dynamic and economic reorganizations. At the level of the countertransference, he was a patient that I felt particularly invested in on account of his intellectual and human qualities and his possibilities for psychic work. For me, his analysis was highly satisfying, in spite of difficult moments, because he was able to develop creativity both in his analytic work and in his life.

I had considered during his treatment the possibility of writing about this case, and in fact did so seven years later in my report for the Congress of French-Speaking Analysts. The text was sent to all the participants two months before the congress. I was then quite astonished to receive a telephone call from Marc the same week as I sent off the text! Without understanding this astonishing coincidence, I thought later that he had perhaps had occasion to read it, that he had recognized himself in one of the clinical cases and wanted to speak to me about it.

I saw him a week later and, to my great surprise, this was not the case at all. He had returned to see me because he had started to experience anxiety again, in particular since the departure of a work colleague with whom he had very close ties and who had played an important role in his professional promotion: he had also helped him cope with his wife's depression in recent years, before she herself undertook an analysis. He was now almost forty, roughly the age of his mother when she died, which undoubtedly aroused his fears of suffering the same fate. Finally, he wanted to tell me that he had taken up writing.

As he did not wish to start an analysis again, I offered to see him once a week face-to-face, and so we worked together in this way for several years more. At the time, I had wondered whether I would show him what I had written about him, but finally decided not to do so in order to avoid a situation of narcissistic collusion. Later on, he brought me a text that he wanted me to read and comment on, which I declined to do, but it did not stop him from speaking to me about it. Marc accepted without difficulty, as he was concerned to respect the conditions of our work.

To be honest, meeting him seven years later under these coincidental circumstances made me feel a sense of uncanniness. Was it to be seen simply as a matter of chance or as a determined event that had occurred without either of us being aware of it? One could be tempted to consider this simultaneity as a magic encounter that had to do with the relationship with his mother before his father's return from the war. How was one to explain that this patient, whose evolution during his analysis I had evaluated very positively, once again found himself faced with phenomena of repetition? Was my sense of uncanniness a countertransference indication of an unresolved transference dimension?

It was at this point that the article by César and Sára Botella (1984) on "unconscious homosexuality" came back to my mind. They link this phenomenon to the danger of non-representation related to the formal regression characteristic of the analytic situation and to the work of the narcissistic double as a possible solution to this danger. According to them, the unconscious homosexual dynamic and the work of the preconscious ego may conceal this work of the double and form a blind point in the transference/countertransference relationship.

The interpretation of the object-related homosexual transference, however right it may be, may impede the emergence of this strange experience, whose repetitive figures Freud had identified, which constitutes in fact an essential and mutative moment in the analytic situation; the tendency to representation thus may have constituted for both of us a soothing solution to distance the anxiety caused by the danger of a loss of the capacity to cathect and represent. This inexpressible anxiety had returned seven years later in a moment of strange coincidence. One could turn to the hypothesis of telepathy to account for this experience, but the danger was then one of short-circuiting a countertransference elaboration; this had enabled me to sense a psychic issue that was still active in my patient and to evaluate both the benefits and risks of a mutual narcissistic fascination, excluding the passivity that is indispensable for the discovery and acceptance of otherness. The alternation of speech and silence is essential here for elaborating this question of the double in the session.

It was probably this experience that Freud (1937) foresaw when, in "Constructions in analysis", he noted that "true hallucinations occasionally occurred in the case of other patients who were certainly not psychotic" (p. 267). It may be that Marc's analysis had raised the problem of both the work of remembering and the reconstruction of the past as a struggle against the waking formal regression of thought and the reliving of the hallucinatory dimension, sources of alteration of the sense of identity, as well as the need for a work of construction that was necessary to continue to the end of the analysis, with the aim of fostering the reliving of the hallucinatory dimension. It is worth considering this possibility given the hypotheses put forward by C. and S. Botella. It may be assumed that the evocation of anxiety linked to *silence* – aggressive silence, a silence of death – and to physical and psychic immobility in the analysis had been evacuated by Marc, both in the efflorescence of his representations and in his various forms of acting out, in particular his multiple absences when he was working through the mourning of his mother.

I recall that during the fifth year of the analysis, I had been attentive to this issue that arises in every analysis, namely, the confrontation with an experience of depersonalization corresponding to the integration of passivity towards the feminine-maternal object. This is the issue of narcissistic regression in analysis, which Michel de M'Uzan (1994) considered to be the essential precondition of an analysis:

> To suffering which, in analysis, is bound up with frustration, must be added a weakening of the boundaries of the ego, a limited and temporary 'failure' of the sense of identity. Otherwise, what is most original, most specific and also most excluded cannot find in the 'self', in the person, an 'organic' place.
>
> (p. 124)

I thought that it was perhaps to escape such controlled and "minor episodes of depersonalization" in analysis that Marc had missed his sessions so often at this time to the point of making me fear that he was going to break off the analysis. He had said, in the first session when he lay on the couch, that he was afraid of going mad and of having hallucinations during the analysis. It was probably this danger experienced this time in the transference that had precipitated the process of ending the analysis, probably an acceptable compromise for both of us, and given rise to this feeling of incompletion that had led him to come back seven years later.

We can see with hindsight the expression in Marc's first dream not only of a phantasy content but also of modalities of his mental functioning. It was a dream in which the patient was going to the cinema, prefiguring the defensive function of depiction; moreover, he climbed up onto the stage, thereby announcing the recourse to acting out. In both cases, these were defensive measures aimed at protecting himself against the risk of non-representation linked to the formal regression engendered by the analytic situation.

This raises the following question: Did the current conditions of the analytic setting – namely, the face-to face situation – foster or impede the elaboration of this fear of immobility and the defensive recourse to the narcissistic double? The face-to-face situation modifies the possibilities of free association and free-floating attention, which customarily are alone capable of bringing about the narcissistic regression authorizing the elaboration of this primordial passivity. However, faced with the danger of non-differentiation, Marc experienced a danger in the face-to-face situation; he was thus able to speak more about the issues at stake in this problem. He stressed the importance of this anxiety which, at certain moments, nailed him to the spot and prevented him from moving or speaking. In order to get out of what he called his "catatonic state", someone had to come and touch him.

He also recalled that during his whole childhood, his mother had had migraines and obliged the entire family, and him in particular, to be silent. He was considered to be a "docile and good child". Protected by the face-to-face situation, he understood that his mother's silence, to which the analyst's silence harked back,[18] had resulted for him in an experience of "terrifying anxiety" corresponding to a withdrawal of cathexis. It may be supposed that, throughout his analysis, he had to struggle against the danger of being faced once again with this silence that was a source of meaninglessness.

Thus, the hypercathexis of the analyst as an external double makes it possible to ward off this danger; but at the same time, this solution represents a major resistance insofar as it can inhibit the elaboration of the processes of secondary identification in favour of the visual incorporation of the material aspects of the object-analyst (Roussillon, 1991): hence the phenomena of imitation of the analyst to the detriment of his internalization as an internal double, the only guarantee of autonomy in relation to the object and of authentic creativity. On the countertransference level, the face-to-face situation seemed to me at certain moments to be a constraint for Marc who tried to immobilize my free floating attention in order to struggle against his own anxiety to do with immobility.

Marc's analytic adventure raises the issues at stake in psychoanalysis and psychotherapy. Clearly, analytic treatment on the couch had allowed him to rely on his capacities to cathect the object to elaborate satisfactorily difficulties to do with sexuality with its attendant affects of shame and guilt. But his return, seven years later, and the resumption of analytic work in the form of face-to-face psychotherapy on a once-a-week basis showed that the couch setting had not enabled him to confront the *destructiveness* linked to his envy of the feminine-maternal dimension. Although this issue implies reliance on the narcissistic double and the organization of primary homosexuality, it is not always possible in analysis on the couch to foster the elaboration of this receptivity towards others, which Freud (1937) thought of as a "biological bedrock". If there is too much destructiveness and drive defusion, there is a risk of taking the patient back to an "invisible maternal dimension", a source of anxiety and intolerable terror, and of engendering transference and even countertransference acting out. Hence, the need for work which gives visual and motor support its place in order to cope with the anxiety of non-representation related to the loss of the capacity to cathect an object.

These patients with whom we suggest working face-to-face are ones whose identity is ill-assured and who make us feel that they will not be able to cope with the experience of losing their boundaries, characteristic of analytic work on the couch, without becoming disorganized and lost. In these cases the analytic work consists in providing them with a setting that allows them to assure themselves as to their identity on the basis of the boundaries and distance in relation to the object that are conveyed by visual perception and motor activity; it is also a means of assuring themselves that the object can resist their destructiveness (Roussillon, 1991). Thanks to this perceptual support, these patients can discover or rediscover capacities for representation and symbolization through topographical and formal regression.

But it is probably necessary to accept the limits of this setting which protects the patient from the experience of depersonalization on the couch and, in the best of cases, reflects a genuine change in the treatment, related to the integration of psychic bisexuality. This is what is at stake in the analysability of every analytic candidate in the lying down position, the derealizing character of which is both a source of anxiety and a special means of elaborating the encounter with the "invisible maternal dimension". It is thus conceivable that certain conceptions of the analytic process and technique, using the couch setting, also have the function of avoiding the elaboration of this experience of the loss of boundaries and identity, without it being possible, however, to deny their therapeutic effect.

Marc's analytic adventure is here an exemplary model of the issues at stake in regression in analysis. The existence of the object can always entail a risk of disorganization, with or without topographical regression. The temptation of the identical can lead both to the solution of self- or hetero-destructive acting out and to that of delusion, which, as Freud points out in connection with organ language in schizophrenia, excludes all topographical regression. The possibility of respecting the difference of others allows for all the substitutions of ideas and affects characteristic of topographical regression, the dream-work and neurosis.

In a certain way, the strange coincidence of Marc's return to analysis opens up a reflection on the conditions of regression in analysis which, it is true, may involve a negative and pathological dimension, even to the point of leading to psychic and somatic disorganizations; but it is also an essentially positive and progressive factor when it allows for the integration of passivity. Robert Barande (1966) insisted on this point by speaking of a "structural disposition of the mind" (p. 401). In any case, it is never a question of returning to an already-experienced earlier state, but of contributing to the constitution of temporality and history in the present. The purpose of the analytic process is to foster the circulation between the psychic systems, which is a consequence of free interplay between the three forms of regression described by Freud.

If Freud seemed to favour temporal regression to the detriment of topographical and formal regression, it was because this hypothesis protected him owing to its linearity against the experience of the timelessness of the unconscious, which returns in these moments of surprise for the analyst and analysand alike. These moments of rupture can lead to a danger of non-representation; but they can also open the way to the resolution of a transference/countertransference enigma which, as Haydée Faimberg (1987) has pointed out, is probably the only criterion of validation for our interpretations-constructions.

For Freud (1919), this "unfamiliar" (*unheimlich*) place is related to what is most "familiar" (*heimlich*), "the former *Heim* [home] of all human beings" (p. 245). If our patients, after an indication of analysis, are capable of confronting this dimension of uncanny strangeness without collapsing, it may be supposed that a successful and deeply mutative analysis should be one that, thanks to regression, makes possible the transference/countertransference encounter with the "invisible maternal dimension" corresponding to the procreative dimension of maternal femininity. This experience, which is correlative with the conditions of the setting and analytic attitude, may certainly result in a vacillation of identity and confront the analysand with the terror of infiniteness, but it is the only one that makes possible the integration of psychic bisexuality as the difference between masculine and feminine, rather than as an opposition between the phallic and the castrated, between the positive and the negative. (Gibeault, 1993). It is certainly an experience of reunion with what Pasche (1960) has called the "personal symbol" with its trail of affects and representations, but also of a symbolic relation that defines the analytic relation and that alone makes possible the gap, the mediation, between the illusion of absolute union and the disillusion of irremediable loss.

Notes

1 Colette Guedeney was the psychoanalyst of this child and I thank her for letting me use this material.

2 These shapes can be bodily substances (faeces, saliva) or non-bodily objects and processes (as in this case the shadow of objects, but also letters, geometrical shapes, etc.); see Tustin (1984).

3 Meltzer et al. (1975) evokes in this connection the function of attention which holds "the senses together in consensuality" (p. 12), following Bion's conception of "common sense" which "apprehends objects in a multifaceted way" (p. 12).

4 An adult anorexic woman patient also expressed one day a similar issue during a psychodrama; her analyst had asked her to draw herself, but she was only

able to produce a filiform representation of herself, without a belly and without volume: the splitting of the body and of the mind was certainly not to be attributed to instrumental difficulties in drawing.

5 It is worth noting that this experience of the touching-touched hand has been used by analysts to show that, in the infant's processes of maturation and learning, it attests to the development of the ego as a distinct organization of the bodily self and to the possibility of distinguishing between the body and the environment (see Hoffer (1952); E. Kestemberg and J. Kestemberg (1966)).

6 For a more detailed presentation of this clinical case, see Gibeault (1995).

7 According to the research carried out by Evelio Cabrejo Parra at the Department of Linguistic Research at Paris VII and at the Centre of the Cognitive Processes of Language of the École des Hautes Etudes en Sciences Sociales (6th section). See also Diatkine (1987, pp. 8–9).

8 The question of the acquisition of language is only mentioned here. For a more detailed elaboration which discusses the issues at stake, in particular with the aim of emphasizing the primacy of identification over imitation in this process see Gibeault, Bouhsira, and Danon-Boileau (1998).

9 According to the expression used by Werner and Kaplan to denote the level of psychic assimilation, the proto-symbol implies a lack of differentiation between the "vehicle" and the "referent", and "presents" a signification directly, unlike the symbol which presupposes a "vehicle" that *represents* a "referent" (an object, a concept, a thought) and implies a difference, even if it is vague, between vehicle and referent (see Werner & Kaplan, 1963, pp. 16–17).

10 Concerning the interpretation of Schreber's delusion as a hypochondriacal delusion, see Macalpine and Hunter (1953).

11 The Lacanian conception of foreclosure presupposes a hiatus between neurosis and psychosis, which rests in fact on a topographical theory of castration; in this connection see Gibeault and Guedeney (1980).

12 E. Laufer and M. Laufer (1984) insist on the importance of this surrender of the adolescent's body to the mother in problems of "breakdown" in adolescence.

13 The present team consists of the following colleagues: group leader: Alain Gibeault (A.G.); psychodramatists: Clément Bonnet, Anne Enguerand, Murielle Gagnebin, Monique Israël, Marina Loukoumskaïa, Pierre Mattar, Laurent Muldworf, Brigitte Reed-Duvaille, Martha Villarino.

14 The Évelyne and Jean Kestemberg Centre for Psychoanalysis and Psychotherapy was founded in 1974 for patients presenting psychotic disorders and severe personality disorders. It is part of the different psychiatric institutions belonging to the Mental Health Association of the 13th area in Paris, which was created in 1958 by a group of psychiatrists and psychoanalysts, including Philippe Paumelle, Serge Lebovici, René Diatkine and Jean Kestemberg, who wanted to provide a deprived population with free mental heath care within a perspective combining psychiatric and psychoanalytic approaches. Following Jean Kestemberg, Évelyne Kestemberg directed the Centre and played a major role in developing reflection on the theory and clinical experience of psychosis.

15 Translator's note: *nuits blanches* can mean both 'white' nights and sleepless nights.

16 According to a relation between incorporation and introjection as defined by Maria Torok following Ferenczi (see Torok, 1968).

17 Unlike Charles for whom the discovery of the phantasy did not suffice to relieve his hypochondriacal anxiety due to the symbolic equation between phantasy and reality.

18 The silence of the analyst here refers more to his neutrality than to an almost total absence of words.

References

Abraham, K. (Ed.). (1924). A short study of the development of the libido, viewed in the light of mental disorders. In: *Selected Papers on Psychoanalysis*. London: Routledge, 2018, pp. 418–501.

Abraham, N. (Ed.). (1978). Manie normale. In: *L'écorce et le noyau* (collaboration and other essays with M. Torok). Paris: Aubier-Flammarion, 1986, pp. 25–87.

Anastasopoulos, D. (1988). Acting out during adolescence in terms of regression in symbol formation. *The International Review of Psychoanalysis*, 15 (2): 177–186.

Angelergues, R. (ed.). (1975). Réflexions critiques sur la notion de schéma corporel. In: *Psychologie de la connaissance de soi*. Paris: Presses Universitaires de France, pp. 215–242.

Angelergues, R. (1981). Variations on hallucination. *Les Cahiers du Centre de Psychanalyse et de Psychothérapie*, 2: 133–143.

Angelergues, R. (1987). Délirer ou rêver. *Les Cahiers du Centre de Psychanalyse et de Psychothérapie*, 15: 1–18.

Anzieu, D. (1975). Le transfert paradoxal. De la communication paradoxale à la réaction thérapeutique négative. *Nouvelle Revue de psychanalyse*, 12: 49–72.

Aulagnier, P. (1985). Le retrait dans l'hallucination: un équivalent du retrait autistique. *Lieux d'enfance*, 3: 149–164.

Barande, R. (1966). Le problème de la régression. Essai critique sur l'histoire et les vicissitudes de l'hypothèse freudienne. *Revue française de psychanalyse*, 30 (4): 351–420.

Bion, W.R. (1957). Differentiation of the psychotic from the non-psychotic personalities. *International Journal of Psycho-Analysis*, 38: 266–275.

Bion, W.R. (1962). *Learning from Experience*. London: Heinemann.

Botella, C., & Botella, S. (1984). L'homosexualité inconsciente et la dynamique du double en séance. *Revue française de psychanalyse*, 48: 687–708; Working as a double, in *The Work of Psychic Figurability: Mental States without Representation*. Hove and New York, Routledge, 2005, pp.67–85.

Bruner, J.S. (1983). *Savoir Faire, Savoir Dire*. Paris: Presses Universitaires de France, 1992.

Chasseguet-Smirgel, J. (1977). Table ronde sur K. Abraham (21 June, 1977): La théorie des stades (roneographed document of the Paris Institute of Psychoanalysis).

Colette, S.-G. (1924). *Fleurs. Aventures quotidiennes. Œuvres, Vol III*. Paris: Gallimard, "La Pléiade", 1991.

Diatkine, R. (1985). Autour du texte de Donald Meltzer. *Lieux de l'enfance*, 3: 111–132.

Diatkine, R. (1987). Essai sur les dysphasies. *Les Textes du Centre Alfred Binet*, 11: 1–127.

Donnet, J.-L., & Green, A. (1973). *L'enfant de ça (Psychanalyse d'un entretien: la psychose blanche)*. Paris: Minuit.

Fain, M. (1983). Réalité du fétiche, réalité de la castration. *Revue française de Psychanalyse*, 47 (1): 325–332.

Freud, S. (1900). *The Interpretation of Dreams*. S.E. 4–5. London: Hogarth.

Freud, S. (1911). *Psychoanalytic Notes on an Autobiographical Account of a Case of Paranoia (Dementia Paranoides)*. S.E. 12. London: Hogarth, pp. 9–82.

Freud, S. (1919). The 'Uncanny'. S.E. 17. London: Hogarth, pp. 217–252.

Freud, S. (1920). *Beyond the Pleasure Principle*. S.E. 18. London: Hogarth, pp. 1–64.

Freud, S. (1924). The Economic Problem of Masochism. S.E. 19. London: Hogarth, pp. 155–170.

Freud, S. (1926). *Inhibitions, Symptoms and Anxiety*. S.E. 20. London: Hogarth, pp. 75–174.

Freud, S. (1937). *Analysis Terminable and Interminable*. S.E. 23. London: Hogarth, pp. 209–253.

Freud, S. (1940). *An Outline of Psychoanalysis*. S.E. 23. London: Hogarth, pp. 139–207.

Freud, S. (1950 [1895]). *A Project for a Scientific Psychology*. S.E. 1. London: Hogarth, pp. 281–397.

Faimberg, H. (1987). Le télescopage des générations. A propos de la généalogie de certaines identifications. *Psychanalyse à l'université*, 12 (46): 181–200.

Fain, M. (1983). Réalité du fétiche, réalité de la castration. *Revue française de Psychanalyse*, 47 (1): 325–332.

Gagnebin, M. (2002). L'image et ses ombres: polysémie et polyvalence. In: M. Gagnebin (Ed.) *L'ombre de l'image. De la falsification à l'infigurable*. Seyssel: Champ Vallon, pp. 7–16.

Gibeault, A. (1986). La symbolique de l'argent. *Les Cahiers du Centre de Psychanalyse et de Psychothérapie*, 12: 63–99.

Gibeault, A. (1988). Étienne or one of today's adolescents. On adolescence and moral masochism. *The International Review of Psychoanalysis*, 15: 195–206.

Gibeault, A. (1990). La *Weltanschauung*: des remaniements de l'idéal du moi et du surmoi à la fin de l'adolescence. In: A.M. Alléon, O. Morvan & S. Lebovici (Eds.) *Devenir adulte?* Paris: Presses Universitaires de France, pp. 157–171.

Gibeault, A. (1993/1988). On the masculine and the feminine. After-thoughts on Jacqueline Cosnier's, book *Destins de la féminité*. In: D. Birksted-Breen (Ed.) *The Gender Conundrum. Contemporary Psychoanalytic Perspectives on Femininity and Masculinity*. London: Routledge, pp. 166–181.

Gibeault, A. (1995). Le malentendu de la répétition. *Adolescence*, 25: Psychodrame, pp. 45–61.

Gibeault, A., Bouhsira, D., & Danon-Boileau, L. (1998). Le dire et le dit dans le fonctionnement symbolique et l'échange. *Revue française de Psychanalyse*, 52 (2): 389–399.

Gibeault, A., & Guedeney, C. (1980). Questions ouvertes. *Les Cahiers du Centre de Psychanalyse et de Psychothérapie*, 1: 73–93.

Gillibert, J. (1985). *Le psychodrame de la psychanalyse*. Seyssel: Champ Vallon.

Green, A. (1971). La projection: de l'identification projective au projet. *Revue française de psychanalyse*, 35 (5–6): 938–960.

Green, A. (1982). La double limite. *Nouvelle Revue de Psychanalyse*, 26: 267–284; Le langage dans la psychanalyse. *Langages*. Paris: Les Belles Lettres, 1984, pp. 19–250.

Green, A. (1986/1980). *On Private Madness*. London: Hogarth.

Grinberg, L. (1979). Projective counteridentification and countertransference. In: L. Epstein & A. H. Feiner (Eds.) *Countertransference*. New York: Jason Aronson, pp. 169–192.

Haddad, G. (2005). *Le jour où Lacan m'a adopté*. Paris: Grasset.

Hoffer, W. (1952). Development of the body ego. *The Psycho-Analytic Study of the Child*, 5: 18–23.

Janin, C. (1990). L'empiètement psychique: un problème de clinique et de technique psychanalytiques. In: *La psychanalyse, questions pour demain* (Monographs of the *Revue française de psychanalyse*). Paris: Presses Universitaires de France, pp.153–160

Jeammet, Ph., & Kestemberg, É. (1981). Le psychodrame psychanalytique. Technique, specificité, indications. *Psychothérapies*, 2: 85–92.

Kestemberg, É. (1957). Quelques considérations à propos de la fin du traitement des malades à structure psychotique. In: *La psychose froide*. Paris: Presses Universitaires de France, pp. 15–54.

Kestemberg, É. (1962). A propos de la relation érotomaniaque. *Revue française de Psychanalyse*, 26 (5): 533–589.

Kestemberg, É. (1978). La relation fétichique à l'objet. *Revue française de Psychanalyse*, 42 (2): 195–214.

Kestemberg, É. (2001). *L'appareil psychique et les Organisations Psychiques Diverses, La psychose froide*. Paris: Presses Universitaires de France.

Kestemberg, É., & Jeammet, Ph. (1987). *Le psychodrame psychanalytique*. Paris: Presses Universitaires de France.

Kestemberg, É., & Kestemberg, J. (1966). Contribution à la perspective génétique en psychanalyse. *Revue française de psychanalyse*, 30 (5–6): 647–649.

Kestemberg, É., Kestemberg, J., & Decobert, S. (1972). *La faim et le corps*. Paris: Presses Universitaires de France.

Kristeva, J. (2002). *Le génie féminin, III. Colettte*. Paris: Fayard.

Kristeva J. (2004), *Colette*. Trans. Jane Marie Todd. New York: Columbia University Press.

Kurts, N. (1988). Alexandre et la conquête du désert ou le mirage de la représentation. Evaluation du changement au cours d'un processus analytique en psychanalyse d'enfants. *Les Textes du Centre Alfred Binet*, 12: 121–140.

Lacan, J. (1949). The mirror stage as formative of the *I* function as revealed in psychoanalytic experience. In: B. Fink (Trans.) *Écrits*. New York: Norton & Co, pp. 75–81.

Lacan, J. (1981). *The Seminar of Jacques Lacan, Book III, The Psychoses, 1955–1956*, trans. R. Grigg. New York: Norton & Co.

Laplanche, J. (1971). Dérivation des entités psychanalytiques. In: *Le primat de l'autre*. Paris: Flammarion, pp. 106–123.

Laplanche, J. (1980). *La sublimation (Problématiques III)*. Paris: Presses Universitaires de France, pp. 50–60.

Laplanche, J. (1987). *New Foundations for Psychoanalysis*, trans. D. Macey. Oxford: Blackwell.

Laufer, L. (2005). De l'irreprésentable à l'hallucination (unpublished). Paper read at the colloquium Image, psychanalyse, société Albi, 11 June, 2005.

Laufer, L. (2006). *L'énigme du deuil*. Paris: Presses Universitaires de France.

Laufer, E., & Laufer, M. (1984). *Adolescence and Developmental Breakdown: A Psychoanalytic View*. London: Routledge.

Lebovici, S., Diatkine, R., Kestemberg, E. (1969–1970). Bilan de dix ans de pratique psycho-analytique chez enfant et adolescent. *Bulletin de psychologie*, 285 (23): 839–888.

Letarte, P. (1990). A partir d'un roc: de la quantité à la qualité. *Revue française de Psychanalyse*, 54 (1): 209–225.

Luquet, P. (1988). Langage, pensée et structure psychique. *Revue française de psychanalyse*, 52 (2): 267–302.

Macalpine, I., & Hunter, R.A. (1953). The Schreber Case: a contribution to schizophrenia, hypochondrai, and psychosoamatic symptom-formation. *The Psychoanalytic Quarterly*, 22: 328–371.

Meltzer, D., Bremner, J., Hoxter, S., Weddell, D., & Wittenberg, I. (1975). *Explorations in Autism*. Strathclyde: Clunie Press.

Meltzer, D., & Williams, M.H. (Eds.) (1988). Aesthetic conflict: its place in the developmental process. In: *The Apprehension of Beauty: The Role of Aesthetic Conflict in Development, Art and Violence.* Strathclyde: The Clunie Press, pp. 7–34.

Merleau-Ponty, M. (Ed.) (1960). Le philosophe et son ombre. In: *Signes.* Paris: Gallimard, pp. 201–228.

Milner, M. (1952). Aspects of symbolism in comprehension of the not-self. *International Journal of Psychoanalysis,* 33: 181–195.

Mondzain, M.-J. (2003). *Le commerce des regards.* Paris: Seuil.

M'Uzan, M. de (1994). *La bouche de l'Inconscient.* Paris: Gallimard.

Pasche, F. (Ed.) (1960). Le symbole personnel. In: *A partir de Freud.* Paris: Payot, pp. 157–159.

Pasche, F. (1975). Réalités psychiques et réalité matérielle. *Nouvelle Revue de Psychanalyse,* 12: 189–197.

Pinol-Douriez, M. (1984). *Bébé agi – bébé actif.* Paris: Presses Universitaires de France.

Quinodoz, D. (2003). *Words That Touch. A Psychoanalyst Learns to Speak.* London: Karnac.

Racamier, P. (1987). De la dépossession du moi à la possession délirante, ou: A la recherche du nouveau monde. *Les Cahiers du Centre de Psychanalyse et de Psychothérapie,* 9: 29–50. Reprinted in: *Psychanalyse et psychose,* Centre de Psychanalyse et de Psychothérapie Evelyne et Jean Kestemberg. vol. 12 (Trauma et vécu catastrophique), 2012, pp. 21–36.

Rose, G.J. (1978). The creativity of everyday life. In: S. A. Grolnick, I. Barkin, & W Muensterberger (Eds.) *Between Reality and Fantasy.* Northvale-London: Jason Aronson, pp. 347–362.

Rosenfeld, H. (1965). *Psychotic States: A Psycho-Analytical Approach.* London: Hogarth Press.

Roussillon, R. (1991). Epreuve d'actualité et épreuve de réalité dans le face à face psychanalytique. *Revue française de Psychanalyse,* 55 (3): 581–596.

Roux, M.-L. (1994). La contrainte à la représentation. In: A. Fine, R. Perron, & F. Sacco (Eds.) *Psychanalyse et préhistoire.* Paris: Presses Universitaires de France, pp. 31–39.

Segal, H. (1957). Notes on symbol formation. *International Journal of Psychoanalysis,* 38: 391–397.

Stein, C. (1986). Figure symbolique de l'enfant. *Les Cahiers de l'IPC,* 3 (Les processus de symbolisation): 61–71.

Tausk, V. (1919). On the origin of the 'influencing machine' in schizophrenia. *Psychoanalytic Quarterly,* 1933, 2: 519–556.

Tisseron, S. (1987). *Psychanalyse de la bande dessinée.* Paris: Presses Universitaires de France.

Tisseron, S. (1989). Des mots et des images: le rôle des images dans la cure. *Revue française de Psychanalyse,* 53 (6): 1993–1997.

Torok, M. (1968). The illness of mourning and the fantasy of the exquisite corpse. In: N. Abraham & M. Torok (Eds.) *The Shell and the Kernel,* trans. N. Rand. Chicago, IL: University of Chicago Press, pp. 107–125.

Tustin, F. (1980). Austistic objects. *International Review of Psychoanalysis,* 7: 27–40.

Tustin, F. (1981). *Autistic States in Children.* London: Routledge.

Tustin, F. (1984). *Autistic shapes. International Review of Psycho-Analysis*, 11 (3): 279–290.

Tustin, F. (1986). *Autistic Barriers in Neurotic Patients*. London: Routledge, 2018.

Weich, M.J. (1978). Transitional language. In: S.A. Grolnick, I. Barkin, & W. Muensterberger (Eds.) *Between Reality and Fantasy: Transitional Object and Transitional Phenomena*. Northvale/London: Jason Aronson, pp. 413–423.

Werner, H., Kaplan, B. (1963). *Symbol Formation*. Hillsdale, MI, and London: Lawrence Erlbaum Associates, 1984.

Winnicott, D.W. (Ed.) (1951). Transitional objects and transitional phenomena. In: *Playing and Reality*. London: Tavistock, 1971, pp. 1–25.

Winnicott, D.W. (Ed.) (1971). Playing: A theoretical statement. In: *Playing and Reality*. London: Tavistock, pp. 38–52.

6 The interplay between symbolization, representation, and sublimation

Symbolization and representation

There is one question underlying many discussions: Is there a difference between the concepts of representation and symbolization? Symbolization is defined in terms of representation understood as a set of relationships where something will represent something else for someone. Is there any interest then in introducing into theory and clinical practice a concept that would only duplicate that of representation?

Roger Perron (1989) proposes to distinguish these two concepts: on the one hand, representation refers to the material, to the content in a term-for-term relationship between a representative and what is represented; on the other hand, symbolization relates rather to a process organizing relations between these different materials. And yet, when Freud (1915a) sets out to give a definition of the thing-presentation, he affirms that it corresponds to "the cathexis, if not of the direct memory-images of the thing, at least of remoter memory traces derived from these" (p. 201). While he refers initially to the idea of a two-term correspondence between the thing and its representation, as the concept of memory-image suggests, he subsequently considers the idea of associative networks between memory traces. Representation and symbolization therefore come together to designate this same processual function, where the substitution between the thing and its representation is necessarily related to the idea of a deviation, of a hiatus between the two terms, and of associations between the representations; this is what Freud (1950 [1895]) had already underlined with regard to the birth of the ego "as a network of cathected neurones, well facilitated in relation to one other" (p. 323) whose function is thus to inhibit the passage of excitation.

According to the model of the experience of satisfaction, which is organized on the basis of the opposition between hallucination and perception, it is indeed necessary to presuppose a cathexis, and, at the same time, perceptual residues to represent it. In certain patients, the inability to use perceptual residues causes an affect of terror. César and Sara Botella (1983) have given the example of a psychotic child who could not represent anything.

DOI: 10.4324/9781003545651-7

The analyst then offered him word-presentations and thing-presentations, while mimicking a terrifying wolf. This child started during the following sessions to play the wolf and come out of this state of non-representation, a source of distress and terror, in which he had previously found himself. The elaboration of separation then became possible, in contrast to what had happened previously when the words of his analyst and their meaning had remained ineffective: an image had been provided, the child had taken it over for himself, which enabled him to get his psychic functioning going again based on the organization of a psychic topography.

The thing-presentation is situated on the boundary between sensation and perception, between affect and the ideational representative. It corresponds to the psychic work of internalization and taking up of memory traces; this is a work of presentation and representation of the object that is at the basis of phantasying and has its roots in a movement of cathexis prior to the perception of the object. It is the moment when, as Freud (1926, pp. 137–138) suggests, automatic anxiety, which functions as an index, becomes fixed in representations: this is a concomitant process of primal repression that allows for the constitution of signal-anxiety. Green (1999) has pointed out that the term "signal" is perhaps not an adequate term here, since we are already in a symbolic dimension: from the moment when excitation is linked to representation we leave the dimension of the signal, which only refers to an immediate reaction.

This is why, if we define representation not as a duplication of the object, in the sense in which empiricist psychology understands it, it is necessarily related to a *process of transformation* of memory traces, which creates a gap, a distance between the thing and its representation. This is what Laplanche (1971) underlines in his own way, evoking a metaphoro-metonymic displacement: both a displacement of the goal of the drive where ingesting becomes incorporating and a displacement of the object, from the milk to the breast. This process is necessarily linked to the idea of a succession of memory systems, and the registration in these different systems of certain aspects of the object related to a drive cathexis: this is what defines the thing-presentation. As for the word-presentation, it is organized in this movement of substitution, since Freud defines it precisely as a substitute for motor images linked to satisfaction with the object. On the psychoanalytic level, the reference to language is part of this work of representation signifying substitution, distancing, a gap between subject and object.

So, what specific meaning should psychoanalysis give to the concept of symbolization? I have already established a distinction between the functions of *signification, representation and symbolization* (Gibeault, 1985), which I will recall here because they will allow me to take these reflections further. Freud had defined the function of signification in his study on aphasia. For him, signification designates the relation between the two systems of representation: "The word acquires its significance through its association with the idea (concept) of the object" (Freud, 1891, p. 77) and not, we might add, in the reference to the thing itself. Signification resides in the difference within language, which can be compared to the Saussurian distinction between the signifier and the signified. The function of representation would then refer to the relation of substitution and would designate the referential function or function of denotation between the sign and the thing, which the signifier/signified relation immanent to the sign had excluded. It is the need to take into account this dimension of the reference that made me give precedence to Peirce's theory of signs rather than that of Saussure.

As for the function of symbolization, it is necessarily part of this movement of substitution that is characteristic of the function of representation. In an oral communication, Serge Lebovici gave a very good example. During a consultation, a mother had told her child: "You suck me, you bite me, you devour me". René Diatkine emphasized that we must take into account the three forms of statements when we want to talk about symbolization. You suck me, that's the informative statement; you bite me, that's the affect; you devour me, that's the metaphor. What we find again here is the dynamic articulation correlative of the displacement and binding of affects through representations: each statement is only of interest due to its position in the sequence which always refers to the gap, to the hiatus between the dimension of need and that of the drive.

But, beyond this relation of substitution between representations, the function of symbolization tends to mark this *reflexive mediation* at both the intrapsychic and intersubjective levels, which the reference to the etymology of the symbol tends to underline as a sign of recognition. The work of representation is part of the dynamic of the sign, where the connection between the terms always seems incomplete, deferred: signifier and signified, representative and represented, represented and perceived are all manifestations of this "something that is instead of something else". The semiotic dimension is organized under the sign of incompleteness and non-coincidence, confirming the Freudian hypothesis of the non-simultaneity of perception and memory. On the contrary, the function of symbolization introduces the idea of a return to oneself restoring completeness: something instead of something else but *for someone*, where the reunion with oneself is equally a reunion with others. Unlike the sign, the symbol contains the idea of a reference "that finds, as it were its own term, a junction with the origin" (Eco, 1984, p. 191, translated from the French) a distance that is not irremediable, but on the contrary is the very condition of proximity. The reference to symbolization as a concept underlines the importance of the work of the subject, who returns to himself in order to better discover otherness and the transcendence of others.

The clinical example given by Roger Perron is exemplary here. A psychotic child whom he saw in a consultation was playing with a mirror to make himself appear and disappear, as in the case of François, the child of the shadows, who staged in the cuckoo game the possibility of representing the relation between presence and absence. When leaving, the child wanted to take the mirror away; faced with the consultant's refusal, he decided to draw the mirror and to take the drawing with him, leaving the paper cut-out, which in a way is a negative mirror. The drawing of the mirror, as well as its cut-out, have the function of depicting the mirror, initiating a relationship of representation with the disappearance and absence of the object: "It is a *figuration*, then an object of perception, a perception whose function is, precisely, to allow representation (the evocation *in absentia* of the lost object, the mirror)" (Perron, 1989, p. 1658). As the protagonists of the scene left each other with a substitute – one positive, the drawing, and the other negative, the cut-out of the paper – we can therefore think of the "symbol" as a means of signifying a link and belonging between them. The symbolization refers to the "link that is lost and yet preserved" between the patient and himself: a recognition in this case that was certainly incomplete, since this child never returned, but which echoes the symbolizing possibilities of analytic work, as much in the analyst as in the patient. If *representation* signifies a relationship of substitution, *symbolization* defines a link between two or more people who will be able, thanks to this reflexive movement, to recognize themselves as having constructed, as Roger Perron emphasizes, a relationship of both belonging and complementarity.

Symbolization also refers to an effect of retroactive reunion with the object, in a correlative movement of rupture with the narcissistic and solipsistic universe, and of elaboration of the loss of the object; the reflexivity of symbolization goes as much with the idea of a process of historization as suggested by the retroactive effect as with that of the transition from a world of private representations to a world of public representations (Athanassiou, 1989). Bion had already insisted on the idea that symbolization implies this social dimension that leaves room for an unsaturated world, open to new meanings, unlike the psychotic who symbolizes, of course, but to an excessive extent, in a narcissistic closure organizing a saturated world (Bion, 1970, pp. 113–127).

At another level, symbolization and hysterical functioning coincide and correspond to triangular, oedipal, and genital elaboration (Bergeret, 1989). These are all ways of indicating that the processes of symbolization aim at the reunion between the masculine and the feminine, psychic bisexuality making it possible to find a completeness; such completeness is never, however, an absolute coincidence, as the Platonic myth of the androgyne evoked by Freud (1920, pp. 57–58) might suggest. Rather, it is a possibility of identifying oneself virtually with the sexual experience of the other sex, without fear of losing one's identity. From this point of view, the processes of symbolization as reflexive mediation lead to a "bisexual mediation" (David, 1975) making it possible to dialectalize all oppositions in terms of difference.

The function of symbolization implies different levels of reflexivity related to the metapsychological approach to psychic functioning. Freud (1939) had thus linked the disposition of thought and the disposition of the drive (pp. 97–99). Bion (1963), in the construction of the vertical axis of his Grid, also attempted a genetic exposition of the different stages in the development of thought, thus supposing an evolution of thought from the most concrete to the most abstract in correlation with instinctual vicis-situdes. Didier Anzieu (1989) also insisted on the importance of "differ-ent logical levels of symbolization" organized around various oppositions, from the most sensory to the most abstract.

Even if one cannot deny the importance of an approach in terms of development, there can be no question of reducing a process to a linear evolution. A metapsychological approach implies taking into account topo-graphical, economic, and dynamic aspects, and refers more to conflicting modalities of cathexis. It is from this perspective that I have evoked the idea not of a succession but rather a conflict between symbolic equation, which would be linked to the non-distinction between ego/not ego and would possibly involve the motor solution, and the birth of symbolization, which, on the contrary, marks the possibility of differentiation and the functioning of thought.

From this perspective, it is important to remember that, for Freud, the presentation or idea *(Vorstellung)* designates a broader concept than visual representation *(Darstellung)*; moreover, he does not use the same terms to designate them. If the presentation/idea can be unconscious as well as conscious, visual representation is essentially a conscious staging, a stag-ing in images, which is found as much in children's play and drawing as in dreams and delusions. It can take different forms – material objects, images, words – which can be considered so many symbols. The emphasis placed on the processes of symbolization certainly leads us to consider a semantics, but also a syntax of these modes of visual representation which will thus have a different meaning according to their function in the mind.

In this work of visual representation, there will necessarily be motivated symbols and arbitrary symbols that we may be tempted to interpret as so many univocal contents. This would, however, be succumbing to a lan-guage trap; by wanting to better control the situation, one is merely led to reify a process and to confine oneself within the register of symbolic equa-tion; as J. Gillibert (1989, p. 1893) remarks, we would be acting like schizo-phrenics in wanting to refer to a univocal code. Above all, this would be forgetting, as Annie Anzieu (1989) has pointed out, that taking into account the dynamics of the function of symbolization leads rather to "tightening as closely as possible the meaning that symbols support in the dialectic of the transference and counter-transference" (p. 1619); it is a question of taking into consideration a cathectic relationship between an analyst and a patient, whose movement is related to multivocity. This means attribut-ing full importance to the distinction between non-linguistic representation and linguistic signification, between the *meaning* which refers to discourse and its referential dimension, and the *signification* which refers to the sign with the risk of a rupture with "things themselves" (Defontaine, 1989).

This is a point on which Green (1984, p. 80) emphasised the need to take into account the double representation (word-presentation and object-presentation), the double significance (sign and meaning), and the double reference (the object of internal reality and that of external reality).

Symbolization and sublimation

Symbolization therefore has close links with sublimation. Unlike the concept of symbolization, Freud very early on sought to describe the concept of sublimation by first emphasizing the *change of aim*: "This capacity to exchange its originally sexual aim for another one, which is no longer sexual but which is psychically related to the first aim, is called the capacity for sublimation" (Freud, 1908, p. 187).

In 1915, he considered writing a metapsychological text about it, just as he did for projection; but faced with his difficulties in exploring the concept more deeply, he gave it up. However, these reservations would not prevent him from including it among the drive vicissitudes alongside repression and reaction formation (Freud, 1915b, pp. 124–125) and, subsequently, from adding two other criteria: the change of object and social valuation: "A certain kind of modification of the aim and change of the object, in which our social valuation is taken into account, is described by us as 'sublimation'" (Freud, 1933, p. 97).

The difficulty would however have a bearing on the mechanism underlying these drive vicissitudes. Although Freud used this concept with reference to the chemical metaphor of the transformation of a solid state body into a gaseous state without passing through the liquid state, he still had to show how this displacement from the sexual to the non-sexual nevertheless retains a connection with the sexual source. We have seen, with regard to symbolism, what was at stake in this debate in the opposition between Freud and Jung. In his work on sublimation, Jean Laplanche (1980) has clearly shown the difficulty that Freud had, in his discovery of infantile sexuality, in simultaneously maintaining – which seems absolutely contradictory – the enlargement of the sexual, which no longer has anything to do with genital sexuality alone, while maintaining within this enlargement the specificity of the sexual.

If infantile sexuality is organized by the reliance of the sexual drives on the functions of self-preservation, testifying to a process of symbolization, Freud found it difficult to describe it as a complete satisfaction in comparison with genital sexuality: hence the importance of preliminary pleasure in the *Three Essays on Sexuality* (Freud, 1905) which cannot be reduced to the sole discharge of the quantity of excitation. It is this status of the genital drives which, because of their inadequacy, opens up another solution in their sublimation; for Freud, they are the source of "virtue" and progress (pp. 237–238). The plasticity of the drive thus gives sublimation the possibility of further freeing itself from the object. This economic issue has given rise to many debates, and both Evelyne Sechaud (2005) and Jean-Louis Baldacci (2005), in their own ways, have sought to offer the analytical community this metapsychological text on sublimation that Freud had wanted to write shortly after his break with Jung.

They both put the emphasis on a sublimatory process organized "from the start", at the birth of the drive itself, which links up with the issues involved in the symbolization process. The changes of aim are part of this movement of the substitution and transformation of representations, corresponding to the passage from the perceived object to the represented object. Symbolization and sublimation differ, however, in the emphasis placed on sublimation on the importance of actual achievements contributing to the development of culture, while symbolization emphasizes the dimension of reflexive mediation. Symbolization is more involved in the work of *representation*, while sublimation is akin to the *creation* of cultural objects whose value depends on very variable social factors.

Symbolization mediates what can be described about a work of representation and a process of sublimation. But the etymology of the word "symbol" reminds us that this process results in social recognition and thus meets the objectives of sublimation in its dimension of social valuation.

Max Kleinman or the crazy night of illusion

Before going any further into the concepts, let us first listen to a story that is rich in lessons and images on which we may reflect. On a winter night shrouded in fog, someone dreams that a man is being pursued by a killer through the dark alleys of a small town: the man who is running away seeks refuge in a house, but all its doors are closed; he goes into a cul-de-sac and sees the murderer coming down a staircase, coming towards him with outstretched arms and strangling him.

At this precise moment, the dreamer is roused violently from his sleep by a group of people who are knocking on his door screaming. So it was just a bad dream, but the reality is just as worrying. There is indeed a serial killer in the city and, faced with the powerlessness of the police force, a mob of citizens has devised a "plan" to track him down. He is asked to leave immediately and join the others. On awaking from his nightmare, our dreamer is immediately gripped by a more tenacious terror: "I was sleeping soundly in my bed", he said, "and here I am caught up in a plan!" Alone in the street on a freezing night, he is overcome by massive anxiety which owes as much to the impossibility of knowing his role in the plan as to the silent threat of an assassin who is prowling the city.

It is with this violence of dreams and reality that Woody Allen's 1991 film, *Shadows and Fog*, begins. It portrays admirably the fundamental questions of the human adventure – Who am I? What can I expect from others? – and the various psychic paths that make it possible to cope with the anxiety they arouse. The tale takes place overnight in a small town in Central

Europe in the interwar period, probably around the 1930s. The hero, Max Kleinman, played by Woody Allen, is a small Jewish bureaucrat, locked into a burdensome daily reality who, on a dark and foggy night, totally loses his bearings in discovering a truth that he had not suspected, and is completely changed in the process. An exemplary metaphor of existential conflict, as highlighted by Freud's discoveries, this film testifies to the vicissitudes of the drive in psychic life and the possible responses in analytic work.

The different stages followed by Max Kleinman in his nocturnal wanderings can indeed all be considered possible solutions to the question posed by the violence of the initial murder. The impossibility of clearly distinguishing between dream and reality corresponds to the total confusion in which our hero is plunged from the moment he finds himself wandering through the dark and icy streets of the city: he does not know why he has been asked to join this group, nor what role he is expected to play, nor the significance of the proliferation of vigilante groups that have begun fighting amongst themselves, as if the extermination of the evil engendered the evil itself.

Kleinman first finds refuge with a forensic doctor responsible for the autopsies of the victims. The latter seeks in the secrecy of the viscera an answer to the questions: What is evil? What can lead a man to commit "serial murders"? Science remains silent and, in guise of an answer, the doctor himself is led to suffer the fate of the victims he has autopsied, during a violent pursuit by the killer, which recalls Kleinman's nightmare.

The contiguity of Kleinman's visit to the doctor and the latter's assassination leads to a kind of contamination which makes our hero a possible culprit who must be pursued. From being the stalker, he becomes the one who is stalked and, in his mad rush, he meets Irmy, a young woman who, like him, has been wandering in the city since the beginning of the night. A sword swallower in a circus, she has fled her lover, the clown, who had betrayed her by falling into the arms of an acrobat, and she found herself in the brothel, the only bright and warm place, which represents life, sexuality and love.

The death and murder that rage in the cold and hostile street are set against the love and sexual pleasure that Irmy discovers at the brothel in the arms of a student, in exchange for a very large sum of money. The proximity of the places of murder and pleasure suggests both their possible contamination in the anonymous sexual crime and their differentiation by the discovery of otherness in love, via sexual pleasure that was intended only to be impersonal and venal.

The intertwining destinies of Max and Irmy are knotted under the sign of flight and guilt. For a short moment, they contemplate together the starry sky, thus suggesting reunion with the absolute and an experience of non-differentiation. But this ideal moment is immediately lost in a whirlwind of violence and fear because the vigilante mob now point their finger at Kleinman, whose guilt is established on the basis of his "smell" picked up by a clairvoyant. This is a barely disguised allusion to the roots of evil equated with the Jewish race which, through Kleinman, has become the scapegoat that has to be eliminated.

In this comedy of errors, with its Shakespearian overtones, the most violent situations are immediately overcome by humour, fantasy and illusion. In a world given over to evil and apparently abandoned by God, there remains the reign of play and illusion, evoked by the world of the circus. Irmy and her lover, the clown, find themselves again through the adoption of a child. Kleinman meets the circus magician who saves him from the strangler by taking refuge with him in the illusionist's mirror. The strangler is himself captured but escapes in turn, probably thanks to this same mirror. There is never an absolute victory over evil.

However, man still has the possibility of facing reality without dying from it thanks to the dream world. "Everyone loves your illusions", says Max to the magician who is about to leave his narrow life as a lonely little bank clerk to go with the circus and definitively reconnect with his sacred childhood. "Worship them?" replies the magician, "they need it just as they need to breathe".

It is an allusion to the world of art and creation which thus appears to be the only valid solution for a man who had until then lived locked into the boring life of a small bureaucrat, apparently without any satisfaction, either in his love life or in his professional work. Caught between a woman, his landlady, who pursues him with her advances, and a boss who rejects him, Max Kleinman suddenly, during this crazy night, loses all his social references and his protective barriers and discovers the world of imagination.

How can we not see in this astonishing film an illustration of what Freud had discovered about the conflict inherent in instinctual life, of the pathological and non-pathological solutions in the individual, as much as in civilizations, and in particular of the crucial issues of symbolization, sublimation, and creation? The murderer of *Shadows and Fog* is clearly a reference and a tribute to Fritz Lang's film, *M.*, in 1931. The expressionist style adopted by Woody Allen and the deliberate choice of black and white demonstrate this just as much as the theme of the two films: how are we to understand evil, as illustrated by the serial murder, apparently the most terrifying and scandalous of all murders? The reference to individual murder is an allusion to the collective murder perpetrated by the Nazis. *M.* was certainly inspired by the murderer Kürten, the vampire from Dusseldorf, whose trial was taking place when the film was released. For the filmmaker, it was an attempt to understand the psychological origin of the murder "whose seed is sown", he said, "in childhood", not only in a few but in everyone. The film was originally to be entitled *The Murderers Are Among Us*, and its distribution, at the time of the rise of National Socialism, quickly emerged as a unique and exceptional document on the genesis of Nazi barbarism.

Drives and sublimation

At the same time, in 1929, Freud wrote *Civilization and its Discontents* (Freud, 1930), in an attempt to understand the relationship between instinctual vicissitudes and the process of civilization. It was an opportunity for him to evoke the question of sublimation, the concept at the crossroads between sexuality and civilized values, which represents one of the possible solutions to what he calls "the search for happiness". In accordance with the regulation of the pleasure/unpleasure principle, this quest is just as much one of the "search for intense pleasures" as of the avoidance of suffering emanating from the body, the outside world and relationships with others: family, State and society. Different psychic solutions are sought to resolve this problem of suffering.

Inasmuch as the sexual drive is, strictly speaking, the only drive, one of the aims of life effectively comes down to seeking love (to love and be loved), and in particular sexual love which thus becomes the "prototype of the longing for happiness". But since the loss of the loved one and their love is always a threat, it is difficult to avoid the resulting suffering. "Pathological" solutions may then be preferred, whether it is withdrawal into drug addiction, isolation or delusions: all of which solutions are intended to deny the source of suffering, whether it be the body, the outside world or others. The recourse to religion is part of the perspective of the delusional solution, no longer individual but collective, where it is a question of "procuring a certainty of happiness – that is to say the satisfaction of impulses – and protection against suffering through a delusional remoulding of reality" (Freud, 1930, p. 81). As such, all these solutions, based on a disavowal of reality, are inadequate.

Then there are "sublimatory" solutions like professional work, science, and art. In all these cases, it is effectively a question of diverting and transforming *sexual aims and objects into non-sexual aims and objects* which will at the same time have a *social valuation* corresponding to the three criteria of sublimation. If simple professional work and social relations favour the displacement of narcissistic, aggressive, and libidinal tendencies, it remains the case nevertheless that, for Freud, "the great majority of people only work under the stress of necessity" (Freud, 1930, p. 80, footnote 1), therefore without pleasure; work is then a sublimation that is not very conducive to the avoidance of suffering. And the narrow professional life of Max Kleinman is illustrative of this "majority of people" evoked by Freud.

It is therefore not surprising that Freud sees in science and art two sublimatory solutions reserved for the "happy few" who possess rare gifts, constituting, alongside ordinary sublimations, exceptional sublimations (Baldacci, 2005). Whether in the solution of problems or the discovery of truths that characterizes the investment in science, or in the possibility of giving substance to phantasies, as in artistic creation, in both cases, it is a type of satisfaction of which Freud (1930) says "we shall certainly one day be able to characterize in metapsychological terms" (p. 79). And yet, he had sought to understand how it worked much earlier, in particular in his study of Leonardo da Vinci (Freud, 1910). Indeed, he believed that sublimation would deliver the secret of this transformation provided one could allow oneself to be permeated by the chemical metaphor, from which the concept originates, and to explore it more deeply in terms of a transition from the non-sexual to the sexual, like the direct transformation of the solid body into a gaseous body, of an upward displacement suggesting a change in values, from the lowest to the highest, according to a socio-cultural valuation.

It is perhaps not so surprising that Freud (1930) made this admission of ignorance insofar as he confined the metapsychology of the process of sublimation within a radical opposition between the *sexual* conceived as "the sating of crude and primary instinctual impulses" on the model of orgasmic discharge, and the *sublimated* whose intensity of satisfaction is infinitely less important… and consequently less likely to procure happiness (p. 79). This hypothesis led Freud to envisage an economy of sublimation that would be inversely proportional to genital sexual satisfaction, which leads, against all clinical evidence, to considering this solution as being likely to involve a risk of an impoverishment of energy; hence the idea that, while an artist may be stimulated in his creativity by sexual activity, a sexually abstinent scientist is more creative.

This economic hypothesis was directly dependent on the conception of sublimation developed by Freud (1923) in *The Ego and the Id*, according to which the "transposition of the object-libido into narcissistic libido… obviously implies an abandonment of sexual aims, a desexualization – a kind of sublimation, therefore" (p. 30). What else can this mean other than that there is a limited quantity of libidinal energy which is distributed between the object-related and narcissistic cathexes, according to a balance between communicating vessels: what one gives to one is withdrawn from the other.

Three observations can be made on this subject. This hydraulic theory, applied to sexuality, suggests a pregenital concept rather than a genital one insofar as the sexual exchange arouses an oral phantasy of emptying and being emptied. In addition, the equation of the concept of happiness with orgasmic discharge leaves out of account all the psychosexual issues on which Freud insisted in respect of the constitution of objectality and the integration of pregenitality under the primacy of the genital sphere. Finally, this economic concept of narcissistic and object-related cathexes is probably too influenced by Freud's positivism and, according to a suggestion by Angelergues (1992), it would be in our interests to take into consideration the modern evolution of thermodynamics to reconsider the importance of the economic order no longer as a mechanical displacement, according to Newtonian dynamics, but as a reciprocal and different transformation of bodies, according to a non-linear concept of the transformation of matter. The identificatory work corresponding to this economic balance of cathexes "is not an addition or a subtraction of good or bad psychic particles", but consists "of a succession of *completely original* new states resulting from the symbiotic work which cannot be reduced to the previous states of both protagonists" (p. 33).

This is what Sophie Mellor-Picaut (1979) suggests when she points out that the relationship between sexual libido and sublimated libido is not one of identity but rather of anaclisis: hence "it is possible for the sublimated libido to rely on sexual activity while detaching itself from it, but at the same time letting it subsist for itself" (p. 473). From this perspective of ana- clisis, it then becomes possible to conceive of a sublimatory outcome that is not incompatible with sexual life, but possibly enriches it thanks to the effect of phantasy activity in return.

In reality, the radical opposition between the sexual and the sublimated leads sublimation to be seen as a theory of defence against the drives along two axes: either a more or less important lack of differentiation from the related defence mechanisms of repression and reaction formation, or the loss of the relationship with drive energy, with the risk of no longer under- standing the process itself. This would be the danger of a conception of sublimation from the perspective of instinctual renunciation rather than of instinctual "derivation", which would not rule out the possibility of instinctual satisfaction.

In his opposition to Jung, Freud had difficulty in explaining the transition from the sexual to the non-sexual, because of this perspective of instinctual renunciation. He criticized Jung for reversing the link established between symbols and repressed sexual impulses, by making the sexual the symbol of something else. For Freud, the Jungian concept of the "libido-symbol" amounted to denying the importance of unconscious factors in the forma- tion of symbols because the libido-symbol meant for Jung "any mental pro- cess substituted for another"; where the libido loses its sexual specificity and where the term "symbol" applies to all forms of direct representation. And yet, at other times, Freud could speak of "symbols of the libido", and Jung did not fail to stress that he took the unconscious into account. The concept of sublimation was a major issue at stake in asserting the specificity of the Freudian discovery of infantile sexuality.

Sexualization and desexualization

Starting from this aporia, in a commentary on Freud's (1932) text "The acquisition and control of fire", Laplanche (1980, pp. 190–191) puts for- ward the hypothesis of a *sublimation not linked to repression* and closer to direct libidinal sources, as evoked by the myth of Hercules, alongside a sublimation linked to repression, as in the Freudian interpretation of the myth of Prometheus. Hence the idea of a "continuous neo-genesis of sexu- ality" which calls into question the principle of a definitive libidinal drive quantity: the succession of quantitative exchanges of this naturally given quantity would then confirm the hypothesis of a complete desexualization in the sublimatory process and thus leave out the link between sublimation and the fate of the sexual drive.

Sublimation actually requires us to take into account a dialectic between sexualization and desexualization, between the objectalizing function and the deobjectalizing function (Green, 1999, pp. 81–88), between binding and unbinding. As Laurence Kahn (2005) reminds us, sublimation has a destructive potential because of this movement of desexualization which Freud says leads to a drive defusion. This is what may have led to questioning the essential link between sublimation and desexualization, hence the suggestion to "define sublimation as sexualization" in order to maintain the link between instinctual plasticity and the "endless finality" of infantile sexuality (André, 2005). Nevertheless, it was on the basis of the reference to desexualization as a mechanism that Freud was able to distinguish sublimation from aim inhibition as in tenderness.

It is therefore more heuristic to conceive of a dialectical interplay between sexualization and desexualization, which leaves open the possibility of a fate that is both positive and negative for sublimation, of which Green was able to say that "it guarantees nothing, protects against nothing", and that it can put itself at the service of deadly tendencies in the individual as in culture (Green, 1999/1993). This is perhaps the interest of symbolization as a process which must be distinguished from symbolic equation; if the latter contributes to the exploration of the world of objects and culture and effectively constitutes a sexualization of thought, symbolization strictly speaking is organized on the basis of a mechanism of desexualization that makes it possible to separate this equation between the symbol and the symbolized object. Symbolization thus becomes the guarantor of *negation,* which alone allows for differentiation between oneself and others and, therefore, makes the movement of recognition possible.

Symbolization helps us to conceive of the gap that is essential for psychic functioning between sexualization and desexualization, between the object and the ego, between the primary process and the secondary process. René Roussillon (2005) also shows the importance in sublimation of a complementary interplay between the sexualization of the primary system, corresponding to the activation of an unconscious phantasy cathected libidinally, and the desexualization of the secondary system, which contributes to changes in aims and objects characteristic of sublimation.

Sublimation in the service of life implies that, when the object is lost, the portion of object libido transformed into a narcissistic libido, in the movement of identification that Freud describes as "a kind of sublimation", is immediately re-objectalized in the cathexis of the sublimated object (Séchaud, 2005). The maintenance of a dialectical relationship between the mechanisms is precisely what makes it possible to preserve the link between sublimation and the "vitality of infantile sexuality" (Baldacci, 2005) and thus to mark the importance of a work of the sexual drive in psychic functioning, albeit at a distance from direct satisfaction.

Finally, in the field of culture, instinctual drive renunciation is inherent in Freud's approach in *Civilization and Its Discontents*, where sublimation is also drawn towards an axiological theory where the task of the process of civilization imposes its ideals and values with the aim of repressing instinctual drive impulses. The exteriority of the sexual and the sublimated would thus be reduplicated by the individual sexual sphere and the collective and civilizing repressive forces, without our being able to understand how they are linked. This was an open door for the idea of "repressive sublimation" introduced by Marcuse (1955) in *Eros and Civilization* to evoke the sublimation generally described in analysis, which, according to him, cannot fail to be accompanied by repression as opposed to non-repressive sublimation, which he suggests is the aim of a sexual revolution. In both cases, we lose sight of what Freud (1930) underlined in *Civilization and its Discontents*: "Sometimes one seems to perceive that it is not only the pressure of civilization, but something in the nature of the function itself which denies us full satisfaction and urges us along other paths" (p. 105). Herein lies the importance of the discovery of infantile sexuality, and understanding of the process of sublimation can only be grasped on the condition of returning to the intrapsychic to perceive the articulation, and not only the opposition, between the sexual and the sublimated, between the individual and collective ideals and prohibitions.

Symbolization and sublimation from the very beginning....to the end

Symbolization and sublimation are therefore two complementary processes that are related to different issues, one referring to the topography of representations, the other to the economic problem underlying the question of change of aim. But ultimately they have a different purpose. Beyond the relationship of substitution between two terms, symbolization designates the *reflexive* mediation between subject and object, between the internal and the external, between the past and the present, and thus coincides with the purpose of the sublimatory process in its function of recognizing and sharing social reality and its values. This is the direction that Bion (1970) pointed to in respect of the social dimension of true symbolization (pp. 64–65).

But both processes are also present from the start, and it would be incorrect to regard one as the condition or the result of the other. The two concepts refer to the constitution of the psychic apparatus as Freud described it starting from the experience of hallucinatory satisfaction. The genesis of symbolization is part of this movement which contributes to the birth of the drive and of its psychic representatives at the moment when the object is perceived as whole and its loss is elaborated; this is a structural moment that creates, retroactively and at the same time, the difference between the sexual and the non-sexual and their reciprocal relations. Symbolization links up here with what Freud wrote about primal repression and about the binding of the drive in representations. But it is also about an economic change which he described in connection with the concept of sublimation and the importance, for "desexualized" psychic functioning, of a change of aim. It is a structural moment which was to be the beginning of a story with a multiplicity of psychic solutions.

This is how we can understand what Freud wrote in his article on Leonardo da Vinci about the transformation of infantile sexual curiosity into intellectual curiosity, according to a process that takes place "from the very beginning" (Freud, 1910, p. 80). But Melanie Klein has clearly shown that it was a process of symbolization that allowed Leonardo to pass over from the cathexis of an infantile sexual memory to the cathexis of a sublimatory activity – in this case, the flight of birds (Klein, 1932, pp. 106–109). This is what is at stake in research and the epistemophilic drive. But this "from the very beginning" concerns not only the conditions of *creation*, certainly Leonardo's artistic creation, but also the *creativity* necessary for "ordinary" psychic functioning which has been defined as "ordinary" sublimation as opposed to exceptional sublimations which have made possible the creation of works of art. J-L Baldacci remarks that Freud uses the expression "from the very beginning", not only for sublimation in respect of Leonardo da Vinci but also for the transition from autoeroticism to narcissism (Freud, 1914, p. 77) and for the link between the sensual trend and the affectionate trend, corresponding to the inhibition of the drive as to its aim (Freud, 1921, p. 115). He concludes with perspicacity by underlining the "uniqueness" of the sublimatory process as the common root of research and creativity (Baldacci, 2005, p. 1406): these are economic, dynamic, and topographical conditions that preside over the constitution of a form of the ego and a presentation of the object that can be said to be related to a process of symbolization. Although Freud did not strictly speaking conceptualize the process of symbolization, it should be noted that he often described the issues at stake by reflecting on the sublimatory process as a drive vicissitude that is associated with, but nevertheless different from, repression.

Symbolization and sublimation are organized in the gap between narcissistic cathexis and object cathexis, which does not however exclude the possibility of a simultaneity between the time of being and the time of having in order to think of the possibility of an encounter, of a "proximity through distance" between the subject and others (Merleau-Ponty, 1960). In *Civilization and its Discontents*, Freud (1930) seeks to understand this question in his critique of Romain Rolland's notion of oceanic feeling. Without delving into this discussion, it is in this connection that he insists on the importance of a time when, "originally, the ego includes everything", introducing into the psyche a "primary ego-feeling", and he adds: "The ideational contents appropriate to it would be precisely those of limitlessness and of a bond with the universe, the same ideas with which my friend [namely, Romain Rolland] elucidated the 'oceanic' feeling. He compares this with 'our present ego-feeling' which is more shrunken and corresponds to the moment when the ego detaches itself from the external world" (p. 68).

This is what he studies again with respect to the necessary but insufficient condition of sublimation – namely, the inhibition of the drive in respect of its aim, in the transition from the discharge of excitation to the experience of the feeling of tenderness. Évelyne Kestemberg (1984) spoke, on this subject, of the importance of primary homosexuality which authorizes, through the experience of tenderness, the experience of a differentiation from the object, like a double according to a modality of *similarity*, thus allowing the passage from the *identical* to *otherness*.

Winnicott insisted for his part on the constitution of an "intermediate area of experience" which can be situated halfway between the hallucinatory discharge and the recognition of others: at this level, narcissistic libido and object-libido, processes of identification and object-cathexis, are reconciled. The difference between orgasmic pleasure and transitional pleasure without a climax makes it possible to resolve the economic aporia between sexual energy and the undifferentiated energy constituting what is sublimated, on condition that the drive is not excluded as Winnicott (1967) was, at times, tempted to do (p. 98). Consequently, "playing" in the transitional area effectively contributes to desexualization, which is not an abandonment of the sexual but represents a turning away from it in favour of what Freud called "the release of still greater pleasure" (Freud, 1908, p. 153).

Sublimation refers to the possibility of organizing thought processes which Freud (1950 [1895]) described in the "Project for a scientific psychology" as relating to the use of small quantities of energy: a pleasurable mode of functioning comprised of an activity that is set up gratuitously, more for pleasure than to escape anxiety and depression, can then be organized, one that is not essentially linked to the discharge of the quantity of excitation according to the principle of inertia. Sublimation is effectively different from repression insofar as it refers to a process of hypercathexis of thing-presentations rather than their countercathexis; this is like the movement described by Freud of the hypercathexis of thing-presentations by word-presentations, authorizing not only the constitution of the preconscious but also and especially circulation between the psychic systems.

This "intermediate area of experience" which calls into question the opposition between the subjective and the objective is also what, according to Winnicott (1953), serves the "mode of external experiencing" that belongs to "the arts and to religion and to imaginative living, and to creative scientific work" (p. 14). It is in this potential space of play which separates and unites both mother and child that he sees "the location of cultural experience" (Winnicott, 1967). This is in line with what Freud had noticed about the wooden-reel game with regard to the links between symbolization, sublimation, and the elaboration of object-loss. The substitution of gesture and speech for immediate satisfaction was indicative of the child's involvement in an activity that was both symbolizing and sublimatory in the service of the ego.

In other words, in the sublimatory realization, access to a cultural and psychic dimension is not opposed to the dimension of nature and the body. Daniel Lagache (1962) also underlined that the cathexis of an object-value is very similar to the love of the object insofar as it testifies to the introjection of the values proposed by the object. There is no doubt that for the child in the wooden reel game, play and language represent essential cultural values offered by the environment in the service of the aims and objects of infantile sexuality. Likewise, the analyst offers the pleasure of psychic functioning as a privileged cultural value in the search for "happiness" which is not essentially linked to the absolute satisfaction of the drives.

Symbolization and creation

It is important not to establish an equivalence between sublimations and high cultural values, as demonstrated by scientific and artistic creation. Although Freud sometimes made this equation, in particular in his text on Leonardo, it is interesting to note that he dealt with discontents in *culture*, (*Kultur*, in German) in the sense of "civilization": the search for happiness in the avoidance of suffering refers to culture in its civilizing dimension, as the "whole sum of the achievements and the regulations which distinguish our lives from those of our animal ancestors and which serve two purposes – namely to protect men against nature and to adjust their mutual relations" (Freud, 1930, p. 89),[1] that is to say to all the systems and symbolic relations – tools, language, dwellings, etc., – which determine and organize a human group, in accordance with Lévi-Strauss' distinction between nature and culture. It stands in contrast with *culture* as such, which is more concerned with the cathexis by the individual of the highest manifestations of social life. Sublimatory processes can certainly lead to exceptional scientific and artistic achievements, but it by no means certain, however, that we can explain the existence of extraordinary gifts and talents in terms of narcissistic and object-related cathexes.

These restrictions do not, however, prevent us from identifying the correspondences between the sublimatory and creative processes. Freud (1910) tried to do this in *Leonardo da Vinci and a Memory of his Childhood*, where the conflict between science and art reflects the psychic risk inherent in aesthetic creation which is related to the undifferentiated world of silence and contemplation, unlike scientific creation which, based on language, establishes itself from the start at a distance from the world in order to better reveal and control it.

To this end, we can compare the *theory* of painting, as Leonardo developed it in his *Notebooks*, with his *practice*. This theory, like any theory of painting, describes an objective world, reified as a third witness would see it, where the technique of perspective claims to give an exact and infallible solution to the imitation of Nature by taking over the data and the position of classical science. And yet his pictorial work is not content with copying nature, but recreates it while never celebrating any enigma other than the experience of vision and human beings.

Thus, in his treatise, Leonardo recommends only painting one emotion at a time, while his work continually demonstrated the opposite by revealing its richness, thanks to the multiplicity of contradictory emotions expressed simultaneously. Freud himself was sensitive to this multivocal symbolism, since he noted that the fascination of Mona Lisa was due to the ambiguity of an unbounded tenderness and at the same time sinister menace (Freud, 1910, p. 115). Moreover, we find the same enigmatic smile in the representations of Saint Anne and Saint John the Baptist, which tends to confirm Kurt Eissler's (1961, pp. 278–279) hypothesis that the expressive richness of these masterpieces is measured by the simultaneous expression, not only of youth and old age, of what is most alive and at the same time moreover immutable and ideal, therefore close to the inert, but also of the masculine and feminine. If the theoretician of painting, like the scientist, tends to think along the lines of grand overviews and only sees the world in terms of its outer envelope, the painter experiences it from within and is included in it.

How can we not think here of the narcissistic regression inherent in the creative act that confronts the artist with the risk of an identification calling into question the boundaries of the ego? If transitionality can be considered a symbolic matrix of the creative experience, we also know that it is a solution to a nameless anxiety corresponding to the danger of non-representation. This is what Leonardo regularly overcame in his various creative activities and depicted particularly at the end of his life in the cycle of his eleven drawings of the Flood where the boundaries between heaven and earth disappear in an indescribable chaos. Eissler hypothesizes that what is involved is "the narcissistic projection of the anticipated dissolution of the Self in the universe" (1961 p. 356) corresponding to the major issue at stake in any artistic creation. This could be seen as a solution to the "blank" experience of psychotic catastrophe as the patient Raphael displayed in his sublimatory conflict over painting. The narcissistic fragility of highly creative people confirms this idea. J.-L Baldacci (2005) remarks that, in exceptional sublimations, we observe, "thanks to the gifts which allow it, repeated attempts aimed at resuming and concluding a sublimatory process that had failed at an early stage" (p. 1419).

The artist may therefore be said to have a particular gift for expressing what every human being experiences: the traumatic irruption of the object and the need to work through this suffering in order to find "happiness", to use Freud's term in *Civilization and its Discontents*. Max Kleinman's adventure illustrates the violence inherent in this experience. He wakes up when, in his nightmare, he is about to be caught by the object carrying his own desires from which he was trying to flee, and when he can no longer escape the traumatic situation. This brutal awakening, which indicates the failure of the dream work, ensures the dreamer obtains a narcissistic triumph over the object and the danger of non-representation. But this triumph is short-lived, since external reality coincides with phantasized reality and calls into question the boundaries of the ego. The only solution remaining is restless wandering in order to take flight from anxiety which can no longer be represented, unless an illusionist magician can be found who proposes both to "deny and to triumph" over this anxiety "in his art" (Freud, 1910, p. 118), play and creation.

This is also the source of the *aesthetic enjoyment* to which the filmmaker invites every spectator, enjoyment which Freud, in *Civilization and its Discontents,* considered an aim-inhibited drive that is essential to man, albeit nonutilitarian, because it allows him to compensate for the sufferings imposed by the absence of absolute satisfaction.

The encounter between Kleinman and the magician shows the importance of *working as doubles* to face the anxiety caused by the danger of losing the capacity to cathect and represent, which is inevitably experienced as a violent excess of excitation of traumatic value. I will take as an example the creative adventure of Freud who needed to rely on external doubles – Wilhelm Fliess, Carl Gustav Jung, Romain Rolland – to find the energy necessary for the discovery of psychoanalysis. At the same time, he knew how to free himself from this and move from an external double to an internal double, allowing him to identify the originality of his thinking (C. Botella & S. Botella, 1984). Henri Vermorel (1982) has clearly shown how the metapsychology of creation can be understood through Freud's fate, in particular in his letter entitled "A disturbance of memory on the Acropolis", addressed to the material double represented by R. Rolland (Freud, 1936). He underlines in particular how the disorder is felt and translated by the perception of two contrasting affects:

> Maternal castration is evoked by the ruins of the Parthenon (and results through identification in a disturbance of memory), whereas it is denied in a narcissistic and nostalgic manner where an identification with the maternal image appears – retrospectively – bearing the attributes of both sexes.
>
> (p. 522)

Creativity draws its source and inspiration from this "oceanic" experience, both lived and overcome, which persists alongside Oedipal and post-Oedipal mental life.

Reliance on the material double is a necessary stage if this primitive maternal identification is to contribute to the genesis of sublimations and creations, the difference between them being a question of quantity and quality. This psychic work confronts the creator with the possible destruction of his ego and of the object. No doubt we should understand the Freudian reference to libidinal and aggressive pregenitality as the source of sublimation as opposed to genitality. But Freud insisted on the importance of the integration of this same pregenitality for a successful genital life, including the possibility of identifying with the sexual experience of the other sex, which may be understood as the necessity of also shouldering this same "oceanic" experience.

This is a major issue in analytic treatment which confronts one with the need to experience formal regression of thought without getting lost through the use of free associative functioning for the analysand and free-floating attention for the analyst. César and Sara Botella have pointed out that the rapprochement of two modes of psychic functioning in the session – perceptual identity and thought-identity – normally designed to be separated, raises a state of uncanniness and loss of identity which is at the origin of the multiple defensive measures of the ego. It is an encounter with "the invisible maternal dimension" relating back to the anxieties and terrors inspired by the procreative dimension of maternal femininity. A successful and deeply mutative analysis should be one that, thanks to narcissistic and formal regression, makes possible the elaboration of this emotional experience that some patients have compared to the road to Damascus, thus enabling them to free up their aptitudes for sublimation and creation.

This is, of course, an asymptotic movement which has never been worked though completely and which represents the essence of all psychic work with regard to the possibility of integrating the *passivity* or *receptivity* that are essential to human experience. The integration of the masculine-feminine polarity becomes the very source of the free functioning of symbolization and sublimation, allowing for an infinite possibility of substitutions characterizing the work of culture and reunions with a conjunction of meaning, as much of the subject with himself as with the world which surrounds him.

Note

1 The German term *Kultur* was first translated into French as *civilisation*, but the translators of the *Oeuvres complètes* made the choice to translate the Freudian concept by "culture" because this term had progressively come to denote not only culture at the individual level but also at the level of societies.

References

André, J. (2005). Les sublimations, finalités sans fin. *Revue française de Psychanalyse*, 69 (5): 1475–1483.

Angelergues, R. (1992). De l'hallucination au langage. Monograph II, *Centre de Psychanalyse et de Psychothérapie E. & J. Kestemberg*.

Anzieu, D. (1989). Note pour introduire l'échelle de symbolisation. *Revue française de Psychanalyse*, 53 (6): 1775–1778.

Athanassiou, C. (1989). Place de la représentation dans le processus de symbolisation. *Revue française de Psychanalyse*, 53 (6): 1701–1706.

Baldacci, J.-L. (2005). "Dès le debut" … la sublimation? *Revue française de Psychanalyse*, 69 (5): 1405–1474.

Bergeret, J. (1989). Symbolisation et aristocratie culturelle. *Revue française de Psychanalyse*, 53 (6): 1797–1778.

Bion, W.R. (1963). *Elements of Psycho-Analysis*. London: Heinemann.

Bion, W.R. (1970). *Attention and Interpretation*. London: Tavistock.

Botella, C., & Botella, S. (1983). Notes cliniques sur la figurabilité et l'interprétation. *Revue française de Psychanalyse*, 47 (3): 765–776.

Botella, C., & Botella, S. (1984). L'homosexualité inconsciente et la dynamique du double en séance. *Revue française de Psychanalyse*, 48 (3): 687–708.

David, C. (Ed.) (1975). La médiation bisexuelle. In: *La bisexualité psychique*. Paris: Payot, pp. 46–72.

Defontaine, J. (1989). Esthétique du sens dans l'analyse. *Revue française de Psychanalyse*, 53 (6): 1971–1976.

Eco, U. (1984). *Sémiotique et philosophie du langage*, trans. from Italian by M. Bouzaher. Paris: Presses Universitaires, 1988.

Eissler, K. (1961). *Léonard de Vinci, étude psychanalytique*. Paris: Presses Universitaires de France, 1980.

Freud, S. (1891). *On Aphasia*. New York: International Universities Press, 1953.

Freud, S. (1905). *Three Essays on the Theory of Sexuality. S.E.* 7. London: Hogarth, pp. 125–245.

Freud, S. (1908). "Civilized" sexual morality and modern nervous illness. *S.E.* 9. London: Hogarth, pp. 181–204.

Freud, S. (1908). Creative writers and day-dreaming. *S.E.* 9. London: Hogarth, pp. 141–154.

Freud, S. (1910). *Leonardo da Vinci and a Memory of his Childhood. S.E.* 11. London: Hogarth, pp. 57–137.

Freud, S. (1914). On narcissism: an introduction. *S.E.* 14. London: Hogarth, pp. 69–102.

Freud, S. (1915a). The unconscious. *S.E.* 14. London: Hogarth, pp. 166–215.

Freud, S. (1915b). Instincts and their Vicissitudes. *S.E.* 14. London: Hogarth, pp. 109–140.

Freud, S. (1920). *Beyond the Pleasure Principle. S.E.* 18. London: Hogarth, pp. 1–64.

Freud, S. (1921). *Group psychology and the Analysis of the Ego. S.E.* 18. London: Hogarth, pp. 65–143.

Freud, S. (1923). *The Ego and the Id. S.E.* 19. London: Hogarth, pp. 1–66.

Freud, S. (1926). *Inhibitions, Symptoms and Anxiety. S.E.* 20. London: Hogarth, pp. 75–175.

Freud, S. (1930). *Civilization and its Discontents. S.E.* 21. London: Hogarth, pp. 57–145.

Freud, S. (1932). The acquisition and control of fire. *S.E.* 22. London: Hogarth, pp. 187–193.

Freud, S. (1933). *New Introductory Lectures on Psychoanalysis. S.E.* 22. London: Hogarth, pp. 1–182.

Freud, S. (1936). A disturbance of memory on the Acropolis. *S.E.* 22. London: Hogarth, pp. 239–250.

Freud, S. (1939). *Moses and Monotheism. S.E.* 23. London: Hogarth, pp. 1–137.

Freud, S. (1950 [1895]). *Project for a Scientific Psychology. S.E.* 1. London: Hogarth, pp. 295–397.

Gibeault, A. (1985). Travail de la pulsion et représentation: représentation de chose et représentation de mot. *Revue française de Psychanalyse*, 49 (3): 753–772.

Gillibert, J. (1989). L'inconscient aux portes de la construction symbolique dans le langage poétique et le langage de la schizophrénie. *Revue française de Psychanalyse*, 53 (6): 1893–1905.

Green, A. (Ed.) (1984). Le langage dans la psychanalyse. In: *Langages*. Paris: Les Belles Lettres, pp. 19–250.

Green, A. (1999/1973). *The Fabric of Affect in the Psychoanalytic Discourse*, trans. A. Sheridan. London: Routledge.

Green, A. (1999/1993). *The Work of the Negative*, trans. A. Weller. London: Free Association Books, 1999.

Kahn, L. (2005). La decomposition. *Revue française de Psychanalyse*, 69 (5): 1389–1395.

Kestemberg, E. (Ed.) (1984). Astrid ou homosexualité, identité, adolescence. Quelques propositions hypothétiques. In: *L'adolescence à vif*. Paris: Presses Universitaires de France, 1999, pp. 239–265.

Klein, M. (Ed.) (1932). *The Psychoanalysis of Children*. In: *The Collected Works of Melanie Klein, Vol. 2*. London: Routledge, 2017.

Lagache, D. (Ed.) (1962). La sublimation et les valeurs. In: *De la fantaisie à la sublimation. Œuvres V, 1962–1964*. Paris: Presses Universitaires de France, 1984, pp. 1–72.

Laplanche, J. (Ed.) (1971). Dérivation des entités psychanalytiques. In: *Le primat de l'autre*. Paris: Flammarion, pp. 106–123; also in *Problématiques III, La sublimation*. Paris: Presses Universitaires de France, pp. 50–60.

Laplanche, J. (1980). *Sublimation: Problématiques III*. Paris: Presses Universitaires de France.

Marcuse, H. (1955). *Eros and Civilization*. Boston, MA: Beacon Press.

Mellor-Picaut, S. (1979). La sublimation, ruse de la civilisation? *Psychanalyse à l'Université*, 4 (15): 447–484.

Merleau-Ponty (1960). *L'oeil et l'esprit*. Paris: Gallimard.

Perron, R. (1989). Représentations, symbolisations? *Revue française de Psychanalyse*, 53 (6): 1653–1659).

Roussillon, R. (2005). Le processus et la capacité sublimatoire. *Revue française de psychanalyse*, 69 (5): 1566–1573.

Séchaud, E. (2005). Perdre, sublimer… *Revue française de Psychanalyse*, 69 (5): 1309–1380.

Vermorel, H. (1982). Un trouble de mémoire sur l'Acropole. *Revue française de Psychanalyse*, 46 (3): 513–526.

Winnicott, D.W. (Ed.) (1953). Transitional objects and transitional phenomena. In: *Playing and Reality*. London: Tavistock, 1971, pp. 1–25.

Winnicott, D.W. (Ed.) (1967). The location of cultural experience. In: *Playing and Reality*. London: Tavistock, 1971, 95–103.

7   The birth of symbolization

Prehistoric art

Graphic representations in prehistory bear witness to the need to develop a "potential space for play" so that creativity and creation are possible. The hypothesis introduced by Winnicott of an "intermediate area of experience" or "transitional area" allowed him to describe a space in which internal reality and external reality are separate but also related to each other.

He first had to designate the dimension in which transitional phenomena and objects are organized – the babbling of the newborn, the child's attachment to the teddy bear, etc. – which make it possible to negotiate the transition from the illusion of an object that is found-created by the subject to the disillusionment of not being the sole creator of the world, and which corresponds to accepting the pleasure given by others. He also sought to define a "potential space for playing" which accounts for the importance of pleasure and play in psychic life and designates the area of the processes of symbolization that are already at work in the organization of phantasy when the child is at the breast, thereby allowing for the creation of an infinite number of symbols that make up the whole field of culture.

In December 1994, the discovery of the Chauvet cave in Ardeche showed that, shortly after arriving in Europe around 40,000 years BP (Before Present), *Homo sapiens* was able to use this ability to play to create graphic representations in indestructible and highly artistic works that are preserved to this day. These date from 36,000 years BP and put us in the presence of figurative masterpieces of great artistic richness, as much through the originality and the diversity of their bestiary – lions, panthers, rhinoceroses, hyenas, owls, and bears – as through the incomparable technical mastery of the artists (drawings, line painting, use of shading to render the relief). The expressive force of this cave is comparable to that of Lascaux (Dordogne), created 15,000 years later and often described as "the Sistine Chapel of prehistory". The Chauvet cave is now one of the oldest artistic testimonies in the history of humanity.

The reference to the Winnicottian concept of a "potential space for playing" should allow us to describe the psychic processes at work in the development of man, as illustrated by the creations of prehistoric man, and to continue thereby the reflection undertaken by François Sacco (2003) on the conditions of creativity in prehistoric art and by Claude Janin (2003) on the issues at stake in primary shame.

DOI: 10.4324/9781003545651-8

First indications of an aesthetic experience

The invention of one tool for making another confirms the appearance of Hominids about 2.5 million years ago. However, the creative power of *Homo sapiens* has been revealed more in the capacity gradually acquired over the past 100,000 years to find aesthetic pleasure in depicting life. The first drawings of aesthetic creation existed in the burial sites of Neanderthal man (*Homo neanderthalensis*) and modern man (*Homo Sapiens*) between 100,000 and 35,000 years ago: the bones of the dead were "decorated" with red ochre, which may be interpreted as a representation of blood and as a symbol of life after death.

Likewise, collecting stones with unusual shapes and colours and fossils was, already at that time, early evidence of this interest in symbolization and imaginary life linked to aesthetic pleasure. For the prehistorian André Leroi-Gourhan (1965), these collections concern "objects that do not directly belong to the living world, but which exhibit its properties or the reflection of its properties [...] and which are in nature like symbols of shapes and movements" (p. 214). This aesthetic research does not exclude the problem that these men had in manufacturing tools with symmetrical and harmonious shapes, referring, as Sacco (2003) remarks, to an early concern with creating more and more functional but also more and more beautiful shapes (p. 587).

In the process of depicting life, it was important to find inert but indestructible materials capable of preserving meaning and fostering transmission. During this evolution towards graphic representation, the earliest surviving evidence dates back to around 60,000 years ago and concerns depictions of rhythm. These are stone slabs and bone fragments marked with regular incisions. According to Leroi-Gourhan, they are the proof of the first intentions to depict life through repetition and rhythm.

Psychoanalysts can see in this an evocation of the psychic conditions of a work of representation. The capacity to create material images (pictures) implies a prior capacity to produce psychic images (images). This is underpinned by drive activity which has its source in the body starting with quantitative and qualitative variations of the affects of pleasure-displeasure. These rhythmic marks, kinds of playful pulsations of the living, which preceded the appearance of the first figurative representations around 36,000 years ago, provide us with information about the conditions that are indispensable for the emergence of psychic and material images.

Squiggles dating back 18,400 years

If we have found primitive traces of figurative representations from 100,000 years ago, it remains the case nevertheless that the most important evidence of the capacity of man to symbolize is artistic creation, as illustrated by the appearance and dissemination of graphic representations and sculptures produced by *Homo sapiens* as early as 36,000 years ago. In Upper Palaeolithic art, it is customary to distinguish three types of graphic units: first, figurative representations corresponding to identifiable anthropomorphic or zoomorphic forms, whether real or imaginary; then *abstract signs*, often repetitive, sometimes associated with animal figures but mainly elementary signs – dots, dashes, straight lines on their own or aligned, panels, circles, etc. – which are totally abstract and inaccessible in the absence of a code, and elaborate and regionalized signs – tectiform, claviform, aviform signs – which probably have semantic and social functions intended to mark the messages specific to each group (Vialou, 1991, pp. 338–339); and finally, unclassifiable drawings – spots, finger-markings, doodles, streaks, etc. – which represent approximately 30% of the parietal graphic units (Lorblanchet, 1986).

The "Hieroglyphic Ceiling" in the Pech-Merle cave in Cabrerets, in the Lot department of France (see Sacco, 2003 for the reproduction of the entire panel), is one of the most famous examples of finger-markings characterizing a particularly remarkable expression of the psychic sources of representational activity (Gibeault & Uhl, 1994). The Pech-Merle cave contains 120 m² of these finger-markings, which appear only on parietal surfaces. They are based on an original technique that differs from engraving and that is closer to modelling insofar as it does not consist in removing material, but in transforming the malleable surface of the support. These finger-markings can be compared to Winnicottian *squiggles*: they are associated with a malleable substance, a simple clay, and are an adaptation to this material. According to Michel Lorblanchet (1992a, 1992b), the prehistorian who made the inventory of this ceiling of the "Hieroglyphs", we can observe, in the main group (Figure 7.1):

1 A set of tracings, apparently unorganized, consisting of parallel bars or sinuous lines drawn by one finger, or more often by two or three, sometimes even with the friction of the whole hand – tracings called macaroni;
2 Three representations of women with elongated breasts and the body tilted forward – two of these representations are headless, the arms being reduced more to stumps;
3 Four representations of mammoths, three of them quite detailed, drawn with a double outline. The legs are parallel and in pairs, except for the largest representation. The fourth on the north side of the group is a simple uni-linear dorsal profile, easily recognized by the bumps on the back and skull, and is identical to all simplified mammoths in the region.

When we look at these markings, we can understand how these forms were created and thus approach the processes of prehistoric thought. Painting and engraving require both technical and psychic preparation, that is to say,

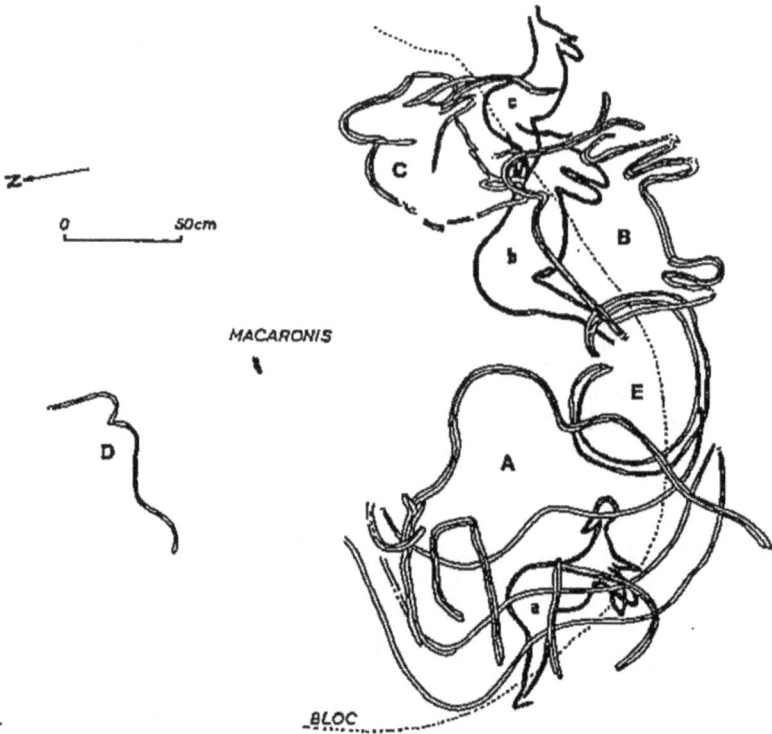

Figure 7.1 Detail of the finger-marking on the Hieroglyphic Ceiling. Pech-Merle
cave, Cabrerets, Lot, 25,000 years BP Three mammoths (A, B, C) drawn
on the three women (a, b, c); D: simplified dorsal profile of a mammoth;
E: circular sign.

© Tracing Michel Lorblanchet

a complete conception of the work to be done before it suddenly appears
on the rock face in its fixed and final state. On the other hand, by contrast,
finger-marking differs from other techniques of representation by the ease
and speed of its execution and by the fact that, according to Lorblanchet, it
is a "marking-imprint requiring direct physical contact with the wall and
with the cave…, an action drawing that allows us to witness the dialogue
between the artist and the cave" (Lorblanchet, 1992a, p. 11). We could see
in this "marking-imprint" a figure of the pliable medium, as defined by
Marion Milner (1955) and taken up by René Roussillon (1988): the properties of the pliable medium – namely, indestructibility, extreme sensitivity,
indefinite transformation, unconditional availability and self-animation –
indeed evoke the matrix role of finger markings in the representative activity of the prehistoric artist.

The finger-markings were not the first expressions of art and painting in
the caves. Carbon-14 dated to about 25,000 years BP, the finger-markings of

the Pech-Merle cave are contemporaneous with the most beautiful paintings of the cave and as such therefore occupy a place among the many techniques used by the prehistoric artist. The finger-markings could be considered a myth representing the genesis both of the world and of graphic creativity. The psychoanalyst can thus follow the intuition of the prehistorian who, without having read Winnicott, suggests that finger- markings are a "mythology of creation": the artist makes creatures emerge from the void and the inextricable (Lorblanchet, 1992b), in a free play, vectorizing the illusion of non-separation from the world and thus constituting, according to the relevant remark of Sacco (2003), "a creative, figurative [and] expressive reserve" (p. 584).

Quasi hallucinatory representations and negative hands

It is remarkable to observe that in prehistoric caves, the artist used the natural relief of the stone to find the proper location of paintings and engravings. This can be seen, for example, from the privileged situation of the spotted horses in the Pech-Merle which follow the contours of the rock; their very particular arrangement evokes a scenic presentation of the cave. The artist found a large rock of about 4 m on which to paint two large horses decorated with spots and accompanied by six negative hands (Figure 7.2).

Lorblanchet, who made the surveys of the paintings and engravings of the cave, emphasizes the thoughtful, composed, and undoubtedly preconceived character of these set images where each element is in its right place, revealing a harmoniously occupied surface. The choice of wall, its relief, its texture, and its colour affect the shape of the painted animals and brings them to life. The artist was also careful to choose an open space in front of the wall with room to stand back; the perception changes and the animals move. And he concludes: "the dialogue of skin tones, lines, support and figures in a theatrical space makes this panel a unique work of art" (Lorblanchet, 1995, p. 218).

Thus, considering the anthropomorphic and animal relief, and the animation that the flickering flame must have given them, it seems that this process was not accidental. In the depths of the cave, it was necessary to create an almost hallucinatory state that confirmed the living presence of the animal spirits already inscribed in the relief of the stone. Even if the use of toxicants and hallucinogens could create true hallucinatory states (Clottes & Lewis Williams, 1996), the reference to hallucinatory activity in the Freudian sense as a condition of any representational activity is heuristic. If the representation requires a prior negation of the world, it is necessary to suppose a process of negative hallucination at the basis of all positive hallucinations and all representations of the world (Green, 1999/1993, pp. 161–214). The graphic representations of prehistory are part of the myths whose precise meaning escapes us in the absence of any written document. But this suggests that the mythology of these hunter-gatherer

Figure 7.2 Panel of spotted horses (length 4 m, Pech-Merle cave) 25,000 years BP.
© Photo: N. Aujoulat; Credit: Centre national de Préhistoire/Ministère de la Culture

peoples was centred on the issues of life and death, and on the representation of omnipotent animal spirits whose powers man may have wanted to appropriate and thereby fight against the terrors provoked by his powerlessness in the face of a hostile nature.

Confirmation of this process can be seen in the testimony of Lorblanchet, who wanted to understand the work of Magdalanian artists by reproducing himself, in a virgin cave in Quercy, the horses of Pech-Merle and the six negative hands surrounding them. He wanted to experiment with what, "in the study of Palaeolithic cave art, allows the prehistorian to place himself in conditions very close to those of the authors of the figurative representations and to try to repeat their gestures" (Lorblanchet, 1995, p. 209). It was a major task because it was necessary to reproduce the panel of horses in life size, with a length of four meters, with the same techniques as those of the prehistoric artist, in particular using the direct spitting with the mouth method.

On this panel of spotted horses as well as on the recess of "Women-Bisons", the negative hands (Figure 7.3) are executed with this stencil technique. On the panel of spotted horses, they belong to the same individual whose right hand and left hand have been reproduced on the wall. Lorblanchet's experiment confronted him with affects that can be compared with the

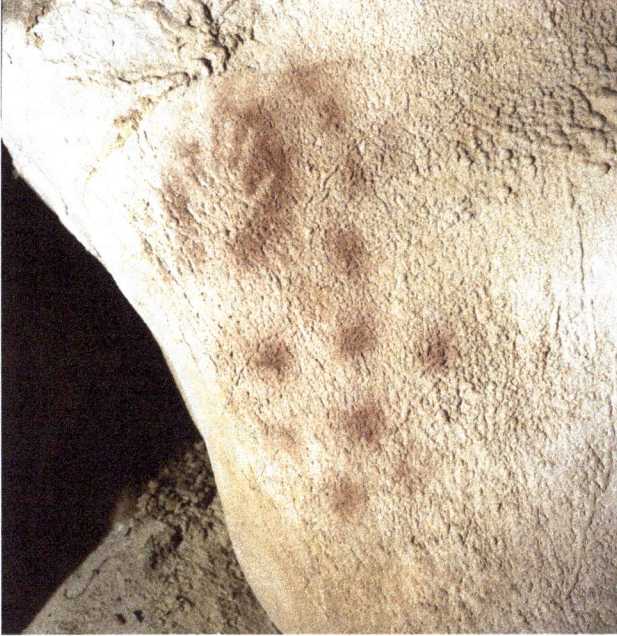

Figure 7.3 Negative hand, Recess of "Women-Bisons", Pech-Merle cave, 25,000 years BP.

© Photo: N. Aujoulat. Credit: Centre national de Préhistoire/Ministère de la Culture

indications given by Claude Janin on primary shame. Let us first quote Lorblanchet:

> The realization of the handprints also gave the operator a surprise; seeing the image of his hand inscribed on the wall, and his individuality, his intimate and personal character exposed to the view of others was disturbing. This was very different to a signature or a name. In the image of his hand, the individual is incomparably present.
>
> (Lorblanchet, 1995, p. 218)

In a personal communication, the prehistorian told me that he actually felt naked.

Acquisition of bipedalism, primary shame, and organic repression

How can we not compare this experience of the prehistorian with what Freud suggested concerning the links between the acquisition of the vertical position in the history of Hominids and the so-called "organic" repression aimed at both the olfactory sensations linked to anality and a source of disgust, and the affects of shame relating to the visibility of the genitals? In his work on the question of shame in psychic life, Claude Janin (2003) quotes the passage in *Civilization and its Discontents* in which Freud evokes the links between the passage to the vertical position, the repression of anal eroticism and the experience of shame:

> The diminution of the olfactory stimuli seems itself to be a consequence of man's raising himself from the ground, of his assumption of an upright gait; this made his genitals, which were previously concealed, visible and in need of protection, and so provoked feelings of shame in him.
>
> (Freud, 1930, p. 99, footnote 1)

This was the occasion for Freud to situate instinctual drive factors alongside biological, ecological, and behavioural factors.

For palaeontologists, the acquisition of bipedalism must be situated in an evolutionary perspective and not as a sudden onset phenomenon. Australopithecus is the first evidence for this acquisition about 3 million years ago; it is believed that the repertoire of this hominid comprised 40% bipedalism and 40% vertical climbing. That of *Homo habilis* (2.5 to 1.7 million years) was little different, and it was only with *Homo ergaster* (1.8 million years) that bipedalism approached that of *Home sapiens* (95% bipedal and 5% vertical climbing) (Gibeault & Uhl, 1994). Many researchers, and in particular Yves Coppens (1983), have interpreted bipedalism as an adaptation to the savannah after the collapse of the Rift Valley in Africa: the cradle of the Hominids was supposedly located to the east of this valley, where a change of climate caused a change of landscape, from the humid and protective forest to the dry and more dangerous savannah. Bipedalism was one of the essential acquisitions of man in the process of natural selection, correlated to a tectonic accident which gradually became an ecological barrier.

This well-known scenario has since been challenged, but the fact remains that palaeontology has mainly sought to make biological and ecological factors prevail over cultural factors. This perspective is all the more understandable since, in the history of human evolution, it was not until 100,000 years ago that cultural development took over from biological development, which is a very short time considering that evolution is calculated in millions of years. It is worth noting in this connection that Leroi-Gourhan (1964, p. 39) made the acquisition of bipedalism one of the four fundamental aspects of humanity, together with the development of a short face, the liberation of the hand during locomotion and the creation of movable tools.

In this context, the interest accorded by Freud to postural repositioning in psychic functioning is part of a more cultural perspective. If he speaks of "organic repression", according to a phylogenetic point of view that the child recapitulates in his ontogenetic development, it nonetheless remains necessary to situate this major issue in the organization of the psyche. Therefore, we must probably bring together organic repression and primal repression in this first stage where the drive becomes fixed to ideas without preconscious counter-cathexis.

For Freud, "the counter-cathexis is the exclusive mechanism of primal repression" and therefore concerns a primal repression of an organic nature, the olfactory linked to anality, a source of disgust, certainly, but also of affects of shame. One of the great merits of Claude Janin is to have drawn our attention to the affect of shame, as well as disgust, in the vertical repositioning of man. Freud referred to it by showing the link between the vertical world, the visibility of the genitals and the affect of shame. Claude Janin evokes the hypothesis of a "primary shame" or "primal shame" which emphasizes not only a developmental sequence but also a metapsychological sequence making the affect of shame constitutive of the human being. Freud is not very precise from a palaeontological perspective when he evokes the moment when "*Homo sapiens* rose for the first time above Mother Earth", whereas the acquisition of bipedalism was well before the appearance of *Homo Sapiens* less than 100,000 years ago. But the Freudian perspective of primitive origins, signified by the prefix "Ur" (*Urverdräng-ung*), is more to mark a transcendental point of view, in the Kantian sense, as a condition of possibility of a scientific domain, correlative of a specific object – namely, the psychic functioning of the human being designated by palaeontologists as *Homo sapiens*.

Thus, one can understand why, in prehistoric art, there are few human representations compared to animal representations. There are in fact 800 human representations including those of negative hands, while animal representations number several thousand. On the other hand, human-like figures are often schematic or partial, and unrealistic in comparison with animal representations, which are more descriptive, even if in prehistoric art, it is less about images representing real objects or beings but rather forms referring to a mythical imagination. From the origins of art, the technical and cultural possibility of representing real sophisticated human figures cannot be excluded, as evidenced by the head of Brassempouy (Landes) (Figure 7.4); but social, cultural, or religious factors have often intervened in human representations which are frequently non-naturalistic and, as Lorblanchet (1986) observes, "most grotesque-looking human images are anti-portraits reflecting a voluntary refusal of the human, and not clumsy tracings that one might describe as archaic" (p. 129).

From then on, *Homo sapiens* surely had multiple reasons not to represent himself in a naturalistic way. Lorblanchet's testimony may lead us to think that, from a psychoanalytic point of view, the affects of shame linked to the visibility of the genitals led the prehistoric artist to conceal the representation of the human body and, under the pressure of repression, to prefer representation of the part rather than the whole – a synecdoche of the body

Figure 7.4 Female head known as "The Dame of Brassempouy". or "the Woman with the Hood", one of the first representations of the human face around 24,000 years BP Dame de Brassempouy (MAN 47019), Musée d'Archéologie nationale.

© MAN/Loïc Hamon

itself – in this case the representation of the negative hand instead of the body as a whole.

If, according to the prehistorian Denis Vialou, "the Palaeolithic imagination concerning the human body makes itself felt through a figurative independence that favours abstraction, either by the schematization and/or the deformation of shapes, or by the segmentation of shapes" (Vialou, 1998, p. 158), this does not mean that human sexuality is eliminated from it. The representations of male and female genital organs are very numerous in Palaeolithic art, but they are part of a general symbolic context that prevents any narrative link between the representations – no scenes of coitus, dance or hunting – like any other realistic representation of the human body. Thus, in the Chauvet cave (Clottes, 2001), a complex Venus/man-bison composition (Figure 7.5) illustrates this abstract representation of woman and man: a typical Venus seen from the front, reduced to the lower body, with a distinctly marked pubis was painted first; then an added representation, using the relief of the stone to represent the dorsal line, shows a composite being, half-man half-animal, nicknamed the Sorcerer at its discovery, which can evoke a prehistoric shaman embodied in the body of a bison. Note here the contrast between the realistic head of the

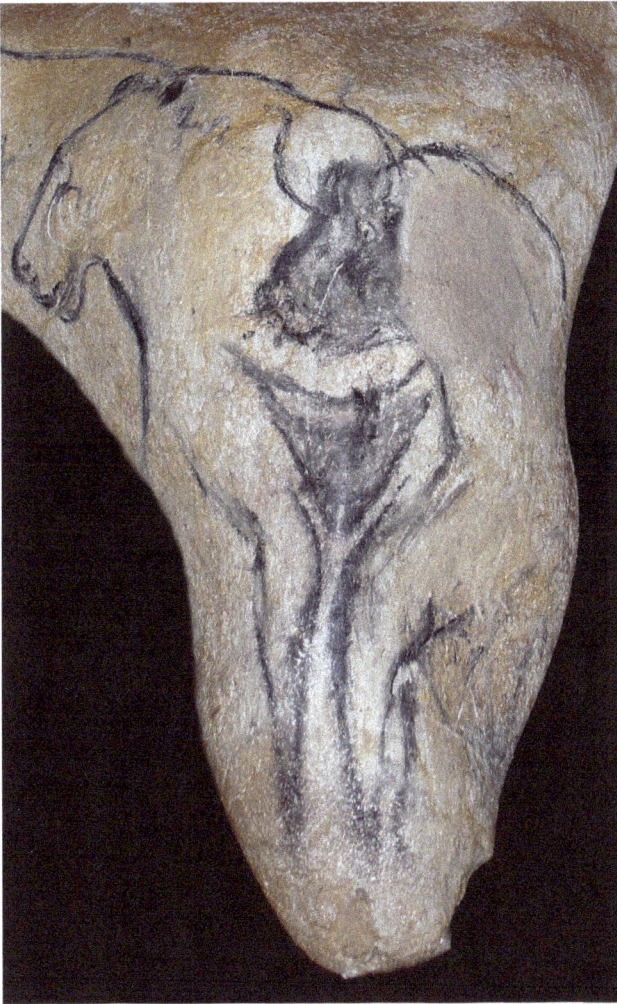

Figure 7.5 Pendant of the Venus, Chauvet Cave, 36,000 years BP. In the centre, a woman reduced to the lower body; on the right man-bison.

bison and the crudely drawn human body, with a human arm, extended by a hand with long fingers that hang downwards, and a penis depicted directly on the rocky ridge by a black line.

If we also consider the scene from the Shaft of Lascaux (Figure 7.6), we can see a wounded bison facing a very schematic ithyphallic man, with the head of a bird and half upside down. It could be interpreted as a realistic hunting scene where a man is mortally wounded by an injured bison. It is more likely a symbolic representation to be interpreted as that of a shaman in an ecstatic trance facing an animal that was dangerous for men and here represented disembowelled or even sacrificed. Sacco (2003) emphasises, with regard to this famous representation of prehistory, that "the difference in the manner of their pictorial treatment is such that they are not placed in the same psychic space" (p. 58) because of the symbolic elements appearing next to the human representation – a man with a bird head, a staff adorned with a bird.

Finally, in the cave of the Trois Frères (Ariège), an engraved scene can be interpreted as a representation of sexual desire in a symbiotic representation of man and animal (Figure 7.7). On this panel, we see a completely vertical man-bison whose lower limbs are human from the feet to the hips, while the sexual body and head are those of a bison. The man-bison is looking forwards, his gaze meets that of a bison's head looking back, but its body is that of a female reindeer whose excited genitalia are very visible. This

Figure 7.6 Scene of the Shaft of Lascaux, Montignac (Dordogne). 17,000 years BP.
© N. Aujoulat/CNP/MC

Figure 7.7 Cave of the Trois Frères, 13,000 years BP. Engraved composition integrating several composite creatures, 23,000 years BP.

© Tracing Henri Breuil, Bégouën Collection

strange bison-reindeer follows another reindeer with male antlers whose forelegs are artificially bent and terminated by some sort of clawed hands.

These representations of composite beings perfectly embody the prehistoric imagination uniting man and animals. According to Denis Vialou (1998), they can be considered "an emblematic image of a myth in which the animal and human actors are linked by the glances exchanged and an active sexuality" (p. 11). The reference to the experience of primary shame makes it possible to give an instinctual drive dimension to the mythical motifs that led the artist to the abstract and symbolic representation of human forms.

Palaeolithic art is as much proof of a mythical imagination, the secrets of which escape us, as of a work of transformation of the drive which both conceals and shows, in a movement of struggle against distress and annihilation by the infinite creation of various substitutes. The emphasis on processes of symbolization rather than on symbolic and social content suggests correspondence between the creators of the past and those of today.

Prehistoric man and contemporary man belong to the same species, *Homo sapiens*, and, as their mental functioning is similar, the processes of symbolization have the function of giving individuals belonging to different eras an opportunity to recognize themselves; this also seems to have been true for hunter-gatherer societies in prehistoric times.

The graphic representations of prehistory are all symbols whose function is to allow the recognition of what is specific in the psychic functioning of the human being. Even if prehistoric art may have had a utilitarian function in the service of rituals, it confirms the acquisition, by *Homo sapiens*, of a potential space for play, of a capacity to play freely with the forms which have allowed, since the dawn of humanity, the multiplicity and richness of artistic representations.

The shamanic interpretation has recently given rise to many discussions among prehistorians (Clottes & Lewis-William, 2001). Without taking up this debate again here (Gibeault & Uhl, 1994) on the interest and the value of a globalizing interpretation in the graphic productions of prehistory, it should be emphasized that the image will never deliver the underlying myth to us, all the more so, as Leroi-Gourhan (1977) has noted, since "the same image was the recipient of spiritual entities with probably radically different mythological contexts" (p. 25). Nevertheless, the prehistoric artist had to become the spokesperson for his social group in order to portray the opposition between life and death. According to the prehistorian Jean-Pierre Mohen (2002), "this opposition of life and death must be overcome so that the group and the individual have a future", and the prehistoric works of art, in their multiple and varied expressions, can thus be considered so many formulas "to find the paths of forgiveness for tomorrow, because the man who can think of death is responsible for it, except when he manages to associate death and birth" (p. 197). The birth of art in prehistoric times actually finds its source in this essential human need to master death and the anxiety and terror it causes.

Palaeolithic art testifies to this essential conflict for the psyche that is correlative to any process of hominization, and that has so often evoked the correspondences between ontogenesis and phylogenesis. The images that prehistoric artists have left us allow us to detect in their creative activity the importance of a transitional activity, of which the finger-markings are a reflection, giving rise to figurative representations. We must not however neglect the social importance of the myths which were the vehicles of these creations, myths probably centred on the life and death of hunters (Vialou, 1991, p. 319). These myths are certainly part of an individual psychic reality, as evidenced by the palaeolithic artist's openness to the dimension of illusion and hallucination, but they are also part of an external social reality which at the same time supports the individual and is transformed by him through his artistic creations. This confirms that the myth is indeed a "collective transitional object" (Green, 1980), that the work of art participates in this "intermediate space" which momentarily suspends the workings of life and death, of the real and the non-real, in order to both represent it and to be able to accept the consequences.

For Freud, the foundations of this symbolic activity presupposed the work of "hereditary memory traces", the origin of which he located in prehistoric times. If he could see there the vestiges of a prehistoric era that was impossible to date, we know that the reference to this material reality could be understood as the need to base the individual adventure on a universal structure. Now it is a fact that these hereditary traces are mainly primal phantasies (primal scene, seduction, castration, return to the maternal womb) which help answer the big questions about origins, where sexuality is prevalent, and thus play the function of collective, universal myths, organizers of the psyche. It is probably not rash to assert that, by producing images often of great beauty, the prehistoric artist was in a way the first witness to this instinctual adventure characteristic of any process of hominization today, as much as 36,000 years BP.

References

Clottes, J. (2001). *La grotte Chauvet. L'art des origines*. Paris: Seuil.

Clottes J., & Lewis-Williams, D. (1996). *Les chamanes de la Préhistoire. Après les chamanes, polémiques et réponses*. Paris: La Maison des Roches.

Clottes, J., & Lewis Williams, D. (1998). *The Shamans of Prehistory. Trance and Magic in the Painted Caves*. New York: Harry N. Abrams.

Coppens, Y. (1983). *Le singe, l'Afrique et l'homme*. Paris: Fayard.

Freud, S. (1930). *Civilization and its Discontents*. *S.E. 21*. London: Hogarth, pp. 64-145.

Gibeault, A., & Uhl, R. (1994). Symbolisation et representation graphique dans la préhistoire. In: A. Fine, R. Perron, & F. Sacco (Eds.) *Psychanalyse et préhistoire*. Paris: Presses Universitaires de France, pp. 117–132.

Gibeault, A., Uhl, R. (1998). De l'outil à l'oeuvre d'art, l'invention de la symbolisation. In: F. Sacco & G. Sauvet (Eds.) *Le propre de l'homme. Psychanalyse et préhistoire*. Lausanne-Paris: Delachaux & Niestlé, pp. 13–40.

Green, A. (Ed.) (1992 [1980]). Le mythe un objet transitionnel collectif. Abord critique et perspectives psychanalytiques. In: *La déliaison*. Paris: Les Belles Lettres, pp. 147–179.

Green, A. (1999/1993). *The Work of the Negative*, trans. A. Weller. London: Free Association Books.

Janin, C. (2003). Pour une théouries psychanalytique de la honte. *Revue française de psychanalyse*, 67 (5): 1657–1742.

Leroi-Gourhan, A. (1964). *Le geste et la parole, I: Technique et langage*. Paris: Albin Michel.

Leroi-Gourhan, A. (1965). *Le geste et la parole, II: La mémoire et les rythmes*. Paris: Albin Michel.

Leroi-Gourhan, A. (1977). Le préhistorien et le chamane. *L'Ethnographie*, 74–75: 19–25

Lorblanchet, M. (1986). *De l'homme aux animaux et aux signes dans les arts paléolithique et australien*. Cultural Attitudes of Animals, vol. 3. Southhampton/London: World Archeological Congress.

Lorblanchet, M. (1992a). Finger markings in Pech-Merle and their place in prehistoric art. In: M. Lorblanchet (Ed.) *Rock Art in the Old World*. New Delhi: Indira Gandhi National Center for the Arts, pp. 451–490.

Lorblanchet, M. (1992b). Le triomphe du naturalisme dans l'art paléolithique. In: T. Shay & J Clottes (Eds.) *The Limitations of Archaeological Knowledge*. Liège: Eraul, pp. 115–139.

Lorblanchet, M. (1995). *Les grottes ornées de la préhistoire*. Paris: Errance.

Milner, M. (1977 [1955]). The role of illusion in symbol-formation. In: M. Klein, P. Heimann, & R. Money-Kyrle (Eds.) *New Directions in Psychoanalysis*. London: Maresfield, pp. 82–108.

Mohen, J.-P. (2002). *Arts et préhistoire*. Paris: Le Terrail.

Roussillon, R. (1988). Le medium malléable, la représentation de la représentation et la pulsion d'emprise. *Revue belge de psychanalyse*, 3: 70–87.

Sacco, F. (2003). La préhistoire aujourd'hui. *Revue française de Psychanalyse*, 67 (3): 576–588.

Vialou, D. (1991). *La préhistoire*. Paris: Gallimard.

Vialou, D. (1997). Singularité des représentations humaines paléolithiques. *Histoire de l'art* (37–38): 3–13.

Vialou, D. (1998). Sexualité et arts préhistoriques. In: F. Sacco & G. Sauvet (Eds.) *Le propre de l'homme. Psychanalyse et préhistoire*. Lausanne-Paris: Delachaux et Niestlé, pp. 151–171.

Conclusion

At the end of this reflection on the process of symbolization, which was intended mainly to mark out the issues at stake and open up perspectives for further thought, many grey areas remain. Symbolization has been demarcated in relation to symbolism, in the relations between a "symbolic mode" (Eco, 1984, pp. 191–236) that favours a "nebulous cloud of contents" and a rule of interpretation that finds in univocity a possible way of limiting the indefinite. Such fixedness of structure would permit creative polysemy: it would be necessary to "decide" to get out of uncertainty, as in the Jewish story told by Freud to Fliess. Faced with the procrastination of a couple who hesitated over whether to kill the cock or the hen, because one or the other was going to pine, the Rabbi said, "So kill the cock"; to the couple's remark: "But then the cock will pine ", the Rabbi replied "So let him pine!" (Letter from Freud to Fliess dated 28 May 1899 in Masson, 1985, p. 353). The necessity for Freud to determine a meaning is transformed by Lacan into a necessity for symbolic castration which fixes and legitimizes the analytical truth by reference to the Other, a secular version of negative theology.

This would be to forget that before the opposition between the sensible and the intelligible, it is necessary to presuppose a cathexis of, and by, the object, which gives the object its existence and grounds discourse. The insistence on transitional space is another way of designating this transcendence of Being that Freud defined in an empiricist approach as the "original reality-ego". It is because the object is given in its reality that negation becomes possible, just as the stage of the illusion of non-differentiation allows for the stage of disillusion and judgment of existence.

Truth in analysis has been the subject of much debate. The error has often been to superimpose the opposition between narrative truth and historical truth on the opposition between psychic reality and material reality, whereas these contrasting pairs must be dialectalized. Material reality implies a construction of the subject according to the hypothesis of the primacy of the hallucination of satisfaction, and thus contains a dimension of narrative truth; conversely, psychic reality is also based on historical facts, just as the hallucination of satisfaction is based on elements coming from perception and material reality.

DOI: 10.4324/9781003545651-9

In our work, our task boils down, as Donald Spence (1982) notes, to increasing the historical truth of the patient's internal world while at the same time widening its phantasy-based and narrative dimension. This is the challenge of a work of symbolization which has been linked more to a three-term operation rather than to a simple two-term substitution. Likewise, it is difficult to distinguish between psychic reality and material reality, even though it is fundamental to maintain their differentiation and to preserve the relations between two dimensions of truth. This is another way of describing the analytic adventure as characterized by the "in-between" and the "back and forth". This is what Haydée Faimberg (1987) underlined when basing the clinical certainty of the construction on the resolution of an enigma in the transference-countertransference relationship.

Thus, the symbolizing function of the treatment coincides with what could not be evoked concerning the "sublimated sublimating" dimension inherent in the situation and in the analytical process (Donnet, 1998, p. 1061). Even if there is no question of making it the objective of the treatment, by promoting the development of creative activities outside the treatment, it is indisputable that the analytical process presupposes, by virtue of its setting, the statement of the fundamental rule and transference on to speech (Baldacci, 2005, p. 1410; Green, 1979), conditions that are favourable to the development of creativity. Symbolization and sublimation are here in the service of elaboration and working through in analysis as possible ways of acquiring a new mode of being, the capacity to associate freely, concerning which Ferenczi (1927) said that it was less the starting point than the end point of analytic work.

It is interesting to note that the very idea of transference as a new experience, rather than as a repetition of the past, certainly presupposes capacities for displacement, but also creative capacities. Freud speaks in this connection of sublimation for these transferences "which are more ingenuously constructed; ... They have undergone an attenuation of their content, a *sublimation...* These, then, will no longer be new impressions, but revised editions" (Freud, 1905, p. 116). Analytical work, in its very essence, implies relying on the symbolizing and "sublimating" (Sechaud, 2005, p. 1337) aptitudes of the analyst and analysand alike.

The very idea of a co-creation (de M'Uzan, 1994) as a result of analytic treatment refers to symbolization and sublimation as fundamental processes of this work of thought, which is also an ability to "play" involving a reversibility of adult-child play (Baldacci, 2005, p. 1418). For Freud, the pleasure of mental functioning and creation is related to children's play: "Every child at play behaves like a creative writer, in that he creates a world of his own, or, rather, re-arranges the things of his world in a new way which pleases him" (Freud, 1908, pp. 143–144). Analytic work should make it possible to acquire this aptitude for play which Winnicott described as "universal", saying that it belongs to "health" (Winnicott, 1971, p. 41).

From this perspective, psychoanalytic interpretation has a symbolizing function first in the context of the treatment, where it is inseparable from the acted repetition of the transference, then in the field of culture, where it has a place alongside other conceptions of the world and interpretative theories. As regards interpretation in analysis, it is desirable not be confined within the opposition of Todorov (1977) between constraint of method and constraint of finality, which can be compared to the contrast between mode of thought and content of thought. Psychoanalysis cannot be identified with hermeneutics and the constraint of finality as Todorov suggests; it is more appropriate to emphasize "the oscillation of the constraints", on the essential articulation in the dynamics of the treatment between the end and the method (Donnet, 1989). It is indeed important to erase the distinction between manifest content and latent content in order to better reveal the conditions of a "work" in the session, as Freud (1900, p. 506, footnote 2) suggested concerning the dream-work. This refers to another way of essentially relating psychic contents to processes, and of situating psychoanalytic interpretation within the movement of the treatment, which implies the maintenance of an indispensable and necessary *gap* between the search for an immediate satisfaction in transference cathexis, and the acceptance of a delay in satisfaction authorizing the elaboration of ideational contents relating to transference displacement.

This involves insisting on the mediating function of symbolization and thereby rediscovering the remarks on interpretation that animated in particular a classic article by James Strachey (1934) on psychoanalytic interpretation. He points out, among other things, that interpretation is a magic weapon, and that it is mutative only on the condition of being essentially transferential and of comprising two phases. In the first, the patient becomes aware of his instinctual cathexis with regard to the analyst, and in the second, he realizes that this cathexis is directed towards an original object of phantasy and not towards a real external object: this work therefore involves the possibility, thanks to the mediation of the analytical function, of marking a gap between the cathexis of the analyst and his person, and the cathexis of an object of phantasy.

Having said that, does the effectiveness of interpretation depend solely on these formal conditions formulated by Strachey? Many articles have since been published on this subject, in particular in the Anglo-Saxon milieu, and have commented on his remarks in different ways. Let us mention in particular the article by John Klauber (1972) who wanted to modify something in this approach to the *explicit* mutative interpretation by evoking an *implicit* mutative interpretation: namely, that which is situated in the context of a relationship where the transference/counter-transference interaction takes place. According to him, three aspects must be taken into account: the content of the interpretations, the subtle understanding of an unconsciously agreed code, and the authority that gives the analyst his conviction and his presence; hence the idea that the content of the interpretation has its place in the field of suggestion. This takes us back to the beginnings of psychoanalysis with Freud and the importance of suggestion with regard to both its positive and negative effects. It is probably necessary to consider these risks of "de-symbolization" in the analyst as well as in the patient. Donnet (1989) reminded us that this constitutes "the threatening and saving background of the analytical enterprise" (p. 1916), in that it leads us to consider analysis as an essentially affective adventure and not as a simple decoding of contents.

What does this mean other than that, if analytic interpretation has to decide, it cannot do so in the mode of "it is" but in that of "perhaps". This mode of "proposing" rather than "imposing" a truth allows the operation of negation to be exercised and to give fresh impetus to thought processes. This is what psychotic patients find it difficult to do because, in order to preserve a minimum of space and thought, they need to settle into the mode of unshakeable certainty when the world is only an "index", as Pasche (1984–1985), referring to Peirce, reminds us; it is then impossible that symbolic thought, as a modality of negation, can find a way to operate. Yet it is this way of thinking that we seek to bear witness to in our work with our patients, and in particularly with psychotic patients: with Charles and Raphaël, it was often a question of encouraging them to return to themselves rather than letting them lock themselves into the system and universality of codes, of arousing in them an interest in their personal history, in relation to what we were sharing, and to imagine a way of thinking other than that which is locked into the "fortress" of univocity and magical thought.

In the case of Marc, whose story was available from the beginning of his analysis, the excitation aroused by the analytical regression found its elaboration in a short and condensed interpretation which made it possible to open the associative process in its self-reflexive dimension. An important moment in the treatment was the reunion, on the occasion of a dream, *A man was hanging from a woman's breast*, and its interpretation, with the phantasy of the maternal breast, no longer as an erotic object but as a tender link to the nourishing breast: whilst he insisted in his associations on the erotic dimension of the breast, I had drawn his attention to the fact that "the breast is also what gives milk". This interpretation had the immediate dynamic effect of sedating the excitation, which naturally was not due to its informative and univocal meaning but to its metaphorical and polysemic value: it was the *image* of analytical work and its function of acting as a stimulus barrier that allowed him to feel the object was non-intrusive and to experience phantasy activity and interpretation as something other than a reciprocal destructive rape. It was in this context of a tender current, and immediately after this session, that Marc was able to tolerate again the narcissistic regression of sleep and to free himself from his insomnia.

Two types of interpretation have often been contrasted: an interpretation-explanation, more external, *breaking* the associative flow, possibly more univocal; and an interpretation in *contact* with the flow of associations, giving free rein to the development of polysemy (Duncan, 1989), as illustrated by the interpretation of the breast in Marc's analysis. This was evoked by Michel de M'Uzan to describe the optimal conditions for the interpretation, "ambiguous and incomplete", causing an economic upheaval, "while leaving the patient with a creative freedom whose effects sometimes surprise the analyst" (M'Uzan, 1983, p. 77). For the latter, the interpretation-explanation is concerned more with the censorship between the conscious and the preconscious, while the allusive interpretation close to dream work is addressed to the censorship between the preconscious and the unconscious (M'Uzan, 1991). Must we necessarily choose, or is it not more heuristic to see in it the need for a dialectic, for a movement between one or the other interpretive modalities, in a relationship between contact and rupture, which ultimately defines the circulation between the psychic systems, as suggested by the metaphor of the "mystic writing-pad"? (Freud, 1925 [1924]).

Hence the importance of space; and space is necessarily linked to temporality which alone can organize the trauma represented by the drive. Between the silent, inassimilable phase of automatic anxiety, and the retrospective phase of the signal anxiety linked to what Freud (1926) calls the displacement "from the economic situation on to the condition which determined that situation, viz., the loss of the object" (p. 138), the process of historicization is put in place which is equally a process of symbolization: this justifies the need for a "period of latency" so that the psychical topography can function, and the need also, in the work with our patients with prevalent psychotic functioning, to foster in our interpretive work the constitution of a "latency period" within the treatment. This movement is related to the integration of anality, which allows symbolization to emerge from repetition and univocity and to take on a polysemic value retroactively in the face of the Oedipus complex; it thus acquires an essentially social dimension and opens out on to new meanings.

The metaphor of origins has permeated different moments of this reflection on the processes of symbolization. Freud opened up the question of origins by referring to phylogenesis, in an empiricist interpretation corresponding to the search for an *original*, primitive origin. But this going back in historical time, first at the level of the individual, then of the human species, also raised the question of the *primal*, as a search for what is first in the very essence of the thing (Perron, 2003, pp. 24–26). This quest for a structure constituting the foundation of psychoanalytic science led Jung to introduce the hypothesis of a collective unconscious and Lacan that of a symbolic order. The Freudian hypothesis of primal phantasies should be interpreted at the junction of structure and history, with reference to the sexual drive, a boundary concept between the psychic and the somatic. Freudian epistemology is not to be understood solely on the basis of manifest expression and, even if Freud insisted until the end of his life on the belief in phylogenetic transmission, it was necessary for him not to separate the essence of the human being from his carnal and instinctual existence.

The "paths of symbolization" have allowed us to temporarily suspend the question of origins and to give priority to the transitional dimension (Roussillon, 1990). But if this is a necessary precondition for metapsychology to work, it should not prevent us from "dreaming" about origins, since clinical work leads us to ask questions about time, birth, and death. This same quest for origins animated the first men when they left traces of burial bearing witness to a search for the absolute and an afterlife. It is also consubstantial with the creation of the first representations in prehistory when *Homo sapiens* arrived. These vestiges are related to the modalities of temporal and social registration in the work of symbolization.

It is this self-questioning that drives the analytical process. It is constitutive of the moment when the subject comes to ask himself: "What does what I have just been thinking about mean?" Whether it is about birth, or death, or the human being as a sexual being, this questioning will lead us to deceive ourselves about ourselves, according to the Freudian expression of the "hysterical proton pseudos" (Freud, 1950 [1895], p. 352) the first lie relating to the action of repression. However, we also know that lies and secrets provoke the conscious, and especially the unconscious movement, not to stop there but to engage in a search for the truth about oneself and about the world. This is probably what the attention given to the process of symbolization in our patients and in ourselves always has to teach us.

References

Baldacci, J.-L. (2005). "Dès le début"... la sublimation? *Revue française de Psychanalyse*, 69 (5): 1405–1474.

Donnet, J.-L. (1989). Symbolisation et règle fondamentale : le « faire-sens ». *Revue française de Psychanalyse*, 53 (6): 1907–1917.

Donnet, J.-L. (1998). Processus culturel et sublimation. *Revue française de Psychanalyse*, 62 (4): 1053–1067.

Duncan, D. (1989). The flow of interpretation. The collateral interpretation, force and flow. *International Journal of Psychoanalysis*, 70 (4): 693–700.

Eco, U. (1984 [1986]). *Semiotics and the Philosophy of Language*. Bloomington: Indiana University Press.

Faimberg, H. (1987). Le télescopage des générations. A propos de la généalogie de certaines identifications. *Psychanalyse à l'université*, 12 (46): 181–200.

Ferenczi, S. (Ed.) (1955 [1927]). The problem of the termination of the analysis. In: *Final Contributions to the Problems and Methods of Psychoanalysis*. London: Hogarth, pp. 77–86.

Freud, S. (1905). Fragment of an analysis of a case of hysteria. *S.E.* 7. London: Hogarth, pp. 7–122.

Freud, S. (1908). Creative writers and day-dreaming. *S.E.* 9. London: Hogarth, pp. 141–154.

Freud, S. (1925 [1924]). A note upon the "Mystic Writing-Pad". *S.E.* 19. London: Hogarth, pp. 227–232.

Freud, S. (1926). *Inhibitions, Symptoms and Anxiety. S.E.* 20. London: Hogarth, pp. 87–174.

Freud, S. (1950 [1895]. *Project for a Scientific Psychology. S.E.* 1. London: Hogarth, pp. 281–397.

Green, A. (1979). Psychanalyse, langage: l'ancien et le nouveau. *Critique,* 381: 127–150.

Klauber, J. (1972). On the relationship of transference and interpretation in psychoanalysis. *International Journal of Psychoanalysis*, 53: 385–391.

Masson, J.M. (Ed.) (1985). *The Complete Letters of Sigmund Freud to Wilhelm Fliess, 1887–1904.* Cambridge, MA: Belknap Press.

M'Uzan, M. de (1983). Interpréter: pour qui, pourquoi? *La Bouche de l'Inconsient.* Paris: Gallimard, 1994 pp. 69–82.

M'Uzan, M. de (1991). Du dérangement au changement. *La Bouche de l'Inconsient.* Paris: Gallimard, 1994, pp. 115–128.

M'Uzan, M. de (1994). *La bouche de l'Inconscient.* Paris: Gallimard.

Pasche, F. (1984–1985). D'une fonction, méconnue (?) de la projection. *Les Cahiers du Centre de Psychanalyse et de Psychothérapie*, 9–10: 1618.

Perron, R. (2003). *La passion des origines. Être et ne pas être.* Lonay: Delachaux et Niestlé.

Roussillon, R. (1990). L'indécidabilité de l'originaire: figures de l'écart théorico-pratique. In: Cl. Le Guen (Ed.) *La psychanalyse: questions pour demain* (Monograph of the *Revue française de Psychanalyse*) Paris: Presses Universitaires de France, pp. 231–239.

Sechaud, E. (2005). Perdre, sublimer… *Revue française de Psychanalyse,* 69 (5): 1309–1380.

Spence, D. (1982). Narrative truth and theoretical truth. *The Psychoanalytic Quarterly,* 51 (1): 43–69.

Strachey, J. (1934). The nature of the therapeutic action of psychoanalysis. *International Journal of Psychoanalysis*, 15: 127–159.

Todorov, T. (1977). *Théories du symbole.* Paris: Seuil.

Winnicott, D.W. (Ed.) (1971). Playing: a theoretical statement. In: *Playing and Reality.* London: Tavistock, pp. 38–52.

Index

Note: *Italic* page numbers refer to figures and page numbers followed by 'n' refer to notes.